The Covenant Theology of Jonathan Edwards

The Covenant Theology of
JONATHAN EDWARDS

Law, Gospel, and Evangelical Obedience

Paul J. Hoehner

FOREWORD BY
Jeong Koo Jeon

⸺PICKWICK *Publications* • Eugene, Oregon

THE COVENANT THEOLOGY OF JONATHAN EDWARDS
Law, Gospel, and Evangelical Obedience

Copyright © 2021 Paul J. Hoehner. All rights reserved. Except for brief quotations in critical publications or reviews, no part of this book may be reproduced in any manner without prior written permission from the publisher. Write: Permissions, Wipf and Stock Publishers, 199 W. 8th Ave., Suite 3, Eugene, OR 97401.

Pickwick Publications
An Imprint of Wipf and Stock Publishers
199 W. 8th Ave., Suite 3
Eugene, OR 97401

www.wipfandstock.com

PAPERBACK ISBN: 978-1-7252-8157-8
HARDCOVER ISBN: 978-1-7252-8156-1
EBOOK ISBN: 978-1-7252-8158-5

Cataloguing-in-Publication data:

Names: Hoehner, Paul J., author | Jeon, Jeong Koo, foreword.

Title: The covenant theology of Jonathan Edwards : law, gospel, and evangelical obedience / Paul J. Hoehner ; foreword by Jeong Koo Jeon.

Description: Eugene, OR : Pickwick Publications, 2021 | Includes bibliographical references and indexes.

Identifiers: ISBN 978-1-7252-8157-8 (paperback) | ISBN 978-1-7252-8156-1 (hardcover) | ISBN 978-1-7252-8158-5 (ebook)

Subjects: LCSH: Edwards, Jonathan, 1703–1758.

Classification: BX7260.E3 H55 2021 (print) | BX7260.E3 H55 (ebook)

Copyrights and Permissions

Scripture quotations taken from the New American Standard Bible® (NASB), Copyright © 1960, 1962, 1963, 1968, 1971, 1972, 1973, 1975, 1977, 1995 by The Lockman Foundation. Used by permission. www.Lockman.org.

Scripture quotations are from the ESV® Bible (The Holy Bible, English Standard Version®), copyright © 2001 by Crossway, a publishing ministry of Good News Publishers. Used by permission. All rights reserved.

For my Dad.

The doctrine of the Covenant lies at the root of all true theology. It has been said that he who well understands the distinction between the Covenant of Works and the Covenant of Grace is a master of divinity. I am persuaded that most mistakes which men make concerning the doctrines of Scripture are based upon fundamental errors with regards to the covenants of law and the covenants of grace. May God grant us now the power to instruct and you the grace to receive instruction on this vital subject.

—CHARLES H. SPURGEON

Table of Contents

List of Tables ix
Foreword by Jeong Koo Jeon xi
Preface xv
Acknowledgments xxvii
Abbreviations xxix

Chapter 1: Reading Jonathan Edwards in Covenant Context 1
Chapter 2: Jonathan Edwards on the Covenant of Works 23
Chapter 3: Jonathan Edwards on the Covenant of Redemption 77
Chapter 4: Jonathan Edwards on the Covenant of Grace 136
Chapter 5: Jonathan Edwards on the Mosaic Covenant 174
Chapter 6: Jonathan Edwards on Justification and Faith 218
Chapter 7: Jonathan Edwards on Evangelical Obedience 260

Summary and Concluding Comments 290
Bibliography 295
Name and Author Index 313
Subject Index 317
Scripture Index 327

List of Tables

Table 4.1. The Structure of Jonathan Edwards's Covenant Theology 173

Table 5.1. The Relationship of the Covenant of Works (Moral Law) to the Old and New Covenants according to Jonathan Edwards 196

Foreword

FOR THE PAST SEVERAL decades, scholars have paid close attention to the development and adaptation of covenant theology that is centered in the distinction between the Covenant of Works and the Covenant of Grace as well as the intratrinitarian covenant, the Covenant of Redemption (*pactum salutis*), in the Reformed tradition. During the Protestant Reformation in Europe, the proper distinction between law and gospel was a decisive hermeneutical guide to interpret and proclaim justification by faith alone (*sola fide*), salvation by grace alone (*sola gratia*), and in Christ alone (*solus Christus*) for both Martin Luther and John Calvin.

The proper distinction between law and gospel was the hermeneutical and theological background of the distinction between the Covenant of Works and the Covenant of Grace among Calvinists in the latter part of the sixteenth and seventeenth centuries. The distinction between the Covenant of Works and the Covenant of Grace was adopted as a confessional form and statement in the Westminster Standards (1643–1648). Ever since, the proper distinctions between law and gospel and the Covenant of Works and the Covenant of Grace stood and fell together in the Reformed tradition. The English Puritan and New England Puritan pastors' and theologians' theology and practice were deeply saturated by covenant theology.

In the twentieth century, Karl Barth quietly dropped a nuclear bomb in the theological playground as a major architect of neoorthodox theology. He deconstructed the bipolar covenant distinction of the Covenant of Works and the Covenant of Grace along with the distinction between law and gospel in light of his Christomonistic concept of grace within an existential ethos. His faithful disciples, including James B. Torrance, Thomas F. Torrance, and Holmes Rolston III, rejected covenant theology, following the lead of Karl Barth in the English-speaking world. In this process, they advocated the falsified and groundless thesis of "Calvin against the Calvinists."

Similarly, the exponents of the New Perspective on Paul reject the common Protestant principle of the proper distinction between law and gospel along with the bipolar distinction between the Covenant of Works and the Covenant of Grace. E. P. Sanders, using the soteriology of Second Temple Judaism, falsely argues that its soteriology was not legalism but "covenantal nomism" which is identified and understood as getting in by grace and staying in by obedience to the law in his famous book, *Paul and Palestinian Judaism* (1977). Following the lead of Sanders' covenantal nomism, James D. G. Dunn coined the term the New Perspective on Paul in 1983. Afterward, N. T. Wright popularized it in his hermeneutics and Pauline theology.

By and large, a significant portion of Jonathan Edwards's handwritten writings and manuscripts were locked in the Beineke Rare Book and Manuscript Library of Yale University until the publication of Perry Miller's landmark book *Jonathan Edwards* in 1949. Ironically, Miller, as a secular historian and sociologist, began to spark scholars' interest in Edwards's writings, philosophy, and theology, although he fundamentally misinterpreted Edwards's theological identity and vision. Contemporary Edwards scholars and researchers approach Edwards's theology and philosophy from several different perspectives. In doing so, some of them inject their own philosophical and theological ideas and ideologies and falsely create diverse versions of Edwards which are foreign and strange from the real Edwards.

In light of contemporary Edwards scholarship, Dr. Hoehner's book is timely. As a gifted medical doctor, scientist, and theologian, he unpacks the backbone of Edwards's theology and philosophy and identifies Edwards primarily as a Reformed pastor and covenant theologian in the context of eighteenth-century New England Puritanism. Moreover, he brilliantly provides the proper window to enter the beautiful and grand mountains of Edwards's theology, philosophy, and doctrinal and practical implications.

Dr. Hoehner insightfully demonstrates that Edwards maintained the distinction between the Covenant of Works and the Covenant of Grace and adopted the Covenant of Redemption as the eternal and covenantal background of the Covenant of Grace which was inaugurated in Gen 3:15 with the proclamation of the primitive gospel (*protoevangelium*). Moreover, according to Dr. Hoehner, Edwards taught the distinction between law and gospel in his exposition of the doctrine of justification, safeguarding against the divergent versions of neonomianism and legalism. Therefore, there is a logical order between justification and sanctification in Edwards's soteriological mind while he harmoniously embraced justification and sanctification under the theological rubrics of the union with Christ (*unio cum Christo*). In addition, he ably defends Edwards's view of justification by faith alone (*sola fide*) and puts "evangelical obedience" in a proper place in light of the elect's good works through the lens of covenant theology. In the end, exploring Edwards's thoughts from the perspective of covenant theology, Dr. Hoehner's thesis sheds light to restore Edwards's theological and philosophical contributions and legacy which are still relevant and beneficial.

Dr. Hoehner's *The Covenant Theology of Jonathan Edwards* will navigate the students and scholars of Edwards's thoughts and writings into the promised land which Edwards envisioned throughout his pastoral ministry and writing. Dr. Hoehner's book is a balanced and proper guide for those who want to dive into Edwards's theological and philosophical world. His book will certainly be a magnificent resource for Edwardsean scholarship for many years to come, providing pastoral, theological, ethical, and philosophical inspiration.

Dr. Jeong Koo Jeon
Professor of Biblical and Systematic Theology
Faith Theological Seminary

Preface

THIS BOOK IS A revision of my doctoral dissertation from the University of Virginia Department of Religious Studies. I had originally set out to write on the theological ethics of Jonathan Edwards. The more I delved into the specifics of Edwards's ethical and moral philosophy in its theological context, the more I realized how it was impossible to understand Edwards's complex and intricate explorations on this subject unless his thought and language were put into the context of his own over-arching biblical theology and the way he interpreted redemptive history according to a covenant framework. Since the emergence of a renaissance in Edwardsean studies beginning in the middle of the last century, catalyzed by the publication of Edwards's corpus and unpublished manuscripts, notes, and sermons by the Jonathan Edwards Center at Yale University, there have been numerous theologians and philosophers, some but not all in Reformed Protestant circles, who have attempted to either appropriate "America's greatest theologian" for specific theological and polemical agendas or interpret Edwards in a way that I thought was either illegitimate or seemed to oppose Edwards's own self-conscious identity as a Reformed pastor and theologian firmly rooted in the historical Reformed Protestant tradition. One of the goals of this study was to understand why this was the case and to offer a positive corrective.

In this volume I maintain that one must read Jonathan Edwards as a Reformed covenant theologian, and that explicating the covenantal framework of his redemptive-historical approach to scriptural exegesis will shed light on and help interpret the more controversial discussions regarding the "ethics" of Edwards, by which I limit to the role of and motive for "good works," or, using the term preferred by Edwards, evangelical obedience, in the salvation and life of the elect believer. In the following chapters I discuss and attempt to clarify Edwards's view of covenant theology, concentrating on his biblical and redemptive-historical theology as it is situated within the Reformed federal scholastic tradition. His view on the Covenant of Works, Covenant of Redemption, Covenant of Grace, and the Mosaic covenant dispensation are examined along with the implications his covenant structure has for the role of evangelical obedience and faith in the believer's justification before God. I will attempt to show how close attention to his covenant theology as a controlling paradigm affords a more authentic and accurate interpretation of Edwards.

The word covenant comes from the Hebrew *berith*, the Greek *diatheke*, and from the Latin *pactum, foedus,* or *testamentum*. At its essence, a covenant is a relationship. In the Bible, covenants are the ways by which God establishes a relationship and interacts with his creation and humanity. Michael Horton notes, "Although qualitatively distinct from the world, God is not distant, aloof, and uninvolved. God created the world as the theater of his unfolding drama, at whose heart is a covenantal relationship."[1] Traditionally, Reformed theology has defined a covenant as an arrangement between two or more parties consisting of binding oaths, with accompanying signs and seals, and governed by stipulations and consequences. O. Palmer Robertson famously defined a biblical covenant as a "bond in blood sovereignly administered."[2] As a bond, it is an oath-bound commitment. As a bond in blood, there is a life and death obligation involved in the covenantal bond. It is also a bond sovereignly initiated and administered by God. It is this absolute sovereignty of God in the reciprocal covenantal relationship which distinguishes this religious-covenantal bond from mere human compacts, agreements, or *quid pro quo* contracts.[3]

Scriptural covenants are also characterized by obligations and sanctions, blessings and curses. Meredith Kline observes, "Every divine-human covenant in Scripture involves a sanction-sealed commitment to maintain a particular relationship or follow a stipulated course of action."[4] A covenant is therefore, according to Kline, a relationship under sanctions. Covenants are also characterized by visible signs and seals of the covenantal promises God has given to those with whom he has

---

1. Horton, *Christian Faith*, 44.
2. Robertson, *Christ of the Covenants*, 4.
3. Kline, "Law and Covenant," 19.
4. Kline, "Law and Covenant," 3.

entered into a covenantal relationship. Examples are the rainbow given to Noah, circumcision given to Abraham, and baptism and the Lord's Supper given to New Testament believers.

Despite the theological difference, it is now well recognized that biblical covenants have many parallels to extra-biblical ANE vassal-suzerain treaties and royal grant treaties, particularly Hittite treaties of the fourteenth and thirteenth centuries BCE.[5] Unlike in ordinary suzerains of the ANE, in Christ the principles of law and promise cooperate for the salvation of God's people. Kline notes that ANE suzerains "were unable in their covenants to guarantee to the vassals the perpetuity of those benefits which were contingent on a continuing display of loyalty. But because the Lord of Adam, Abraham, Moses, and Paul is the God of sovereign election and grace, the God who gives Christ as a covenant to his people, he is able to guarantee an everlasting realization of the beatitude of this covenant to his covenant-breaking vassals even while he reaffirms that the fulfillment of the holy demands of his law is the prerequisite of the promised blessings."[6]

The Covenants of Works, Redemption, and Grace, to use Edwards's own tri-covenantal distinction and terminology, are the three unified but distinct divine covenants that organize biblical revelation. They are sometimes referred to as the theological covenants in distinction from the other "biblical" covenants such as the Noahic, Abrahamic, Mosaic, and Davidic. These "biblical" covenants, being organically connected as different administrations of the one eternal Covenant of Grace, along with the prophecies of Jeremiah and Ezekiel, build upon each other as successive increasing revelations of what will ultimately be brought to completion in the New Covenant of Christ.[7]

The theological covenants are said to be distinct from the biblical covenants because they are "derived" from Scripture, whereas the biblical

---

5. Rad, *Old Testament Theology*, 131–32; Eichrodt, *Theology*, 37, 54, 63.

6. Kline, "Law Covenant," 12.

7. New England Puritans in Edwards's day also recognized two other covenants, a national covenant and a church covenant, which they linked to the Covenant of Grace. However, since these covenants concerned both the regenerate and unregenerate, they are to be distinguished from the Covenant of Grace which deals only with the elect or true believers. Yazawa, while recognizing this distinction, also concludes, "Since the church covenant and the national covenant are areas where eternity and time intersect, it is possible to hear even in this earthly turmoil repercussion echoing down from eternity. Creation, justification and sanctification, issues of church and national membership all take place within history." Yazawa, *Covenant of Redemption*, 161.

covenants are explicitly presented in the Bible. This distinction can be pushed too far and risks digging too great a chasm between biblical and systematic theology. Especially when treating the divine covenants, it is difficult to distinguish the functions of biblical theology and systematic theology. As Kline reminds us:

> To analyze these covenants is to trace the history of revelation and divine-human relationship, which is precisely the domain of biblical theology. Certainly, too, biblical theology involves the systematization of the covenantal data under relatively broad historical epochs. The task of systematic theology is hardly distinctive if it consists merely in the summary of the results of biblical theology, and if systematics were to de-historicize its treatment of covenant, distilling from the data general truths of divine-human relationship, it would radically misrepresent the object it was defining.[8]

For Edwards, the theological covenants were not merely an inspired inference from the Scriptures, but the way the Bible explicitly structures all redemptive history. The "biblical" covenants were part of the on-going historical revelation of the one Covenant of Grace that runs from Gen 3:15 to the consummation of history at Christ's Parousia. It is for this reason I have chosen to structure this book around Edwards's thinking on these three biblical-theological covenants, along with the Mosaic dispensation of the Covenant of Grace.

I will discuss Edwards's covenant theology under four main headings: The Covenant of Works, the Covenant of Redemption, the Covenant of Grace, and the Mosaic covenant. Each chapter will begin with a brief review of the Reformed development of each covenant to situate Edwards in his own historical context. I will then follow with a detailed examination of Edwards's own covenant theology. The final two chapters will bring Edwards's covenant theology to bear on specific questions regarding justification, faith, and the role of evangelical obedience. I will conclude that understanding Edwards's covenantal structuring of redemptive history puts his theology of works and faith in proper perspective, emphasizing the non-meritorious necessity of works in the life of the believer without compromising the Reformed doctrine of *sola fide*, while at the same time avoiding (mis)readings of Edwards that would conclude otherwise.

---

8. Kline, "Law Covenant," 9 n. 15.

In the first chapter I will discuss the importance of this topic, both for current Edwardsean studies as well as for contemporary theological and hermeneutical discussions. I will present Edwards as a New England Puritan biblical theologian and pastor in the Reformed tradition, one who prioritized the authority and centrality of Scripture over philosophical speculation in theology.[9] I will then follow with a brief overview of the development and historiography of Reformed covenant theology up to Edwards's own time to situate Edwards's own ideas in historical perspective.

In the second chapter I will discuss Edwards's view of the Covenant of Works. The Covenant of Works, sometimes referred to as the *foedus operum*, was the first covenant made by God with man at creation and instituted before man's fall into sin. For many Reformed theologians (and certainly this can be found in Calvin) the Tree of Life and the Tree of the Knowledge of Good and Evil in the beginning of the Genesis narrative are sacramental (covenantal) signs of the grace available, on condition of obedience, to the first human pair under the Covenant of Works. Since this initial command, therefore, has a broad federal significance, Reformed theologians invariably interpret the violation of the Covenant of Works as more than a violation of a simple token command not to eat of a particular fruit, but as a violation of the entire moral law (covenant of nature or *foedus natural*). In the twentieth century, John Murray questioned the use of the term "Covenant of Works," preferring the term "Adamic administration," to underscore his claim that all covenants between God and man are at their core gracious and not legal.[10]

Edwards had a robust view of the prelapsarian Covenant of Works and the antithesis between the Covenant of Works and the Covenant of Grace. Likewise, his contrast between law and gospel stand or fall together in his covenantal hermeneutics. Despite this, Edwards could say that both the Covenant of Works and the Covenant of Grace are based on faith and obligation. With respect to the Covenant of Works, there was faith in the promises of God that would be fulfilled by Adam's obligation (as federal head). In the Covenant of Grace, there was faith in the promises of God

---

9. Adriaane Neele appropriately characterizes Edwards as, "a remarkable preacher, revivalist, and struggling pastor who reflected theologically and philosophically in the immediate context of ministry" and conducted all his labors "in the service of preaching." Neele, *Before Jonathan Edwards*, 67, 180.

10. Murray, "The Adamic Administration," 2:47–59. See also Jeon, *Covenant Theology and Justification*, 3–25.

that the obligations required would be fulfilled by another (Christ, the federal head of the new Covenant of Grace). For Edwards, the Covenant of Works was not strictly abrogated but fulfilled by Christ. As an "eternal rule of righteousness" it remains in effect for the believer as the goal of salvation (and chiefly as God's end in creation itself). This distinction between abrogation and fulfillment was central to Edwards's arguments against forms of Arminianism and perfectionism.

In the third chapter I will look at Edwards's formulation of the Covenant of Redemption and its implications. The Covenant of Redemption, sometimes referred to as the *pactum salutis*, is the pretemporal, intratrinitarian agreement between God the Father and the Son concerning the Covenant of Grace and its ratification in and through the work of the Son incarnate. The Son covenants with the Father, in the unity of the Godhead, to be the temporal sponsor of the Father's *testamentum* in and through his work as Mediator.

The origin of this doctrine appears for some scholars to have arisen *de novo* as a piece of speculative doctrine, particularly associated with the seventeenth-century Dutch Reformed theologian Johannes Cocceius (1603–1669). However, Richard Muller has shown that the concept of the *pactum salutis* had a pedigree of origin within medieval scholastic concepts, possibly in Martin Luther (1483–1546), and later in extended exegetical and doctrinal precedents and parallels over the course of several generations of Reformed scholars, ultimately leading to the actual formulation of the *pactum salutis* in Cocceius.[11]

In his later writings Edwards developed a clear doctrine of the Covenant of Redemption that was both distinguished from (specifically in terms of the parties of the covenant) and at the same time contained the Covenant of Grace within its boundaries. As far as sinners are concerned, the Covenant of Redemption is the eternal basis for the Covenant of Grace. For Christ, the Covenant of Redemption is a Covenant of Works rather than a Covenant of Grace. The Covenant of Grace for sinners is simply the Covenant of Works fulfilled by Christ as the covenant head, meriting eternal life for those united to his mystical body.

Edwards's concept of the Covenant of Redemption has several implications. First, his formulation of the subordination of the Son to the Father is worked out in its intratrinitarian context in a way that does justice to the voluntary *ad extra* subordination of the Son to the Father

---

11. Muller, "Toward the *Pactum Salutis*," 11–65.

in his humility, while not reducing the *ad intra* trinitarian relations to one of subordinationism. While the Holy Spirit is not formally one of the parties of the *pactum*, Edwards retains a full trinitarian view of the covenant which defines more precisely the Holy Spirit's role in redemptive history. The Holy Spirit provides the faith for its application, as well as the surety for the performance of all the promises of God relating to salvation. Second, and because of this work of the Holy Spirit, the assurance and comfort of the Covenant of Grace is anchored in the Covenant of Redemption. Third, the certainty of the Covenant of Redemption is relevant for the elect believer because the believer participates in the covenant by being united to Christ and considered together as one mystical person. Fourth, the Covenant of Redemption undergirds the eternal divine plan in redemptive history. Finally, because Edwards viewed the Covenant of Redemption as ultimately a Covenant of Works (fulfilled by Christ on behalf of those given to him by the Father, his bride the Church), the holiness of God as reflected in his moral law ("the eternal rule of righteousness") is ratified as an obligation (though never meritorious) in the life of the Christian under the Covenant of Grace, even while abrogated insofar as the justification of the sinner is concerned. Each of these issues and formulations have profound implications for Edwards's view of justification, sanctification, and the role of works in salvation.

In the fourth chapter I will discuss Edwards's view of the Covenant of Grace and some unique distinctions Edwards makes regarding this doctrine. The Covenant of Grace (*foedus gratiae gratuitum* or *foedus gratiae evangelicum*) is a way of describing an elect believer's relation to God, a doctrinal feature that has been present in differing degrees of elaboration throughout the history of Reformed theology. In scholastic definitions it is the pact made by God first revealed in the *protevangelium* (Gen 3:15), confirmed and revealed more fully to Abraham, and finally fulfilled in Christ. It is a gracious covenant of salvation given to fallen humanity apart from any consideration of any man or woman's ability to respond to it or fulfill it and apart from any human initiative. The entire biblical history is one of gracious promise. Obedience under covenant, accompanied by saving fulfillment in Christ, becomes a central structure and pattern of salvation directly applicable to the life of God's people. In this chapter I will also show Edwards to be rightly placed among orthodox Reformed theologians with his acceptance of the scriptural correlation between divine sovereignty and human responsibility represented by that tradition. Edwards not only maintained the doctrine of the Covenant of Grace but did so within the framework of distinctive Reformed or Calvinistic doctrines.

The fifth chapter will address the Mosaic covenant as an important "test case" for understanding both the biblical unity of the covenantal structure in Edwards's theology as well as the role of works and faith in covenantal perspective. A central issue in present debates in Reformed theology, both within and outside of confessional orthodoxy, is the interpretation of the Mosaic covenant (or Mosaic dispensation under the Covenant of Grace).[12] Even in Edwards's day there were several different interpretations of the role of the Mosaic covenant in redemptive history. Edwards acknowledges such in a treatise addressing the controversy surrounding the "half-way covenant": "There is perhaps no part of divinity attended with so much intricacy, and wherein orthodox divines do so much differ, as the stating the precise agreement and difference between the two dispensations of Moses and of Christ."[13] Within the historic Reformed tradition, the hermeneutical key to the relationship between justification and sanctification, as well as the role of the works in salvation, is the proper biblical assessment of the symbolic-typical aspect of Old Testament revelation and the recognition of the dual principles of law and grace operative in the Mosaic administration of the Covenant of Grace. Viewing the Mosaic administration in some sense as a Covenant of Works in Edwards is instrumental in interpreting his views of justification and the law-gospel distinction. Edwards uniquely characterized the Mosaic administration (and Sinaitic administration with Israel) as the "cortex" or "shell" that covers the "medulla" of the Covenant of Grace. As such the Covenant of Grace is cloaked in a "republication" of the Covenant of Works that acts as a tutor or "schoolmaster" to drive the Israelites to the need of a covenant redeemer. While clearly having unique aspects, Edwards's view is consistent with the majority of Reformed theologians in the early history of federalism.

The last two chapters will examine particular aspects of faith and works, or evangelical obedience, that have been particularly controversial in Edwardsean studies with the view to a revised reading of Edwards that situates him more firmly in his own Reformed tradition as a federal theologian. The relationship between justification and sanctification, or

---

12. For an overview of some of the issues, see Ferry, "Works," 76–108; Karlberg, "Reformed Interpretation," 1–57; Woolsey, *Unity and Continuity*; McGiffert, "From Moses to Adam," 131–55; Karlberg, "Mosaic Covenant."

13. Edwards, "Humble Inquiry," *WJE* 12:279. See also Ferry, "Works," 76–108.

the distinction between law and gospel, has defined in good measure Protestant polemical discourse ever since Luther's reformation, yet not without subsequent intramural polemical controversies and confusions. The challenges raised by antinomian and neonomian theologies, as well as the ever-present Arminian "heresy," helped focus Edwards's thinking and exposition. In assessing Edwards's use of "evangelical obedience" as a soteriological category within the context of these debates, such issues as defining the meritorious value of works, the conditional nature of New Covenant obedience, the priority of justification over sanctification, and imputation versus impartation of the righteousness of Christ became central and defining concerns.

I believe that one of the reasons some corners of the Reformed church struggle with matters related to the doctrine of justification and its relation to sanctification is because of their unfamiliarity with key elements of classic covenant theology. For example, Christ's identity as a covenant surety, a key pillar of the Covenant of Redemption, provides important data regarding the material cause of justification. The Covenant of Redemption also delivers important information regarding the priority of the forensic to the transformative benefits in redemption and why justification precedes sanctification in the *ordo salutis*. According to Fesko, the entire system of doctrine lies in seminal form within the Covenant of Redemption.[14]

Edwards's biblical theology, particularly the covenantal structure of redemptive history, provides insights and clarifications for interpreting his earlier systematic and polemical works on these important theological topics. His ability to synthesize and unify biblical historical-redemptive theology with systematic theology, correlating the *historia revelationis* and the *ordo salutis*, is exemplary and solves many of the perceived conundrums in his earlier theology that have been difficult to interpret without this perspective.

Edwards expounded a unique eschatological vision for the Christian moral life and the role of "holiness" as the ultimate end of both the Christian life and, ultimately, of God's glorification of himself in creation. Within this context, the role of perseverance has been a controversial issue, particularly with regards to the conditional/unconditional status

---

14. Fesko, *Trinity*, xix. In a parallel way Mark Beach has argued that Turretin set forth his doctrine of the twofold covenant (works and grace) as a defense and exposition of divine grace and justification, his federalism highlighting what he judged to be the gospel in its purest expression. See also Beach, *Christ and the Covenant*.

of the life of the believer under the New Covenant. How to interpret Edwards's view of "final" or "second" justification based on works in the context of his overall theology is treated in the final chapter. Understanding Edwards is again aided significantly by paying close attention to his redemptive-historical and covenantal framework.

One of Edwards's stated goals was to write a new kind of theology, "a body of divinity in an entirely new method,"[15] that was historically based instead of relying on the traditional systematic *loci*. While his untimely death shortly after accepting the presidency of Princeton College precluded the completion of his future *magnum opus*, there is a general tendency in his later works towards a more redemptive-historical approach to theology, probably best exemplified in his sermon series *History of the Work of Redemption* and later *Miscellanies*. I will endeavor to show that Edwards's covenantal structuring of biblical history, and his correlating that historical perspective to the specific categories of individual salvation, is a relatively untapped resource for understanding Edwards's theology, especially with regards to the role of "evangelical obedience" in the life of the justified believer.

I do not intend to present covenant theology as the overarching motif or meta-thematic center of Edwards's theology (a "central dogma" approach). Edwards employed several themes, including divine sovereignty, typology, God's glory, beauty, ethics, etc. in his thinking and writing. As a Reformed biblical pastor and theologian, however, he did give central precedence to the covenant structure of biblical redemptive history. This was no dry academic exercise for this Northampton pastor and revivalist, but a glorious discovery of the great drama of redemption of what God ordained from eternity past, what Christ accomplished on the cross, and what the Holy Spirit will complete in the church, Christ's bride.

Edwards's theology, even when rigorously expounded in all its systematic and painstakingly detailed and logical exposition, remains immensely practical. Whether taking the form of systematic or biblical theology, "divinity," according to Edwards and his Puritan tradition, was simply the doctrine of living to God by Christ. "It comprehends all Christian doctrines as they are in Jesus, and all Christian rules directing us in living to God by Christ. There is nothing in divinity, no one doctrine, no promise, no rule, but what some way or other relates

---

15. Edwards, "Letter to the Trustees," *WJE* 16:727.

to the Christian and divine life, or our living to God by Christ."¹⁶ The purpose of all doctrine, according to Edwards, is to promote our living to God here in this world, in a life of faith and holiness, and to bring us to a life of perfect holiness and happiness, in the full enjoyment of God in eternity. The covenant theology of Jonathan Edwards, as it shows forth the wonder, joy, and relevance of the Christian faith unfolding in history, continues to be spiritually significant, pastoral, and comforting for today's modern church.

---

16. Edwards, "The Importance and Advantage of a Thorough Knowledge of Divine Truth," *WJE* 22:86.

Acknowledgments

THIS WORK IS DEDICATED to my wife, Sheryl, who never gave up on my dreams and sacrificed so much of herself to make this possible. Without her, this undertaking would not have been conceivable or desirable. It is her faithful commitment to such an "uncommon union" of ours that this work is as much hers as it is mine. She has truly been my "Sarah." It is also dedicated to my children: Christian, Timothy, and Carolyn. More than just a constant source of encouragement and inspiration, they have been my closest friends throughout. And especially, to my mother, Sharon Hoehner, for her endearing support and love.

I owe many thanks to those scholars and friends who have made this accomplishment possible. My sincerest appreciation goes to Michael Payne, who first encouraged me to pursue doctoral studies as I was finishing my seminary degree at Reformed Theological Seminary in Jackson, Mississippi. I owe an enormous debt of gratitude to James Childress, my initial graduate advisor and mentor at the University of Virginia who stayed on my dissertation committee even after his retirement. Jim took an interest in my work and stuck with me from the very beginning of my time in Charlottesville and beyond, and without whose patient, gentlemanly, and persevering encouragement this would not have been possible. Charles Matthewes is an exemplary teacher and scholar who patiently guided my graduate work and chaired my dissertation committee, which also included James Davison Hunter and Paul Dafydd Jones. I am exceedingly grateful for my good friend, colleague, and greatest encourager, Jeong Koo Jeon. Thank you for all your prayers and fellowship. Our frequent all-morning breakfast discussions at Bob Evans kept me on track, focused, and fed, both nutritionally and spiritually. It is an honor to call you my brother in the faith.

And finally, I want to express my gratitude to the Mustard Seed Foundation for the financial support I received as a Harvey Fellow during my graduate studies and to the Jonathan Edwards Center at Yale University for allowing me to participate in their Global Accelerated Sermon Editing Project in editing Jonathan Edwards's unpublished sermon manuscripts.

Abbreviations

AV	Authorized King James Version of the Bible, 1769 Blayney Edition of the 1611 King James Version the English Bible.
ANE	Ancient Near Eastern
ANF	*The Ante-Nicene Fathers: Translations of the Writings of the Fathers Down to A.D. 325.* 10 vols. 1885–1887. Edited by Alexander Roberts and James Donaldson. Peabody: Hendrickson, 2004.
BCE	Before the Common Era
BS	*Bibliotheca Sacra*
c.	circa
CH	*Church History*
CTJ	*Calvin Theological Journal*
d.	died
EQ	*Evangelical Quarterly*
ESV	*The Holy Bible, English Standard Version.* Wheaton: Crossway, 2016.
GB	*Geneva Bible of 1599*
HTR	*Harvard Theological Review*
JE	Edwards, Jonathan. *The Works of Jonathan Edwards.* 2 vols. 1834. Reprinted, Peabody: Hendrickson, 2007.
JEH	*Journal of Ecclesiastical History*
JES	*Jonathan Edwards Studies*

JTS	*Journal of Theological Studies*
JR	*Journal of Religion*
LW	Luther, Martin. *Luther's Works*. 75 vols. Edited by Jaroslav Pelikan, Helmut T. Lehmann, and Christopher Boyd Brown. Philadelphia: Muehlenberg and Fortress, and St. Louis: Concordia, 1955–.
Misc.	*Miscellany*
MJT	*Mid-America Journal of Theology*
NASB	*The New American Standard Bible*. La Habra, CA: The Lockman Foundation, 1995.
NPNF	*A Select Library of Nicene and Post-Nicene Fathers of the Christian Church*. 28 vols. in 2 series. Edited by Philip Schaff and Henry Wace. 1886–1889. Peabody: Hendrickson, 2004.
SCJ	*Sixteenth Century Journal*
SJT	*Scottish Journal of Theology*
TJ	*Trinity Journal*
WA	Luther, Martin. *D. Martin Luthers Werke, Kritische Gesamtausgabe [Schriften]*. 73 vols. Weimar: Herman Böhlaus, 1883–2009.
WA DB	Luther, Martin. *D. Martin Luthers Werke, Kritische Gesamtausgabe [Deutsche Bibel]*. 12 vols. Weimar: Herman Böhlaus, 1883–2009.
WCF	*Westminster Confession of Faith*
WJE	Edwards, Jonathan. *The Works of Jonathan Edwards*. General Editor Harry S. Stout. 26 vols. (1–26). New Haven: Yale University Press, 1957–2008.
WJEO	Edwards, Jonathan. *The Works of Jonathan Edwards Online*. 46 vols. (27–73). Jonathan Edwards Center, Yale University. Edwards.yale.edu/research.
WLC	*Westminster Larger Catechism*
WSC	*Westminster Shorter Catechism*
WTJ	*Westminster Theological Journal*

Scripture

Gen	Genesis
Exod	Exodus
Lev	Leviticus
Num	Numbers
Deut	Deuteronomy
Josh	Joshua
1 Sam	1 Samuel
2 Sam	2 Samuel
Neh	Nehemiah
Job	Job
Ps	Psalm
Prov	Proverbs
Cant	Canticles (Song of Solomon)
Isa	Isaiah
Jer	Jeremiah
Ezek	Ezekiel
Dan	Daniel
Hos	Hosea
Hab	Habakkuk
Zech	Zechariah
Matt	Matthew
Mark	Mark
Luke	Luke
John	John
Acts	Acts
Rom	Romans
1 Cor	1 Corinthians
2 Cor	2 Corinthians
Gal	Galatians

Eph	Ephesians
Phil	Philippians
Col	Colossians
2 Tim	2 Timothy
Titus	Titus
Heb	Hebrews
Jas	James
1 John	1 John
Rev	Revelation

1

Reading Jonathan Edwards in Covenant Context

Introduction

MODERN CONTROVERSIES IN AMERICAN conservative and confessional Reformed and Presbyterian denominations underscore the importance of the perennial tension between works and salvation in Western Protestant Christianity. The writings of Jonathan Edwards, the great eighteenth-century New England Puritan pastor, are frequently enlisted to support different and sometimes contrary positions in recent scholarship on such central topics as justification and sanctification. By focusing on his more speculative writings, several interpreters of Edwards's theology have read into the Northampton pastor's works many of their own theological preconceptions and biases. Concentrating on his earlier more systematic and polemical writings has at times resulted in categorical confusion regarding certain passages, resulting in a misreading of isolated statements of this committed New England defender of Reformed orthodoxy that have on the surface sounded less than truly "Reformed." Few studies have examined Edwards's covenant theology as a means to clarify his writings, which is interesting considering that covenant thinking was such a central point in this New England Puritan's discussions concerning legalism and antinomianism. The central purpose of this volume is to show how re-examining Jonathan Edwards's biblical covenant theology in its redemptive-historical context provides a more nuanced and clearer reading of his theology, particularly his views on justification, sanctification, and the role of works in salvation. It will show that Edwards, while occasionally original in his language and formulations, remained in full continuity with the broader orthodox Reformed tradition and his own eighteenth-century Puritan heritage.

Importance of the Topic

Reformed Christian theology, a major and important branch of Protestant Christian thought, has long been fascinated by the relationship between those dynamics in the Christian life that it labels "justification" and "sanctification," or the relationship between "grace" and "works" in salvation (sometimes discussed under the rubric of "law and gospel"). Throughout scholastic Reformed, Calvinist, and English Puritan theology there exists a creative tension, in both systematic theology and biblical exegesis, between faith and works, along with several trajectories as to the role "good works" play in the drama of salvation.

From a Reformed perspective at least four major trajectories on the relationship between works and grace can be broadly discerned within the major western Christian traditions.[1] In Roman Catholicism there is a material cooperation with the workings of grace by good works. In Lutheranism good works are evidence of gratitude for the gift of grace from God, and in themselves contribute little if anything to salvation outside of forming a life of gratitude. In the Anabaptist/Pietistic traditions works are the way in which a Christian patterns his or her life after Christ and thereby gives evidence of their faith and the working of the Spirit in their lives. Sanctification is a means to participate with grace in the work of salvation. There is more of an emphasis on how the faithful conduct their lives in view of the example and teachings of Jesus found in Scripture. In the Reformed tradition the continued perseverance of the saints in the face of the trials and temptations of life are a sign of God's electing grace. The capacity to persevere in good works is a sign of the electing grace of God working in the lives of the faithful. Instead of preceding, cooperating, or simply responding to God's grace, their perduring presence in the life of faith follows the effectual electing work of grace in salvation. Although discrete traditions represent the normalization of a particular emphasis, echoes of each are found in each of the other trajectories. The major question regarding the value of good works in God's scheme of

---

1. This is my own construal from a Reformed perspective. Different representatives of these positions may dissent from this admittedly broad categorization.

salvation is not whether good works are essential, but rather how they are essential to the Christian life.

These four different approaches to the question of the place of "good works" in the scheme of salvation have created a moral field of vision for the Christian tradition in the West since the Reformation. Scholars looking to Jonathan Edwards, a central pillar in the history of Reformed Christian thought, for assistance and insight have often come away with remarkably diverse and contradictory conclusions. Edwards's corpus is vast, variegated, and daunting in its intellectual acumen and precision. Getting lost is easy and focusing on a select area of Edwards's writings can inadvertently lead one astray. It has been tempting for many scholars to begin with Edwards's more speculative and philosophical works or earlier more systematic and polemical writings to look for insightful clues to unpack his underlying theology. While fruitful and interesting in many aspects, these approaches have led to conclusions that have in some cases made Edwards appear more Catholic, ecumenical, or even Arminian than orthodox Reformed, a strange conclusion for one who saw himself and his life work as an apologist and champion against just such heterodox (from a Reformed perspective) positions. Maybe these are the wrong places to start.

A perspective that has not been emphasized as much as a central theme is Edwards's redemptive-historical approach to biblical interpretation, particularly his covenant theology, a perspective that presents and clarifies the distinction between faith and works (Edwards prefers the term "evangelical obedience"), and justification and sanctification. In fact, Edwards's writings on justification, sanctification, and the role of works in salvation may be most intelligible through the lens of his covenant theology. The evidence for this is more visible in his later works, which shifted their overall genre or "center of gravity" from speculative/systematic to biblical historical-redemptive approaches. A central theme of this book is that reading Edwards's work through his late articulated covenant theology clarifies his contributions to the Reformed discussion on justification and sanctification.

While a study of Edwards's covenant theology is interesting in its own right, there are several reasons that make a renewed study of Edwards and his covenant view of biblical redemptive-history particularly relevant, needed, and long overdue. First is the paucity of recent studies. Over fifty years ago Conrad Cherry was one of the first Edwards scholars to unapologetically restore Edwards's connection with his Calvinist legacy, resisting attempts to "modernize" Edwards and maintaining that his Calvinism was central to the whole of his intellectual endeavor and germane to his major works. Cherry highlighted the importance of covenant theology in Edwards's doctrine of faith, particularly God's "debt" to man in the Covenant of Grace and man's faith as the "condition" of the covenant with God.[2] A decade later Carl Bogue surveyed Edwards's published works and many of his unpublished sermons to further argue against the flow of Perry Miller's influence that Calvinism and the Covenant of Grace are consistent and do not exclude one another.[3] The Covenant of Grace was not a Puritan device to allow man to act autonomously, but a provision of a sovereign, electing God working out his eternal plan in history. Edwards's Calvinism and covenant theology went hand-in-hand.[4] Bogue's work concentrated on the Covenant of Grace and drew mostly from Edwards's earlier *Miscellanies* and sermons. It has now been over forty years since Bogue's seminal study on Edwards's Covenant of Grace appeared without a single published monograph addressing this aspect of Edwards's theology in the interim, with the exception of Reita Yazawa's recent study that concentrates on the trinitarian aspects of the Covenant of Redemption and its implications in Edwards.[5] Furthermore, Edwards's own particular contributions to a biblical understanding of the covenants in redemptive history is noticeably absent in works surveying Puritan contributions to Reformed theology, especially on the critical issue of the role of the Mosaic covenant in the Old Testament and its relationship to the Covenants of Works and Grace.[6]

2. Cherry, *Theology of Jonathan Edwards*. See also Cherry, "The Puritan Notion," 328–41.

3. Bogue, *Jonathan Edwards*.

4. Edwards never mentions John Calvin's commentaries in his works and Calvin is "conspicuously absent" from the "Catalogue" and the "Account Book." According to Peter Thuesen, "This does not mean that Edwards never read Calvin: he cites the *Institutes* three times in *Religious Affections*, and we may assume that in many matters, Calvin's authority was simply taken for granted in New England." Thuesen, "Editor's Introduction," *WJE* 26:57. See also Neele, *Before Jonathan Edwards*, 115.

5. Yazawa, *Covenant of Redemption*. Some general aspects of Edwards's views on the covenants have been recently addressed in passing in Douglas Sweeney's review of Edwards's biblical exegesis. Sweeney, *Edwards the Exegete*, 56–57, 83–85, 144–45, 208–9. A chapter in Michael McClymond and Gerald McDermott's systematic summary of Edwards's theology entitled "Edwards's Calvinism and Theology of the Covenants" reviews the relationship between Edwards's covenant theology and predestination. McClymond and McDermott, *Theology of Jonathan Edwards*, 321–38.

6. For example, see Mark Karlberg's surveys which uniformly go directly from the

Second, there have been a great many studies on Edwards's views of justification, sanctification, and the role of works in salvation that have been published in the last few decades.⁷ Many of these studies have questioned whether Edwards indeed stood firmly within the Reformed tradition in relation to these loci, some even making Edwards's theology to be more Catholic than Protestant with regards to these very subjects, subjects that stood at the very heart of the Protestant-Catholic divide. Some of these studies interpret Edwards through his more speculative writings (e.g., his ontology of dispositions) and attempt to "re-read" or "re-interpret" Edwards in ways that seem inimical to his own Reformed theological heritage. Examining Edwards's theology, particularly aspects of faith, justification, and the role of works in salvation, through the lens of a further exposition of the nuances of Edwards's covenant theology promises to shed more and clearer light on these controversial statements of Edwards from a Reformed perspective.

Third, there is a large amount of evidence that suggests Edwards shifted his thinking from a more systematic approach to a more historical-redemptive approach in his theology. Central to his historical-redemptive approach is his use of the covenants which served as a central organizing hermeneutical principle and framework. One indicator of Edwards's increased interest in a biblical-redemptive approach to theology is his increased interest in "covenantal thinking" in his writings.⁸

Westminster Standards to the Princetonian Charles Hodge: Karlberg, "Reformed Interpretation," 1–47; Karlberg, "Justification in Redemptive History," 213–46; Karlberg, *Mosaic Covenant*. See also Rohr, *Covenant of Grace*.

7. A few of the more influential studies include Hunsinger, "Dispositional Soteriology," 107–20; Morimoto, *Jonathan Edwards*; McClymond and McDermott, *Theology of Jonathan Edwards*, 389–409; McClymond, *Encounters with God*; McDermott, "Jonathan Edwards on Justification," 92–111. See also Fesko, *Trinity*, 30–31; Fesko, *Covenant of Redemption*, 127–38; Horton, *Covenant and Salvation*, 288, especially n. 98. Foundational for many of these studies is Schafer, "Jonathan Edwards," 55–67.

8. Although present even in his earliest writings, Edwards seems to have a greater and greater interest in this overarching theme. An "unscientific" search of Edwards's works for the word "covenant" using the on-line search feature of Yale University's Jonathan Edwards Center (www.Edwards.Yale.edu/archive) showed that between the years 1720 and 1729 there were 533 occurrences, between 1730 and 1739 1,386 occurrences, and between 1740 and 1750 2,347 occurrences of the word "covenant" (a near linear increase over those three decades). If one were to look at the years up to November, 1734 (the year Edwards gave his two public lectures on justification by faith, which he attributes to the beginning of the Connecticut Valley revivals, and which are entirely systematic and polemical in nature) there are a total of 1,081 occurrences. After that time (beginning generally with the preaching of his redemptive

This development is most clearly shown in his *Miscellanies*. The topic is entirely absent in the first years, then first introduced in several headings under the topic *The Work of Redemption*, and finally in a whole series of entries titled *The History of Redemption*.[9] If one looks at his later works, particularly those concentrating on a redemptive-historical framework, things take on a new cast and become more exegetically clear, especially regarding the fraught doctrinal topic of justification and sanctification.

Current controversies within American Reformed denominations and seminaries are highlighting once again the contentious nature of interpretations of Reformed covenant theology in relation to justification and sanctification. A majority of faculty at Westminster Seminary in Philadelphia, for example, have in recent years promoted a form of "mono-covenantalism" under the rubric of "the union with Christ school,"[10] the results of which have already begun to influence "new readings" on Edwards's views of justification and works.[11] The prolific writings of N. T. Wright, enormously influential in a wide context of New Testament studies, has generated much discussion regarding his view of covenant nomism which has challenged the traditional Reformation distinctions between justification and sanctification in subtle but important ways.[12]

---

history sermons in 1738, later published posthumously as *The History of the Work of Redemption* in 1774) there are 3,357 occurrences. This cursory survey did not distinguish and stratify between individual treatises or sermons which may have had multiple occurrences, or stratify for the use of "covenant" in unrelated contexts such as the "national covenant" or the "half-way covenant" with regards to Edwards's sacramental controversies in Northampton. Even given these limitations, the increased use of "covenantal language" in Edwards's sermons and writings is remarkable.

9. Wilson, "Editor's Introduction," *WJE* 9:11–17.

10. Foundational works contributing to the "union with Christ school" are Shepherd, *Call of Grace*; Lillback, *Binding of God*; and Gaffin, *By Faith*. For a summary of the controversy see Jeon, *Covenant Theology*. For a response and critique see Wenger, "New Perspective," 311–28.

11. For example, Christopher Atwood in a study of Edwards's doctrine of justification concludes that, "while God sees the faith that brings a believer into union with Christ as *naturally* fit, that same faith also produces holiness which in turn makes him *morally* fit; since God sees the two together, God, in a sense, justifies a person on account of both." Atwood, *Jonathan Edwards's Doctrine of Justification*, 132. Statements like these only contribute to a confusion of law and gospel that is characteristic of the "union with Christ" school. It is noteworthy that Atwood concentrates on Edwards's earlier systematic writings exclusive to his later redemptive-historical writings.

12. Wright, *Climax of the Covenant*; Wright, *What Saint Paul Really Said*; Dunn, "The Justice of God," 1–22; Dunn, *Theology of Paul*. For a response to these studies, see Carson et al., *Justification and Variegated Nomism, Volume 1*; Carson et al., *Justification and Variegated Nomism, Volume 2*.

Within traditionally conservative and confessional denominations in the United States, a form of neonomianism, sometimes referred to as the Auburn Avenue Theology (or Federal Vision), has generated a great deal of intramural controversy.[13]

It is not the aim of this dissertation to appropriate Edwards for either side of these disputes, or to read back into eighteenth-century New England Puritanism the specific issues of contemporary American Reformed theological debate. However, these contemporary issues underscore that discussions of "evangelical obedience" and the nature of ethics (sanctification) as a soteriological category is an important ongoing issue in the Reformed theological tradition. A study of Edwards, especially focusing on his covenant theology, could help shed light on the underlying nature of these issues within the broad contours of historic Reformed theology.

Recognizing that covenant understandings of redemptive history have significant ramifications for systematic formulations of doctrine, a more thorough understanding of Edwards's covenant theology is essential. Explicating Edwards's covenant theology promises to shed light on and help interpret the more controversial discussions regarding the relationship of justification to works and obedience in Edwards's writings, particularly his earlier more polemical discussions.[14] Edwards maintained a nuanced tripartite distinction between the Covenant of Redemption (sometimes referred to as the *pactum salutis*), the Covenant of Works (*foedus operum*), and the Covenant of Grace (*foedus gratiae*). Furthermore, the Mosaic covenant was clearly subordinate to the Covenant of Grace established in the Old Testament, being a republishing or "displaying" of the Covenant of Works as a tutor or "schoolmaster" to drive the Israelites to the need of a covenant savior as typologically represented in its cultic temple sacrifices and ceremonies. In a covenantally unifying approach to the Old and New Testaments, Edwards maintained a clear distinction between law and gospel[15] while simultaneously and

---

13. For a summary of the issues see Beisner, *Auburn Avenue Theology*; Jeon, *Calvin and the Federal Vision*.

14. Precedent for this type of analysis can be seen in Myer's study of the Marrow Controversy in Scotland and the respective differences in covenant or federal theology that generated many of the doctrinal misunderstandings between Ebenezer Erskine (1680–1754) and James Hadow (1667–1747). Myers, *Scottish Federalism*.

15. The law-gospel distinction refers to two opposing principles of inheritance, appropriate to St. Paul's teaching on the two Adams in Rom 5. The forensic contrast between the order of law and the order of grace is one of opposition. This is not to oppose law and grace, but to recognize that a works principle of "do this and live" is

without contradiction explicating a clear and necessary role for works in salvation (avoiding antinomianism) that are not meritorious or contributory to one's justification (avoiding any incipient Arminianism or confusion of law and gospel). Edwards's covenant approach to redemptive history was not at odds with but rather maintained and undergirded the traditional Reformed *ordo salutis* with its logical priority of justification over sanctification and the non-meritorious necessity of "evangelical obedience" in salvation.

None of this is to suggest that Edwards was not creative in his discussions of Reformed theology. Indeed, the creative and innovative aspects of his covenant theology, especially as it applies to the relationship between faith and obedience, will be highlighted. The question is: Was Edwards being creative in form but essentially traditional in content within his Reformed and English Puritan tradition or was he being creative on both levels? In other words, was Edwards saying something "novel" or something in a "novel way" regarding the role of works and obedience in the life of the regenerate and justified Christian? I believe the latter is truer of Edwards and that a renewed study of his covenant theology bears this out. Edwards was not trying to develop a novel theology based on philosophical principals but was attempting to selectively use the best of then current philosophical thinking in defense of a traditional and orthodox theology. In his words, "to obviate cavils" (remove objections) and to satisfy that what Scripture taught, while at times not fully comprehensible, was not "unreasonable." I will be taking the presumptive view that Edwards should be included as part of the trajectory of what E. Brooks Holifield has called "catholick theologiens" who "proposed no alteration of Calvinist doctrine," but who "subtly modified and expanded the older vocabulary in order to make more room for natural causes and moral virtues."[16]

Edwards as a Biblical Theologian

While many academics laud Edwards as a speculative theologian of the highest caliber ("The greatest philosophical mind America has produced," to cite the oft-quoted Perry Miller), Edwards was supremely a

---

fulfilled either "by man" as a law to be fulfilled or "for man" as a gracious gift to be received.

16. Holifield, *Theology in America*, 82.

biblical theologian. According to Neele, Edwards did not reject speculative (philosophical) knowledge entirely, but rather assigned significant importance to it. Yet this speculative knowledge did not come at the expense of but in support of spiritual knowledge or practice.[17] In a sermon on Christian knowledge, Edwards tells his congregation in Northampton that "having a right speculative notion of the doctrines contained in the Word of God" is not exclusive of "having a due sense of them in the heart." However, "it is intended that we should seek the former [speculative] in order to the latter [practical]." This was a crucial point for Edwards, because "a speculative knowledge of [the Word of God], without spiritual knowledge, is in vain and to no purpose . . . Yet a speculative knowledge is also of infinite importance in this respect, that without it we can have no spiritual or practical knowledge."[18]

A key statement of Edwards, and one I think is central to his thinking, is contained in his treatise *Concerning The End for Which God Created the World*, a treatise considered by many to be his most intensely speculative. At the end of the first section, which is devoted to a reasoned analysis of God's ends in creation, and immediately preceding the final section devoted to a biblical exposition of the doctrine, Edwards provides an important synopsis of his overall methodology:

> I confess there is a degree of indistinctness and obscurity in the close consideration of such subjects, and a great imperfection in the expressions we use concerning them; arising unavoidably from the infinite sublimity of the subject, and the incomprehensibleness of those things that are divine. Hence *revelation is the surest guide in these matters*, and what that teaches shall in the next place be considered. Nevertheless, the endeavors used to discover what the voice of reason is, *so far as it can go*, may serve to prepare the way, by obviating cavils insisted on by many; and to satisfy us that what the Word of God says of the matter, is not unreasonable; and thus prepare our minds for a more full acquiescence in the instructions it gives, according to the more natural and genuine sense of words and expression we find often used there concerning this subject.[19]

---

17. Neele, *Before Jonathan Edwards*, 169.

18. Edwards, "The Importance and Advantage of a thorough Knowledge of Divine Truth," *WJE* 22:86–87.

19. Edwards, "Concerning the End," *WJE* 8:462-3 (emphasis mine).

The central importance of this passage for understanding Edwards, especially in his more speculative and philosophical works, is underscored by the editor's note that, "These words and paragraph should be taken quite seriously."[20] These words are equally applicable to understanding those more systematic and polemical passages in Edwards with regards to justification and the role of works or evangelical obedience, which is why an integration of Edwards's redemptive-historical approach to his more systematic and polemical writings on these issues is so vital. One must read Edwards's biblical theology as driving his speculative and philosophical thoughts and not vice-versa.

In his first year of pastoral ministry in New York City in 1722, Jonathan Edwards penned several resolutions that would guide both his life and ministry. Number twenty-eight read, "Resolved, to study the Scriptures so steadily, constantly and frequently, as that I may find, and plainly perceive myself to grow in the knowledge of the same."[21] This statement reflects Edwards's own self-conscious biblicism that would guide his life, study, and pastoral ministry during his lifetime. Perry Miller famously claimed that Edwards was America's greatest philosopher and theologian yet did not share his faith in redemptive history or belief in the veracity of Scripture. Moreover, Miller characterized Edwards's biblical exegesis, among the few references of the Bible in his important and seminal biography, as "fixing upon texts which the Arminians were constantly citing," arguing "in a literalistic—and to us unrewarding—vein."[22] Yet, according to Stephen Stein, it has only been since the 1990s that serious attention has been given to Edwards as a biblical theologian.[23] New studies confirm that Edwards immersed himself in a close study of primary sacred texts, particularly the Bible, as well as biblical commentaries and original word studies. According to Stein, this failure to understand Edwards's biblical centrism in his theology has "led some in the past to ignore, if not dismiss, the scriptural side of Edwards' thought,"[24] resulting in a skewed view of Edwards devoid of his biblical centrism. Cherry argues that "Jonathan Edwards was preeminently a biblical theologian," and that it is "precisely because of his commitment to biblical exegesis" that he "contributed to

---

20. Edwards, "Concerning the End," *WJE* 8:462 n. 7.
21. Edwards, "Resolutions," *WJE* 16:755.
22. Miller, *Jonathan Edwards*, 297.
23. Stein, "Editor's Introduction," *WJE* 24:4.
24. Stein, "Editor's Introduction," *WJE* 24:4.

the emergence of modern thought."[25] Karen Stetina acknowledges that, "It's time for scholars to turn their attention back to the influence that Scripture and faith had on Jonathan Edwards."[26] Robert Brown's study of Edwards's use of the Bible further supports the idea that focusing on Edwards's biblical writings and his biblical interpretation is key to understanding his broader engagement with critical thought and provides a unifying thread to his theological work.[27]

Studies of Edwards's use of the Bible have demonstrated a far-more nuanced and complex exegesis than mere "proof-texting." Edwards used a conglomeration of textual references combined with complex typological and metaphorical correspondences between biblical types and antitypes, and between biblical symbols and the Christocentric reality they mirror. This multifaceted use of Scripture is a classic example of what is today called "pre-critical" exegesis. This does not mean Edwards was "uncritical," but refers to the exegetical methodology of the period before modern "critical" methods. Edwards's continuity with the ongoing tradition of interpretation of previous Reformed theologians and scholastics is marked by this "pre-critical" exegesis.[28] Edwards is situated during the period that Muller characterizes as "late orthodoxy."[29] This is the period roughly after 1725 following the period of "high orthodoxy"—a transition of increased pressure on the pre-critical textual, exegetical, and hermeneutical model of orthodoxy. It is a period characterized by a departure from a Christian Aristotelian philosophical model used by older theologians and a turn to either variants of rationalism or to a virtually a-philosophical dogmatics. It also represents a period of internal divisions over the Reformed confessions raised by the issues of the *Nadere Reformatie*,[30] particularly over issues of piety, and by the expelling of English and French Reformed Protestants. By 1725, a fairly uniform and unified confessional subscription had faded both in England and in Switzerland. This was the era of theologians who would be most influential on Edwards, including Wilhelmus à Brakel (1635–1711), Petrus van

25. Cherry, "Symbols of Spiritual Truth," 263–64.
26. Stetina, *Jonathan Edwards' Early Understanding*, ix.
27. Brown, *Jonathan Edwards and the Bible*.
28. Muller, *Post-Reformation Reformed Dogmatics*, 1:40.
29. Muller, *Post-Reformation Reformed Dogmatics*, 1:32.
30. *Nadere Reformatie* refers to the Dutch "second" or "further" Reformation, roughly equivalent to the English Puritanism and German Pietism movements, c. 1600–1750.

Mastricht (1630–1706), Herman Witsius (1636–1708), Thomas Boston (1676–1732), and Francis Turretin (1623–1687).[31]

Stein suggests that typology is the unifying dimension of Edwards's "Notes" on Scripture.[32] In another article, he shows that Edwards recognized multiple levels of meaning in the biblical text, identifying both literal and spiritual levels, while giving primacy to the spiritual.[33] But even these labels for defining Edwards's method fall short of his diverse handling of Scripture. A more recent work by David Barshinger on Edwards's work on the Psalms underscores his methodological complexity, locating it within the broader contours of the redemptive-historical model.[34] This is a more theologically grounded method, recognizing that Edwards had

---

31. Edwards admired Turretin and Mastricht, referring to "the great Turretine," and again to "the great Mastricht." Edwards, "Religious Affections," *WJE* 2:289 n. 2 and 337. Edwards references both "Turretinus" and "Mastricht" and their works on predestination. Edwards, "Misc. 292," *WJE* 13:383. In a letter to Joseph Bellamy in 1746 Edwards says about Turretin and Mastrich, "They are both excellent. Turretine is on Polemical divinity; on the Five Points, and all other controversial points; and is much larger in these than Mastricht; and is better for one that desires only to be thoroughly versed in controversies. But take Mastricht for divinity in general, doctrine practice and controversie; or as an universal system of divinity; and it is much better than Turretine or any other Book in the world, excepting the Bible, in my opinion." Edwards, "To the Reverend Joseph Bellamy," *WJE* 16:217. For Edwards's use of Mastricht, see Neele, *Before Jonathan Edwards*, 159–68.

32. Stein, "Editor's Introduction," *WJE* 15:2. Sweeney has shown that while Edwards often went beyond what other Protestants had said about the Christological meanings of the Old Testament texts, he refused to go beyond what the rule of Scripture and the rule of faith allowed. The twin pillars that supported classic Protestant exegesis included the "analogy of Scripture" or *analogia Scripturae* in which Scripture is interpreted in light of other texts in other parts of Scripture, and the "analogy of faith" or *analogia fidei* in which more difficult texts were read in view of simpler texts of the kerygmatic core and doctrinal drift of the Bible. Sweeney, *Edwards the Exegete*, 102. According to Edwards, "Spiritually to understand the Scripture is rightly to understand what is in the Scripture, and what was in it before it was understood: 'tis to understand rightly, what used to be contained in the meaning of it; and not the making of a new meaning." Fabricating "new meaning" would be tantamount, in Edwards, to "making a new Scripture: it is . . . adding to the Word; which is threatened with so dreadful a curse." Edwards, "Religious Affections," *WJE* 2:280.

33. Stein, "Quest for the Spiritual Sense," 19–113.

34. Barshinger, "Making the Psalter," 3–29. See also Barshinger, *Jonathan Edwards and the Psalms*. Barshinger identifies seven major themes in Edwards's use of the Psalms: God's glory, human depravity, Christ and his broad work, the heralding of the gospel by the Spirit, the Church, vital piety, and eschatological judgment and hope.

a great concern for redemptive history. Other case studies of Edwards's exegesis come to similar conclusions.[35]

Perry Miller's evaluation of Edwards's as having "brushed aside the (by his day) rusty mechanism of the covenant to forge a fresh statement of the central Protestant definition of man's plight in a universe which God created"[36] clearly misreads the biblical and covenantal centrality of Edwards's theology. This "rusty mechanism of the covenant" was, in the words of John Gerstner, "oiled, greased and made to swing Edwards' whole theology."[37] Edwards always saw himself, and proved himself, to be a federal or covenant theologian. Edwards viewed the Bible as witnessing to a unitary vision of the message of salvation, which the covenant or federal scheme operated as the scaffold supporting a unified biblical narrative of redemption. Edwards taught this scheme from his earliest ministry. In one of his earliest sermons to the congregation of Northampton in 1729, Edwards preached, "the Covenant of Grace is that Covenant which G[od] has Revealed to man since he failed of life by the Covenant of Works, Promising Justification & Eternal life to all that believe in J[esus Christ]."[38] To read Edwards as a biblical theologian is to read him as a covenant theologian.

Reformed Covenant Theology

Federal or covenant theology has been a central and important paradigm or organizing principle for interpreting biblical *loci* within Reformed theological systems, particularly since the seventeenth century. Covenant theology is not a Puritan or even a sixteenth-century phenomenon, but can be traced back as early as the ante-Nicene theologians, earlier than most patristic research or general surveys of the history of the covenant idea in the Christian tradition have often recognized. For example, J. Ligon Duncan has shown that covenant arguments are used in interpretive schemes and in structuring redemptive history in Irenaeus (c. 130–c. 202), Justin Martyr (100–165), Tertullian (c. 155–c. 240?), Lactantius (c.

---

35. For examples, see Yoo, "Jonathan Edwards's Interpretation," 160–92; Stein, "'Like Apples of Gold,'" 324–37; Abernethy, "Jonathan Edwards," 815–30; Tooman, "Edwards's Ezekiel," 160–92.

36. Miller, *Errand*, 48.

37. Gerstner, *Rational Biblical Theology*, 2:81.

38. Edwards, "2 Sam 23:5," *WJEO* 44, L. 3r.

250–c. 325), and Clement of Alexandria (c. 150–c. 215). These arguments are also found in Augustine (354–430), who learned his theology of the covenant primarily from Irenaeus and his contemporaries.[39] Surveys of early Christian covenant thought have shown that the pre-Nicene theologians usually took the Old Testament covenant passages as the starting point in their applications of the covenant concept to Christian living. The early Christian use of the covenant idea shows that they understood the covenant to be both unilateral and bilateral, both promissory and obligatory, and to bring divine blessings and entail human obedience. These writings also show that these early Christian authors, following Old Testament and New Testament examples, employed the covenant idea as a key structural idea in their presentations of redemptive history. The covenant idea functioned to stress moral obligations incumbent upon Christians, to show God's grace in including the Gentiles in the Abrahamic blessings, to deny the reception of these promises to the Israel of the flesh (Israel considered merely as an ethnic entity), and to demonstrate and explain continuity and discontinuity in the divine economy.

As Latin became the *lingua franca* in the western Christian church, the covenant concept faded into the background theologically, but subsequently become more prominent in the late medieval nominalist tradition. While there is no evidence that Martin Luther employed a covenantal interpretive scheme, or that it played any significant role in post-reformation Lutheran scholasticism, it became more prominent in the Reformed branch of the Reformation. This is particularly evident in the writings of Ulrich Zwingli (1484–1531), who made much use of the covenant concept in his writings against the Anabaptists. Despite Perry Miller's opposition of Edwards's "harsh" predestinarian Calvinism with the supposed "kinder and gentler" Puritan Covenant of Grace, one can indeed trace a covenant structure in John Calvin (1509–1564), specifically in his commentaries. While Calvin did not use the covenant as an organizing principle of the *Institutes*, he did develop his doctrine of the sacraments in light of the covenants. Calvin's argument was that where there is a sacrament there must be a covenant because a sacrament is a covenant sign. For Calvin, the Tree of Life in the Garden did not in itself convey eternal life but was a sign and a seal of a covenant promise. This gives credence to those who see in Calvin a rudimentary and

39. Duncan, "Covenant Idea."

undeveloped yet real understanding of a covenant structure in scripture, including the existence of a covenant prior to the fall of Adam.

Post-reformation developments in Reformed theology gave central precedence to the covenant structure of biblical redemptive history and a robust federal theology became an established and characteristic theme among Reformed theologians. Despite the long tradition of using a covenant framework within Reformed exegesis and a general overall accepted covenant scheme, there was no monolithic or uniform consensus within the broader Reformed tradition on the exact nature and arrangements of the distinct covenants and their dispensations within English Puritanism.[40] Furthermore, despite the importance of covenant theology to Reformed doctrine, Muller reminds us that the actual and declared *principia* of Reformed systems were the doctrines of Scripture and God, which had an absolute determinative effect on the structure and contents of their theological system. A principle or foundation of knowing (*principium cognoscendi*) and a principle or foundation of being (*principium essendi*) were the two *principia theologiae* of Protestant scholastic prolegomenon. The first is Scripture, God's own self-revelation. The second is God himself, the self-existent ground of all finite existence. Muller therefore argues that it is a mistake to see any "central dogma" such as the divine decrees or predestination in Reformed Protestantism that is not first and foremost present as a topic (*locus*) in the biblical revelation. This applies even to covenant theology. Covenant theology was not a doctrinal or philosophical construct imposed on Scripture but was derived from Scripture.[41]

The "Reformed tradition" is not as easy to define and delineate as would seem at first glance. There exists a spectrum of thought and exposition within the broad contours of this tradition. For instance, the exact theological and intellectual relationship of Calvin's work to the later Reformed tradition concerns the nature of a tradition as well as the character and variety of continuities and developments within a tradition.

40. The differences within Reformed orthodoxy are summarized in Peterson, "Continuity and Discontinuity," 17–34.

41. Muller, *Post-Reformation Reformed Dogmatics*, 1:125–32. Muller cites Althaus, *Die Prinzipien, der deutschen reformierten Dogmatik in Zeitalter der aristotelischen Scholastik* (Leipzig: Deichert, 1914), where Althaus, "tries to elicit from select doctrinal *loci*, typically the *loci de praedestinatione, de Deo, de providential*, and *de foedere* what he believes to be underlying principles and tendencies, without paying particular attention to what the Protestant scholastics themselves say about *principia*." Muller, *Post-Reformation Reformed Dogmatics*, 1:129–30.

All these concepts require careful nuancing.[42] There are, however, fundamental continuities of the basic tradition of ecumenical and creedal catholicity that can be acknowledged. There are broad continuities belonging to specific Reformation and post-Reformation era confessional traditions and common theological ground enunciated in the major confessional works of the mid-sixteenth century, namely the Gallican, Belgic, and Scots Confessions, the *Heidelberg Catechism*, and the *Thirty-Nine Articles* of the Church of England. These were all written in communities either in dialogue with or in one way or another indebted to Calvin and which, more importantly, represent the international community of Reformed belief to which Calvin belonged. Particularly important to this tradition is the *Westminster Standards*, which Edwards is known to have agreed with in at least its general system or "substance" of thought.[43]

Reformed "orthodoxy" and "scholasticism" are terms that also need to be clarified. Orthodoxy, or "right teaching," was the goal of the Reformation from its inception. The early reformers waged a polemical discussion on specific disputed points that are embodied in such confessions as the *Augsburg* and *Tetrapolitan* confessions. Later Protestant confessionalism attempted to compile more comprehensive statements of the whole body of doctrine, which became characteristic of institutionally established Protestantism. Orthodoxy and institutionalization are two aspects of one development consisting in the adjustment of a received body of doctrine and its systematic relations to the needs of the established Protestant church, in terms dictated by the teachings of the Reformers on Scripture, grace, justification, and the sacraments.

The terms "scholasticism" or "scholastic" have a narrower reference, referring to the technical and academic side of the process of institutionalization and professionalization of Protestant doctrine in the universities of the late sixteenth and seventeenth centuries. "Scholasticism" has a history of being used as a derogatory term, sometimes indicating a "tradition-bound, logic-chopping mentality, involving a slavish adherence to Aristotle . . . laden with ideological baggage."[44] It is

---

42. Trueman, "Reception of Calvin."

43. "As to my subscribing to the substance of the Westminster Confessions, there would be no difficulty," Edwards in a letter to John Erskine in response to his question whether Edwards could subscribe to *The Westminster Confession* and Erskine's offer to assist Edwards in finding a congregation in Scotland. Edwards, "To the Reverend John Erskine," *WJE* 16:355.

44. Vos, "Scholasticism," 621.

often used to characterize the medieval period of Catholic theological systematization that was self-consciously indebted to Aristotelian philosophy, especially in the synthesis of philosophy and theology in Thomas Aquinas (1225–1274).[45] In the past century, it has become customary in historical theological studies to apply these same stereotyped perspectives to the development of Protestant scholasticism in the sixteenth and seventeenth centuries, in which it is conceived as "not much more than a rigid and inflexible complex of dogmas involving a regression to outdated medieval patterns of thought."[46] German historians such as Paul Althaus (1888–1966), Hans Emil Weber (1882–1950), and Heinrich Heppe (1820–1879), began to promote a view of Protestant scholasticism as a deviation from the "pristine" theology of John Calvin. James B. Torrance argued that in the *Westminster Confession*, "the pattern is no longer the trinitarian one of the Creeds or Calvin's *Institutio* of 1559, but is dominated by the eternal decrees and the scheme of Federal Theology," arguing further that the entire system is framed deductively from the doctrine of election.[47] Heiko Oberman and David Steinmetz argued for a reevaluation of this period and a need to recognize a greater continuity between the Reformation and the scholasticism of the Middle Ages than had been previously acknowledged.[48]

Muller, building on this foundation, applied these studies to later Protestant orthodoxy, finding greater continuity between the Reformation and the later Reformed scholastic period. He argues that after the first generation of Reformers the needs of the movement shifted from polemics to systematization, with the task of sharpening definitions, clarifying boundaries, and, most importantly, developing institutions where this new theology would be taught and defended. Scholasticism, according to Muller, is bound up with the institutionalization of Protestantism: "Orthodoxy and institutionalization are but two aspects of one development—indeed, they are corollaries of one another."[49] Hence, "the term *scholasticism* well describes the technical and academic side

---

45. Protestant orthodoxy appropriated the scholasticism of late Renaissance humanism, not the scholasticism of Thomas Aquinas.

46. Asselt and Dekker, *Reformation and Scholasticism*, 11.

47. Torrance, "Strength and Weaknesses," 455–56.

48. Oberman, *Dawn of the Reformation*, 39–120, 234–58; Oberman, *Harvest of Medieval Theology*, 423–28; Oberman, "The Shape of Late Medieval Thought," 3–25; Steinmentz, *Luther in Context*.

49. Muller, *Post-Reformation Reformed Dogmatics*, 1:37.

18   THE COVENANT THEOLOGY OF JONATHAN EDWARDS

of this process of the institutionalization of Protestant doctrine," being, "preeminently a school-theology."[50] Muller defines scholasticism as a theology designed to "develop a system on a highly technical level and in an extremely precise manner by means of the careful identification of topics, division of these topics into their basic parts, definition of the parts, and doctrinal or logical argumentation concerning the divisions and definitions."[51] This is distinct from other genre and approaches, namely catechetical, biblical-exegetical, and simple didactic or ecclesial methods. Carl Trueman and R. Scott Clark agree with Muller's conclusions, stating that, "scholasticism was the attempt to adapt the Reformation to the demands of the academy in terms of a pre-critical worldview."[52]

The latter part of the twentieth and early twenty-first centuries, particularly in Reformation and Puritan studies, saw an increased interest in and research devoted to the idea of covenant in theological formulations.[53] Two historiographical landmarks are particularly significant and form the backdrop for any discussion of the covenant in the history of doctrine from the perspective of modern theology. The first is the work of Perry Miller on Puritanism.[54] Writing in a day that had little interest in Calvin or Calvinists, Miller managed to rehabilitate the Puritans by depicting them as the authors of a "revision of Calvinism."[55] The Puritans, according to Miller, mollified the harsher characteristics of Calvinism by the "invention" of covenant or federal theology. This covenant theology supposedly had the effect of creating a space for human responsibility in an oppressive predestinarian system. In Miller's presentation, the covenant idea was a theological tool used by the Puritans to change Calvinism for the better. Miller's work has exerted a tremendous influence on

---

50. Muller, *Post-Reformation Reformed Dogmatics*, 1:33.

51. Muller, *Post-Reformation Reformed Dogmatics*, 1:33.

52. Trueman and Clark, *Protestant Scholasticism*," xvii. For further favorable defenses of post-Reformation scholasticism see Muller, "Scholasticism Protestant," 193–205; Muller, "Giving Direction to Theology," 183–93.

53. This is not to neglect that the historiography of the covenant idea in the nineteenth and early twentieth centuries was considerable. See Zandt, "Doctrine of the Covenants," 28–39; Lindsay, "Covenant Theology," 521–38; Girardeau, "Federal Theology," 96–130; Rainy, "Federal Theology," 341–49, 427–34; Vos, "Doctrine of the Covenant," 234–70. For an extensive bibliography of nineteenth-century treatments of the development of covenant theology, see Woolsey, *Unity and Continuity*.

54. Miller, *New England Mind*.

55. See Marsden's analysis of Miller's work on the Puritans, in Marsden, "Perry Miller's Rehabilitation," 91–105.

subsequent writing on the idea of covenant in the Reformed tradition. Marsden puts it well when he says, "As for the thesis that the covenant of grace represented a revision of Calvinism, Miller has created a myth that has been so elegantly presented and widely repeated that it will be difficult to destroy."[56] While more recent studies have certainly allowed scholars to go beyond Miller's thesis, one certainly cannot go around it, especially with regard to Miller's subsequent role in the rehabilitation of Edwardsean studies in the twentieth century.

A second catalyst for modern historical consideration of the covenant idea may be found in Karl Barth's criticism of the older covenant theology.[57] Whereas other modern theologians tended to ignore the Reformed theology of the seventeenth century, Barth appreciated and interacted with the covenant theologians of that period. He also recognized that the covenant idea that had attained such a prominent place in their system was not absent from the earlier Reformers.[58] But Barth was very critical of these federal theologians at certain points.[59] He was particularly displeased with the concept of a pre-fall Covenant of Works and the use of covenant theology to maintain a doctrine of limited atonement.[60] These "later developments" in covenant theology, Barth suggested, were given confessional status for the first time in the *Westminster Confession*.[61] Since Barth made these observations, a large number of studies have sought to substantiate historically his theological critique of covenant theology.[62] According to writers in this school, the systematization

56. Marsden, "Perry Miller's Rehabilitation," 105. Miller's influence can be seen in the work of Leonard J. Trinterud whose "two-tradition" theory of the development of covenant theology was a modification of the Miller thesis; see Trinterud, "Origins of Puritanism," 37–57. See also McGiffert, "Grace and Works," 463–502; McGiffert, "Tyndale's Conception of the Covenant," 167–84. Baker, *Bullinger and the Covenant* is an expansion of the Trinterud thesis. For similar approaches, see Henderson, "The Idea of the Covenant," 2–14; Møller, "Beginnings," 46–67. For helpful correctives to this interpretation, see Rohr, *Covenant of Grace*; Stoute, "Origins and Early Development"; Calhoun, "Covenant in Bullinger and Calvin."

57. For a distillation of Barth's views on covenant, see Barth, *Church Dogmatics*, 4/1:1–78, esp. 54–66, where he discusses Federal Theology.

58. Barth, *Church Dogmatics*, 4/1:54–55.

59. For an elaboration of Barth's own covenant theology and his criticism of the Cocceian school, see Scott, "Covenant," 182–98; McCormack, "Scholastic of a Higher Order," 2:626.

60. Barth, *Church Dogmatics*, 4/1:57–63.

61. Barth, *Church Dogmatics*, 4/1:59.

62. See McClelland, "Covenant Theology," 182–88; McCoy, "Cocceius," 352–70;

of the "unbiblical" concept of covenant led to a revision of Calvinism (similar to Miller's thesis), but for the worse (contra Miller). Some of the recurring themes is these historical examinations of covenant theology include the conditionality or unconditionality of the covenant,[63] the role of law and its relation to covenant,[64] the question of single versus multiple traditions of covenant thought in Reformed theology,[65] and the role of covenant in the structure of redemptive history.[66]

Much more can be said about the trajectories of interpretation of Reformed covenant theology, especially in its post-Barthian developments. The ramification of these developments has been a reinterpretation of Reformed orthodoxy in fundamental ways. One argument has pitted "Calvin against the Calvinists," interpreting Calvin "as a theologian of grace to be distinguished from the legalism of later 'Calvinist' covenantal or federal theology."[67] Muller summarizes this neoorthodox

---

Rolston, "Responsible Man," 129–56; Rolston, *John Calvin*; Torrance, "McLeod Campbell," 295–311; Torrance, "Covenant Concept," 225–243; Torrance, "Covenant or Contract?," 51–76; Bell, *Calvin and Scottish Theology*. David Weir also tends to follow this line in Weir, *Origins of Federal Theology*; cf. Duncan, "Review of *The Origins of Federal Theology*," 55–57. For a critique of this historical approach, see Karlberg, "Original State of Adam," 291–309; Lillback, *Binding of God*; Lillback, "Continuing Conundrum," 42–74; Muller, "Covenant of Works, 75–101; Woolsey, *Unity and Continuity*, 129–98.

63. McCoy, "Cocceius," 362–64; Torrance, "Covenant or Contract?," 54–57. The same preoccupation with conditionality/unconditionality may be noted in Torrance, "Covenant Concept," 228–31. Because of the influence in Protestant circles of Barth's strongly monergistic bent on the covenant, and the subsequent equation of conditionality with "works salvation," almost all contemporary discussion of covenant thought breaks down into "either/or" categories: conditional/unconditional, bilateral/unilateral, and synergistic/monergistic. This affects the historical study of the idea in the Reformation and post-Reformation eras as well. For a thorough evaluation of this pattern, see Woolsey's historiographical survey of covenant thought in the nineteenth and twentieth centuries in Woolsey, *Unity and Continuity*, 101–98.

64. Rolston, "Responsible Man," 129–56; Lyall, "Metaphors and Analogies," 1–17; Eusden, "Natural Law and Covenant Theology," 1–30.

65. For presentations of the "two-tradition" hypothesis, see Trinterud, "Origins of Puritanism," 37–57; McGiffert, "Grace and Works," 463–502; Baker, *Bullinger and the Covenant*. For alternative evaluations of the development of covenant theology, see Woolsey, *Unity and Continuity*; Lillback, *Binding of God*; Rohr, *Covenant of Grace*.

66. Lincoln, "Development of the Covenant Theory," 134–63; Kaiser, "Old Promise," 11–23; Feinberg, *Continuity and Discontinuity*, 37–62.

67. Muller, "Calvin and the 'Calvinists,'" 349. Various arguments have been employed by different writers, but they all come down to something like the following: whereas Calvin's presentation of the Christian gospel was warm, exuberant and

interpretation of Calvin as "the attempt to identify Calvin as the direct ancestor of neoorthodox Christocentrism and to discredit theologically the Reformed orthodox teaching as incompatible both with Calvin and with Barth."[68]

One of the most important aspects of the traditional orthodox Calvinist teaching on the covenant is the use of the law-gospel distinction. The antithesis between law and gospel reflects two opposing principles of inheritance corresponding to the Pauline teaching on the two Adams in Rom 5. Much of recent neoorthodox Reformed theology has openly denied the importance of the law-gospel distinction (maintaining that this distinction is a peculiarly "Lutheran" hermeneutical principle), substituting in its place the Barthian notion of "law in grace." This neoorthodox school of interpretation maintains only one order or covenant, the Covenant of Grace, comprehending both creation and redemption. Repudiation of the law-gospel antithesis registers itself in other critical and related areas of Reformed exposition, particularly that of justification by faith, the atonement of Christ, sanctification, and the relationship between grace and works.

---

thoroughly evangelical, his so-called Calvinistic successors presented what was in effect another gospel that was formal, introspective, and legalistic. Some have held that later Calvinists distorted the teaching of Calvin by giving a greater prominence to predestination than he did. R. T. Kendall suggests even further that the Puritans, supposedly followers of Calvin, were actually opposed to the teaching of Calvin in its central emphases. Kendall, "Nature of Saving Faith." These studies, which have attempted to draw a sharp distinction and extreme discontinuity between the thought of Calvin and later reformed scholastic theologians, are challenged by Muller. Muller refutes the generalizations and arguments of nineteenth- and early twentieth-century German historians and theologians such as Alexander Schweizer, Heinrich Heppe, Paul Althaus, and Hans Emil Weber who discussed the development of predestination as a central dogma within Reformed, and particularly Calvin's, theology and the purportedly significant differences between Calvin and Bullinger ("Genevan" and "Rhineland" theologies respectively) on the topic of covenant, arguing that covenant theology acted as a counterpoise to "rigid" seventeenth-century predestinarianism. The more recent "Calvin against the Calvinists" school, which draws upon the arguments of Schweizer, Heppe, Weber, and Ernst Bizer, argues that later Reformed theology is a predestinarian system, but that this development of predestination is a "departure" from the thought of Calvin. This approach is grounded in neoorthodox assumptions concerning revelation, Scripture, the relation of law and gospel, and the principal function of Christ in theology as well as a negative, theologized understanding of "scholasticism." See Muller, *Christ and the Decree*; Muller, *Unaccommodated Calvin*; Muller, *After Calvin*; Muller, *Calvin and the Reformed Tradition*.

68. Muller, "Calvin and the 'Calvinists,'" 353.

With this background in mind, this work will situate Edwards's own covenantal thinking within the broader Reformed tradition that he inherited as an eighteenth-century New England Puritan. A discussion of Edwards's covenant theology is not mere prolegomena to his views on faith, works, and salvation, but embodies that very theology.

2

Jonathan Edwards on the Covenant of Works

Introduction

As stated in the previous chapter, I maintain that Jonathan Edwards's theology of evangelical obedience is best understood in the context of his covenant theology. This chapter is the first of four that will examine the main contours of Edwards's covenantal thought. These chapters set the context for understanding the role of works in the life of the believer under the New Covenant. Central to this exposition will be the role of covenant theology, in both the Reformed tradition up to Edwards and in Edwards himself, in defining the distinction between law and gospel.

Before discussing Edwards's own covenant theology, each of the following four chapters begins with a brief discussion of the history and historiography of the covenants in post-reformation Reformed theology up until the time of Edwards. I do this for several reasons. First, it sets Edwards within his own historical context to evaluate the continuities and occasional discontinuities between Edwards and the broader Reformed tradition. In doing so it will support the conclusion that Edwards's own formulations were well within the bounds of Reformed confessional orthodoxy. Second, it will provide a basis for looking at the implications of his covenant theology for evangelical obedience, especially as it relates to faith and justification. Finally, since in many cases Edwards more-or-less assumed the basic overall confessional structure of Reformed orthodoxy, it will provide a necessary background to Edwards's own covenantal thinking.

I begin with a discussion of the Covenant of Works for several reasons. First, if covenant theology can be considered the architectonic[1] principle of both the systematizing of the Christian faith as well as a biblical hermeneutic to structure the relationship between the Old and New Testaments, the first of the covenants, commonly referred to as the Covenant of Works, is the foundational cornerstone of that structure in Edwards's thought. In this sense it has a certain logical priority. It is the first covenant made by God with man, instituted before the fall with Adam when Adam was still in the state of moral perfection (*status integritatis*). As such it forms a foundation for ordering and understanding both the nature of the second covenant (of redemption) and its outworking within the history of redemption (Covenant of Grace). It therefore provides a clear picture of the principle of "works" that informs the entire structure of covenant redemption and provides a key principle for systematizing the Christian faith in Edwards. While the Covenant of Redemption is an "eternal" covenant that precedes in time (or is rather "above it" in eternity), God's covenant with Adam, the Covenant of Works, is the first in the biblical narrative of redemption. Beginning with the Covenant of Works also has precedence in Reformed scholastic theology. Moreover, Edwards did not pose a radical dichotomy between biblical theology and systematic theology. His covenantal structure, of which the first Covenant of Works defines the subsequent relations among the future covenants, is the integrating thread that ties together the themes of redemptive history and the *ordo salutis* of individual salvation in Edwards's writings, particularly with regards to the law-gospel distinction.

In this first chapter I intend to show that Edwards held to a fully developed view of the Covenant of Works and that this view was consistent with and in continuity with the Reformed scholastic tradition of his time. I will first present an overview of the history and historiography of the origin and development of the Covenant of Works in post-reformation Reformed scholasticism, examining the continuities and discontinuities that existed between this period and the early Protestant reformers. It must be remembered that the Reformed tradition was never monolithic in terms of formulating a consistent covenantal or federal theology. Despite several intramural debates, however, a broad tricovenantal structure

---

1. Referring to covenant or federal theology as the architectonic principle of Reformed theology was first used by B. B. Warfield: "The architectonic principle of the Westminster Confession is supplied by the schematization of the Federal theology, which had obtained by this time in Britain." Warfield, *Works*, 56. See also MacLeod, "Covenant Theology," 214.

and outline was formulated and incorporated in many of the Reformed confessions. This is important for both situating Edwards within his own tradition, showing the continuities and discontinuities within Edwards's own formulation.

In the next section I will discuss Edwards's own view of the Covenant of Works in his writings. I intend to show that the Covenant of Works was crucial for maintaining the law-gospel distinction in Edwards. I will do this by concentrating on explicit discussions in his *Miscellanies* as well as several of his sermons, developing his view of the Covenant of Works in detail, focusing on the centrality of the works principle and its implications.

An understanding of Edwards's theology of the Covenant of Works is not only important for Edwardsean historiography, but also has important implications for current controversies in Reformed scholarship. As discussed in the previous chapter, the Covenant of Works has come under scrutiny in recent conservative Reformed teachings. While it would be anachronistic to fully insert Edwards into these contemporary disputes, the central importance of Edwards in the history of the Reformed theological tradition would provide strong historical arguments in this intramural debate.

The Covenant of Works in Reformed Theology

In this section I will provide a brief overview of the Covenant of Works as developed by Reformed theologians leading up to Edwards. This will be important to put Edwards's own covenantal views in their historical perspective. I will begin by briefly discussing the specific terminology used by Reformed theologians and the logical priority they gave to a Covenant of Works, followed by a review of the history and historiography of the first covenant in post-reformation Reformed federal theology. I will make the argument that the Covenant of Works did not develop out of an increasing scholastic "legalism" in opposition to the more "gracious" theology of John Calvin. Rather, the Covenant of Works developed out of a post-reformation biblical hermeneutic that was explicitly connected to the law-gospel distinction and acts to undergird the principle of salvation by grace alone. I will also examine the "two traditions" theory first put forward by Leonard Trinterud, who distinguished two separate strains of covenant theology arising in the sixteenth century.[2] According to

2. Trinterud, *Origins of Puritanism*, 37–57.

Trinterud and other scholars, a bilateral or two-sided covenant scheme arose with Ulrich Zwingli (1484–1531) and Heinrich Bullinger (1504–1575) in Zurich and the Rhineland that became a point of tension or conflict with the unilateral covenant theory and predestinarianism associated with Calvin and the Genevan Reformation. These conclusions were refuted by Muller, and I will look at the works of some of the architects of Reformed federal theology, particularly Theodore Beza (1519–1605), Zacharias Ursinus (1534–1583), Robert Rollock (1555–1599), and Petrus van Mastricht (1630–1706), in support of Muller's critique.

Terminology

Reformed federal theologians have used various terms to describe this prelapsarian covenant with Adam, including the covenant of nature (*foedus naturale*), the Covenant of Works (*foedus operum*), the covenant of life, and sometimes the covenant of innocence, among others.[3] These different terms reflected the different ways in which the original prelapsarian covenant relationship with Adam was construed. As the original relationship to be fulfilled through use of the endowments given Adam it may be called the covenant of *creation* or *nature*. As a covenant made with Adam before sin it may be called the covenant of *innocence*. As a covenant made between parties who were friends it may be called the covenant of *friendship* or of *love*. The blessing in view may lead one to call it a covenant of *life*, while the requirement of obedience to God suggests the term *legal* covenant or covenant of *law* or of *works*. Consideration of the tender love and generosity suggests the term covenant of *favor*. Others have opted for a neutral term, the *Adamic* administration.[4] In the seventeenth century, Reformed theologians preferred the term Covenant of Works in distinction from Arminians who tended to retain the term covenant of nature because of their emphasis on the natural capacity for obedience among all redeemed and unredeemed humanity. For important and similar reasons, Edwards used the term Covenant of Works consistently and almost exclusively in his writings, recognizing the subtle distinctions these other terms (covenant of creation, law,

---

3. Asselt, *Federal Theology*, 254–57. Asselt lists the following terms: *foedus naturae* (covenant of nature), *foedus natural* (natural covenant), *foedus creationiss* (covenant of creation), *foedus legale* (covenant of law), *amicitial cum Deo* (friendship with God), and *foedus operum* (covenant of works).

4. Murray, "Adamic Administration," 49.

works, life, innocence, etc.) give to the nature and theology of this first covenant in the writings of other Reformed theologians.

Logical Priority

A discussion of the Covenant of Works is a logical starting point for a discussion of Edwards's covenant theology. While the *pactum salutis*, or Covenant of Redemption, is the eternal pretemporal covenant between the members of the Trinity *ad intra* that forms the foundational ground for God's covenantal relationship with humanity *ad extra*, many Reformed scholastics recognized a logical, if not temporal (at least in terms of its biblical revelation in Genesis), priority to the Covenant of Works as a basis for their understanding Reformed covenantal structure in general.

Wilhelmus à Brakel, reflecting the concerns of many Reformed theological systematicians, maintained that, "Acquaintance with this covenant is of the greatest importance, for whoever errs here or denies the existence of the Covenant of Works, will not understand the covenant of grace, and will readily err concerning the mediatorship of the Lord Jesus. Such a person will readily deny that Christ by His active obedience has merited a right to eternal life for the elect . . .Whoever denies the covenant of works, must rightly be suspect to be in error concerning the covenant of grace as well."[5] For à Brakel, there is a logical and systematic connection between the covenants. He warns that a logically consequent doctrinal *locus* could all too easily become the basis of a retroactive misconception of a primary or logically prior doctrinal *locus*. Herman Witsius also drew connections between rejecting or misunderstanding the Covenant of Works with a series of Christological and soteriological errors.[6] More recently, Geerhardus Vos (1862–1949) observed, with respect to the *pactum salutis*, "how a denial of the covenant of works sometimes goes hand in hand with a lack of appreciation for the counsel of peace."[7]

Recognizing the systematic interrelatedness of the different covenants is essential for understanding Reformed theology and cannot be ignored. For Edwards, especially, the grand redemptive scheme of the biblical narrative, of God's revelation of his sovereign judgment and saving grace,

---

5. Brakel, *Christian's Reasonable Service*, 1:355.
6. Witsius, *Economy of the Covenants*, 1:17–24; cf. 1:57–58, 1:64, and 1:73–75.
7. Vos, "Doctrine of the Covenant," 245.

hinges on a right understanding and correlation between the covenants, of which the Covenant of Works, the initial covenant of God with man in his created innocence, is foundational. Edwards's systematic and rigidly logical mind dissected to the marrow the structure of Reformed covenantal thinking and, while maintaining a system well within the bounds of Reformed orthodoxy, creatively reconstructed covenantal formulations in nuanced ways that would have profound consequences for his theology, both practical as well as polemical, within the historical milieu of his own eighteenth-century New England Puritanism.[8] This is particularly significant with regards to the Covenant of Works, given the historiographical controversies surrounding the origin of the concept of the Covenant of Works, as well as current controversies and discussions regarding the definition, place, and role of the Covenant of Works within Reformed theology.

Historiography and Debate

In this section I will briefly review the debate that has ensued over the last century and a half over the origins and development of covenant (federal) theology. While historians have provided considerable clues and pieces to the puzzle, it has been claimed that no one has adequately explained the origin of the Covenant of Works within Reformed theology. David Weir states that "no real reason has been given as to why the [prelapsarian covenant] idea arose or how it came to prominence."[9] Weir himself has proposed that the idea arose in Reformed discussions during the 1550s within the context of the predestinarian controversies. These discussions involved the place of Adam's fall in the sovereign decree of God. In other words, the Covenant of Works was a means to account for the perceived "contradiction" between the Calvinist assumption of "the utter sovereignty of God over human action, without God being the author of sin" and the assumption of "the utter responsibility of man for his conduct."[10] Weir goes on to say that, "The prelapsarian covenant with Adam was a means by which orthodox Calvinists of the late sixteenth

---

8. It has been debated whether Jonathan Edwards deviated from his tradition in this regard (among others). Carl Bogue's detailed study of Edwards's Covenant of Grace provides a comprehensive and convincing assessment that Edwards, "is clearly within the Reformed and Covenant family." Bogue, *Jonathan Edwards*, 52.

9. Weir, *Origins of the Federal Theology*, 34.

10. Weir, *Origins of the Federal Theology*, 15–16.

century . . . could maintain the tension between prelapsarian Adamic responsibility and divine sovereignty . . . This covenant gave moral responsibility to Adam, and yet it was also the means by which the sovereign decrees concerning Adam were carried out."[11] The Covenant of Works arose primarily as a theodicy, argues Weir, originating in the German Palatinate between 1560 and 1590 with the first appearance of Zacharias Ursinus's *Major Catechism* of 1561 or 1562. It later evolved into a mature theological *locus* within Reformed theology in the works of Kaspar Olevianus (1536–1587), Thomas Cartwright (c. 1535–1603), and Dudley Fenner (1558–1587) between 1584 and 1590 and finally in a fully developed system in Robert Rollock's *Tractatus de vocatione efficacy* (1597).[12]

Lyle Bierma and Richard Muller have argued that Weir's conclusions are without any clear historical warrant, and that Weir only hypothesizes a connection between the predestinarian debate and Ursinus's covenant language without offering any clear explicit historical connection.[13] Muller provides historical evidence that the debate was not concerned with covenant concepts at all and that Ursinus did not link covenant concepts with the contradiction that Weir sees underlying the Reformed position in the debate.[14] That contradiction in Ursinus's thought, as well as in other Reformed theologians, was resolved throughout the Augustinian tradition and in the sixteenth century on other grounds. This tradition either employed the category of divine permission or used formulations in terms of divine *concursus*, which undergirds but does not negate human willing (or by combining these two approaches with an emphasis on the mediation of the divine will in and through secondary causes). In either case, the formulation of a prelapsarian Covenant of Works does not appear necessary to the predestinarian issue.[15] Muller critiques Weir's basic presupposition as following an old "central dogma" thesis, with its

---

11. Weir, *Origins of the Federal Theology*, 16.

12. Weir notes that the phrase "covenant of works" occurs as early as 1596 in Rollock's *Questiones et Responsiones aliquot de Foedere Dei*, (1596) but is more developed in his *Tractatus* (1597), and later in *A Treatise of God's Effectual Calling* (1603). Weir, *Origins of the Federal Theology*, 16.

13. Bierma, Review of *Origins of the Federal Theology*, 483–85.

14. Muller, Review of *Origins of the Federal Theology*, 597–98.

15. Muller further argues that in order for the doctrine of a prelapsarian covenant to function at all the concepts of divine permission and the mediation of the divine will in and through secondary causes must be presupposed.

view of Beza's *Tabula* as a paradigm for theological system and assuming the debate over the supposed central dogma of predestination controls virtually all other discussions.

Alternative perspectives on the origin of the Covenant of Works within Reformed theology include those of Robert Letham, who argues a clear relationship in early Reformed theology between a covenantal understanding of the Mosaic law and the identification of the natural law known to Adam before the fall with the Mosaic law. He also explains the emergence of the two-covenant scheme with the popularization of Ramist dichotomies.[16] Michael McGiffert, following on the theme of two diverging tendencies in Reformed theology posited originally by Trinterud,[17] argues that late sixteenth-century covenant theology represented a stronger legal orientation over against the theology of grace taught by Calvin and his contemporaries.[18] Holmes Rolston III, James Torrance, and David Poole also view the rise of the concept of a works covenant within post-reformation Reformed theology as a developing form of legalism and a deviation from the theology of the reformers, particularly John Calvin. The Covenant of Works was an "illegitimate" addition which disturbed the priority of grace over works, asserting a historical (and potentially theological) priority of law over grace, while misunderstanding the biblical concept of *berith* as a purely legal contract.[19]

---

16. Letham, "*Foedus Operum*," 457–67.

17. Trinterud, "Origins of Puritanism," 37–57. Trinterud posits two traditions in Reformed theology that diverged after Calvin. The first stemmed from Heinrich Bullinger and the Rhenish Reformers who accented the bilateral nature of the covenant between God and humanity, and the other from John Calvin, who emphasized the unilateral and predestinarian nature of the covenant. See also Møller, "Beginnings," 46–67; Greaves, "Origins and Early Development," 21–35; Baker, "Bullinger," 359–76.

18. McGiffert, "Grace and Works," 463–502; McGiffert, "From Moses to Adam," 131–55.

19. Rolston, *John Calvin;* Rolston, "Responsible Man," 129–56; Torrance, "Strengths and Weaknesses," 51–56; Torrance, "Calvin and Puritanism," 264–77; Torrance, "McLeod Campbell," 295–311; Poole, *History of the Covenant.* See also Muller, Review of *History of the Covenant*, 217–18. Reading Reformed orthodox writers' sophisticated linguistic analysis of the use of the term "covenant" does not support Torrance's claims that the perceived problem is a confusion of its meaning. Stephen J. Casselli cites, for example, Anthony Burgess's facility with the Hebrew, Greek, and Latin terms, as well as an awareness of other relevant Semitic languages. Casselli, *Divine Rule Maintained*, 56–57. Casselli also highlights John Ball's exposition of the doctrine of the covenant beginning with an analysis of the Hebrew term *berith* in which he interacts with various opinions regarding the proper root of the term, employing comparisons with the Septuagint and other Greek classical writers, noting the term's use throughout the

Even earlier, Donald Bruggink asserted that there is a complete absence of any intimation of a Covenant of Works made with Adam in Calvin's writings.[20] Bruggink cites Calvin's statement in his commentary on Jer 31:31–34, "God has never made any other covenant than that which he made formerly with Abraham, and at length confirmed by the hand of Moses." But he misses the immediate context of Calvin, who is seeking to show that the "New Covenant" is not contrary to the first covenant, i.e., the Mosaic covenant, which was in turn a confirmation of the covenant with Abraham. This quote by Calvin can just as easily mean that God has in essence only made one Covenant of Grace, which he continues to reestablish in history. Calvin is stressing the essential unity of the covenantal dispensations rather than the first moment of confirmation of the covenant. Such a literalistic interpretation of Calvin at this point negates the very point he is attempting to make, namely, that if God only made a covenant with Abraham and Moses, he did not make a "new" covenant.

Another argument advanced by Bruggink is that Calvin insisted upon one gracious covenant with Adam, and understood Adam, even as he existed before the fall, to be sustained by God's grace. Federal theologians brought in the concept of attainment by works—albeit works before the fall. Nevertheless, the seriousness with which these pre-fall works were proclaimed set the stage for putting works between man and God, prioritizing the legal over the relational. The federal constructs which further denominated both parties fulfilling certain conditions as prerequisites to a valid covenant, with a corresponding triple Covenant of Works, Redemption, and Grace, led to a demand of works on the part of fallen humanity to fulfill the conditions of the Covenant of Grace, which would seem a contradiction, or at least a danger leading to a righteousness based in some aspect on works.[21] John Murray recognized, however, that this question was not discussed until the seventeenth century, thereby exempting Calvin from such a view of covenant and conditions.[22]

Heinrich Heppe considered German Reformed theology to be a rejuvenation of the Lutheran theologian Philip Melanchthon's

---

Old Testament while referencing commentators both medieval and Reformed, and considering rabbinic approaches to the question. Ball, *Treatise of the Covenant*, 1–6.

20. Bruggink, "Calvin and Federal Theology," 15–22.

21. Bruggink, "Calvin and Federal Theology," 20. The same thoughts respecting the question of the mutuality of covenant obligations in Calvin's idea of the covenant can also be found in Trinterud, "Origins of Puritanism," 56 n. 20.

22. Murray, "Covenant Theology," III:208.

(1497–1560) theology in opposition to the Calvinistic doctrine of predestination.[23] According to Heppe, the doctrine of absolute predestination resulted in arid scholastic disputes and a loss of piety. Federalism was an outgrowth of Melanchthon's desire to protect the human will from the excesses of absolute predestination. This opposition of predestination to the interests of covenant theology as interpreted by Heppe was influential in twentieth-century interpretations of Edwards, especially as pioneered by Perry Miller.

In a series of influential works, Muller has effectively rebutted the arguments of those who would pit Calvin against later covenant theologians, in that "they typically proceed as if Reformed federalism were a monolith with little variety of formulation and no clear sense of the relationship of the concept of a Covenant of Works to the doctrines of grace, Christ, and salvation."[24] He also cites Poole's work as heavily reliant on secondary sources and for its failure to deal with contemporary scholarship's reinterpretation of Protestant orthodoxy.[25] Any significant discontinuity in substance at this point between Calvin and later Reformed covenantal theologians, as argued in Rolston's and Torrance's work, comes only at the expense of exaggerating Calvin's views on the prelapsarian graciousness of God and by minimizing his comments on Adam's duties before God and God's law, and then by arguing the opposite distortion in the thought of other covenantal theologians (such as Witsius). For Rolston and Torrance, Calvin is seen to emphasize grace far beyond law and the later covenantal theologians are seen to emphasize law to the virtual exclusion of grace.[26]

While Calvin did not explicitly use covenant language, he did see a relationship between the natural order and the divine law as grounded in the goodness and sovereignty of God.[27] This is a corrective to the arguments of Rolston, Torrance, and Poole who all insist on a radical priority of grace over law and interpreting the entire prelapsarian order as an act of pure grace (without law or as opposed to law). Bierma also shows how

23. Heppe, *Reformed Dogmatics*, 296–98.
24. Muller, "Covenant of Works," 75–100. See Muller, "Diversity in the Reformed Tradition," 11–30; Muller, "Calvin and the 'Calvinists'"; Muller, *Calvin and the Reformed Tradition*; Muller, *Unaccommodated Calvin*; Muller, *After Calvin*; Muller, *Christ and the Decree*.
25. Muller, Review of *History of the Covenant*, 217–18.
26. Mark W. Karlberg, "Reformed Interpretation," 1–57.
27. Schreiner, *Theater of His Glory*, 22–28, 77–79, 87–90.

Calvin's language of a *ius creationis* or "right of creation" foreshadows Olevianus's explicitly covenantal use of the term.[28] Peter Lillback has shown that Calvin highlights several concepts that clearly anticipate the later language of a Covenant of Works or nature. These concepts include an emphasis on the legal relationship between God and Adam, an identification of the Tree of Life as sacramental, along with the assumption that sacraments are covenantal signs, an identification of the Mosaic laws as a *pactio legalis*, and by explicating the relationship between Adam and Christ as the basis of Christ's redemptive satisfaction of the law.[29] Muller concludes (citing Calvin's *Institutes* and *Commentary of Genesis* 2:16) that, "If Calvin did not speak of the prelapsarian state as bounded by covenant he certainly assumed that it was governed by Law."[30] Even if the exact language of a Covenant of Works cannot be found in Calvin, a theology that undergirds a *foedus opera* is certainly present, and that the "broad lines of the reformer's thought were refined and developed rather than distorted" by his theological successors.[31]

Reformed theologians acknowledge that the Scriptures nowhere apply the term "covenant" to the relationship between God and Adam.[32] The doctrine of the Covenant of Works is, according to Muller, an example

---

28. Bierma, Review of *Origins of the Federal Theology*, 483–85.

29. Lillback, "Ursinus' Development," 247–88. See also Lillback, *Binding of God*, 276–304. Lillback notes that the relevance of this argument for connecting Calvin's doctrine with the later more clearly developed doctrine of the Covenant of Works of the federal theologians in the seventeenth century can be ascertained by comparing Cocceius's and Witsius's studies on the covenants where they both lay a great deal of stress on the Tree of Life as being the sacramental sign of the Covenant of Works. Witsius, for example, states: "God also granted to man such symbols under the covenant of works; concerning which we are now to speak, that nothing may be wanting in this treatise; and if I mistake not, they were four in all, which I reckon up in this order. 1. Paradise. 2. The Tree of Life. 3. The Tree of Knowledge of Good and Evil. 4. The Sabbath." Witsius, *Economy of the Covenants*, 1:105. The disagreement over the number of the sacraments of the Covenant of Works as well as other related questions are well illustrated in Heppe, *Reformed Dogmatics*, 296–98.

30. Muller, "Covenant of Works," 88–89.

31. Horton, *God of Promise*, 85. For a further defense of Calvin's biblical theological concept being fully congruous with the later developed doctrine of the Covenant of Works, see Jeon, *Covenant Theology*, 14–20.

32. For example, John Barrett writes, "I confess the Covenant of Works made with Adam in innocency, is more darkly spoken of than the Covenant of Grace." Barrett, *Good Will*, 2. Although Charles Hodge describes the prelapsarian relationship as a Covenant of Works, he also notes that it "does not rest upon any express declaration of the Scriptures." Hodge, *Systematic Theology*, 2:117.

of a doctrinal construct, not explicitly stated in Scripture, but drawn as a conclusion from the examination and comparison of a series of biblical *loci* or *sedes doctrinae* (secondary or derivative, albeit still fundamental, category of doctrine).[33] It is an example of what the *Westminster Confession of Faith* calls, "good and necessary consequences" deduced from Scripture.[34] The theological setting of the doctrine in mature federal theology is that of law and grace in its relation to the first and second Adam—Adam and Christ—as set forth in St. Paul's epistle to the Romans, along with supporting citations of St. Paul's use of covenant language in the epistle to the Galatians. Muller emphasizes that Reformed covenantal theologians of the sixteenth and seventeenth centuries did not take their exegetical starting point to be the opening chapters of Genesis, nor such "proof texts" usually cited such as Hos 6:7 ("But they like men [or Adam, *adam*] have transgressed the covenant") and Job 31:33 ("If I have hid my sinne, as Adam, concealing mine iniquitie in my bosome").[35] Rather, the doctrine was a conclusion drawn from the integration of a large body of texts, among them Gen 1:26–27, Lev 18:4–5, Matt 19:16–17, 22:37–39, Rom 1:17, 2:14–15, 5:12–21, 7:10, 8:3–4, 10:5, Gal 3:11–12, 4:4–5, with Hos 6:7 and Job 31:33 offered only as "collateral" arguments.[36] Poole's point "that nowhere in Scripture is a covenant with Adam mentioned"[37] imposes a standard of "proof texting" on the seventeenth century that was not held and does not give due justice to the exegetical and interpretive process of seventeenth-century Reformed scholasticism.[38] For Muller, an

33. Muller, "Covenant of Works," 75.

34. "The whole counsel of God, concerning all things necessary for His own glory, man's salvation, faith and life, is either expressly set down in Scripture, or by good and necessary consequence may be deduced from Scripture." WCF 1.4. Anthony Burgess (d. 1664), a member of the Westminster Assembly, in a lecture on the exposition of Gen 2:17, says about the doctrine: "That God did not only, as a Lawgiver, injoyn obedience unto Adam; but, as a loving God, did also enter into covenant with him." Burgess admits that this covenant with Adam is "more obscurely laid down, then the covenant of grace after the fall," but "must only be gathered by deduction and consequence . . . We are not therefore to be so rigid, as to call for expresse places, which doe name this Covenant. . . That which is necessarily and immediately drawn from Scripture, is as truly Scripture, as that which is expressly contained in it." Burgess, *Vindiciae Legis*, 123.

35. Both citations are taken from the 1599 Geneva Bible.

36. Witsius, *Economy of the Covenants*, 1:58–60, and Brakel, *Christian's Reasonable Service*, 1:355–67. See Muller, *Post Reformation Reformed Dogmatics*, 2:436–41 for a discussion of the interpretation of Hos 6:7 in this context.

37. Poole, *History of the Covenant*, 254.

38. This would also apply to other fundamental Christian doctrines, such as the

understanding of the nature of God's covenant with Adam was the result of:

> A complex of exegetical, etymological, theological, and legal considerations that evidence concern for the text of Scripture, the culture of the Jews and other ancient Near Eastern peoples, the linguistic and cultural transition from Hebrew into Greek and Latin, the Christian exegetical tradition and the doctrinal appropriation of ancient covenant language in the light of other fundamental theological questions—notably the relationship of Adam and Christ, the *imago Dei*, the problem of original righteousness and original sin, the history of salvation recorded in Scripture, and the distinction of law and gospel.[39]

The Law-Gospel Distinction

In the development of Reformed covenant theology, the concept of a prelapsarian covenant rooted in the order of creation instituted by God was explicitly connected to the basic distinction of law and gospel and was constructed for the sake of undergirding the Reformation principle of salvation by grace alone. The recent tendency in Reformed studies to relegate the law-gospel distinction to a "Lutheran" hermeneutic is not supported by Reformed confessions and the writings of Reformed theologians.[40]

---

trinity.

39. Muller, *After Calvin*, 177.

40. Horton, "Law, Gospel, and Covenant," 279–87, and Horton, "Calvin and the Law-Gospel Hermeneutic," 27–42. Wilhelm Niesel, in his *Reformed Symbolics*, observes that, "Reformed theology recognizes the contrast between Law and Gospel, in a way similar to Lutheranism. We read in the Second Helvetic Confession: 'The Gospel is indeed opposed to the Law. For the Law works wrath and pronounces a curse, whereas the Gospel preaches grace and blessing.'" Niesel, *Reformed Symbolics*, 217. Recent theologians have also divided Luther and Calvin in terms of justification. David Garner is an example: "Calvin and Luther shared much in common in the Protestant movement, but their respective hermeneutical and theological differences must not be discarded. To do so is to confuse Reformed theology and Lutheranism, and to read into Calvin a Lutheran concept of justification by faith. In truth, Luther and Calvin differed not only on the Lord's Table, but also on the very heart of *sola fide*!" Garner, Review of *Binding of God*, 291–94. Among other issues, this directly ignores Calvin's own words of admiration for Luther and Melanchthon, specifically in their theological agreements, despite the differences they had. As witness, Calvin not only signed the *Augsburg Confession*, but acknowledged as late as 1557 that, "in regard to the *Confession of Augsburg* my answer is, that it does not contain a word contrary to

The distinction between the law and the gospel is a distinguishing feature of Luther's hermeneutic and was the warp and woof of the *sola fide* fabric that drove his break with Rome, becoming the centerpiece of his mature theology and a veritable litmus test for the true Christian faith. This is no more clearly and emphatically taught than in a sermon by Luther on Gal 3:23–24:

> What St. Paul has in mind is this: That throughout Christendom preachers and hearers alike should teach and should maintain a clear distinction between the Law and the Gospel, between works and faith. He so instructed Timothy, admonishing him (2 Tim. 2:15) to "divide rightly the word of truth." Distinguishing between the Law and the Gospel is the highest art in Christendom, one that every person who values the name Christian ought to recognize, know, and possess. Where this is lacking, it is not possible to tell who is Christian and who is pagan or Jew. That much is at stake in this distinction.[41]

Luther further extracts the necessity of the distinction from the Old Testament in a sermon entitled, "How Christians Should Regard Moses":

> We must know what the law is, and what the gospel is. The law commands and requires us to do certain things. The law is thus directed solely to our behavior and consists in making requirements. For God speaks through the law, saying, "Do this, avoid that, this is what I expect of you." The gospel, however, does not preach what we are to do or to avoid. It sets up no requirements but reverses the approach of the law, does the very opposite, and says, "This is what God has done for you; he has let his Son be made flesh for you, has let him be put to death for your sake." So, then, there are two kinds of doctrine and two kinds of works, those of God and those of men. Just as we and God are separated from one another, so also these two doctrines are widely separated from one another. For the gospel teaches exclusively

---

our doctrine." Calvin, *Selected Works*, 2:355. In response to just how faithfully he was to the words of the *Confession* he said, "As to their meaning…to whom can I better appeal than to the author himself? If he declares that I deviate in the smallest from his idea, I will immediately submit" (referring to Philip Melanchthon as the author and in the context of interpreting the presence of Christ in the Lord's Supper). Calvin, *Selected Works*, 2:277.

41. Luther, *The Distinction Between the Law and the Gospel* (1532). I am using the translation provided by Bruce, "Distinction," 153–62. The original German can be found in Luther, "Predigten 1532," WA 36:8–42.

what has been given us by God, and not—as in the case of the law—what we are to do and give to God.⁴²

These exact sentiments find their parallel in several representative Reformed theologians.

Theodore Beza stated that, "Ignorance of this distinction between Law and Gospel is one of the principle sources of the abuses which corrupted and still corrupt Christianity."⁴³ In his discussion of "the Word," he divides it into two parts, "The Law" and "The Gospel":

> We divide this Word into two principal parts or kinds: the one is called "The Law," the other the "Gospel." For, all the rest can be gathered under one or the other of these two headings. What we call Law (when it is distinguished from Gospel and is taken for one of the two parts of the Word) is a doctrine whose seed is written by nature in our hearts . . . What we call the Gospel ("Good News") is a doctrine which is not at all in us by nature, but which is revealed from Heaven (Matt. 16:17; Jn. 1:13), and totally surpasses natural knowledge. By it God testifies to us that it is his purpose to save us freely by his only Son (Rom. 3:20–22), provided that, by faith, we embrace him as our only wisdom, righteousness, sanctification and redemption (1 Cor. 1:30).⁴⁴

Zacharius Ursinus discusses the doctrine in the ninth question of his *Larger Catechism* where he explicitly brings it to bear on the contrast between the Covenant of Works and the Covenant of Grace. It is also explicit in his commentary on the *Heidelberg Catechism*:

> The doctrine of the church is the entire and uncorrupted doctrine of the law and gospel concerning the true God, together with his will, works, and worship . . . The doctrine of the church consists of two parts: The Law, and the Gospel; in which we have comprehended the sum and substance of the sacred Scriptures . . . Therefore, the law and gospel are the chief and general divisions of holy Scriptures, and comprise the entire doctrine comprehended therein . . . for the law is our schoolmaster, to bring us to Christ, constraining us to fly to him, and showing us what the righteousness is, which he has wrought out, and now

---

42. Luther, "How Christians Should Regard Moses," *LW* 35:155–74, 162. See also Luther, "Reihenpredigten über 2. Mose 1524/27," *WA* 16:363–93.

43. Beza, *Christian Faith*, 41.

44. Beza, *Christian Faith*, 41.

offers unto us. But the gospel, professedly, treats of the person, office, and benefits of Christ. Therefore we have, in the law and gospel, the whole of the Scriptures comprehending the doctrine revealed from heaven for our salvation . . . The law prescribes and enjoins what is to be done, and forbids what ought to be avoided: whilst the gospel announces the free remission of sin, through and for the sake of Christ . . . The law is known from nature; the gospel is divinely revealed . . . The law promises life upon the condition of perfect obedience; the gospel, on the condition of faith in Christ and the commencement of new obedience.[45]

In the English Puritan Presbyterian tradition, Robert Rollock, a pioneer of Reformed federal theology, specifically developed the Covenant of Works/Covenant of Grace scheme in view of the law-gospel antithesis.[46] In his *Art of Prophesying*, William Perkins (1558–1602) asserted that, "The basic principle in application [of proper biblical interpretation] is to know whether the passage is a statement of the law or of the gospel. For when the Word is preached, the law and the gospel operate differently. The law exposes the disease of sin and as a side-effect stimulates and stirs it up. But it provides no remedy for it . . . The law is, therefore first in the order of teaching; then comes the gospel."[47]

Representing Dutch Reformed theologians, Petrus van Mastricht, an important influence on Jonathan Edwards, recognized the intrasystematic importance of the doctrine of the Covenant of Works and the law-gospel distinction:

> To very many heads of the Christian religion, e.g., the propagation of original corruption, the satisfaction of Christ and his subjection to divine law Rom. 8:3–4 (what the law could not do, in that it was weak through the flesh, God, sending his own Son in the likeness of sinful flesh and for sin, condemned sin in the flesh, that the requirement of the law might be fulfilled in us, who walk not after the flesh, but after the Spirit) Gal. 3:13 (Christ redeemed us from the curse of the law, having become a curse for us . . .), we can scarcely give suitable satisfaction, if the covenant of works be denied.[48]

---

45. Ursinus, *Commentary*, 32, 34–45.
46. Rollock, "Treatise," 33–37.
47. Perkins, *Art of Prophesying*, 54.
48. Cited in Heppe, *Reformed Dogmatics*, 290. Of note is that Mastricht, following his teachers Gisbertus Voetius and Johannes Hoornbeeck, did not see the use of

The architects of covenant theology developed their Covenant of Works-Grace structure from their prior commitment to this distinction between law and gospel. "In the writings of subsequent generations of Reformed theologians, the idea of an initial fundamental, prelapsarian covenant was rooted in the concept of creation as an order instituted by God and it was also connected with the basic exposition of the doctrine of law and grace in its relation to the problem of the creation of man according to the *imago Dei*."[49] A pattern of rendering "law-gospel" and "Covenant of Works-Covenant of Grace" interchangeable continued throughout Reformed theology up to Louis Berkhof's *Systematic Theology*, under the heading "The Two Parts of the Word of God Considered as a Means of Grace."[50] Students as they were of the Church Fathers, Reformed federal theologians may also have recognized this connection in the works of Irenaeus, who distinguishes between "an economy of law/works" and a "Gospel covenant."[51] The basic elements of the covenant of creation can even be discerned in Augustine's claim: "The first covenant was this, unto Adam: 'Whensoever thou eatest thereof thou shalt die the death,'" and this is why all his children "are breakers of God's covenant made with Adam in paradise."[52]

By the time of Jonathan Edwards's ministry, the two-fold Covenant of Works-Grace scheme had been explicated in fully developed forms by such theologians as Johannes Cocceius (1603–1699) in *Summa Doctrinae de Foedere et Testamento Dei Explicata*, (1648), Herman

---

scholastic theological method as antithetical to the practical use of theology for Christian piety. See Mastricht, *Best Method of Preaching*, 8, 12.

49. Muller, "Covenant of Works," 89, referencing Ursinus's *Summa theologiae*, qq. 10–19.

50. Berkhof, *Systematic Theology*, 612.

51. Irenaeus, "Against Heresies," *ANF* 1:495–96, 554. See also Duncan, "Covenant Idea."

52. Augustine speaks of "the origin which is common to all mankind, since all have broken God's covenant in that one man in whom all sinned." There are various covenants, "But the first covenant, made with the first man, is certainly this: 'On the day you eat, you will surely die'... For the covenant [curse] from the beginning is, 'You will surely die.' Now, seeing that a more explicit law was given later, and the Apostle says, 'Where there is no law, there is no law-breaking,' how can the psalm be true, where we read, 'I have counted all sinners on earth as law-breakers'? It can only be true on the assumption that those who are held bound by any sin are guilty of a breach of some law." Thus even infants are "recognized as breakers of the Law which was given in paradise." He goes on to clearly distinguish this covenant from the gracious covenant made with Abraham. Augustine, *City of God*, 688–89.

Witsius (1636–1708) in *De Oeconomia Foederum Dei cum Hominibus* (1677), John Preston (1587–1628) in *The New Covenant* (1629), John Ball (1585–1640) in *A Treatise of the Covenant of Grace* (1645), and Thomas Boston (1676–1732) in *A View of the Covenant of Grace from the Sacred Records* (1734) and became the foundational principle undergirding the system of theology exposited by the *Westminster Standards* of 1648 in which it received confessional status. The *Westminster Confession of Faith* defines the "first covenant," the covenant God made with Adam: "The first covenant made with man was a covenant of works, wherein life was promised to Adam, and in him to his posterity, upon condition of perfect and personal obedience."[53] In a later chapter entitled, "Of the Law of God," the confession goes on to state that: "God gave Adam a law, as a covenant of works, by which He bound him and all his posterity to personal, entire, exact, and perpetual obedience; promised life upon the fulfilling, and threatened death upon the break of it; and endued him with power and ability to keep it."[54]

Jonathan Edwards on the Covenant of Works

In this section I will discuss Edwards's theology of the Covenant of Works from his own writings, concentrating on his *Miscellanies* and sermons. I will begin by examining Edwards's distinction between the covenants, followed by his biblical derivation of a prelapsarian covenant with Adam. I will then argue that the Covenant of Works was crucial for maintaining the law-gospel distinction in Edwards. This distinction between "what needs to be done" and "what has been done for you" is not only a systematizing theme in Edwards's covenant theology, it also undergirds his theology of justification by faith alone as well as the role of "good works" under the gospel dispensation (evangelical obedience). I will also show that Edwards held to a view that did not oppose law and grace when grace is used in a non-soteric sense. His theology was not a mere graceless legalism, as some have caricatured federal theology. Law and grace, as well as law and love, are not contradictory categories but rather are complimentary and go hand-in-hand in his theology. In this context I will address several misconceptions regarding the concept of merit in Reformed theology and in Edwards. I will conclude that for Edwards the

---

53. *WCF* 7.2.
54. *WCF* 19.1.

first covenant is essentially a covenant of "works" and is the basis for the "works principle" which forms the overarching internal structure of Edwards's biblical narrative of redemption. As the Covenant of Works was an eternal covenant reflecting God's own holy nature and character, it was never abrogated. Its eternal and abiding character therefore informs the nature of Christ's redemptive work as well as the believer's response in evangelical obedience.

Distinguishing between the Covenants

Edwards accepts a tricovenantal[55] structure inherited from his Puritan Reformed background, albeit with some qualifications in terminology and the specific way he relates the Covenants of Redemption and Grace. This "first covenant," the Covenant of Works, is "first" in the chronology of historical revelation. The Covenant of Grace, though founded in eternity in the Covenant of Redemption, is called the second covenant or the New Covenant.[56] For Edwards, this distinction takes the Covenant of Redemption and the Covenant of Grace in their unity rather than in their dual aspect and compares it as one covenant beside the Covenant of Works. Sometimes this terminology can be confusing in Edwards's

---

55. Bicovenantal refers to the broad outline of redemptive history as composed of a Covenant of Works and Grace. This is distinguished from monocoventalism which subsumes even God's covenanting with Adam under a covenant of grace (not works). Tricovenantalism includes the Covenant of Redemption in its overall structure. These can be somewhat artificial distinctions, as in the case of Edwards, in which the relationship of the Covenants of Redemption and Grace could be viewed both in their unity and in their distinction.

56. Edwards distinguishes between God's eternal (supralapsarian) decrees to glorify his "exceeding abundance and overflowing fullness" of "goodness and love," which he calls God's "ultimate ends," and his eternal (infralapsarian) decrees to glorify his mercy and grace, which are "means" to God's ultimate ends. God's glorifying his love and communicating his goodness stands prior to the subject and does not presuppose it. The goodness of God gives the being as well as the happiness of the creature. Contrariwise, the glorifying of God's mercy presupposes the subject to be miserable, and the glorifying his grace presupposes the subject to be sinful, unworthy and ill-deserving. These decrees of mercy and love are "infralapsarian" in the sense they are not to be considered as prior to the decree of the being and permission of the fall, and the decree of election. "A decree of glorifying God's mercy and grace considers man as being created and fallen, because the very notion of such a decree supposes a great sin and misery." Edwards, "Misc. 704," *WJE* 18:317. Yet both decrees are eternal. Here Edwards clearly distinguishes God's decree of grace in a postlapsarian sense that clearly belongs to the Covenant of Grace in distinction to the Covenant of Works.

writings. Does Edwards speak of one, two, or three covenants? The distinction between the Covenant of Works and the Covenant of Grace, viewed from a peculiar Edwardsean perspective, can be collapsed into a "single" covenant.

> Towards the rectifying of what has been already said about the covenants [Nos. 2, 30]. The covenant of grace or redemption (which we have showed to be the same) cannot be called a new covenant, or the second covenant, with respect to the covenant of works; for that is not grown old yet but is an eternal immutable covenant, of which one jot nor tittle will never fail. There have never been two covenants, in strictness of speech, but only two ways constituted of performing of this covenant: the first constituting Adam the representative and federal head, and the second constituting Christ the federal head; the one a dead way, the other a living way and an everlasting one.[57]

Even within the Covenant of Grace, Edwards is careful to emphasize this works aspect which forms the basis for his polemics against both neonomianism and antinomianism. What distinguishes these two covenants (as Edwards generally did, following the usual way of expression in Reformed covenant thought) was the way of performing or fulfilling each and the covenant headship represented within each. Both were covenants of works by strict definition, the first made by God with Adam as federal representative of all mankind before the fall, the second with Christ (and his "mystical body," i.e., the elect) who fulfills the original covenant made with Adam on behalf of the elect. This is explicit in an earlier *Miscellany*:

> With reference to what has been before spoken of the covenant [No. 2]. Covenant is taken very variously in Scripture, sometimes for a divine promise, sometimes for a divine promise on conditions. But if we speak of the covenant God has made with man stating the condition of eternal life, God never made but one with man to wit, the covenant of works; which never yet was abrogated, but is a covenant stands in full force to all eternity without the failing of one tittle. The covenant of grace is not another covenant made with man upon the abrogation of this, but a covenant made with Christ to fulfill it. And for this end came Christ into the world, to fulfill the law, or covenant of works, for all that receive him.[58]

---

57. Edwards, "Misc. 35," *WJE* 13:219.
58. Edwards, "Misc. 30," *WJE* 13:217.

Another way of expressing this distinction is made by Edwards in a sermon on Zech 4:7 entitled "Glorious Grace," whereby the first covenant is fulfilled by what we do, the second is fulfilled by what has been given freely. Not only are the covenant requirements fulfilled, but the judgment procured on the first Adam is taken by the second Adam:

> When we were fallen, it was come to this: either we must die eternally, or the Son of God must spill his blood; either we, or God's own Son must suffer God's wrath, one of the two; either miserable worms of the dust that had deserved it, or the glorious, amiable, beautiful, and innocent Son of God. The fall of man brought it to this; it must be determined one way or t'other, and it was determined, by the strangely free and boundless grace of God.[59]

Continuity is maintained by the gratuitous character and works aspect in both covenants. There is discontinuity in that the first covenant is terminated as a means of attaining eternal life. This important distinction lay at the foundation of Edwards's law-gospel distinction and the central role of the imputation of Christ's active righteousness in justification.

While Edwards in one sense distinguishes three covenants (works, redemption, and grace), in another sense he does not separate them, treating them as three aspects or three perspectives of one covenant. The term "Covenant of Grace" (between Christ and the believer), while a distinct covenant relation, is sometimes used by Edwards to refer to the historical progressive revelation and outworking in time of the (eternal intratrinitarian) Covenant of Redemption. And since in the Covenant of Redemption Christ fulfills the condition of righteousness, both these covenants can be viewed as aspects of the Covenant of Works fulfilled by two covenant heads. The intricacies of the relationship between the Covenants of Grace and Redemption, as those terms are used by Edwards, will be more fully explicated in the following chapter.

Edwards discusses the Covenant of Works throughout his writings in terms of the need for a "mediator." The "first covenant" that God made with man in the Garden of Eden stating the condition of eternal life was the only covenant God ever made with man distinctly by themselves without the necessity of a mediator for eternal life. It was made with Adam as federal head in his original state of righteousness or innocence, i.e., without sin. The second Covenant of Grace is made with Christ

---

59. Edwards, "Glorious Grace," *WJE* 10:393.

as man's mediator, and is only made with man indirectly as he is in union with Christ, or as Christ's "mystical body," a union that Edwards frequently describes as a "marriage" union or "marriage covenant."⁶⁰ The clear implication is that after the fall, after the initial relationship between Adam (and his posterity with him) and God was destroyed by Adam's disobedience, God will no longer enter directly into covenant relationship with man except through a mediator.

Edwards does not deny the overall unity of the covenants, but distinguishes, in modern terms, a tricovenantal structure of the history of redemption. God deals in a very different manner with pre- and post-fall man. The Covenant of Works is prior to sin and God does not have to provide a mediator to enter into relationship with man. After the fall, a mediator is provided out of the graciousness of God under a covenant of redemptive grace by which the (never abrogated) Covenant of Works is fulfilled by the "second Adam" on behalf of the elect.

Scriptural Proofs

Edwards is clearly convinced that the Covenant of Works is a doctrine derived from Scripture but spends little time proving the existence of the Covenant of Works exegetically in his writings. Mentioning in passing Hos 6:7 in *Original Sin*, Edwards accepts the Vulgate Latin rendering of the Hebrew *berith* as *pactum* and the English translation as "covenant."⁶¹ He references Hos 6:7 in *Misc. 884* ("Covenant Made with Adam")⁶² and cites Isaac Watts approvingly in *Misc. 1074*.⁶³ There are also passing references in his *Notes on Scripture* (mentioning the use of "Adam" and "covenant")⁶⁴ and the *"Controversies" Notebook*.⁶⁵ Nowhere in his writings

---

60. For instance: "The soul is espoused and married unto Jesus Christ; the believing soul is the bride and spouse of the Son of God. The union between Christ and believers is very often represented to a marriage. This similitude is much insisted on in Scripture—how sweetly is it set forth in the Son of Songs! Now it is by faith that the soul is united unto Christ; faith is the bride's reception of Christ as a bridegroom." Edwards, "Misc. 37," *WJE* 13:219–21.

61. Edwards, "Original Sin," *WJE* 3:264, 343; cf. Edwards, "Original Sin Notebook," *WJEO* 34.

62. Edwards, "Misc. 884," *WJE* 20:140.

63. Edwards, "Misc. 1074," *WJE* 20:458–59, citing Isaac Watts, *The Ruin and Recovery of Mankind* (London, 1740), 145–47.

64. Edwards, "Notes on Scripture," *WJE* 15:444.

65. Edwards, "Controversies Notebook," *WJEO* 27, where he renders the phrase,

does he reference Job 31:33, the other classic "proof text" for the covenant with Adam. Edwards otherwise either assumes the doctrine or draws necessary inferences from a wide range of biblical texts.⁶⁶

Rather than relying on "proof texts," Edwards draws many of his conclusions regarding the Scriptural basis for the Covenant of Works from inferences regarding the use of the term "covenant" in Scripture. In *Misc. 1215* Edwards maintains this first covenant with Adam was truly a covenant according to the way Scripture uses the word in that it was conditional, requiring perfect and complete obedience, with attached blessing or judgment rendered to Adam's obedience or disobedience. There was a promise of favor (life) in case of compliance as well as a threatening of wrath (death) in case of disobedience: "Concerning the declaration or manifestation which God made of his mind to Adam concerning the rule of his duty to God, and what [God] expected of him, enforced with threatenings of his displeasure in case of a violation of that rule and promises of his favor in case of a compliance, especially Adam's consent being supposed—I say, as to this being called a COVENANT."⁶⁷ The blessing of the commandment's fulfillment being "life" is also inferred from what Scriptures says about the Tree of Life and what the Apostle Paul says in Rom 7:10 (also referencing Rom 10:5 and Rev 22:14). In his notes on Gen 1:27–30 the covenantal nature of God's relationship with Adam is also emphasized: "God's making them in his own image, and then blessing them, implies his bestowing these blessings pronounced on the subject blessed, as [if it] continued such an excellent subject as he had made it."⁶⁸ The result of compliance was blessed and eternal life, the result of disobedience was "death."⁶⁹

Also consonant with the nature of covenant is Adam's consent, since "consent to a covenant is necessary to the very being in that covenant; a man can't be in any covenant till he consents to it,"⁷⁰ and, again, in a sermon on Isa 1:18–20 preached in Northampton entitled, "All God's Methods

---

"they like men have transgressed the covenant."

66. For example, Rom 3:27 in Edwards, "History of the Work of Redemption," *WJE* 9:309, and Rom 7:10, Rom 10:5, and Rev 22:14 in Edwards, "Misc. 1074," *WJE* 20:458–59 and Edwards, "Misc. 1215," *WJE* 23:147.

67. Edwards, "Misc. 1215," *WJE* 23:147.

68. Edwards, *"Notes on Scripture," WJE* 15:395.

69. Edwards, *"Misc. 1215," WJE* 23:147. See also Edwards, *"Misc. 400," WJE* 13:465–66; Edwards, "Misc. 401," *WJE* 13:466; Edwards, "Misc. 720," *WJE* 18:350.

70. Edwards, "Misc. 299," *WJE* 13:386.

Are Most Reasonable," "In every covenant there is required the consent of both parties: in the first covenant it was required of Adam that he should accept and consent on his part to the covenant proposed by God; but after he had consented, he was yet to do that work which was the condition of the covenant: he had yet to perform perfect obedience."[71] While not explicit in the Genesis narrative, Edwards infers Adam's consent, since "his dissent would have been sin, which, to suppose before he sinned, is a contradiction."[72] Furthermore, Adam understood his role in consenting as a federal head, the stipulations, blessings, and curses of the Covenant of Works being given to him "as the public head of mankind" and "given him in the name of the whole race."[73] The concept of covenant obligations by means of covenant heads is brought out in a manuscript sermon on Ps 111:5. Edwards mentions two kinds of covenant engagements: "1) Those that he enters into with the covenant head ... wherein promises are made to man indirectly in their representatives, or 2) those that he enters into with men."[74] Of the first sort Edwards cites two examples: "That which was made with the first Adam" and "that which was made with the second Adam" (the Covenant of Redemption). The covenant was with Adam and his posterity, and Adam knew this in his consenting to the terms of the covenant, so that "when Adam is threatened with being deprived of all these in the case of his disobedience, Adam must understand it in like manner as a calamity to come on the whole race."[75]

The idea of consent is so closely tied to faith that Edwards insists that it was a condition of the first covenant as well as the second. There must be a believing in and trusting in God's word as prerequisite for

---

71. Edwards, "All God's Methods are Most Reasonable," *WJE* 14:182. Edwards goes on to compare this with the Covenant of Grace, which also requires consent (which he equates with faith), but in which there are no further obligations or requirements, having already been performed by Christ; cf. Edwards, "Misc. 299," *WJE* 13:386. Edwards frequently returns to the requirement of consent within any covenant. He uses the concept not only in his systematic treatment of covenant theology, but also in his practical theology and ecclesiology. For instance, Edwards employs the necessity of consent in his sacramental arguments during the "half-way covenant" controversy. See Edwards, "Misrepresentations Corrected and Truth Vindicated," *WJE* 12:485.

72. Edwards, "Misc. 1215," *WJE* 23:147.

73. Edwards, "Notes on Scripture," *WJE* 15:395.

74. Edwards, "Sermon 788. Ps. 111:5. God never fails in any instance of faithfulness to the covenant engagements he has entered into on behalf of any of mankind" (Aug. 1745 Quarterly lecture), as quoted in Bogue, *Jonathan Edwards*, 105.

75. Bogue, *Jonathan Edwards*, 105. See also Edwards, "Misc. 717," *WJE* 18:348-49.

consenting with or accepting the covenant obligations. In his *Miscellaneous Remarks* on the subject of faith, Edwards says:

> The condition both of the first and second covenant is a receiving compliance with or yielding to a signification or declaration from God or to a revelation made from God. A receiving or yielding to a signification of the will of God as our sovereign Lord and lawgiver is most properly called obedience. The receiving and yielding to a strange and mysterious revelation and offer which God makes of mercy to sinners, being a revelation of things spiritual, supernatural, invisible and mysterious, through an incredible power, wisdom and grace of God, is properly called faith.[76]

And in another *Miscellanies* entry he states that under the Covenant of Works "keeping the commandments of the Lord" is the "yielding to the authority of a mere Lawgiver, demanding what is due to him from us for his pleasure and honor."[77] This "hearing and yielding to the voice of God" is common in both covenants, equally in complying with the precepts of pure law and in complying with the calls and offers of the gospel.

Law and Gospel

Edwards maintains the distinction between the two covenants, and their respective condition, in the same manner as within mainstream Reformed covenant theology with a contrast between law and gospel.

> There is indeed obedience in the condition of both covenants, and there is faith or believing God in both. But the different name arises from the remarkable different nature of the revelation or manifestations made. The one is a law; the other a testimony and offer. The one is a signification of what God expects that we should do towards him, and what he expects to receive from us; the other a revelation of what he has done for us, and an offer of what we may receive from him.[78]

---

76. Edwards, "Miscellaneous Remarks," *WJE* 21:440–41.

77. Edwards, "Misc. 1354," *WJE* 23:517. Edwards goes on to contrast this with "keeping the commandments of the Lord" under the new covenant, which is an "adhering to and attending the directions of a Redeemer and spiritual head and husband, following a captain of salvation, obeying his word of command in order to our deliverance from our enemies, as a manifestation of trust in him."

78. Edwards, "Writings on the Trinity, Grace, and Faith," *WJE* 21:441.

The condition of the first covenant consisted in works to be done. It is something offered by man to God in terms of perfect and complete obedience to the positive and negative precepts of God's law, his eternal rule of righteousness. While faith is a condition[79] of entry into the covenant, or more strictly faith *is* the entry or consent to the covenant, it is not part of the work of that covenant or the condition of covenant blessing. The distinction that marks out the first covenant is that there is a work to be done, i.e., complete and perfect obedience for the blessing of eternal life to apply. Faith, while in one sense a necessary "condition" of consenting to the covenant itself, is not the condition of the covenant to be fulfilled. That is why the first covenant is not of faith but of works.

Edwards will contrast this to the second covenant, whereby faith is likewise a "condition" of consent (this time consent to the "marriage covenant" with Christ). But herein is the crucial difference: there is no further work to be done (having already been done by Christ). Just as in the Old Covenant, faith is not a "work" that must be accomplished for the covenant blessing of eternal life to apply. That is why the second covenant is of faith (alone) and not of works. Faith is not a "new work," a "new law" of obedience, or a "work" that replaces the Old Covenant "works" of obedience. This very misunderstood aspect of Edwards's use of "condition" as applied to faith and works under both covenants will need to be more fully addressed in chapter 7.

Law and Grace

The language of "works" or even "law" is consistently and universally used by Edwards in describing the first covenant. Never does he use the terms "covenant of nature" or "covenant of creation" in describing God's first covenant with Adam. In a few (three) select instances he uses the term "covenant of life" when he wants to emphasize that particular blessing of eternal life that was promised by the fulfillment of the covenant stipulations.[80] Edwards is not reserved, and indeed is emphatic, in his insistence that the covenant was one of works or law. As will be seen later, Edwards held that a right understanding of the Covenant of Works to be

---

79. Edwards uses the term "condition" in various ways, and so it is important to note his distinctions. This will become extremely important when discussing the "conditionality" of the covenants in a later section.

80. Edwards, "Misc. 880," *WJE* 20:239; Edwards, "Misc. 1074," *WJE* 20:459. See also Edwards, "Drafts of Professions of Faith," *WJEO* 39.

essential in its outworking within covenant theology and consequently to a right understanding of the relationship of law and gospel. It was central to the core gospel doctrine of the imputation of the active righteousness of Christ in the Christian's justification.

In this section I will show that Edwards's emphasis on "law" and "works" does not imply a barren "legalism" in Edwards. I will do this by showing how law and grace are not opposed in Edwards's theology. I will then show how the "law," far from an arbitrary legal obligation, is an analogical revelation of God's own holy nature and character that was mercifully given to man out of the condescending goodness and love of God. The "law" in covenant perspective, when obeyed, becomes the means of having communion with God. As such, law and love are not opposed in Edwards's theology.

For all the emphasis on "works" and "law" in this first covenant, it does not mean that Edwards was reticent to acknowledge the gracious nature of the first covenant (if by "gracious" one distinguished a pre- and postlapsarian use of the term) or that it was a covenant that was strictly based on merit (also rightly distinguished and understood). That God's covenant with Adam before the fall can be appropriately denominated as a "gracious" covenant in a certain sense is acknowledged in the *Westminster Confession*: "The distance between God and the creature is so great, that although reasonable creatures do owe obedience unto Him as their Creator, yet they could never have any fruition of Him as their blessedness and reward, but by some voluntary condescension on God's part, which He hath been pleased to express by way of covenant."[81] Edwards uses similar language in describing the nature of the first covenant in an unpublished sermon on Rom 4:16: "The goodness of God appeared in the first covenant which proposed justification by works. It was an act of God's goodness and condescension toward man to enter into any covenant at all with him and that he would become engaged to give eternal life to him upon his perfect obedience."[82] If graciousness is defined by and delimited to God's goodness and condescension to his

---

81. WCF 7.1; see also WLC Q. 20.

82. Edwards, "153. Sermon on Rom. 4:16," *WJEO* 45, L. 2r (my transcription of Edwards's sermon notes). Edwards's original manuscript reads: "The Goodness of G. appeared in the first Coven. Which Proposed Justif by works. it was an act of Gods Good ness ~~towards men to Enter into an~~ & Condescension towards man to Enter into any Cov at all to with him. & that he would become Engaged to Give Eternal life to him upon his Perfect Obed."

creature, then Edwards would have no dispute. In one of Edwards's most powerful sermons he explains the gracious nature of the first covenant: "If Adam had stood and persevered in obedience, he would have been made happy by mere bounty [and] goodness; for God was not obliged to reward Adam for his perfect obedience any otherwise than by covenant, for Adam by standing would not have merited happiness."[83] God's way of entering into a personal relationship with Adam was through covenant, and the ontological distance between God and man necessitated God initiating and condescending to providing, making, offering, and establishing such a covenant as a way of revealing himself to his creation. This reflects Rollock's argument that every relationship between God and man is thoroughly covenantal since "God speaks nothing to man without covenant."[84] God's revelation of himself within creation, and to a certain extent creation itself, always has a "giveness" that is central to it.[85] This "giveness" or "giftedness," which Edwards would equate with the overflowing goodness of God, which presumes a creation but is in no way dependent on anything in creation, may be a better term to use than "gracious," which has only led to a great deal of confusion.

Confusion arises when this "graciousness" or undeserved "giveness" is not properly distinguished from the redemptive graciousness of God that presupposes man as sinner, justly under condemnation, that marks the distinction between law and gospel in Reformed theology. It is not simply true, as Torrance argues, that there can be nothing prior to grace or that bicovenantal (or tricovenantal) schemes involve a radical dichotomy between the sphere of nature (Covenant of Works) and the sphere of grace (Covenant of Grace).[86] There is always something that stands prior to grace (something to which is "given"), whether it is "creation" (and the ontological separation it implies) in terms of a condescending goodness, or "sin" in terms of redemptive grace. And there is always something (law) which is prior to sin. It is anachronistic to require redemptive or

---

83. Edwards, "Glorious Grace," *WJE* 10:390.

84. Rollock, "Treatise," 33.

85. There is a certain underlying "giveness" to all of creation, that all of life is based on the reality of "grace." As Josef Pieper reminds us, "that something given, something free of all debt, something undeserved, something not-achieved—is presumed in everything achieved or laid claim to; that what is first is always something received," Josef, *Leisure*, 20.

86. Torrance, "McLeod Campbell," 295–311, which also reflects Barth's criticisms of federal theology in Barth, *Church Dogmatics*, 4/1:22–99.

merciful grace as the foundation of creation and covenant in the beginning.⁸⁷ While not ignoring the condescending goodness of God in his taking the initiative to establish ("give") a covenant relationship with man, Edwards, and Reformed theologians before him, took the biblical concept of "grace" in its more restricted sense to refer exclusively to the merciful, redemptive, and therefore exclusively postlapsarial work of God. Tying the grace of God to its outworking in the history of redemption, Edwards begins this history immediately after the fall, continuing up until the return of Christ at the end of the world.⁸⁸ The Covenant of Grace, specifically as the progressive revelation of and outworking of in history of the Covenant of Redemption, is always to be contrasted in Edwards with the "non-gracious" Covenant of Works.

Law as Revelation

The nature of the covenant was not one of imposing a set of arbitrary "do's" and "don'ts" to test Adam's fidelity (although a probationary test of Adam's perseverance in obedience and faithfulness was certainly a component). It was rather an analogical revelation of God's own holy nature and character, an expression of his very being, a sharing of which was necessary for communion and fellowship between God and man. Far from arbitrary, that law is the expression of God's very being. It is simply a false caricature of Edwards's and many Reformed theologians' views of the law to see it as an "impersonal legalism" that is "interposed" within the original relation of God and man.⁸⁹ Fellowship with God and the law of God are not at odds. There is no antithesis between "law" and love. To

---

87. Horton, *God of Promise*, 84. See also Edwards's distinction between the decrees in Edwards, "Misc. 704," *WJE* 18:315.

88. Edwards, "History of the Work of Redemption," *WJE* 9:116. Accordingly, Edwards will also have a role for "grace" in the prelapsarian role of the Holy Spirit's upholding Adam in his original righteousness. But, again, this is a "giveness" that does not presuppose Adam as sinner, but only in his *status integritatis*.

89. For example, see Berkouwer, *Sin*, 207–8: "We err if we interpret this distinction as though God's original covenant had to do with *our* work or *our* achievement or *our* fulfillment of his law, while the later covenant of grace has reference to pure gift of his *mercy* apart from all *our* works . . . We interpose the notion of an impersonal legalism within the original relation of God and man . . . Therefore whoever burdens the so-called 'covenant of works' with the notion of achievement and presumes that we gain God's favor in that way, must endorse the idea of a 'nomological' un-existence of man and must cut asunder the law of God from the fellowship of God."

love God is to love his holy nature and character, and to love his nature and character is to reflect, as the *imago Dei,* his holy character and nature by conforming to his righteousness as it is revealed to man through his "law."[90] Michael Horton writes, "When we hear the divine benediction on the creation of humanity, 'It is very good,' we are meant to see that here God saw himself in the mirror."[91] The law was natural not only for God, but for his image-bearer, who was to reflect that image.

Law as Merciful

In his sermon *There Is Much of the Goodness and Mercy of God Appearing in the Commands He Has Given Us,* Edwards expands on the Deuteronomic admonition to keep the commandments of the Lord "for thy good" (Deut 10:13).[92] In the giving of the law, God does not only exercise his authority, but also shows his "mercy." Edwards, again, is making a clear distinction in the use of "mercy." In this context Edwards is not referring to God's gracious mercy in view of man as sinner, nor to the redemptive use of the law in revealing sin and providing a rule of life, not leaving man to "do what is right in his own eyes." In this context mercy is the condescending goodness and love of God in revealing to Adam a rule for "what tends to our own good and benefit." God has given us these commands "out of respect to our good":

> "What doth the Lord thy God require of thee but to keep the commandments of the Lord . . . for thy good?" This is as much as to say, "What does God require of you but to seek your own advantage, to do what is your perfection and your happiness to do?" The Lord your God is so far from imposing any grievous burden or task upon you that He only requires you to be happy, and to do what tends to your happiness. The commands He has given He has given from goodness to you, out of respect to your happiness. Your God has sought your benefit therein.[93]

These commands "don't only tend to our benefit by divine constitution or because he has been pleased to annex a glorious reward to obedience,

---

90. Edwards expresses the covenant requirement as requiring "holiness and sincere and universal compliance and actual conformity to God's nature and will." Edwards, "Notes on Scripture," *WJE* 14:393–94.

91. Horton, *God of Promise,* 84.

92. Edwards, *Puritan Pulpit,* 236–59.

93. Edwards, *Puritan Pulpit,* 237.

but they are such as in their own nature tend to our good and would do if God had promised no reward at all."⁹⁴ The law, for Edwards, is a blessing and remains so even after its abrogation as a means of meriting eternal life under the Covenant of Works. In this aspect the law, now having lost its condemning power, continues under the second covenant as a rule for righteousness and as a guide to evangelical obedience in preparation for ultimate eternal communion with God.

Law as Communion

Obedience to the law is a means of having communion with God. The focus of Edwards's sermon above is on the New Covenant obedience of the Christian, which does not contribute in any manner to one's salvation (it "isn't the righteousness that is the price of eternal life"), but as a preparation for the enjoyment of eternal life, to prize it and receive it in thankfulness. The context also reflects on the purpose of the original giving of the law under the old (first) covenant with Adam, as a means to enjoy communion with God and to fit him for the further enjoyment of eternal life which would be confirmed in his persevering obedience. Obedience requires the soul for the enjoyment of eternal life, says Edwards, and it "fits and prepares the soul for the happiness of heaven . . . it puts the soul into a suitable capacity for the enjoyment of the heavenly place . . . [and] it makes way for the vision and fruition of it."⁹⁵

Law and Love

Law and love are not opposed in Edwards's theology, and the giving of the law under the Covenant of Works can reflect simultaneously a "law" motif as well as a love by which God seeks mankind's goodness and happiness. There is no inherent radical dichotomy between the two. Or, in more specific Edwardsean parlance, it is God's own eternal intratrinitarian love for himself and his holiness that overflows in his self-communication to his creation, for the purpose of reflecting back his own holiness and happiness in his creatures for his own glory.

---

94. Edwards, *Puritan Pulpit*, 240.
95. Edwards, *Puritan Pulpit*, 245.

Law and Merit

The role of "merit" in Edwards and Reformed theology has been a source of contention by critics of Reformed federal theology. Edwards's own position, which helps clarify certain misconceptions regarding the role of "merit," is made clear in his sermons on Luke 17:9 and Zech 4:7.

When the Torrance school of neo-Barthians claims that merit is not an appropriate category in the Adamic relationship it misconstrues the historic position in Reformed theology as well as its use by Edwards by illegitimately conflating the various ways the term "merit" is used in covenant theology. To merit can mean either "to gain" or it can mean "to earn," a distinction clearly taught in the seventeenth century by Francis Turretin: "The word 'merit' is used in two ways: either broadly and improperly; or strictly and properly. Strictly, it denotes that work to which a reward is due from justice on account of its intrinsic value and worth. But it is often used broadly for the consecution of anything. In this sense, the verb 'to merit' is often by the fathers put for 'to gain,' 'to obtain,' 'to attain.'"[96] Within the Reformed tradition the use of merit-as-earning from strict justice is avoided with regards to Adam's having "merited" eternal life through his obedience to the Covenant of Works.[97] Thus Robert Rollock: "It is a question here, whether in the first creation, good works in the covenant of works, were required of man as meritorious for the promised life? I answer, not so. But they were due in the creation as pledges of thankfulness in man to his creator, for that excellent work of his creation, and to glorify God his creator."[98] Adam, by virtue of creation, owes perfect obedience to God and merits nothing from God for that obedience owed. Any "reward" comes when God graciously chooses to reward on the basis of the covenant established by him and not by anything that Adam would strictly deserve. John Ball also explains why the arrangement with Adam was not one of strict merit:

> For it is impossible the creature should merit of the Creator, because when he hath done all that he can, he is an unprofitable servant . . . The Covenant is of God, and that of his free grace and love: yet it was of grace that God was pleased to bind

---

96. Turretin, *Institutes*, 2:710.

97. Charles Hodge may be the lone, relatively undogmatic, advocate of the merit-as-earning viewpoint among Reformed theologians. Hodge, *Systematic Theology*, 2:364–65.

98. Rollock, *Treatise*, 37.

himselfe to his creature, and above the desert of the creature: and though the reward be of justice, it is also of favour. For after perfect obedience performed according to the will of God, it had been injustice in God, as he made the creature of nothing, so to have brought him unto nothing: it was then of grace that he was pleased to make that promise, and of the same grace his happiness should have been continued . . . God promiseth freely to recompence the good of obedience, which is already due, and might be exacted without promise or reward.[99]

William Ames (1576–1633), in *The Marrow of Theology* in the chapter on God's "Special Government of Intelligent Creatures," makes the point pertaining to government that this covenant is not between equals but between lord and servant. He writes:

> 9. From this special way of governing rational creatures there arises a covenant between God and them. This covenant is, as it were, a kind of transaction of God with the creature whereby God commands, promises, threatens, fulfills; and the creature binds itself in obedience to God so demanding. Deut. 26:16–19 . . .
>
> 10. This way of entering into covenant is not between those who are equal before the law but between lord and servant. It, therefore, rightly pertains to the government. It is very rightly called the covenant not of man but of God, who is the author and chief executer. Deut 8:18 . . .
>
> 11. In this covenant the moral deeds of the intelligent creature lead either to happiness as a reward or to unhappiness as a punishment. The latter is deserved, the former not.[100]

Based on the Creator-creation distinction in the pre-fall state, John Owen (1616–1683) affirmed that God offered no other reward for obedience other than the covenant. While the governing principle of the Covenant of Works was the law, the original covenant was based upon God's "infinite holiness, wisdom, righteousness, goodness, and grace."[101] Owen indicates that God annexed "promises and threatening or reward and punishment";

---

99. Ball, *Treatise of the Covenant*, 7. See also Rutherford, *Covenant of Life Opened*, 10, 22–23.

100. Ames, *Marrow*, 111.

101. Owen, *Works*, 6:472.

the first of grace, the other of justice.[102] Francis Turretin, also based on the Creator and creature distinction, asserted that the covenant of nature was gratuitous, and depended on a "pact" or gratuitous promise of God.[103] Ernest Kevan, in a survey of this topic in the Puritans, concludes that, "nearly all the Puritans concurred in the view that whatever good Adam would have received by his obedience was of grace," not of strict merit.[104] John Ball, with many others, cites the commonly received understanding of Luke 17:10 as a proof text for this position.[105]

Deserved punishment (justice) and undeserved happiness (grace) is a scriptural contrast relevant to both covenants in Edwards's thought as much as it is in the Reformed Puritan tradition. Reformed theologians wanted to distinguish between Adam's earning eternal life through his perfect obedience to God's natural law and gaining eternal life through perfect obedience to the covenant stipulations (natural and positive law) of the Covenant of Works. The point is that Adam could not have "merited" eternal life in any other way than by the covenant promises

---

102. Owen, *Works*, 5:275. Jeon explains how "the distinction between the Creator and creature in the prefall state of Adam can be seen in Owen's penetrating discussion on 'the theology of Adam' and is based on natural theology where the law was a controlling motif in the Covenant of Works and Adam's eschatological life was dependent upon his perfect obedience to the law. Therefore, the Covenant of Works was based upon 'God's gracious will' and 'His free choice' because God is absolutely sovereign over all things." Jeon, *Covenant Theology*, 47 n. 113. Based upon this distinction between Creator and creature, Owen can use this non-soteric concept of grace in the original status of Adam: "The creation of man in original righteousness was an effect of divine grace, benignity, and goodness; and the reward of eternal life in the enjoyment of God was of mere sovereign grace." Owen, *Works*, 5:277.

103. "If therefore upright man in that state had obtained this merit, it must not be understood properly and rigorously. Since man has all things from and owes all to God, he can seek from nothing as his own by right, nor can God be a debtor to him—not by condignity of work and from its intrinsic value..., but from the pact and the liberal promise of God." Turretin, *Institutes*, 1:578.

104. Kevan, *Grace of Law*, 112. One can add the witness of Samuel Rutherford, who also held that God showed grace to Adam in establishing a covenant with him. "He believed that Adam could have served God perfectly forever and never earned a right to confirmation of eternal life. Therefore God's promise was to reward obedience above what it merited and, for Rutherford, this demonstrated that even the covenant of works contained grace... This acknowledgment of grace in the covenant of works did not prevent Rutherford from sharply distinguishing that grace from the grace shown in the *foedus gratiae*, stating that there was 'no Gospel-Grace' in the covenant of works." MacLean, "Missing, Presumed Misclassified," 261–78. See Rutherford, *Covenant of Life*, 23.

105. Ball, *Treatise of the Covenant*, 10.

under the Covenant of Works, of which the condition was perfect obedience. In like manner we can then speak of Christ meriting eternal life by his perfect obedience under the Covenant of Redemption. While Adam would certainly have deserved death for sinning, he would not have earned a greater reward such as eternal life outside of the covenant blessings.

God's covenant with Adam before the fall was appropriately regarded as a "gracious" covenant by almost all Reformed theologians. But there was also the recognition of the need to distinguish the different meanings of "grace" between the pre- and postlapsarian dispensations. There were those who were reluctant to call the pre-fall arrangement one of "grace" because of the exclusive nature of the redemptive-historical use of the word "grace" in Scripture, particularly in the New Testament. Anthony Burgess (d. 1664) is exemplary, when he recognizes that, "because the Scripture makes that onely grace which comes by Christ, and when the subject is in a contrary condition, as we are; but it was not so with Adam."[106] Turretin, who acknowledged the gracious component of the first covenant, maintained that the pre-fall state was meritorious "from that covenant in a broader sense" and that this notion was drawn from the distinction between the principles of the covenants of works and grace. In the end, the legal condition has the relation of a meritorious cause (*ex pacto*, not of congruity or of condignity)[107] of the promised thing (namely, of life)—"Do this and live." Thus life would have been granted to Adam because of what he had done and on account of his obedience.[108] Turretin designates the original covenant as a covenant of

---

106. Burgess, *Vindiciae Legis*, 115. Burgess would go on to say, "I cannot tell whether this be worth the while to dispute." Burgess, *Vindiciae Legis*, 116.

107. *Meritum de condigno* (merit of condignity or condign merit) is a full merit as opposed to a half-merit or *meritum de congruo* (merit of congruity). The medieval scholastics distinguished between a merit of condignity which deserved grace, and a merit of congruity, a half-merit or act not truly deserving of grace, but nevertheless receiving grace on the basis of the divine generosity. Muller, *Dictionary of Latin and Greek*, 191–92. The "merit" accepted of God according by way of covenant (*ex pacto*) is not of the same order, it is an "improper merit"; *ex pacto* "merit" is not *meritum de congruo*, as suggested by Karlberg. Karlberg, "Recovering the Mosaic Covenant," 233–50. Oberman sees a precursor or remnant of a latent covenant theology in the medieval scholastic idea of *pactum*, but not its equivalence. Oberman, *Forerunners of the Reformation*; Oberman, *Harvest of Medieval Theology*; Oberman, *Dawn of the Reformation*.

108. Turretin, *Institutes*, 2:189, 1:575. Turretin rejects the Covenant of Works as meritorious "in a strict sense." He argues that there "can be no merit in man with God

nature, works, and law: "The covenant of nature is that which God the Creator made with innocent man as his creature, concerning the giving of eternal happiness and life under the condition of perfect and personal obedience . . . It is also called 'legal' because the condition on man's part was the observation of the law of nature engraved within him; and of 'works' because it depended upon works or his proper obedience."[109] Confusion has resulted from the failure to appreciate the careful distinctions that were made regarding specific terms, such as merit and grace, as well as to which particular aspect of the covenant relationships they were being applied.

In a sermon on Luke 17:9 Edwards makes his own position clear by the title, *God Doesn't Thank Men for Doing Those Things He Commands Them*. In the doctrinal section of this sermon Edwards expounds on the parable of the servant in Luke 17. In the Lucan narrative the rhetorical question is posed by Christ to his disciples as to whether the servant's master should thank the servant for merely doing what was commanded of him. The obvious answer is, "No, he is an unprofitable servant: he has done that which was his duty to do." Edwards's lesson for his congregation from this text is that by analogy God, as master and creator of the universe, likewise "doesn't look upon Himself as being in any way obliged to men for their obedience." In God's dealing with mankind, there is no room for any concept of strict merit-as-earning. The main lesson in this sermon is that no good works or obedience of man obligates God in any way to save them under the New Covenant, to pardon their sins, hear their prayers, accept them as righteous, deliver them from condemnation and hell, or bestow heaven upon them. Obedience to God deserves no reward from him, much less a reward so exceedingly great. In like manner, obedience under the Covenant of Works does not merit (either by *meritum condigni* or *meritum congrui*) or put God under obligation

---

by works whatsoever, either of congruity or of condignit . . . Hence also it appears that there is no merit properly so called of man before God, in whatever state he is placed. Thus Adam himself, if he had persevered, would not have merited life in strict justice, although (through a certain condescension [*synchatabasin*]) God promised him by a covenant life under the condition of perfect obedience (which is called meritorious from that covenant in a broader sense because it ought to have been, as it were, the foundation and meritorious cause in view of which God had adjudged life to him)." Turretin, *Institutes* 2:712. In reference to the new covenant, Turretin says, "For if innocent man could merit nothing with God, how much less the guilty sinner?" Turretin, *Institutes*, 2:175.

109. Turretin, *Institutes*, 1:575.

to reward eternal life in any other way than by graciously administered covenant (*ex pacto*). Any promise of reward or blessing annexed to the requirements for obedience must come by way of covenant promise: "If He is pleased to oblige Himself by promising that upon such and such conditions He will reward them, it is His promise that obliges Him. It is not their services, for He is in no way obliged to make such a promise, nor is He obliged to give any reward for any other reason but merely because He was pleased to lay Himself under obligation, and not because man's service lays Him under obligation."[110] If Adam had perfectly obeyed the law and performed the condition of the Covenant of Works he would not have deserved eternal life other than by the virtue of God's covenant.[111] It was no more than what the person of Adam was obliged to do, i.e., to obey the law. Edwards goes on to exhort his congregation not to trust in their own righteousness for acceptance with God, presuming ("foolishly" and "unreasonably") to endeavor to work out a righteousness that obliges God or draws him to show mercy. Likewise, in a sermon on Zech 4:7, he says God was not obliged to make man happy even if he persevered in obedience, and goes on to say how the second covenant is a Covenant of Grace in a way quite different from the first.[112]

It is in this context that Edwards puts forward the distinction between law and gospel. It was Christ's perfect obedience that merited eternal life for the believer, and this in a higher way than Adam's obedience would have done, since, according to Edwards, the person of Jesus Christ was not obliged to obey the law in any other way than by his own condescending agreement to put himself under such obligation by virtue of the Covenant of Redemption.[113]

---

110. Edwards, *Puritan Pulpit*, 40.

111. Edwards's sermon notes reads: "Adams Obedience if he had Perfectly Obeyed the Law, and Performed the Con-dition of the covenant of works would no Otherwise have deserved Eternal life than by virtue of Gods Covenant. If he had strictly Required Obedience in to not only to the moral Law but many Positive and the Abstaining from the forbidden fruit but many other Positive precepts without any Promise of or hopes of Rewards the pa it would have been most Reasonable that he should Obey and God Could no way be Accused of Injustice if he had be-stowed no Reward." Edwards, "Sermon on Luke 17:9," *WJEO* 42, L. 2r.

112. Edwards, "Glorious Grace," *WJE* 10:391–92.

113. "Indeed, when He was born and had become man, the man Christ Jesus was obliged to obey the Law, but Christ was not obliged to subject Himself to the Law by becoming man. He did this for the honor of God's Law, which He was not obliged to do. He was an infinite and infinitely glorious Person, equal with the Father. Yet He became a servant to the Law that men had broken, and perfectly obeyed and hereby

The doctrine of the covenant did not pit love against law or argue for a priority of one over the other. There was no such dichotomy strictly speaking. The Covenant of Works was both a legal and gracious (loving) relationship initiated by God, and it bound Adam to respond in love. "Love and obedience, so often set against one another by modern critics of the Westminster tradition, do rather 'sweetly comply with' one another."[114]

The Works Principle is Foundational to the Biblical Narrative of Redemption

In this section I will argue that the first covenant was primarily a "Covenant of Works" for Edwards. I will discuss five aspects of this "works principle" in Edwards. First, that this works principle is foundational to Edwards's biblical narrative of redemption; second, that the demands of the Covenant of Works are unchangeable and eternal; third, the reasonableness and justice of God in punishing sin with eternal death in Edwards; fourth, the necessity for complete and perfect obedience; and finally, that sense in which the Covenant of Works was never abrogated.

Edwards recognized the gracious "condescending" nature of any covenant relationship initiated by God with his creatures, and the non-meritorious nature of the promise of life entailed in the first covenant with Adam. Despite this, his preferred terminology unambiguously emphasizes the "works" nature of this first covenant. The "grace" inherent in the first covenant God made with Adam needs to be distinguished from the grace of the gospel. In fact, nowhere in his writings does Edwards use the term "grace" to describe the first covenant. Citing Rom 11:6, Edwards distinguishes the Covenant of Works from the grace of the gospel based on what he (Adam) himself did, whereas the grace of the gospel is given altogether freely based on the reception of what is given. In another sermon on Rom 6:14, he distinguishes the grace of the gospel from that of the covenant with Adam: "By grace is meant the dispensation of God's grace in Christ or the covenant of grace . . . If you see to be justified by the covenant of works, then you have departed from the gospel or the

---

merited eternal life from the Father for all who come to Him." Edwards, *Puritan Pulpit*, 52.

114. Casselli, *Divine Rule Maintained*, 77, quoting Burgess.

covenant of grace."[115] He goes on to define grace as, "God's free love and kindness to his creatures . . . That for which principally the kindness and bounty of God is called grace in the freeness of it. The freeness of love and kindness consists in its exercise being unmerited, not what can be demanded, and secondly in its being disinterested . . . and not from self-interest."[116] In the same sermon Edwards considers the ways in which the new Covenant of Grace is to be distinguished from the first as to their natures:

> The grace of the new covenant is distinguished from that of the first, both as to its freeness and as to its greatness. 1. It is distinguished as to the freeness of the grace . . . in its being offered and given to those that had no excellency and in its being offered to offenders without satisfaction made by them. Eternal life was not offered to offenders by the first covenant . . . Neither was eternal life offered to a creature that was not excellent . . . 2. The last covenant is distinguished in the greatness of the grace: (1) The gift is greater in itself, communion with Christ; (2) but abundantly greater if compared with the state that we were found in by the first covenant.[117]

Edwards acknowledges the condescending grace of God in covenanting with man at all in a sermon on Zech 4:7. While it was a gracious act of God to provide a Covenant of Works, or any covenant, Edwards points to an important difference: "But yet this grace would not have been such as the grace of the gospel, for he would have been saved upon the account of what he himself did, but the salvation of the gospel is given altogether freely. Romans 11:6. 'And if by grace, then it is no more of works: otherwise grace is no more grace. But if it be of works, then it is no more grace: otherwise work is no more work.'"[118] Edwards is not opposing law and grace if grace is used in the fullest sense of the term (condescending love and mercy). Grace is a factor in both covenants. But there is also a works-grace distinction that is absolute. It is the basis for the covenantal redemptive-historical distinction between law and gospel in Edwards's history of redemption (that he also correlates to the individual *ordo salutis*). That is why it is so important for Edwards to maintain the Covenant of Works nomenclature exclusively. The concept behind

---

115. Edwards, "Sermon on Romans 6:14," *WJEO* 44, L. 1v.
116. Edwards, "Sermon on Romans 6:14," *WJEO* 44, L. 1v.
117. Edwards, "Sermon on Romans 6:14," *WJEO* 44, L. 1v.
118. Edwards, "Glorious Grace," *WJE* 10:392.

a covenant of *works* provides the substratal principle and overarching internal structure to the biblical narrative of redemption. In simple gospel parlance, it becomes the difference between "what is required" and "what is given," or between "what you need to do" and "what has been done for you." In *Misc. 69, On Perseverance*, Edwards writes:

> 'Tis a Covenant of Works and not a covenant of grace that suspends eternal life on what is the fruit of a man's own strength. Eternal life was to have been of works in these two respects, viz. as it was to have been for man's own righteousness and as it was suspended on the fruit of his own strength. For though our first parent depended on the grace of God— the influences of his Spirit in their hearts— yet that grace was given him already, and dwelt in him constantly and without interruption, in such a degree as to hold him above any lust or sinful habit or principle. And eternal life was not merely suspended on that grace that was given him and dwelt in him, but on his improvement of that grace, his persevering by his own strength with that grace which he already had: for, in order to his perseverance, there was nothing further promised beyond his own strength; no extraordinary occasional assistance was promised. It was not promised but that man should be left to himself as he was (though God did not oblige himself not to afford extraordinary assistance on occasion, as doubtless he did to the angels that stood). But the new covenant is of grace in a manner distinguishing from the old in both these respects, that the reward of life is suspended neither on his own strength or worthiness.[119]

Another way of stating this fundamental distinction is that the covenant blessing of eternal life is fulfilled through the conditional obedience of only one of two federal heads, either through the first man Adam or through the "second Adam," the God-man Christ.[120] In a sermon on Ps 111:5, Edwards says that they (the Covenant of Works and the Covenant of Redemption) are "both Covenants of works . . . or rather being different ways of fulfilling one Covenant of Works . . . both the Covenant of Works and the Covenant of Redemption fulfill one eternal rule of

---

119. Edwards, "Misc. 695," *WJE* 18:278. See also Edwards, "Charity and Its Fruits," *WJE* 8:346.

120. "There have never been two covenants, in strictness of speech, but only two ways constituted of performing of this covenant: the first constituting Adam the representative and federal head, and the second constituting Christ the federal head; the one a dead way, the other a living way and an everlasting one." Edwards, "Misc. 35," *WJE* 13:219.

righteousness."[121] In Edwards's distinction, grace of the gospel is the unconditional offer of those benefits procured solely by Christ's perfect fulfillment of the covenant obligations, obligations that Adam failed to fulfill in the original Covenant of Works. Moreover, the curse (eternal death) imposed upon Adam due to his failure to fulfill both the natural and positive precepts of the original Covenant of Works (and imposed on the rest of humanity through his federal representation and imputed guilt) is taken upon the "second Adam," Christ, as well. This emphasis on Christ's fulfilling the work which Adam (and the rest of mankind in him) failed is clearly taught in Edwards's treatise on justification.

> If Adam had finished his course of perfect obedience, he would have been justified; and certainly his justification would have implied something more than what is merely negative; he would have been approved of, as having fulfilled the righteousness of the law, and accordingly would have been adjudged to the reward of it: so Christ our second surety (in whose justification all who believe in him, and whose surety he is, are virtually justified), was not justified till he had done the work the Father had appointed him, and kept the Father's commandments, through all trials, and then in his resurrection he was justified: when he that had been put to death in the flesh was quickened by the Spirit (1 Pet. 3:18), then he that was manifest in the flesh was justified in the Spirit (1 Tim. 3:16).[122]

The condition of the Covenant of Works was contained in the condition of the Covenant of Redemption and Christ fulfilled those conditions, not as a private person, but as a representative like Adam.

> The Covenant of Works and the covenant of grace, as to their condition, or that which they propose to be complied with by us in order to eternal life, are in some respects the same, though in other respects exceeding diverse. They propose the very same duties. 'Tis the same law, the revelation of the same holy God, and, in general, the same holy acts and exercises that are now proposed to us as the way to our possession of eternal life that was before in the Covenant of Works.[123]

---

121. Edwards, "God Never Fails in Any Instance of Faithfulness," sermon manuscript in Beinecke Library, Yale University, Box 3, Folder 178.

122. Edwards, "Justification by Faith Alone," *WJE* 19:150–51.

123. Edwards, "Misc. 1030," *WJE* 20:367.

The difference is that in the first covenant (of works) we give to God "something acceptable and well pleasing to him," but in the second covenant (of grace) there is only "an expression of acceptance of something offered by God to us most profitable and good for us."[124]

Unchangeable and Eternal

Despite the difference between the first and second covenants, Edwards insists on the unchangeable and eternal demands of the Covenant of Works.

> But yet, the dispositions and acts by which both one and the other of these covenants is complied with are fundamentally the same, because it is still the same God that we have to do with in both, a God of the same nature, and there is implied an agreeableness between us and this God in either case, whether we offer to God that which is acceptable, amiable to the will of his infinite majesty and holiness, or whether we, on the other hand, entirely and sincerely yield to the offers he makes of himself to us as our beneficent friend, Savior and all-sufficient portion. This can't be without an agreeableness between us and him. So that 'tis the same agreeableness to the same glorious God that is requisite in both cases, but this agreeableness includes all holiness and all our duty that we are directed to, both under the covenant of works and the covenant of grace.[125]

The holiness and justice of God cannot be compromised in any covenant, whether the covenant is between God and man, between God the Father and the Son, or ultimately even in the marriage covenant between Christ and the believer.

The condition of the Covenant of Works is perfect and complete obedience to both the natural law and the positive command not to eat of the Tree of the Knowledge of Good and Evil or, as Edwards puts it, "holiness and sincere and universal compliance and actual conformity to God's nature and will."[126] In *Misc. 1030* he says, "Hence we may see the reason why perfection is insisted on in the former covenant . . . Because in the former case, an offering is made to infinite majesty and holiness, as a

---

124. Edwards, "Misc. 1030," *WJE* 20:367.

125. Edwards, "Misc. 1030," *WJE* 20:367–68.

126. Edwards, "Notes on Scripture" *WJE* 14:393–94. See also Edwards, "'Controversies' Notebook: Justification," *WJE* 21:329.

compliance with demands of those perfections of the supreme Lord of the universe, which can't be satisfied without the most spotless perfection."[127] It is a "moral excellency" that in itself is agreeable to God, "amiable and beautiful in his eyes," that is absolutely necessary. Furthermore, obedience of the soul is required for the enjoyments of communion with God in his moral excellency.[128]

Reasonable and Just

While some see it unreasonably harsh that God saw fit to condemn Adam and his posterity to eternal death for the breaking of even a single commandment, Edwards argues that God is consummately reasonable. Sin, however small, deserves everlasting punishment because it is an "infinitely aggravated" injury to God's infinite majesty and disobedience to his authority. In a sermon based on Isa 1:18–20 entitled, *All God's Methods are Most Reasonable*, Edwards tells his congregation: "Sin is an affront and injury to an infinite majesty, and therefore merits an eternal punishment. If an injury to a finite person deserves finite punishment, it will follow that an offense to an infinite person or being deserves infinite punishment. If an injury is aggravated at all in any proportion whatsoever by the degree, merit and excellency of the person injured, it will most surely follow that the offense that is committed against one of infinite excellency is infinitely aggravated."[129] In Edwards's calculus (which is "certain and without dispute"), the grievousness of the sin is proportional to the majesty and authority of the one offended by the sin. Punishment is not simply proportional to the crime, but to the honor and majesty of the victim. A sin against an infinite and holy God, "a Being of infinite holiness and goodness, of infinite amiableness and excellency," merits a punishment proportional, which is likewise infinite and eternal punishment.

Eternal punishment is not only proportional to the nature of sin but is also fitting to the nature of God. This is not, for Edwards, to say that because God is righteous he is obliged to punish sin. The punishment of sin is a mere act of justice, yet if he did not punish it "nobody could charge God with any wrong." Edwards does not like this manner of phrasing.

---

127. Edwards, "Misc. 367," *WJE* 20:367.
128. Edwards, *Puritan Pulpit*, 236.
129. Edwards, "All God's Methods are Most Reasonable," *WJE* 14:188.

Rather it is more proper to say that God is obliged in holiness and wisdom to punish sin. "It would not be a prudent, decent and beautiful thing for a being of infinite glory and majesty, and the sovereign of the world, to let an infinite evil go unpunished. And as God's nature inclines him [to] order all things beautifully, properly and decently, so it was necessary that sin should be punished; God in his infinite wisdom saw that there was such a necessity as this."[130] Certainly God is both just and merciful, but they are subservient (subordinate) decrees to the decree to express his holiness and wisdom, his majesty and glory.[131]

Moreover, sin "in its own nature" brings everlasting misery upon the soul. Eternal death is not only the wages but the proper fruit and natural end of sin itself. Sin brings the soul into such a condition, "so destroys and ruins the nature, so corrupts and poisons the heart," that it can never recover itself. It so "kills the soul," that it never to all eternity can restore itself. It so "infects the mind and brings such a distemper upon it," that it never will of itself be cured. Pain and misery is the natural fruit of the "poison" of sin and unavoidably follows as long as the soul remains corrupted, which, because it cannot recover itself, remains forever.[132] The reality of eternal punishment has a further end to "awe men to obedience" and to an "awe of the infinite majesty of God." Hard-hearted sinners need no less than such a punishment threatened to deter them in their sinning and drive them to obedience.

> If they were to be punished a thousand years, or a million, or however long, yet if it were to have an end they would take encouragement that it would not last always, that sometime or other it would be over, and so they would be bold in sin.
>
> This is very evident, in that though now eternal punishment is threatened, it has so little effect upon men, that they are so little awakened by it, that thousands and millions nevertheless give themselves a full swing in iniquity and go on securely in a way of disobedience to God; and it's a difficult thing, by telling

---

130. Edwards, "Misc. 306," *WJE* 13:391.

131. Edwards's discussions on the ordering of God's decrees is found in Edwards, "Misc. 348," *WJE* 13:419; Edwards, "Misc. 700," *WJE* 18:282–83.

132. Edwards, "All God's Methods are Most Reasonable," *WJE* 14:187. Edwards goes on to answer the question as to why sinful souls in this life are not always so tormented in this way. His answer is that souls are anesthetized ("benumbed and kept asleep by the body of flesh"). "The flesh that they carry about with them keeps them in a stupid condition, like a person in a lethargy; but when they awake in another world, it will be otherwise," Edwards, "All God's Methods are Most Reasonable," *WJE* 14:188.

men of everlasting burnings, to make them bethink themselves and leave off a way of allowed sinning. How would it be, then, if it were only a temporal punishment was threatened, a punishment that is infinitely less dreadful than an eternal one, as every temporal punishment is, however long it is continued?[133]

Edwards, in a foreshadowing of a more famous sermon preached later (*Sinners in the Hands of an Angry God*), implores his congregation, "to let those [who are afraid of being dammed] see and own that it would be most just with God forever to cast them into hell. Don't be inventing these and those excuses for yourselves, don't meditate upon the good things you have done, the care you have taken to avoid sin, and the pains you have taken to do as God commands; but own that God may justly cast you into hell forevermore, notwithstanding all that you have done, notwithstanding all your care and pains."[134] For Edwards, these warnings were not to just terrify, but to awaken sinners to God's remedies and prepare them for conversion. The warnings of God's just eternal damnation of sinners were every bit as part of the gracious mercy of God to drive them to the "precious remedy" of the gospel as the announcement of the free offer of that remedy.

Requirement of Complete and Perfect Obedience

The condition of complete and perfect obedience is of foremost importance in the Covenant of Works for Edwards. The covenant agreement bound man to a perfect obedience to the divine decree, and the slightest infringement or momentary lapse of obedience was sufficient to immediately cancel the promises of eternal life and incur the promised curse. In his capacity as a public person, or a federal head, all men now share in both the guilt and resultant curse of Adam's disobedience. Edwards would go on in a more speculative vein in his treatment of the imputation of Adam's sin by attributing the unity of the race to the "arbitrary constitution" of divine wisdom, a notion dependent upon his metaphysical philosophy of idealism. However much commentators of Edwards critique or misunderstand his speculations in this regard,

---

133. Edwards, "All God's Methods are Most Reasonable," *WJE* 14:190.

134. Edwards, "All God's Methods are Most Reasonable," *WJE* 14:191. See also Edwards, "The Torments of Hell are Exceeding Great," *WJE* 14:301–29; and in the same sermon series, Edwards, "The Warnings of Scripture are in the Best Manner Adapted to the Awakening and Conversion of Sinners," *WJEO* 47:330–37.

speculations that are quite "reasonable" to the Edwardsean mind and worldview, it does not challenge the essential teaching in Reformed theology regarding Adam as the federal head with the result that all men are taken up in Adam's sin.[135]

The obedience required of the Covenant of Works included both the natural law as well as the positive precept of not eating of the Tree of the Knowledge of Good and Evil. In his sermon on Luke 16:24, Edwards states that, "both according to the law of God and according to the reason and nature of things, the law fixes death as the wages of every sin. 'In the day that thou eatest thou shalt [surely] die' [Gen. 2:17]. Which does not only refer to that one particular sin, but to every other thing that God has forbidden."[136]

Miscellany 884, Covenant Made With Adam is an extended response to Jonathan Dickinson (1688–1747) who argued that Adam had only to obey the one precept of not eating of the fruit of the tree in order to justify himself and his posterity.[137] Edwards argues that God's explicit command to Adam to not eat of the tree does not imply that other commands were not part of the covenant and that the same punishment would not follow for breaking those commands as well. Those commands

---

135. Edwards, *Original Sin*, WJE 3:389–412. See also Holbrook, "Editor's Introduction," WJE 3:41–60. Edwards's doctrine of original sin *per se* was not based on his speculative philosophical theology, but on biblical exegesis and his Reformed and Augustinian doctrinal heritage. It is worth noting that the bulk of *Original Sin* is a biblical, historical, and empirical argument for the doctrine. The philosophical notions of Edwards's realist "identity" of Adam and his progeny as founded in God's "idea" was an attempt to defend the doctrine "rationally" (or at least to show that the doctrine was not "irrational") from its Enlightenment detractors who insisted that an individual cannot be blamed or praised for something he did not himself (God's appointment notwithstanding) choose to do. While adding a layer to the concept of federal headship that was admittedly "new ground" for Reformed theology, it did not negate it. Edwards taught and preached the orthodox doctrine of federal headship in many of his sermons and treatises in the same vein as orthodox Reformed confessional theology, using the terms "surety" and "covenant head" most often. John Gerstner, while not necessarily siding with Edwards's thinking in the matter, nevertheless called it "federal theology with a vengeance." While traditional Reformed orthodoxy never did (and still doesn't) accept Edwards's philosophical doctrine of "identity," it, like Charles Hodge, sees Edwards as traditionally orthodox though by an "untraditional" route. Gerstner, *Rational Biblical Theology*, 3:333–34. See also Hodge, *Systematic Theology*, 2:208.

136. Edwards, "The Torments of Hell are Exceeding Great," WJE 14:309.

137. Dickinson, *True Scripture-Doctrine*. Edwards is addressing the discourse entitled, "Nature and Consequences of Original Sin."

were a "rule already given, and known, and now standing forth in the law written on men's hearts." In the very command of not eating the forbidden fruit, there was presupposed the sum of the law of nature "to have been already established and known by Adam," that is, "that man owed God a supreme and perfect respect, and to be regarded above all other things." Edwards reasons from Rom 5:13–14 that up until a law was given in an express revelation in Moses, there still existed a law of nature that was known, even if at times faintly and obscured by sin and spiritual blindness, from Adam until the time of Moses. Therefore, "how much more was it sufficiently plain, as written on the heart of Adam, who was created in knowledge after the image of him that created him, without one deceitful lust to blind his reason and conscience, and [with] the Spirit of God dwelling in him, as a principle of perfect holiness, to enlighten him."[138] He goes on to say:

> The Apostle speaks of this law of nature written on the hearts of men, with its sanction or threatening made know with sufficient clearness to condemn men and bring on death, not only after it had been obscured by the fall and with the help of tradition from Adam in the first ages of the world, but even many ages after, among the heathen, where sin and Satan and a barbarous education had actually prevailed to obliterate the light of nature to a very great degree indeed [Rom 1:18–32]. Therefore, surely it was plain enough to have justly brought on condemnation and death on Adam, in all his light and perfection.[139]

According to Edwards, the precept of not eating the forbidden fruit was not the only part, nor even the "main rule," given to Adam for his obedience. This "main rule" was that "great rule of righteousness written in his heart" when God first made him, which it "must be supposed" that he knew sufficient. This, Edwards reasons, Adam knew sufficiently before God gave the positive precept of not eating from the tree. Otherwise, when God did give that precept to Adam, "[He] would have been at a loss whether he ought to submit to it or not, for this could be known only by the law of nature, the sum of which is that God is to be fervently regarded and loved, and his will to be universally complied with. And this was the grand rule given to Adam."[140] The positive precept was given to see

---

138. Edwards, "Misc. 884," *WJE* 20:142.
139. Edwards, "Misc. 884," *WJE* 20:143.
140. Edwards, "Misc. 884," *WJE* 20:144.

whether Adam would keep God's commands, to try him in his obedience to the law of nature or moral law. Edwards sets this forth in a sermon on Gen 3:11 (taken from a transcript of his notes), where he states that:

> There were other commands that Adam was obliged by. He was obliged by every precept of the law of nature. But God established this command as the especially manifestation of his authority and sovereignty over Adam, forbidding one tree among many he pleased, to be a trail of his submission to God's authority. Neither was that the only sin that was forbidden and threatened with death in the Covenant of Works. For that required perfect obedience and forbid all sin whatsoever and therefore all those other sins that Adam committed were breaches of the Covenant of Works.[141]

This "main rule" encompassed all other positive and revealed laws and is summed up by the great commandment that required one to love God with all one's heart, with all one's soul, with all one's mind, and with all one's strength, and to "regard his authority and glory, and submit themselves wholly to him, and yield themselves up to him, and obey and serve him as their God."[142]

Eternal and Never Abrogated

Edwards insists that the Covenant of Works is an eternal covenant that was never abrogated. Understanding what Edwards means by this and the careful distinctions and qualifications he makes is extremely important for understanding almost all of his subsequent thoughts regarding covenant theology as he reads it in Scripture. Edwards maintained the Covenant of Works was a covenant "forever established." By this he meant that while it was abrogated in terms of its fulfillment by Adam, it was not abrogated in terms of its judgment, neither was it abrogated in

---

141. Edwards, "Sermon on Gen. 3:11," *WJEO* 54, L. 25r, 25v (my transcription of Edwards's sermon notes). Edwards's original manuscript reads: "there were other Commands that adam was obliged by [-] he was ---- by every precept of the law of nature. but G. established this Command as the Especially manifesta. of his Authority . in order & sovereignty over adam forbidding one tree among many in which he pleased . to be a trial of his submission to Gods Authority neither was that the only sin that was forbidden in the Cov of works & threatned with Death in the Cov. of works for that Required Perfect obed & forbid all sin Whatsoever & theref all those other sins that Adam Committed were breaches of the Cov. of works."

142. Edwards, "Sermon on Gen. 3:11," *WJEO* 54, L. 25r, 25v.

terms of "an eternal rule of righteousness" in distinction from the specific covenant with Adam.

In his sermon on Num 23:19 entitled *God Never Changes His Mind*, Edwards presents the doctrine that God "never repents of anything that he has done" and "never changes his mind with respect to the rules which he fixed for himself to act by."[143] Edwards has principally in mind "the covenants that God has entered into with his reasonable creatures." Specifically, he cites the Covenant of Works as that "which God entered into with angels and men, is what God will never depart from." The Covenant of Works is never abrogated, "but as a covenant stands in full force to all eternity without the failing of one tittle."[144] Edwards's main target with these and other sentiments is a class of Arminians (or neonomians) that proposed Christ abolished the requirements and demands of the Covenant of Works and established a "new law" of faith and sincere, albeit imperfect, obedience.[145] By effectively turning faith into a "work," the New Covenant became nothing more than the Old Covenant of "works" reincarnated, but with less stringent demands. The distinction between law and gospel was blurred, if not abolished. For Edwards, an abrogation of the Covenant of Works in this sense was the equivalent to the abrogation of the distinction between law and gospel.

In terms of the specific covenant with Adam, as a covenant unto eternal life promised to him and to his prosperity on condition of obedience, it was abrogated the moment Adam sinned in terms of its fulfillment. Adam lost the federal headship of his race and incurred the judgment of

---

143. Edwards, "God Never Changes His Mind," *WJEO* 44, L. 3r. Also published in Edwards, *Puritan Pulpit*, 1–13.

144. Edwards, "Misc. 30," *WJE* 13:215.

145. Edwards discusses this in numerous places in his works, most clearly in his lectures on justification in Edwards, "Justification by Faith," *WJE* 19:147–242, and in several *Miscellanies*, most clearly in Edwards, "Misc. 2," *WJE* 13:197–98. Cherry notes that Edwards maintains that "the essence of Arminianism is its neonomianism," which "conceives faith as a new kind of obedience and the gospel as a new kind of law." Cherry, *Theology of Jonathan Edwards*, 187. Morimoto lists three claims that Edwards uses to define the Arminian doctrine of justification: 1) "to justify means to pardon"; that "there is no imputation of Christ's righteousness"; and that "sincere obedience is sufficient in order to receive justification," for God "regards our imperfect human effort as perfect." Morimoto, *Jonathan Edwards*, 76. Thomas Schafer notes, "There was probably not, in 1734, an avowed Arminian in the Puritan pulpit of New England; but the works of English divines like Samuel Clarke, John Tillotson, Isaac Barrow, and Daniel Whitby were beginning to be read." Schafer, "Jonathan Edwards," *CH* 20, 55–67.

God's wrath immediately upon the first act of eating the fruit. "[The] sentence of condemnation was already immediately passed upon Adam, and on his posterity with him, when he had broken the covenant, agreeable to the threatening contained in the covenant. The covenant was immediately acted upon. And he that gave the covenant proceeded to judgment, and so the whole affair of trying of mankind upon that covenant with Adam was determined. Judgment is the final issue of God's transacting with man in a covenant established."[146] The matter of man's obedience was decided and he failed. The means is closed by way of that covenant forever and "'tis absurd to suppose that God still treats with man upon that covenant."[147] The judgment is passed and the sentence is in the process of being carried out. "The covenant with Adam was acted upon and done with."[148] God can no longer covenant directly with a sinner, apart from a mediator. In that manner, the specific Covenant of Works with Adam and his posterity *as a means to eternal life* is "abrogated" and hence serves only to condemn.

> God, not only after Adam had violated the covenant, presently acted upon it and proceeded to judgment; but he before, in the making of the covenant, declared that he would do so. "In the day that thou eatest thereof," said God, "thou shalt surely die" [Gen 2:17]. So that the very establishment, or covenant itself, as God revealed and stated it, implied that the first, overt, explicit violation should be the abolishing of the covenant as to future proceedings, because that was in the establishment, that on the first violation God would immediately proceed to judgment.[149]

It is much clearer to say that the covenant with Adam can never be rescinded and no other covenant with man can alter that final covenant verdict. This is the thrust of Edwards's statement that "God never made but one [covenant stating the condition of eternal life] with man to wit, the Covenant of Works; which never yet was abrogated, but is a covenant stands in full force to all eternity without the failing of one tittle."[150] In essence, there is only one way to eternal life, yet that way is forever barred through Adam's covenant disobedience. The implication is that

---

146. Edwards, "Misc. 717," *WJE* 18: 348–49.
147. Edwards, "Misc. 717," *WJE* 18: 349.
148. Edwards, "Misc. 717," *WJE* 18: 349.
149. Edwards, "Misc. 717," *WJE* 18: 349.
150. Edwards, "Misc. 30," *WJE* 13:217.

any other way to eternal life must come by some other way of fulfilling that covenant, i.e., through "another Adam."

In terms of its judgment, the Covenant of Works is *not* abrogated. The condemning nature of the now broken Covenant of Works stays in force and is never abrogated. As Edwards says, we are indeed still now under the Covenant of Works in its condemnation. Not only is there no provision for salvation, but the law now increases sin and man's hostility toward God. This is expanded in his sermon on Gen 3:11: "They have lost their love to God and instead of love there is a slavish and hatred. Instead of embracing opportunities of conversing with God as their best friend, they fly from him as an enemy."[151] In his *Notes on the Bible*, on Rom 6:14, Edwards explains what it means to be "under the dominion of sin," contrasting being "under the law" and "under grace":

> The law, or Covenant of Works is not a proper means to bring the fallen creature to the service of God. It was a very proper means to be used with man in a state of innocency but it has no tendency to answer this end in our present weak and sinful state; but on the contrary, to have been kept under the law would have had a tendency to hinder it, and would have been a bar in the way of it, and that upon two accounts. 1. It would have tended to discourage persons from any attempts to serve God, because under such a constitution it must necessarily have been looked upon as impossible to please him or serve him to his acceptance; and one in despair of this would have been in no capacity to yield a cheerful service to God, but would rather have been far from any manner of endeavors to serve him at all, but to have abandoned himself to wickedness. By such a despair the dominion of sin would have been dreadfully established, and all yielded up to it, as in the damned in hell. 2. God must necessarily have been looked on as an enemy, which would have tended to drive from him and stir up enmity against him. A fallen creature held under the Covenant of Works can't look on God as a father and friend, but must necessarily look on him as an enemy, for the least failure of obedience by that constitution, whether past or future, renders him so. But this would greatly establish the dominion of sin or enmity against God in the heart. And indeed, it is the law only that makes wicked men hate God. They

---

151. Edwards, "Gen 3:11," *WJEO* 54, L. 1v (my transcription of Edwards's sermon notes). Edwards's original manuscript reads: "they have lost their love to G. & instead of Love there [is] a slavish & hatred instead of em-[embr]acing opportunities of Conversing with G. as [thei]r Best friend they fly from him as an Enemy."

hate him no otherwise than as they look upon [him] as acting, either as the giver or judge of the law, and so by the law opposing their sins, and the law tending to establish the hatred of God.[152]

"Why is it that we need to know this?" asks Edwards. It is primarily in order to know the remedy. There is such an intimate linkage between the covenants that the knowledge of the first leads to the second. The remedy meets the failed demands of the first under a second head and this knowledge drives us to that remedy. According to Edwards, "It is of infinite importance that we should know both, for their first is our own by which we are undone and the second must be our own if ever we are saved, and we must know the former in order to know the latter."[153] It is just as important for sinners to be sensible of their sin and guilt by the first Adam, so as to know their righteousness and recovery by the second Adam, Christ.

Distinct from this specific covenant with Adam, the Covenant of Works as "an eternal rule of righteousness that God had established between himself and mankind . . . that is the covenant" continues to stand forever as a rule of judgment.[154] It is the "original and eternal rule of righteousness which we call the law, or Covenant of Works."[155] In his lectures *Justification by Faith Alone*, Edwards says, "The law is the eternal and unalterable rule of righteousness, between God and man, and therefore is the rule of judgment, by which all that a man does shall be either justified or condemned; and no sin exposes to damnation, but by the law."[156] These are important statements. The immutability of the Covenant of Works "as an eternal rule of righteousness and judgment" is the basis for the grace of the New Covenant and the unity of the covenant structure in Edwards's theology. The Covenant of Redemption, which is the foundation for the

---

152. Edwards, "Notes on Scripture," *WJE* 15:198.

153. Edwards, "Sermon on Genesis 3:11," *WJEO* 54, L. 3v (my transcription of Edwards's sermon notes). Edwards's original manuscript reads: "it is of Infinite Importance that we should know both for the for the first is our own by which we are undone & the second must be our own if ever we are saved & we must Know the former in order to Know the latter [-] & so that is of as Great moment [-] us to Kno be sensible of our sin & guilt by the first Adam as tis [-] Know our Righ. & Recovery by the second."

154. Edwards, "History of the Work of Redemption," *WJE* 9:309.

155. Edwards, "Misc. 589," *WJE* 18:122.

156. Edwards, "Justification by Faith Alone," *WJE* 19:197.

Covenant of Grace, is based on fulfilling the Covenant of Works via a new surety or covenant head:

> The covenant of grace or redemption (which we have showed to be the same) cannot be called a new covenant, or the second covenant, with respect to the Covenant of Works; for that is not grown old yet but is an eternal immutable covenant, of which one jot nor tittle will never fail. There have never been two covenants, in strictness of speech, but only two ways constituted of performing of this covenant: the first constituting Adam the representative and federal head, and the second constituting Christ the federal head; the one a dead way, the other a living way and an everlasting one.[157]

And, again, in *Misc. 717*:

> Though the law or covenant of works stood in force, still yet the covenant with Adam was acted upon and done with . . . were it not that there is still a possibility and a trial for obtaining by that covenant under a new head, even under Christ. The voice of that covenant still is directed to us, viz. that if we sin in ourselves, or in our surety, we shall die. But if we obey in ourselves, or in our surety, without sin we shall live.[158]

Both the unity of the covenants as well as the distinctions between the covenants in Edwards is founded on a right understanding of the nature of the Covenant of Works.

Conclusion

Edwards's tricovenantal structure of covenant or federal theology was in continuity with the broader Reformed tradition to which he was heir. He embraced a Covenant of Works that emphasized the unchanging and eternal nature of God's holy rule of righteousness that demanded perfect and complete obedience. While Edwards insisted on the "works" nature of the covenant by which a "work" had to be accomplished by Adam as the covenant mediator (or surety) of mankind, it was not a law opposed to (condescending) grace. The law for Edwards was not a mere arbitrary and grace-less set of burdens, but a revelation of God's own holy nature and character and a means of communion with God. As such law and grace,

---

157. Edwards, "Misc. 35," *WJE* 13:219.
158. Edwards, "Misc. 717," *WJE* 18:349.

or law and love, are not opposed in Edwards's theology. The Covenant of Works was a covenant never abrogated in terms of its establishment of the conditions for eternal life ("Do this and live!"), even after Adam's probationary failure and the imputation of the guilt of that failure to his progeny, whereby the conditions are now impossible to fulfill. A right and proper view of the Covenant of Works was foundational for Edwards's attack on the twin errors of antinomian lawlessness and neonomian legalism that he saw as threatening the very nature of the gospel message.

The following chapters will show that the eternal and never abrogated "eternal rule of righteousness" of perfect obedience that is at the heart of the Covenant of Works is foundational for understanding Edwards's view of the Covenants of Redemption and Grace. It forms the basis for the redemptive role of Christ as the second mediator or "surety" in the Covenant of Redemption in the face of Adam's failure. It is also the basis for the doctrine of the imputation of the active righteousness of Christ, as perfect and complete fulfillment of the "eternal rule of righteousness," as the only basis of salvation in the Covenant of Grace. The doctrine of the Covenant of Works and the imputation of the active obedience of Christ stand or fall together in Edwards's soteriology.

Misunderstandings of or failures to appreciate the significance of Edwards's view of this doctrine has resulted in subsequent confusion regarding Edwards's theology and its practical implications. The Covenant of Works in Edwards, as it was in the entire history of Reformed thought up to Edwards, was founded upon the biblical witness in its entire redemptive-historical aspect and in the vital distinction between law and gospel that permeated Edwards's biblical hermeneutics. The covenant structure of Scripture gave shape to Edwards's law-gospel soteriology. The foundational cornerstone of this structure was the "eternal rule of righteousness that God had established between himself and mankind," a rule that was a gracious rule and the basis of man's communion with God and his eternal happiness. Edwards's covenant distinctions have profound implications for his practical theology and provide a covenantal foundation for the real necessity of "evangelical" (gospel) obedience in the Christian life.

3

Jonathan Edwards on the Covenant of Redemption

Introduction

IN THE PREVIOUS CHAPTER, I showed how Edwards's doctrine of the Covenant of Works was rooted in the "works" principle of complete and perfect obedience to God's covenant stipulations. While the covenant was abrogated in terms of its fulfillment by Adam, it was not abrogated in terms of its judgment. In this chapter I will show how the works principle is rooted in the intratrinitarian relationship. In other words, Adam's sin makes Christ's perfect obedience according to the intratrinitarian Covenant of Redemption the only basis of salvation. In historical Reformed covenant theology, the Covenant of Redemption roots the gospel message in the eternal council of the Trinity and connects the eternal decrees to their outworking in the history of redemption. It is a doctrinal argument for the *ad intra* ("to within") trinitarian grounding of the *ad extra* ("to without") work of salvation as it terminates on the individual divine persons of the Trinity.

Like the Covenant of Works, Edwards inherited from his Reformed tradition a well-established conceptual framework that included the Covenant of Redemption, albeit not without variations in its expression. In many formulations it is the key link between the eternal decrees and the Covenant of Grace, and this is no less true for Edwards. The Covenant of Redemption, as Edwards articulates the doctrine, is central and crucial to his concept of the history of the work of redemption.[1] For Edwards, the

---

1. Yazawa, *Covenant of Redemption*. Yazawa's study underscores many of the

Covenant of Grace is not only the historical outworking and application of the Covenant of Redemption as it impacts the history of redemption as it progresses from the fall of Adam to the second coming of Christ, from the Old Testament to the New Testament, it also informs the *ordo salutis* in the individual elect believer. In other words, the Covenant of Redemption, properly understood in its relationship to the Covenants of Works and Grace, links Edwards's biblical and systematic theologies and is the foundation for the law-gospel distinction in his theology. Edwards's trinitarianism involves the whole Trinity in this work. He shows how the Covenant of Redemption is founded upon, and not opposed to, the eternal decrees of election. Finally, Edwards's theology of the Covenant of Redemption has important implications for evangelical obedience. This chapter, along with the previous and the two subsequent, form an extended prolegomenon to understanding the role of works in Edwards's theology.

The Covenant of Redemption in Reformed Theology

The Covenant of Redemption is a special new arrangement that exists only between the Father and the Son, entered by mutual and free consent, to undertake the work of redemption. This "new" covenant is fundamentally the "old" covenant with a new mediator, the Second Person of the Trinity. The Covenant of Redemption (*pactum salutis*) was not a speculative doctrine of philosophical theology, as proposed by some historians, but a conclusion of Reformed theologians' comprehensive biblical exegesis. It was also an integral aspect of a systemizing of theology, especially in relation to the divine decrees.[2]

A Speculative Doctrine

The Covenant of Redemption (*pactum salutis* or *foedus redemptionis*) is admittedly the most speculative element in Reformed doctrine. But, according to Richard Muller, it represents that most basic issue of the Reformed system: "the eternal, divine, and consistently gracious ground

---

conclusions of this chapter. For a critique of Edwards's view of the *pactum salutis*, see Fesko, *Covenant of Redemption*, 122–26.

2. For an overview of the historic origins of the Covenant of Redemption in early modern Reformed theology, see Fesko, *The Covenant of Redemption*.

of the plan of salvation, the resolution of the seemingly unbridgeable gap between the eternal and the temporal, the infinite and the finite, undertaken redemptively and by grace alone from the divine side."[3] Despite its seeming centrality, the doctrine in its full explication does not fully appear until the middle of the seventeenth century. This has caused historians of theology to question its origins and basis within Reformed doctrine. Does its sudden appearance on the stage of church history expose its novelty as a theological innovation and belie its veracity, or were there antecedents and reasons for its appearance at this stage of the development of Reformed theology?

The name Johannes Cocceius has been so associated with the Covenant of Redemption that Wilhelm Gass believed (in a bit of overstatement) that Cocceius invented the concept.[4] However, Cocceius himself recognizes the influence of Johann Cloppenburg (1592–1652) on his theology[5] and Gottlob Schrenk discusses the presence of the Covenant of Redemption in Cloppenburg's theology just prior to Cocceius.[6] Heppe argued that it was fully present even earlier than Cloppenburg, e.g., in Kaspar Olevianus's *De substantia foederis* (1585).[7] More recently Bierma also located the roots of the doctrine in Olevianus.[8]

Muller notes the potential for even earlier antecedents of the *pactum salutis*.[9] There are hints, for instance, of the concept even in Luther in his 1519 lectures on Galatians. There he notes that Christ, as immortal God, "made a *pactum*." While as one who was to become mortal, "made a *testamentum*."[10] His point is that equals can compact together while a testament "can only be made by one who is capable of dying." Luther does not explicitly formulate an intratrinitarian covenant, but there is by implication a *pactum* made by the Son prior to the *testamentum* that Christ undertook as the incarnate Mediator. The language of *Iesus Christus, deu immortalis . . . quia futurus mortalis* places both the

---

3. Muller, "Toward the *Pactum Salutis*," 11–65.

4. Gass, *Geschichte der protestantishen Dogmatic*, 4:264.

5. Asselt, *Federal Theology*, 228.

6. Schrenk, *Gottesreich und Bund*, 61, 79.

7. Heppe, *Dogmatik des Deutschen Protestantismus*, 2:215–20; Heppe, *Geschichte des Pietismus*, 211.

8. Bierma, *German Calvinism*, 107–12.

9. Muller, "Toward the *Pactum Salutis*," 12–14.

10. "Thus Jesus Christ, the immortal God, made a covenant." Luther, "Lectures on Galatians (1519)," *LW* 27:368; cf. *WA* 2:521.

testament and the prior *pactum* in eternity. Andrew Woolsey sees a foreshadowing of the concept in Johannes Oecolampadius (1482–1531): "In what can only be regarded as a foreshadowing of the later covenant of redemption idea, Oeclampadius spoke of God's covenant with his people in Christ as based on a '*pactum cum filio sua*.' Just as God entered into a covenant with his Son, so according to his larger promises (*ampliores promissiones*) there will be an everlasting covenant (*foedus sempiternum*) made with his people."[11] Paul Helm traces antecedents of the doctrine in the thought of John Calvin.[12] Herman Witsius, while maintaining that the *pactum salutis* was not found among the Reformers and their immediate successors, finds the doctrine first appearing, surprisingly, in Jacobus Arminius (1560–1609).[13] He also cites William Ames who, while refuting Remonstrant theologians, noted that the particular distinction made by them "denies that the covenant entered into by Christ (*He shall see his seed . . . and the pleasure of the Lord shall prosper in his hand*), had been ratified."[14] Franciscus Gomarus (1563–1641) is also mentioned, referencing the doctrine in his exegesis of the baptism of Christ: Christ's Baptist was, "the sign and seal of the covenant between God and Christ; namely, that God would be his God . . . [and] he himself was bound to perform obedience."[15] David Dickson (c. 1583–1663) in his speech before the General Assembly of the Church of Scotland in 1638 made explicit use of the eternal Covenant of Redemption for the refutation of Arminianism—with no hint that the doctrine was a new or novel concept:

> [The Arminian's] main errour is this (let me speak it with reverence towards your learning)—not knowing the Scriptures, and the power of God in the matter of the Covenant of redemption betwixt God and Christ; yet there is enough of it in the Scripture. They pointed at it themselves, which, if they should have followed, they might sein all their matter in the midst; for the

---

11. Woolsey, *Unity and Continuity*, 211–12.

12. Helm, "Calvin and the Covenant," 68–71.

13. Witsius, *Economy of the Covenants*, I:176–77. See also Arminius, "Priesthood of Christ," 2:416–17. Witsius goes on to discuss the concept as found in Cloppenburg ("not only slightly mentions this subject, but fully and accurately handles it"), Voetius, Essenius, and Owen (he omits Cocceius and appears not to have known of the formulations in Oecolampadius or Olevianus).

14. Witsius, *Economy of the Covenants*, 1:176, citing Ames's *Anti-Synodalibus, de morte Christi* and Isa 53:10.

15. Witsius, *Economy of the Covenants*, 1:176, citing Gomarus on Matt 3:13 and Luke 2:21.

Covenant of Salvation betwixt God and man is one thing, and the Covenant of Redemption betwixt God and Christ is ane uther thing.[16]

In fact, according to Muller, Dickson presented the doctrine as a standard and already accepted point in theology, foundational to a right understanding of the Reformed view.[17]

Biblical Foundations

Richard Muller notes how little opposition there was to what seemed a relatively new idea with a "rather shaky pedigree," especially in an era of orthodoxy and fairly strict confessionalism. He raises the question of whether the concept might have had other precedents. "Worlds may arise *ex nihilo*, doctrinal formulae probably do not."[18] Muller provides several elements of Reformed exegesis, textual criticism, philology, and doctrinal discussion that laid groundwork or provided a backdrop to the formulation, even prior to the first use of the term *pactum salutis* or *foedus redemptionis*. Of central importance to the Reformation movement was a series of shifts that occurred in the exegesis of the Old and New Testaments during the sixteenth and early seventeenth centuries. These shifts arose largely by departing from Vulgate-dependent exegesis and engaging the new critical editions of the Hebrew and Greek texts of the Old and New Testaments respectively that had become available. These texts were re-examined in light of specific doctrinal issues raised during the Reformation.

For instance, Theodore Beza rendered Luke 22:29 as "*Ego vero paciscor vobis, prout pactus est mihi Pater meus regnum*," translating the Greek *diatithemi* as the Latin *paciscor*, "to make a covenant," and given the tenses of the verbs, is taken as: "I make a covenant with you [present] . . . as my father has made a covenant with me [past]." The Vulgate, according to Beza, "badly" rendered *diatithemi* as *dispone* (as Calvin used this reading). Beza also cross-references this verse to Heb 9, connecting the *pactum* in Luke 22 with the eternal *testamentum* in Heb 9.[19] According

---

16. Quoted in Muller, "Toward the *Pactum Salutis*," 17. Dickson's speech is recorded in Peterkin, *Records of the Kirk of Scotland*, 156–59.
17. Muller, "Toward the *Pactum Salutis*," 16–20.
18. Muller, "Toward the *Pactum Salutis*," 14.
19. Beza, *Iesu Christi*, n. p., ad loc. Luke 22:29.

to J. V. Fesko, "Beza dropped this exegetical pebble into the theological pond and it rippled well into the seventeenth century."[20] The implication was that theologians began thinking more in terms of Christ's office of mediator as being covenantally appointed. It was in the context of biblical exegesis, not philosophical speculation, that the Covenant of Redemption was formulated.

The biblical exegesis employed by the scholastic Reformers, especially with regards to covenant theology, was no mere proof-texting, as is often claimed.[21] Muller notes that no single verse or text provided the exegetic foundation for the Covenant of Redemption.[22] It was rather a conclusion drawn from the juxtaposition of texts and doctrinal considerations about the nature of the work of redemption. For example, in the case of Old Testament texts, it was assumed under a broadly Christological hermeneutic that Christ was the fulfillment of Old Testament prophesies of redemption and was the ultimate anti-type of the various Old Testament types or figures. The New Testament texts provided the hermeneutical foundation for the work of Christ, understood both as the fulfillment of prophecy and as the realization of God's eternal plan of salvation. Adriaane Neele likewise affirms that "the hermeneutical, philological, and text-critical work of the post-Reformation period disproves the so-called proof-text characterization so often alleged—that is, that biblical exegesis was confined to the confirmation of established doctrine."[23]

---

20. Fesko, *Trinity*, 5.

21. Louis Berkhof is an example when he states that, "exegesis became the handmaid of dogmatics and degenerated into a mere search of proof-texts." Berkhof, *Principles*, 29.

22. For instance, modern commentators find no support for the *pactum* doctrine in Zech 6:13, which is usually identified as a proof-text for the doctrine. However, this text played no role in the initial formulations of the doctrine and was only brought in by later theologians. While it is true that the phrase "Counsel of Peace" was taken from this passage and applied to the concept of the Covenant of Redemption, and it is also true that it is a misunderstanding of what the verse is talking about (which is referring to the harmony of Christ's roles as priest and king, not a covenant to redeem among the Father, Son, and Spirit), this is not where the concept of the Covenant of Redemption originated. Rather, it was simply an idea applied to it later. See Muller, "Toward the *Pactum Salutis*," 11–65.

23. Neele, *Before Jonathan Edwdards*, 110–11.

In Systematic Theology

From the very beginning, formulations of the Covenant of Redemption also concerned a complex integration of doctrinal issues, e.g., the Trinity, Christology, covenant, and predestination, within a debate concerning the relationship between the eternal decrees and the Covenant of Grace. It was not simply a covenant alternative to the doctrine of the divine decrees or predestination.[24] The question was rather one of distinguishing but not separating the *pactum salutis* and the eternal decrees in Reformed theology. The *archetypal/ectypal* pattern of discerning an *ad intra* divine foundation in knowing and willing for all divine work *ad extra* was a base assumption of Reformed thought.[25] The doctrine of the *pactum* was employed to answer questions not dealt with in the doctrine of the decrees. For instance, it addresses the issue of how humanity, in its inability and having violated the Covenant of Works, can be given a new federal head as a foundation of a new covenant relationship without removing the legal foundations of the Covenant of Works. Muller notes that this issue is present in all the early formulations of the *pactum salutis* and is reflected in the formulator's biblical exegesis.

The Covenant of Redemption also deals with the question of how the Son, as the Second Person of the Trinity and fully God, could submit to and obey the will of the Father without falling into the errors of subordinationism or tritheism. The Dutch Calvinist theologian Gisbertus Voetius (1589–1676) approached the question in terms of how Christ could be subject to the law as mediator and surety.[26] Voetius rejects the answer given by Chrysostom, who maintained that Christ never actually

---

24. Bierma, "Federal Theology," 304–22; Bierma, "Role of Covenant Theology," 453–62.

25. Asselt, "Fundamental Meaning of Theology," 319–35. According to Francis Junius, archetypal theology deals with matters that pertain to the wisdom of God beyond strict human comprehension (knowing). Ectypal knowledge is the shadow or copy of the archetype, but is nevertheless true, finite, and revealed knowledge of God suited for human capacity for their salvation. Junius, "*Vera Theologia*," 51–52. See also Horton, *Covenant and Eschatology*, 183, and Muller, *Dictionary of Latin and Greek*, 299–301. Edward Leigh (1602–1671) explains the terms: "Archetypal knowledge, or divinity in God, of God himself," is that "by which God by one individual and immutable act knows himself in himself, and all other things out of himself, by himself." On the other hand, "Ectypal and communicated" theology is "expressed in us by divine revelation after the pattern and idea which is in God, and this is called *theologia de Deo*, divinity concerning God." Leigh, *System*, 2.

26. Voetius, "Problematum De Merito Christi," 2:266.

received a command that required submission, but merely agreed to act as such.[27] Rather, Voetius looked to Augustine's comments on Christ's words in John 14:28: "The Father is greater than I." Augustine stressed both the ontological equality of the Father and the Son, but also underscored the Son's status as servant, pointing to the two-fold designation of the Son in Phil 2:8–9 as both "in the form of God" and the "form of a servant." While not employing the exact terms, the concept of distinguishing between the ontological and the economic Trinity is nevertheless well formulated in Augustine's understanding.[28] Voetius uses this insight to explain Christ's roles of mediator and surety as covenantally established.

Development and Confessionalization

The specific use of the Covenant of Redemption, as the first statement concerning salvation after the failure of Adam under the Covenant of Works, becomes fully developed in the theologies of David Dickson, Peter Bulkeley (1583–1659), Johannes Cocceius, and Herman Witsius. The doctrine was soon codified in church confessions. The collective witness is not to a doctrine generated *ex nihilo* out of philosophical speculation, but one of refinement and refocus of a number of biblical texts which mention the Son's full divinity while acknowledging his submission and obedience to his Father's will.

The *Westminster Standards* alludes to the doctrine as it touches on the person and work of Christ, although the connection is not obvious. The *Westminster Confession* speaks of Christ's appointment as a mediator in Chapter VIII in terms that reflect the Covenant of Redemption: "It pleased God, in His eternal purpose, to choose and ordain the Lord Jesus, His only begotten Son, to be the Mediator between God and man; the Prophet, Priest, and King; the Head and Saviour of His Church; the Heir of all things; and Judge of the world; unto whom He did from all eternity give a people, to be His seed, and to be by Him in time redeemed, called, justified, sanctified, and glorified."[29] The *Westminster Larger Catechism* Q. 30 introduces the covenant doctrine as a category to structure the relationship between Christ as Mediator and the elect: "God doth not leave all men to perish in the estate of sin and misery, into which they fell by

---

27. Chrysostom, "Homilies on St. John," *NPNF* 1/14:218.
28. Augustine, "On the Holy Trinity," *NPNF* 1/3:33–34.
29. *WCF* 3.1.

the breach of the first covenant, commonly called the Covenant of Works; but of his mere love and mercy delivereth his elect out of it, and bringeth them into an estate of salvation by the second covenant, commonly called the Covenant of Grace."[30] The *Westminster Larger Catechism* Q. 31 states that the Covenant of Grace is made with Christ (and in him all the elect as his seed), originating the Covenant of Grace in eternity with Christ as the second Adam.[31] While the Covenant of Grace was revealed in history immediately after the fall, it is rooted in the eternal counsel of the Trinity.

The relationship and dynamic between the covenant made with Adam (Covenant of Works) and the elect (Covenant of Grace), particularly in terms of the covenanting parties, was explained in two ways, which may explain some of the ambiguity in the *Westminster Standards*. Unlike the *Westminster Larger Catechism's* answer to Q. 31, the *Westminster Confession* in Chapter VIII states that the Covenant of Grace was made only with the elect, not mentioning Christ.[32] The Puritan preacher Thomas Watson (1620–1686), in his commentary on the *Shorter Catechism*, underscores that the Covenant of Grace was made with the elect, rather than with Christ, as the *Westminster Shorter Catechism* appears to state: "[God] did enter into a covenant of grace to deliver them [the elect]."[33] For Thomas Watson there is a "Compact and Agreement made between God and fallen Man, wherein the Lord undertakes to be our God, and to make us his People."[34] While there is no other Mediator of the covenant with Christ, Watson does not explicitly mention God's covenant with Christ as the second Adam, and concentrates on the Covenant of Grace made with believers: "For who is this Covenant made with? Is it not with Believers? And have not they Coalition and Union with Christ; Christ is the head, they are the Body. Ephesians 1.23."[35] William Perkins emphasizes a similar structure in his commentary on Gal 3:16: "Christ as Mediatour, is first of all elected, and we in him."[36]

Conversely, other Westminster divines underscored a Covenant of Redemption (*pactum salutis*) whereby God covenants with Christ, the

30. *WLC* Q. 30.
31. *WLC* Q. 31.
32. *WCF* 7.1.
33. Watson, *Body of Divinity*, 154.
34. Watson, *Body of Divinity*, 154.
35. Watson, *Body of Divinity*, 154.
36. Perkins, *Works*, 242. See also Muller "Toward the *Pactum Salutis*," 43.

second Adam. Samuel Rutherford (1600–1661), a Scottish Presbyterian Commissioner to the Westminster Assembly, argued that the covenant made with Christ and the covenant made with the elect were distinct covenants, yet inseparably joined together. The two chief parties of the Covenant of Redemption were God the Father (representing all three members of the Godhead) and God the Son as covenant surety (as the Second Person of the Trinity). The Covenant of Grace was between God and fallen humanity. God, out of free love and mercy, engaged in another covenant to repair the now broken Covenant of Works and redeem the elect. The former Covenant of Redemption was the cause of the Covenant of Grace.[37] Other members of the Westminster Assembly who were strong proponents of the *pactum salutis* included Thomas Goodwin (1600–1680) and Obadiah Sedgwick (1600–1658).[38]

Shortly after publication, the *Westminster Standards* were officially adopted by the Scottish Kirk and several brief doctrinal treatises were annexed to them. One of those treatises, *The Sum of Saving Knowledge* (1649), was authored by David Dickson and James Durham (1622–1658). In this document, the Covenant of Redemption is explicitly affirmed and defined:

> The sum of the Covenant of Redemption is this, God having freely chosen unto life, a certain number of lost mankind, for the glory of his rich Grace did give them before the world began, unto God the Son appointed Redeemer, that upon condition he would humble himself so far as to assume the humane nature of a soul and body, unto personal union with his Divine Nature, and submit himself to the Law as surety for them, and satisfie Justice for them, by giving obedience in their name, even unto the suffering of the cursed death of the Cross, he should ransom and redeem them all from sin and death, and purchase unto them righteousness and eternal life, with all saving graces leading

---

37. Rutherford, *Covenant of Life Opened*, 308–10.

38. The ambiguity within the *Westminster Standards* represents the diversity of views present among the divines. Fesko reminds us of the need to understand the *Westminster Standards* in their historical perspective. The plurality of views "confirms that the divines never intended the *Confession* to be a doctrinal straightjacket but instead a corporate confession for the church, not the manifesto of one particular party. To be sure, some teachings were deemed beyond the line of orthodoxy, such as Crisp's two covenants of grace. But as much as the *Confession* excludes this one view, its silence speaks volumes regarding the permissibility of other views held among the members of the assembly." Fesko, *Theology*, 167.

thereunto, to be effectually, by means of his own appointment, applied in due time to every one of them.[39]

Dickson, in an outline of his speech before the General Assembly of the Scottish Kirk (1638), argued that the chief failing of the Remonstrant (Arminian) doctrine was their unfamiliarity with the "Covenant of redemption betwixt God and Christ."[40] Dickson brings up the Covenant of Redemption in this polemical context because he believed it undergirded the inviolability of the Covenant of Grace. He lists five theses to explain this: 1) there is a covenant between God and Christ, which is the ground of all that God does to redeem fallen man, 2) in the Covenant of Redemption, whereby the elect were personally designated in terms of individuals in name and number as well as the time in which they would be saved, 3) the price of redemption was established, i.e., Christ's "holden captive of death, &tc.," 4) the mediator was ensured of his success and the elect were given to him, and their salvation placed in his hand, and 5) no one would truly take God's grace for granted or be robbed of the assurance of salvation given God's wise dispensation of the gospel, the fruit of the Covenant of Redemption.[41]

The co-publication of the *Westminster Standards* and *The Sum of Saving Knowledge* indicates, at least to the Church of Scotland, that the *Standards* and the Covenant of Redemption are compatible and not contradictory. Soon after, modified versions of the *Westminster Confession of Faith* were adopted by Reformed Congregationalists (1658)[42] and Particular Baptists (1677),[43] explicitly inserting the Covenant of Redemption. It can also be seen in the *Formula Consensus Helvetica* (1675) authored by Francis Turretin and Johann Heinrich Heidegger (1633–1698).[44]

---

39. Dickson and Durham, *Summe of Saving Knowledge*.

40. Peterkin, *Records of the Kirk of Scotland*, 156–57. Dickson poignantly reminds them that "they pointed at it themselves," likely referring to Arminius's earlier statements regarding the doctrine.

41. Peterkin, *Records of the Kirk of Scotland*, 156.

42. Dennison, *Reformed Confessions*, 466.

43. Dennison, *Reformed Confessions*, 542.

44. Dennison, *Reformed Confessions*, 518–30.

Jonathan Edwards on the Covenant of Redemption

In this section I will undertake to describe Edwards's own theology of the Covenant of Redemption. Because this doctrine was so intimately linked to his doctrine of the Trinity, I will begin by discussing the trinitarian background of Edwards's theology. To do this I will first examine the philosophical principles that converged upon his biblical centrism to forge his trinitarian theology, including his idea of God as communicative, his philosophical idealism, and his aesthetics. I will then survey his view of the *ad intra* immanent trinitarian relationships as they are reflected and exhibited in the *ad extra* redemptive work of each member of the Trinity, and I will discuss Edwards's view that the divine activity of redemption parallels and communicates the structure of the immanent divine life.

Next, I will look at specific aspects of Edwards's doctrine. I will first discuss the role of the Holy Spirit in Edwards's covenant theology, an area that he saw deficient in standard orthodox discussions of the economy of the Trinity in redemption. Second, I will show how Edwards defended the work of redemption as the work of the whole Trinity. Finally, it will be shown that Edwards, far from opposing a Calvinistic "predestinarian" theology with a Puritan covenant scheme, viewed the Covenant of Redemption as founded upon the eternal decrees of the Godhead. I will conclude by summarizing a few of the implications of Edwards's views in relation to the works principle and evangelical obedience, implications which will be more fully discussed in subsequent chapters. I will draw from a wide selection of Edwards's writings including his *Miscellanies*, sermons, and larger essays such as *Discourse on the Trinity* and *Treatise on Grace*.

The historical tradition of covenant theology that Edwards inherited as a Reformed biblical theologian was certainly not a monolithic tradition and there were several variations on a theme within Reformed standards of orthodoxy. Within this tradition, however, Edwards was consistent within the broader context of orthodoxy, but also critical and creative when it came to the nuances of language and formulation, especially as it impacted his theology of justification and faith, law and gospel. This is also apparent in how he constructed the trinitarian background to the Covenant of Redemption.

Trinitarian Background

Edwards's interpretation of covenant theology and his exposition of the Trinity are intimately linked in his thoughts and writings. In his introduction to Edwards's sermon on 1 Cor 11:13, Wilson Kimnach says that, "Edwards links the doctrine of the Trinity to that of the work of redemption, identifying his favorite theological mystery with his favorite paradigm of theology."[45] The Trinity, as Edwards's "favorite theological mystery," is the foundation of the entirety of Edwards's theological thought concerning the nature, purpose, and works of God. Edwards's "favorite paradigm" is the means by which God accomplishes his ultimate purpose in all things: to display his glory in the person and work of Christ and communicate his glory in redeeming sinners to a participation in the love and glory of the Trinity. Craig Biehl puts Edwards's doctrine of the Covenant of Redemption in perspective when he states, "In the work of Christ in redemption, in His meritorious obedience to God's unalterable rule of righteousness, in His accomplishment of the ultimate Trinitarian purpose of the display and communication of God's glory, we have arrived at the center of Edwards's theology."[46] In Edwards's theology, God's glory is the flowing forth of his excellence (his attributes) and happiness. God's ultimate purpose is his glory in the display and communication of his excellence and happiness to his creatures. Christ's perfect obedience is the ultimate trinitarian work to display God's glory and to communicate God's glory in the purchase of his bride, the elect. In Edwards's historical-redemptive narrative, as encapsulated in his covenant theology, God's ultimate purpose will be complete in the happiness of the elect in their viewing and enjoying God's excellence forever in heaven.

While his orthodoxy with respect to the Trinity is maintained, Edwards developed his presentation of the inner-trinitarian relationship in a manner notably different from other typical orthodox Christian, particularly Reformed, theologians. Amy Plantinga Pauw underscores the importance of Edwards's trinitarian thought, noting that it "is rich and original, and deserves more attention than it has received in other treatments of his theology."[47] But as Richard Weber reminds us, Edwards never left a full systematization of his trinitarian theology, and much of his writings arrived posthumously and late on the scene. Therefore,

---

45. Kimnach, "Editor's Introduction," *WJE* 25:143.

46. Biehl, *Infinite Merit*, 26.

47. Pauw, *Supreme Harmony*, 18.

it is important to consider the entire breadth of Edwards's thought as expressed in his major treatises, shorter theological works, sermons, and private notebooks as a whole.[48] Weber maintains Edwards's orthodoxy while at the same time finds him both creative and critical, presenting the Trinity in a manner that is sometimes strikingly different from typical Reformed writings.[49]

Edwards noted deficiencies in the formulations proposed by covenant theology in his own received Reformed tradition, which led him to develop his own unique exposition of the doctrine of the Trinity. Edwards felt that the view of grace espoused by many Reformed writers in the context of covenant theology did not adequately represent the biblical witness regarding the nature of grace, especially the view that the Holy Spirit merely applied the benefit of grace purchased by Christ. Such a view limited the role of the Holy Spirit to merely the agent of application of a benefit purchased by the sacrifice of Christ which, according to Edwards, unnecessarily limited the Spirit's role in the work of redemption. It improperly withheld equal glory from the Spirit that was afforded to the Father and the Son in the trinitarian economy.[50] "If we suppose no more than used to be supposed about the Holy Ghost [merely applying to us the blessing purchased by Christ] the concern of the Holy Ghost in the work of redemption is not equal with the Father's and the Son's."[51] He seems to have the *Westminster Confession* and *Catechisms* as well as other Reformed creeds in mind and clearly regards his account of the Trinity as an improvement on standard Reformed theology.

---

48. An example of the danger of not holding to the entire extent of Edwards's corpus is that of Paul Helm. In his introduction to Jonathan Edwards's *Treatise on Grace and Other Posthumously Published Writings*, Helm accuses Edwards of certain "dubious" distinctions with regards to the generation of the Son. However, Helm does not interact with specific entries in the *Miscellanies* in which Edwards explains these distinctions. Edwards, *Treatise on Grace*, 20–21. Pauw also fails to interact with the entire range of Edwards's writings. In her discussion, she cites several of Edwards's *Miscellanies*, but restricts the remainder of her references to one sermon manuscript, a single citation from Edwards's *Essay on the Trinity*, and a few citations from other works. She does not cite his *Treatise on Grace*, any of his other sermons, or his philosophical writings on the nature and excellency of God. Pauw, "'Heaven Is a World of Love," 392–400.

49. Weber, "Trinitarian Theology," 297–318.

50. Stout, "Editor's Introduction," *WJE* 13:29.

51. Edwards, *Treatise on Grace*, 125.

Edwards's exposition of the Trinity is also notable in his "un-Reformed" view that such an exposition was open to human reasoning.[52] "I think that it is within the reach of naked reason to perceive certainly that here are three distinct in God, each which is the same [God]."[53] This is not to presume that Edwards had a "profound confidence in naked reason" to apprehend the Trinity apart from Scripture,[54] but rather that certain reasoned conclusions could be made from what Scripture already revealed. In other words, he is not using reason as a starting point in isolation from Scripture, nor is he going beyond the bounds of Scripture, but is using reason and Scripture to deduce further implications from what has been said of these "mysterious matters."[55] Edwards did not presume to fully grasp the mysteries of the Triune God. Indeed, he readily admitted his own limitations of both language and understanding. In his *Essay on the Trinity*, he wrote, "I am far from pretending to explaining the Trinity so as to render it no longer a mystery. I think it is the highest and deepest of all divine mysteries still, notwithstanding anything that I have said or conceived about it. I don't intend to explain the Trinity."[56] In his earliest

---

52. "Un-Reformed" in the sense that most Reformed theologians viewed the Trinity as a doctrine that comes by revelation alone and is beyond human reason or natural theology. "But as this mystery far transcends the reach of the human reason, so it can be solidly demonstrated from the revealed word alone. Whatever proofs of it some are wont to adduce from nature and reason, or from the perfection and power of God, or from his understanding, or from the communication of good (although on the supposition of revelation, they may with respect to believers serve in some measure to illustrate it), yet they cannot convince and obtain the force of solid proof. The same is the case with the various similitudes usually employed here: from the human soul, the rainbow, a tree, a fountain, the sun and light. These seem to afford some resemblance to the Trinity, though very obscure as they always labor under a great dissimilitude. Thus they out to be proposed soberly and cautiously, not for the purpose of convincing adversaries, but for confirming the believers and showing them the credibility at least of this great mystery." Turretin, *Institutes*, 2:266. Summarizing Reformed scholasticism, Heppe asserts, "For human reason this doctrine remains an eternally inexplicable mystery. —Generally the inconceivability of the doctrine of the Trinity is recognized by all dogmaticians. Therefore, the use of analogous phenomena from the world of nature or from the ideas of similar appearance belonging to the realm of a heathen outlook is disapproved of . . . In a word, this doctrine [thus shrouded in mystery] rests simply on revelation." Heppe, *Reformed Dogmatics*, 105, 100.

53. Edwards, "Misc. 94," *WJE* 13:357.

54. Robert W. Caldwell, *Communion in the Spirit*, 30–33.

55. Gerstner puts it this way: "When Edwards speaks of 'naked reason' he does not mean *de novo* thinking but rather speculation about what has been revealed to show many of its implications with certainty." Gerstner, *Rational Biblical Theology*, 2:66.

56. Edwards, *"Essay on the Trinity," WJE* 21:134; cf. Edwards, "Misc. 308," *WJE* 13:393; Edwards, "The Threefold Work of the Holy Spirit," *WJE* 14:401.

extant manuscript on the Trinity (from which the above quote is taken), and which is fundamental to his future expositions, Edwards states:

> There has been much cry of late against saying one word, particularly about the Trinity, but what the Scripture has said; judging it impossible but that if we did, we should err in a thing so much above us. But if they call that which necessarily results from putting [together] of reason and Scripture. Though it has not been said in Scripture in express words—I say, if they call this what is not said in the Scripture, I am not afraid to say twenty things about the Trinity which the Scripture never said. There may be deductions of reason from what has been said of the most mysterious matters, besides what has been said, and safe and certain deductions too, as well as about the most obvious and easy matters.[57]

Edwards's opponents in these remarks are those who were refusing to say anything about the Trinity apart from what Scripture explicitly stated.[58] If one begins with Scripture and divine revelation, then there are safe and certain deductions that can be made. As Richard Weber notes, Edwards assumed the orthodox doctrine and was only seeking to make it more intellectually satisfying.[59] This is consistent with the Reformed and Puritan theology of the use of faith and reason.[60] Edwards did engage in "philosophical" thought, both of the natural and metaphysical, in all areas of his theology, but he can only strictly be said to be a philosophical

---

57. Edwards, "Misc. 94," *WJE* 13:256–57.

58. Both Hubert Stogdon (1692–1728) in his *Seasonable Advice Relating to the Present Disputes about the Holy Trinity, Address'd to Both Contending Parties* (London, 1719) and Isaac Watts (1674–1748) in his *The Christian Doctrine of the Trinity . . . Asserted and Prov'd [and] . . . Vindicated by Plain Evidence of Scripture, without the Aid or Incumbrance of Human Schemes* (London, 1722) condemned giving the status of fundamental doctrines to "Unscriptural Terms and Phrases" justified as "Scripture consequences," arguing that only what is "plainly reveal'd in 'express Scripture' is necessary to salvation." Stogdon, *Seasonable Advice*, 23–24. See also Watts *Christian Doctrine*. The background to these writing is the controversy over Arianism that was raised by Samuel Clark. Clarke, *Scripture-Doctrine and the Trinity*. As Stout notes, Edwards was not directly concerned with the controversy *per se* and assumed the truth of the orthodox doctrine and only sought to make it more "intellectually satisfying." But he was aware of the debate over "Scripture consequences," e.g., as it affected the licensing of ordinands. Edwards, "Misc. 94," *WJE* 13:263 n. 2.

59. Weber, "Trinitarian Theology," 297–318.

60. See *WCF* 1.4 with regards to the "good and necessary consequence may be deduced from Scripture" as in keeping with the Reformed concept of *sola scriptura*.

thinker in the Puritan sense of the word. It was never his aim to construct a system of thinking to supplant plain biblical understanding, but rather to search into the lengths and breadths of human knowledge, i.e., "philosophy," confident that therein would be found a description of the activities of God already asserted in the Bible. Edwards was a consistent Anselmian in his appropriation of the maxim *"credo ut intellegam."* Such was the normal certainly of Puritan thought. The perfect doctrine contained in Scripture "comprehends the doctrine of God's works, which is called philosophy."[61]

Philosophical Principles

Three philosophical principles converged on Edwards's biblical centrism to forge his trinitarian theology. These would also become the foundational matrix for his covenant view of redemption. These principles included Edwards's view of the "communicative" nature of God's being, Edwards's philosophical idealism, and his theory of excellency. These philosophical influences had a decidedly apologetical thrust. Edwards was recommending the Trinity to a rational age that was quickly dispensing with the central truths of the Christian faith. While the Trinity was certainly in many senses "above" reason, it was not against reason, properly situated within the bounds of revelation. This was no mere speculation. For Edwards, Scripture more than confirmed his philosophical starting points. His Scriptural starting points were no mere proof-texts, but rather a conglomeration of textual references combined with complicated typological and metaphorical correspondences between biblical types and antitypes, and between biblical symbols and the Christocentric reality they mirrored.[62] As such, Edwards could present a multifaceted argument (e.g., the Second Person of the Trinity is truly God's infinite idea of himself) and provide rational arguments that confirmed this same idea. Edwards was a classic example of a "pre-critical" exegete and "Puritan" philosopher.

---

61. Miller, *New England Mind*, 14–15.
62. Caldwell, *Communion in the Spirit*, 30 n. 45.

God's Self-Communicating Nature

Edwards's trinitarian treatment of God's self-communicating (relational) nature and love may serve as a starting point.[63] Following Augustine,[64] Edwards believed that the Scriptural declaration that God is love implies plurality within God's being: "That in John God is love shows that there are more persons than one in the deity, for it shews love to be essential and necessary to the deity so that his nature consists in it, and this supposes that there is an eternal and necessary object, because all love respects another that is the beloved."[65]

Though God does not have any need to express his love outside of the "family of three" or the "society of three persons," this intratrinitarian self-communication is the eternal background for God's self-communication (or self-giving) to creatures. It is tightly bound up in his reflections on God's purpose in creating the world.[66] For instance, in *Misc.* 332 Edwards says, "The great and universal end of God's creating the world was to communicate himself. God is a communicative being."[67] Likewise, in *End of Creation*: "Thus it appears reasonable to suppose that it was what God had respect to as an ultimate end of his creating the world, to communicate of his own infinite fullness of God; or rather it was his last end. That there might be a glorious and abundant emanation of his infinite fullness *ad extra*."[68] God, being a communicative being, desires to communicate to creatures.[69]

---

63. Leithart, "Trinitarian Anthropology," 58–71; Pauw, *Supreme Harmony*, 19–36; Jenson, *America's Theologian*, 91–98; Lee, *Philosophical Theology*, 107–10; Holmes, *God of Grace*, 31–76.

64. Augustine expressed similar arguments in his *On the Trinity*. Whether Edwards saw himself as a continuation of the Augustinian tradition or not, he was aware of it in Chevalier Ramsey's work from which he quoted with apparent approval. Edwards, "Misc. 1253," *WJE* 23:184.

65. Edwards, "Misc. 94," *WJE* 13:257.

66. Edwards, "Misc. gg," *WJE* 13:185; Edwards, "Misc. 22," *WJE* 13:211; Edwards, "Misc. 87," *WJE* 13:251–52; Edwards, "Misc. 92," *WJE* 13:256; Edwards, "Misc. 104," *WJE* 13:272–74.

67. Edwards, "Misc. 332," *WJE* 13:410.

68. Edwards, "Concerning the End," *WJE* 8:433. Later in this work (445–50) Edwards carefully nuances his discussion to preserve God's immutability. This emanation is of God's holiness (love) and not ontological essence, so as not to be confused with any pantheistic tendencies.

69. It is interesting to compare Edwards's account to that of the anonymous fourteenth-century mystical author of the *Theologia Germanica*: "To God, as God, belongs

Edwards extends the analogy to claim that the purpose of creation and redemption was to extend the family: "The end of the creation of God was to provide a spouse for His Son Jesus Christ, that might enjoy him and on whom he might pour forth his love."[70] Or again: "Heaven and earth were created that the Son of God might be complete in a spouse."[71] And again: "There was, as it were, an eternal society or family in the Godhead, in the Trinity of person. It seems to be God's design to admit the church into the divine family as his son's wife."[72]

Not only did Edwards emphasize that God as Trinity was inherently communicative, inherently loving, inherently ecstatic, but he also emphasized that this pattern is imprinted on the creation. Creation as a whole, and the divine-human relationship in particular, are echoes of the eternal music of Triune life. Emanation is inherent in the trinitarian life: The Father outflows in love to the Son, and the Son returns love to the Father in the Spirit. And so it is with creatures of this God: "in the creature's knowing . . . loving . . . and praising God, the glory of God is both . . . received and returned. Here is both emanation and remanation."[73] In redemption, because the bride is united to the eternal husband, she comes to participate in the eternal flow of gift and return that is the Son's life with the Father and the Spirit.

Redemption thus necessarily takes a social and interpersonal form, not only a harmony of relation between the Triune God and his people, but a manifestation of this harmony in the life of the saints together. There is a trinitarian background to Edwards's use of musical analogies in ecclesiology, and to his efforts to describe eschatological life, history, and creation. As Robert Jenson said, "Edwards' paradigmatic art is music . . . If we ask what art was most immediate to Edwards, and provided

---

the desire and ability to express Himself, and to know and love Himself, and to reveal Himself to Himself . . . and without created beings, this would lie in His own self as a substance or well-spring, but would not be manifested or wrought out into deeds. Now God desires and wills it to be exercised, expressed, acted out, and clothed in a form . . . and this must take place in created beings." "But it belongs to God as God to revere Himself, to know and to love Himself, to reveal Himself to Himself—and all this still in God, all still in God as being, not as manifested work, for He is still the Godhead without created beings. It is in this reverence and this revealing that distinction between persons arises." Anonymous, *Theologia Germanica*, 101, 139.

70. Edwards, "Misc. 702," *WJE* 18:298.
71. Edwards, "Misc. 103," *WJE* 13:271.
72. Edwards, "Misc. 741," *WJE* 18:367.
73. Edwards, "Concerning the End," *WJE* 8:531.

the metaphor of his aesthetic descriptions, the answer is unambiguous: singing."[74] This is manifest in Edwards's own famous description of his picture of human happiness: "The best, most beautiful and most perfect way that we have of expressing a sweet concord of mind to each other, is music. When I would form an idea of a society in the highest degree happy, I think of them . . . sweetly singing to each other."[75] This perfect harmony awaits realization in the new creation, in which the "spiritual proportion" will be a "very complex tune, where respect is to be had to the proportion of a great many notes together."[76]

Such notions of harmony also helped Edwards express his high Calvinistic conviction that all creation is guided and directed to a single end. In explicit polemic against the Newtonian view of dead matter in empty space, Edwards spoke instead of creation as a place of harmony, where "the whole course of nature . . . [is] subservient to the affair of redemption." Indeed, "Every atom in the universe is managed by Christ so as to be most to the advantage of the Christian."[77] This is ultimately an ontology (or "physics") of love, in which gravity is conceived on the model of trinitarian attraction and difference. "The whole material universe," Edwards claimed, "is preserved by gravity or attraction, or the mutual tendency of all bodies to each other." This gravity is universal so that "the beauty, harmony and order, regular progress, life and motion, and in short all the well-being of the whole frame depends on it." Edwards thus expresses what Pauw calls a "relational ontology," in which, in Edwards's words, "Every real being must, as a condition of its reality, stand in some relation to other things, and even to all other things."[78]

Many see in Edwards's emanationist language of communication a tendency towards pantheism,[79] or at least panentheism. But Edwards's position is more nuanced than might first appear. Oliver Crisp argues that Edwards's language of a divine disposition to create some world is consistent with one understanding of a "pure act" account of the divine

74. Jenson, *America's Theologian*, 19.
75. Edwards, "Misc. 188," *WJE* 13:331.
76. Edwards, "Misc. 188," *WJE* 13:331.
77. Edwards, "Misc. ff," *WJE* 13:183–85.
78. Anderson, "Editor's Introduction," *WJE* 6:85.
79. Riley, *American Philosophy*, 126–187; Woodbridge, "Jonathan Edwards," 401–6. More recent studies include Cooper, *Panentheism*, 74–77; Lee, *Philosophical Theology*, chapters 7–8; Wainwright, "Jonathan Edwards, 119–33; Colacurcio, "Example of Edwards," 72.

nature, and maintains that Edwards's doctrine is much more in keeping with that tradition than has sometimes been thought, e.g., on Sang Hyun Lee's account. Edwards, at least for Crisp, turns out to be something like a "pure act panentheist." God is pure act and must create some world because he is essentially creative. However, Crisp views Edwards's position as more problematic than this because he claims that God *must* create a world and God must create *this* world. That is, Edwards seems to be committed to the idea that God must create the best of all possible worlds.[80] Crisp notes that this was an idea "in the air" at the time of Edwards's writing (Leibniz died around the time Edwards matriculated to Yale).

The Neoplatonic language of Edwards's later writings certainly comes close to identifying God with the world. In his *Dissertation Concerning the End for Which God Created the World* (1755), he writes of creation as an emanation from God, an enlarging of the divine being through communication. Even in an earlier *Miscellany*, he writes:

> Many have wrong conceptions of the difference between the nature of the Deity and created spirits. The difference is no contrariety, but what naturally results from his greatness and nothing else, such as created spirits come nearer to, or more imitate, the greater they are in their powers and faculties. So that if we should suppose the faculties of a created spirit to be enlarged infinitely, there would be the Deity to all intents and purposes, the same simplicity, immutability, etc.[81]

But Edwards also protected the distinction between God and the world. The world is utterly dependent on God, and yet remains separate from God. The world of created spirits, especially, retained a separate identity. Yazawa notes that while the above statement would be surprising for a Reformed mind that emphasized the unequivocal distinction between God and creation, "this is Edwards's way of specifying that human beings are created in the image of God. They are hence equipped to perceive God's self-communication in a parallel way that God the Father perceives himself in the Son as his perfect image."[82] Douglas Elwood maintains that Edwards is a traditional theist who posits an ontological distinction between God and creation without denying God's immanent presence as

---

80. Crisp, "Jonathan Edwards on the Divine Nature," 175–201.
81. Edwards, "Misc. 135 (151)," *WJE* 13:295.
82. Yazawa, *Covenant of Redemption*, 110.

the ongoing source of creation.⁸³ Edwards's God is not the horizon of created beings, which have their being in him as "panentheism" suggests. For Edwards, God is not one being among many, but is that Being itself who, simple considered, is so supreme that all and every other being together are but as "dust in the balance." The problem is reconciling Edwards's absolute transcendence with his simultaneous unwavering commitment to God's supreme immanence in upholding and governing all parts and acts of creation.⁸⁴

A search on the words "transcendent" and "transcendence" in the online works of Jonathan Edwards at the Jonathan Edwards Center at Yale University (www.edwards.yale.edu) reveals that he employs the terms in his major works, such as *Religious Affections,* and in his sermons always in reference to deity. The word "ineffable" also appears in contexts such as this from *Religious Affections*: "The things that appertain to the Supreme Being, are vastly different from things that are humane; that there is a godlike, high, and glorious excellency in them, that does so distinguish them from the things which are of men, that the difference is ineffable . . . "⁸⁵ Rather than labeling Edwards with a variety of panentheism, a more modest resolution is found in the text of *Nature of True*

---

83. Elwood, *Philosophical Theology*, 6–7, 21–22.

84. Kathryn Tanner discusses the Christian theistic position of the "noncontrastive" nature of God's divine transcendence and immanence. According to Tanner, radical transcendence does not exclude God's positive fellowship with the world or presence within it (that aspect of God's nature that permeates the world in creating, sustaining, and providential power), it rather guarantees it. Tanner, *God and Creation*, 81–119. David Bently Hart sounds very "Edwardsean" in defining the nature of God: "To speak of 'God' properly, then is to speak of the one infinite source of all that is: eternal, omniscient, omnipotent, omnipresent, uncreated, uncaused, perfectly transcendent of all things and for that very reason absolutely immanent to all things. God so understood is not something posed over against the universe, in addition to it, nor is he the universe itself. He is not a "being," at least not in the way that a tree, shoemaker, or a god is a being: he is not one more object in the inventory of things that are, or any sort of discrete object at all. Rather all things that exist receive their being continuously from him, who is the infinite wellspring of all that is, in whom (to use the language of the Christian scriptures) all things live and move and have their being. In one sense he is 'beyond being,' if by 'being' one means the totality of discrete, finite things. In another sense he is 'being itself,' in that he is the inexhaustible source of all reality, the absolute upon which the contingent is always utterly dependent, the unity and simplicity that underlies and sustains the diversity of finite and composite things. Infinite being, infinite consciousness, infinite bliss, from who we are, by whom we know and are known, and in whom we find our only true consummation." Hart, *Experience of God*, 30.

85. Edwards, "Religious Affections," *WJE* 2:299.

Virtue. "Object" language is applicable to God only when comparison is made to other objects of human dispositions. Edwards is well aware of the danger of reducing God to the same scale or ontological category as other "beings." "If the Deity is to be looked upon as within that system of beings which properly terminates our benevolence, or belong in to that whole, certainly he is to be regarded as the head of the system and the chief part of it; if it is proper to call him a part, who is infinitely more than all the rest, in comparison of whom, and without whom all the rest are nothing, either as to beauty or existence."[86] No actual comparison of the creature with the Creator is possible, because the distance between image and reality is so great. The image is not a competitor but only a shadow.[87]

E. Brooks Holified illustrates how Edwards's eschatological view of heaven and hell is a way in which God enhances the revelation of his transcendence. While many modern interpreters of Edwards have focused on his treatment of God's immanence—as the source of all being—this has caused them to downplay his equal concern for maintaining God's transcendence above the human world. God's transcendence, Holified argues, can be seen especially in Edwards's teaching about heaven and hell, which distinguishes Edwards from any pure form of pantheism or panentheism.[88] The elect believers, chosen for "an infinitely perfect union" with God in eternity, would never attain a perfect oneness, "the time will never come when it can be said it [union with God through the elect's union in Christ] has already arrived at this infinite height."[89] In the New England pastor's personal correspondence, Edwards concluded that when the saints unite with God and become "partakers of his holiness," it means the Holy Spirit "communicates something to the saints... without imparting to them his essence."[90] Even more so, the reprobate in hell would remain eternally separate from the divine being.[91] Paul Ramsey concludes: "God alone is immutable, unchanging. All creatures are the opposite of that by virtue of their finitude. We ought not to suppose that

---

86. Edwards, "Nature of True Virtue," *WJE* 8:553.

87. Spohn, "Sovereign Beauty," 394–421.

88. Holified, "Edwards as a Theologian," 148. See also Davidson, "Glorious Damnation," 809–22.

89. Edwards, "Concerning the End," *WJE* 8:534.

90. Edwards, "Related Correspondence," *WJE* 8:639.

91. Edwards, "Misc. 27a," *WJE* 13:213; Edwards, "Misc. 94," *WJE* 13:213, 256–63; Edwards, "Misc. 697," *WJE* 18:281–82; Edwards, "Misc. 880," *WJE* 20:121–39; Edwards, "Concerning the End," *WJE* 8:436–38, 455–56, 460–62, 536.

in the end of the end time of redemption in heaven men become gods and that the good angels . . . also become gods, i.e., become no longer creatures. Therefore we must not suppose that heaven is inherently an unchanging society."[92] While the divine and human never merge together, there is an ever-increasing communication of the divine diffusiveness and the elect's participation in God's happiness. Because God is infinite and elect human beings are finite, heaven is full of wonders and new discoveries each day and each moment for eternity.[93]

Philosophical Idealism

Edwards's philosophical idealism can be summarized by the phrase, "nothing can be without being known."[94] Existence and consciousness are necessarily connected for Edwards: "We know there was being from eternity, and this being must be intelligent. For how doth one's mind refuse to believe, that there should be being from all eternity without its being conscious to itself that it was."[95] Edwards's version of idealism was his response both to the atheistic materialism of Thomas Hobbes (1588–1679) as well as Enlightenment deists. "Idealism reflected a theocentric strategy of 'turning the tables' on materialism, making God in his immateriality into the central and defining reality, and rendering 'matter' a merely derivative phenomenon of consciousness."[96] By undermining their metaphysical foundation, Edwards's idealism was also a direct challenge to the attack on biblical Christianity by rationalist thinkers.

A word must be said about Edwards's relationship to George Berkeley (1685–1753). Although Edwards's idealism bears superficial resemblances to that of Berkeley, there is no clear evidence that Edwards was directly influenced by him.[97] Both Gordon Rupp and Wallace Anderson argued for similarities and differences between Berkeley and

---

92. Ramsey, "Heaven is a Progressive State," *WJE* 8:711.

93. Yazawa, *Covenant of Redemption*, 190.

94. Anderson, "Editor's Introduction," *WJE* 6:75, Danaher, *The Trinitarian Ethics*, 18–35.

95. Edwards, "Misc. pp," *WJE* 13:188.

96. McClymond, "God the Measure," 43–60.

97. Edwards refers to the works of George Berkeley in his catalogue of books, but it is not clear which of the books recorded he had read, which he intended to read, and which he merely had heard of and showed some interest in. See Edwards, "Catalogue of Books," *WJE* 26:184.

Edwards but not derivation.[98] More recently Richard Hall attempted to make a case for the conceptual similarity of their ethical discussions which would imply direct derivation. Hall admits, however, that such a link cannot be established with relation to Edwards's idealism and that even with regard to his ethics the evidence falls short of proof.[99] Josh Moody maintains that Edwards's theory is neither derived from Berkeley, nor are their theories coincidentally the same.[100]

Despite their similarities, there is a greater discontinuity between Edwards and Berkeley. It is true that for both Berkeley and Edwards "perception" is that which gives existence "reality." For Berkeley, however, it is perception in general: *esse* is *percipi*. But for Edwards it is specifically God's perception: *esse* is *percipi deo*. This difference is crucial. Existence is not a human idea for Edwards, as it is for Berkeley, but an idea of God, one where the only "real" is God. While Berkeley may sound like Edwards (or make Edwards sound like a "Puritan" Berkeley) when he posits his aim as to "inspire my readers with a pious sense of the presence of God,"[101] the difference lies in Berkeley's use of "sense." For Edwards, human sense perception is not foundational, rather God's perception is the essential basis for the reality of the universe. This is important as Berkeley's idealism has often been the straw-man of skepticism, derided for its caricature in the face of the certainly of physical reality in believing "that all material objects and space and time are an illusion."[102] Berkeley

98. Rupp, "Idealism," 209–26; Anderson, "Immaterialism," 181–200. See also Fiering, *Jonathan Edwards's Moral Thought*, 39.

99. Hall, "Did Berkeley Influence Edwards?" 101, 115.

100. Moody, *Jonathan Edwards*, 96.

101. Berkeley, *Treatise*, 162.

102. Hawking, *Brief History*, 18. Stephen Hawking goes on to illustrate this with the famous (apocryphal) anecdote of Dr. Johnson who, when told of Berkeley's opinion, cried, "I refute it thus!" and stubbed his toe on a large stone. This anecdote can be found in James Boswell's biography, Boswell, *Life of Johnson*, 333. Johnson may have understood Berkeley better, writing in his *Autobiography* that, "His [Berkeley's] denying matter at first seemed shocking, but it was only for want of giving a thorough attention to his meaning. It was only the unintelligible scholastic notion of matter he disputed, and not anything either sensible, imaginable or intelligible; and it was attended with this vast advantage, that it not only gave new incontestable proofs of a Deity, but moreover the most striking apprehensions of His constant presence with us and inspection over us, and of our entire dependence on Him and infinite obligations to His most wise and almighty benevolence." See Flower and Murphey, *History of Philosophy*, 84. For a recent defense of the orthodoxy of Berkeley, see Spiegel, "Theological Orthodoxy," 216–35.

counters the subjectivism of his idealism by arguing that it is not just one mind that perceives "but all Minds whatsoever."[103] The role of God is merely to excite ideas in our minds, and to view God to be the "perceiver" is a notion that "seems too extravagant to deserve a confutation."[104] Yet it is just these extravagancies that undergird Edwards's theocentric view of God's role. God is the "prime empiricist." It is his perception that gives objectivity. Edwards avoids Berkeley's relativism by posing a theocentric idealism in which reality is objective (without denying individual subjective perception) because God is the true perceiver, unlike Berkeley's anthropomorphic idealism in which man is the perceiver.[105] As such, Edwards aspires to transcend the subjective-objective dichotomy of modern though by advancing an altogether different theory of truth. Edwards "found a universe that avoids the crisis of modernity and the relativism of postmodernism . . . as material objects are ideas, they can be theory-laden, inseparable from the reading of the viewer, without being relative . . . The inescapability of individual and cultural interpretation, the hermeneutic of life, entails not relativism but 'perceptivism.'"[106] Even though humans are limited to a finite perception of the real, the divine vision transcends such cultural and historical barriers to view reality as an entirety. It is God's subjective perception which ultimately provides objectivity.

According to Edwards, there are no "substances" if one means by "substance" an independent, self-perpetuating "being." All being is dependent on God and, as such, God is the only true "Substance." Many of the misappropriations of Edwards stem from a failure to understand the way in which he uses the word "substance." "Substance" for Edwards is that which "philosophers used to think subsisted by itself, and kept up solidity and all other properties."[107] Because God, for Edwards, is immediately active, to believe in a substance that "keeps up" the world is to usurp the place of God, for only God is self-existent and directly (immediately) supports the world. As such to deny "substance" and to affirm an ideal world is not to deny reality but independent reality. If there

103. Berkeley, *Treatise*, 119.

104. Berkeley, *Treatise*, 128.

105. For a further analysis of Edwards's theocentrism, see McClymond, "God the Measure," 43–60.

106. Moody, *Jonathan Edwards*, 94–95.

107. Edwards, "Of Atoms," *WJE* 4:215. The idea of a substratum of supporting substance may be drawn from Locke, *Essay*, 208–26.

is a "substance" that produces solidity (which is equivalent to "infinite resistance" in Edwards) than "that 'something' is he by whom all things consist."[108]

The perceptivism of Edwards, in which God is the only active power of the universe, does not lead by another route to pantheistic or panentheistic tendencies, as even Perry Miller recognized against the criticisms of William Ellery Channing (1780–1842):

> Critics like Chauncy Whittelsey never understood Edwards, but their instinct was not far wrong when they accused him of atheism—except that they could not conceive an atheism more profoundly conscious of God than they could experience. Channing came closer to the truth when he said that by making God the only active power of the universe, Edwards annihilated the creature, became in effect an 'atheist,' and obliged men at least to question whether any such thing as matter exists. Rational liberals do not want the creature annihilated, and they want matter to remain matter. I believe no one aware of recent physics and logic can be so confident as was Channing, or certainly so confident as were his colleagues and followers in liberal Protestantism, that matter is as solid as he would have it. As for annihilation of the creature, sociology and anthropology as well as history do not exactly enhance his independence of circumstances.[109]

While there is an intriguing similarity between Edwards's doctrine of God as the only substance and that of Spinoza, the differences in the two philosophies are important. When Edwards says that "God is proper entity itself"[110] and that "God and real existence are the same,"[111] he is only concerned with matter in the sense of "proper," "real," or "strictly," indicating by these important qualifiers that "substance as independent existence" is what he has in mind (no pun intended). By saying that the world is an "ideal one,"[112] or that it is a "shadow of being,"[113] Edwards is describing a world utterly dependent upon God, where God is the only independent.[114] The *sine qua non* of Edwards's view of reality is the de-

---

108. Edwards, "The Mind," *WJE* 6:380.
109. Miller, *Jonathan Edwards*, 292.
110. Edwards, "The Mind," *WJE* 4:380.
111. Edwards, "The Mind," *WJE* 4:345.
112. Edwards, "The Mind," *WJE* 4:350.
113. Edwards, "The Mind," *WJE* 4:335.
114. This goes beyond Calvin's statement that, "our very being is nothing but

pendent relation of the universe upon God. The universe is not God but is projected by God to be real or, according to Edwards, it is a "shadow" of the divine being. Edwards understanding of perception, that perception is somehow inherent to reality, is an attempt to establish the coherence of this position.

Edwards's theocentric idealism is foundational for his trinitarianism and is intimately bound up with creation itself. In relation to God himself, infinite being (God) must be infinitely self-reflective, for not even God can be without being known. This becomes the ontological foundation for the eternal generation of the Second Person of the Trinity. In relation to creation, Edwards notes the "senseless matter . . . would be useless if there were no intelligent beings at all . . . for what would it be good for? Intelligent beings are created to be the consciousness of the universe, they they [sic read 'that they'] may perceive what God is and does."[115]

Aesthetic Vision

The aesthetic character of being is an important theme in Edwards, which was not only foundational to his ethics, but also to his trinitarian ontology. His understanding of aesthetics circles around the concepts of beauty and excellence, and both are defined in explicitly trinitarian terms. "One alone," he argues, "cannot be excellent, inasmuch as, in such case, there can be no consent. Therefore, if God is excellent, there must be a plurality in God; otherwise, there can be no consent in him."[116] For Edwards, excellent divine being thus cannot be an undifferentiated unity, but necessitates a plurality within that unity, "One alone without any reference to any more, cannot be excellent; for in such case there can be no manner of relation no way, and therefore, no such thing as consent."[117]

---

subsistence in the one God." It is not just that we only exist in God but that God is the only independent existent. Calvin, *Institutes*, 1:35.

115. Edwards, "Misc. 87," *WJE* 13:252. Moody maintains that Edwards's perceptivism is not strictly based on his idealism but that immediate action of God on which also the universe is founded. Moody, *Jonathan Edwards*, 98. There is some unease in the history of Edwardsean scholarship regarding his idealism. Perry Miller denied that Edwards was an idealist at all, seeing him rather as describing reality as a sequence of events with God as the one cause. Miller, *Jonathan Edwards*, 91–92.

116. Edwards, "Misc. 117," *WJE* 13:283–84.

117. Edwards, "The Mind," *WJE* 6:337.

"Consent" here is virtually interchangeable with 'harmony,' and this musical notion is at the foundation of Edwards's aesthetics. Without a plurality of persons in God, there would be no harmony because there would be no difference, and there would be no beauty because harmony is the keynote of beauty. Edwards concedes that simplicity can have a beauty, but he sees that as beauty of a very limited sort. By contrast, when "thousands of different ratios at once . . . make up the harmony," the beauty produced is "far the sweetest."[118] The trinitarian argument becomes even more explicit in Edwards's links between love and beauty: "'Tis peculiar to God that he has beauty within himself, consisting in being's consenting with his own being, or the love of himself in his own Holy Spirit; whereas the excellent of others is in loving others, in loving God, and in the communications of his Spirit."[119] Edwards's view that love is not love without an object implies that God's eternal love requires some eternal plurality in his being. Similarly, since beauty consists in love, beauty depends on the trinitarian nature of God. Without a harmony of difference, a harmony of Father, Son and Spirit, there would be no beauty in God.

Edwards does say things like, "There are but these three distinct real things in God [viz. God the Father, the 'idea of God' = the son, and 'love and delight' = the Holy Spirit]; whatsoever else can be mentioned in God are nothing but mere modes or relations of existence."[120] What Edwards means by "real" distinctions here amounts to no more than what the Reformed orthodox are getting at when they allow "modal" distinctions in the Godhead, pertaining to the so-called relations of origin distinguishing the divine persons. Oliver Crisp argues that, "while Edwards uses different terminology than his Reformed forbearers, and goes about distinguishing the divine persons differently from, say, Van Mastricht or Turretin, it is not clear that his strategy for individuating the divine persons yields a substantially different account of the individuation of the divine persons."[121]

---

118. Edwards, "Original Sin," *WJE* 3:194.
119. Edwards, "The Mind," *WJE* 6:365.
120. Edwards, "Discourse on the Trinity," *WJE* 21:131.
121. Crisp, "Jonathan Edwards on the Divine Nature," 175–201.

The Immanent Trinity

The terms economic and immanent have been used in trinitarian discussions since Augustine and their subsequent augmentation and development by Aquinas. The economic Trinity is that knowledge of God which is revealed to us by his presence and action in the economy of salvation history as Father, Son, and Holy Spirit. The immanent Trinity refers to the interior life and nature of the Triune God without reference to creation. In other words, the economic Trinity relates to what God "does," while the immanent Trinity relates to what God "is" and "how" he experiences himself as a tri-unity.

It is necessary to understand Edwards's trinitarian background of the Covenant of Redemption because, for Edwards, the divine activity of redemption parallels and communicates the structure of the immanent divine life. This is not to say that Edwards would have appropriated Karl Rahner's *Grundaxiom* that the "economic" Trinity and the "immanent" Trinity are one in the same. The primary implication of Rahner's axiom is that one can discover God's triune character *ad intra* through God's action *ad extra* in history even if God does not disclose this through verbal revelation (in Scripture). Edwards's starting point was always Scriptural revelation, of which the covenant structure of redemptive history was foundational. God can (and does) disclose the doctrine of the Trinity in Scripture[122] (it is not mere philosophical speculation), and the ectypal economic structure can also reveal to (some extent) the archetypal immanent Trinity, but only insofar as it is informed by verbal revelation in Scripture.[123]

While Rahner's dictum is helpful for retrieving the inherent bond between the doctrine of the Trinity and soteriology in his epistemological approach, contemporary trinitarian theologies have appropriated it in ways that practically eliminate the distinction between the immanent and the economic Trinity altogether. Because the immanent Trinity concerns the divine perfection in God's self-sufficient independence from the world and the economic Trinity refers to God's relation to the world in history, blurring or eliminating the distinction between the immanent

---

122. Edwards argues that it was because of the atonement that the doctrine of the Trinity had been revealed in Scripture. See Edwards, "History of the Work of Redemption," *WJE* 9:125–26, and his manuscript sermon on Eph 3:10 in *JE* 2:150.

123. For a critique of Rahner's axiom in this context, see Jowers, "Exposition and Critique," 165–200.

and economic Trinity risks losing the distinction between the triune God and the world and between the Creator and creation. The "immersion" of the economic Trinity into the immanent Trinity, according to Joseph Bracken, essentially amounts to panentheism.[124] Recognizing the distinction between the two, without separating them, is important for understanding the true nature of God's transcendence and immanence, as it was in Edwards. According to Ted Peters:

> On the one hand, to affirm the immanent-economic distinction risks subordinating the economic Trinity and hence protecting the transcendent absoluteness at the cost of genuine relatedness to the world. On the other hand, to collapse the two together risks producing a God so dependent upon the world for self-definition that divine freedom and independence are lost.[125]

Chung-Hun Baik reaffirms the importance of this for contemporary theology when he says that "both the distinction and unity between the immanent and the economic Trinity need to be acknowledged simultaneously, in order to establish the equilibrium between God's relatedness to the world and God's gracious freedom."[126]

A better model for properly relating the economic and immanent Trinity that Edwards foreshadows is that by Kevin Vanhoozer. Vanhoozer, much in the mindset of Edwards, employs the key category of *communication* when he states that "the economic Trinity is, or rather communicates, the immanent Trinity."[127] He mounts an argument that we can indeed describe the inner Trinitarian life of God on the basis of the revelation in the economy: "We begin, then, with a brief description of the inner life of the triune God—the eternal doings of Father, Son, and Spirit—to the extent that it can be discerned from the communicative patterns that comprise the economy."[128] We come closest to understanding God's inner life by attending to the intratrinitarian communicative action in the economy, particularly the dialogical interaction between the Father and Son that is revealed in the Gospels (particularly and most clearly in the Gospel of John). Vanhoozer highlights three main topics

---

124. Bracken, *Trinity*, 7–22; Bracken, *Panentheism*, 7–28; Baik, *Holy Trinity*, 163–65.
125. Peters, *GOD*, 108–9.
126. Baik, *Holy Trinity*, 183–84
127. Vanhoozer, *Remythologizing Theology*, 294.
128. Vanhoozer, *Remythologizing Theology*, 243.

in these Father-Son dialogues: mutual glorification, the giving of life, and the sharing of love. In doing so, Vanhoozer rearticulates his project of understanding the story of Scripture ("the divine drama") as a real revelation of who God is. "Because the way God is in the economy corresponds to the way God is in himself, we may conclude that the Father, Son, and Spirit are merely continuing in history a communicative activity that characterizes their perfect life together... Hence this triune dialogue in history fully corresponds to the conversation God is in himself."[129] According to Vanhoozer, "God is the communicator, communication, and communicatedness. The triune God is the agent, act, and effect of his own self-communication."[130] While Edwards would use different categories, his overall underlying argument is nearly identical: the economic Trinity communicates and reveals the immanent Trinity in redemptive history as revealed in and interpreted by the biblical narrative. Covenant theology, as the structure of that biblical narrative, provides the *ad extra* economic movement to and communication of the *ad intra* immanent Trinity.

An example of additional ways Edwards derives Scriptural support for his Trinitarian formulations is his discussion of the word *Elohim* (as pleural and joined to a pleural verb) in Gen 20:13, citing other instances in Gen 1:26, 3:22, 11:7, 35:7, Exod 2:4, Neh 9:18 and Isa 16:6. He discusses this in relation to the other names of God:

> In the original [Deut 6:4], it is *Jehovah Elohenu Jehovah Ehadh*; the more proper translation of which is, *Jehovah our God is one Jehovah*. The verb *is* is understood, and properly inserted between *Jehovah Elohenu* and *Jehovah Ehadh*, thus, *Jehovah Elohenu is Jehovah Ehadh*; which, if most literally translated, is thus, *Jehovah Our Divine Persons is one Jehovah*; as though Moses, in this remark, had a particular reference to the word *Elohim* being in the plural number, and would guard the people against imagining from thence that there was a plurality of Essences or Beings, among whom they were to divide their affections and respect... Not only is the word *Elohim* properly plural, the very same that is used, ver. 15. The gods which your fathers served, &c.—but the adjective *holy* is plural. A plural substantive and

---

129. Vanhoozer, *Remythologizing Theology*, 251.

130. Vanhoozer, *Remythologizing Theology*, 261. It is also worth noting how Vanhoozer uses his root metaphor of communication to turn the tables on Feuerbach: "Projection is first and foremost a divine communicative activity. Jesus Christ is the God-projected word and image of God into the created order." Vanhoozer, *Remythologizing Theology*, 271.

adjective are used here concerning the True God, just in the same manner as in 1 Sam. iv. 8. "Who shall deliver us out of the hands of these mighty Gods." And in Dan. iv. 8. "In whom is the Spirit of the holy Gods." So ver. 9, 18. And chap. v. 11. That the plural number should thus be used with the epithet *Holy*, agrees well with the doxology of the angels, "Holy, holy, holy, Lord God of Hosts," &c.—Isa. vi. and Rev. iv. §64. It is an argument, that the Jews of old understood that there were several persons in the Godhead, and particularly, that when the cherubim, in the 6th of Isaiah, cried, "Holy, holy, holy, Lord of Hosts," they had respect to three persons: that the seventy interpreters, in several places, where the Holy One of Israel is spoken of, use the plural number; as in Isa. xli. 16."[131]

Edwards also discusses the Trinity in his exegetical sermons, particularly on John 16:8 and John 14:23, a sermon Gerstner describes as a "practical and warm application of the Trinity doctrine to the Christian life."[132] Because of this Scriptural background and foundation, and not in isolation from it, Edwards can proceed to derive the intratrinitarian relationships from a number of perspectives.

God the Father

Edwards begins his discussion of the immanent Trinity with a notion of God the Father as the "Deity subsisting in the Prime, unoriginated and most absolute manner."[133] The Father is Deity in direct existence; infinite, universal, and all comprehending existence.[134] It is impossible, according

---

131. Edwards, "Miscellaneous Observations on Important Theological Subjects," *JE* 2:510.

132. Both sermons are unpublished and cited along with the quote in Gerstner, *Rational Biblical Theology*, 2:68.

133. Edwards, "Discourse on the Trinity," *WJE* 21:131. Edwards gives his fullest single development of the Trinity in his very early *Misc. 94*. Even before this, Edwards laid the foundation for the doctrine of "Excellence" in his first entry in *The Mind*: "In a being that is absolutely without any plurality, there cannot be excellence, for there can be no such thing as consent or agreement." Edwards, "The Mind," *WJE* 6:337. *Misc. 94* was written c. 1722, possibly before *The Mind* and well before the beginning of his Northampton ministry in 1727.

134. Edwards says relatively little of the Father in Himself. Almost all Edwards's remarks concern the Father's thinking of Himself in the generation of the Son. He says much more of the Son but pays greatest attention and makes his greatest contribution to the concept of the Holy Spirit.

to Edwards, for God to be anything but infinitely excellent and consenting. To be infinitely excellent demands another. He writes, "One alone cannot be excellent, inasmuch as, in such case, there can be no consent. Therefore, if God is excellent, there must be a plurality in God; otherwise, there can be no consent in Him."[135] But to be infinitely excellent and consenting from eternity also means to be infinitely happy from eternity. The conclusion for Edwards is that the infinite excellence of God results in his infinitely enjoying himself and being infinitely happy in his own direct existence. Furthermore, it is the Father who possesses both knowledge and love. These are the only two "real attributes" and "faculties" in God.[136] This psychological triad of God, his knowledge, and his love is that which provides the ontological basis for the subsistent persons in the Godhead.

God the Son

Edwards discusses the eternal generation of the Second Person of the Trinity in terms of God's knowledge and his love. Since "God is infinitely happy in the enjoyment of Himself,"[137] this happiness arises from God perfectly beholding and infinitely rejoicing in his own excellent essence and perfection. God has an idea of his own essence and perfection. But unlike human ideas, God's ideas are not merely shadows of things, imperfect and incomplete as mere likenesses of things upon the mind. For Edwards, God's ideas, being perfect and complete in knowledge, *are the things themselves.* "An absolutely perfect idea of a thing is the very thing, for it wants nothing that is in the thing, substance nor nothing else ... God's idea, being a perfect idea, is really the thing itself."[138] In the Father's reflecting on himself and having in view a perfect idea of himself, "there is a substantial image of God begotten."[139] God's idea of himself must be the very essence of God, the very same perfection and

---

135. Edwards, "Misc. 117," *WJE* 13:284; cf. Edwards, "Nature of True Virtue," *WJE* 8:562.

136. Edwards, "Discourse on the Trinity," *WJE* 21:113, 132.

137. Edwards, "Discourse on the Trinity," *WJE* 21:113.

138. Edwards, "Misc. 94," *WJE* 13:.257. Edwards says in *Misc. 238*, "If we diligently attend to our minds we shall find that [these ideas] are not properly representations, but are indeed repetitions of those very things." Edwards, "Misc. 238," *WJE* 13:353. To think about "thought" or "love" is actually to repeat the ontological reality of thought and love in the mind.

139. Edwards, "Misc. 94," *WJE* 13:258.

substance. By God's thinking of himself, Edwards concludes, the deity itself is generated in distinct subsistence and is described in Scripture as the "Word of God." This "Deity generated by God's understanding" is the Son of God, the Second Person of the Trinity. Through self-reflection, God generates himself again, not outside of himself, but within his own being, so that there is a "duplicity" within himself, i.e., God and his divine self-knowledge.[140]

Edwards draws on such Scriptural passages as Col 1:14, 2 Cor 4:4, Phil 2:5, and Heb 1:3 where Christ is described as the "image of the invisible God." Edwards also draws upon Exod 33:14, "My presence will go with you, and I will give you rest." He notes how "presence" can mean "face, look, form or appearance." Hence, "now what can be so properly and fitly called so with respect to God as God's own perfect idea of himself, whereby he has every moment a view of his own essence? This idea is that face of God which God sees, as a man sees his own face in a looking glass."[141] Christ is often denoted in Scripture by concepts closely associated with "ideas," such as the Wisdom of God (wisdom being identified with knowledge, e.g. 1 Cor 1:24 and Prov 8), the *Logos* or "Word" of God (John 1), or the "amen" of the truth of God (John 14:5).[142] Christ is also described in Scripture as the "light and refulgency" of the Father (Heb 1:3, John 1:1 and 8:12, 1 John 1:5). As the Father is the infinite fountain of light, so the Son is the communication of that light to the world. "The property of light is to make manifest; that is, to cause things to appear and be seen; without light, nothing can be seen; all things lie hid; nothing can be discerned by the most perceiving without some light. But when light comes, then things are made to appear . . ."[143] It is through the Son alone, as the light of the world, that the true wisdom and knowledge of God are imparted to the human mind.[144]

---

140. Paul Helm charges Edwards with a form of tritheism. "What God's Idea of Himself will be will be not another person of the Godhead but another God . . . implicitly tritheistic." Helm, "Editor's Note," in Edwards, *Treatise on Grace*, 21. Yet Edwards clearly taught that identity of essence does not preclude distinction of persons. Edwards also meets the objection that this could then prove an infinite number of persons in the Godhead, for each person has an idea of other persons. Edwards says this is "color without substance." See Edwards, "*Misc. 94.*" *WJE* 13:259–63, and Edwards, "Misc. 308," *WJE* 13:392–93 for Edwards's full response.

141. Edwards, "Discourse on the Trinity," *WJE* 21:118.

142. Edwards, "Discourse on the Trinity," *WJE* 21:119–120.

143. Edwards, "Christ the Light of the World," *WJE* 10:538.

144. Edwards, "God Glorified in Man's Dependence," *WJE* 17:201.

God is love (1 John 4:8, 16), which is for Edwards the perfection and happiness of being and therefore essential and necessary to the deity. In *Misc. 11*, Edwards says that God has infinite love.[145] But this love must be more than mere self-love, for even the devils have that, i.e., a desire for their own pleasure and their aversion to pain.[146] Therefore there must have been an object from all eternity which God infinitely loves. God's love demands a beloved. There must be another to which God is infinitely consenting and this object must be infinitely agreeable to him (i.e., infinitely consenting). This can only be God's very same essence. Thus, the object of God's infinite love is none other than God's own essence again, i.e., the eternally generated Second Person of the Trinity.

God the Holy Spirit

The Holy Spirit is the Deity breathed forth. Edwards states that the love which the Father loves the Son is an infinite, holy, sacred love. This love is not merely shed forth upon the Second Person of the Trinity, it is also returned: "If love be not mutual, it is a torment and not a pleasure."[147] There is an infinite love and delight in each other (Prov 8:30). It is through this perfect love—the breathing forth of God's essence in an infinite act of mutual love between Father and Son—that another manner of subsistence stands forth, namely the Third Person of the Trinity, the Holy Spirit.[148] God himself *is* this act of infinite love, breathing forth his own divine essence in love, joy, and delight upon the Son. It is a mutual love which also receives the same from the Son.[149] It is an *ad extra* expression of an *ad intra* inclination of the Father and Son to communicate in mutual love. This subsistence is distinct from the Father and Son. Edwards argues that the delight and energy that results in humans from their own ideas is distinct from the ideas themselves. In the same manner, the delight and energy that is communicated between God and the idea of God is distinct from the idea itself. It must therefore be a third, distinct substance. Edwards draws on a number of Scriptural passages to

---

145. Edwards, "Misc. 117," *WJE* 13:283–84.
146. Edwards, "The Mind," *WJE* 6:337.
147. Edwards, "Application on Love to Christ," *WJE* 10:617.
148. Edwards, "Discourse on the Trinity," *WJE* 21:121.
149. This is contra Helm who understands it as only "the personal love of God the Father." Helm, "Editor's Note," in Edwards, *Treatise on Grace*, 12.

support this, whereby the grace of Christ *is* the love of God, which *is* the communion and love of the Spirit (1 John 4:12–13, 4:18, Acts 2:32–33, Titus 3:5–6, Rom 5:5, and 2 Cor 3:14).[150] In *Misc. 336*, for instance, the dove descending on Jesus' baptism coincides with what is proclaimed, "This is my beloved Son," in that the Dove, which *is* the Spirit, *is* the proclamation, and that proclamation *is* the Divine Love itself.[151]

The Spirit himself *is* God's love for the regenerate. He is not simply the *agent* who applies God's love to the regenerate. Edwards does not find anywhere in Scripture that refers to the Son loving the Spirit, nor of the Spirit's love for human beings, nor of fellowship with the Spirit. One reads of the Father's love for the Son and the Son's love for the Father, but not of the Spirit's love for the Father and Son (because the Spirit *is* the love of the Father and Son). The Spirit is the love of the Father and Son poured out upon the saints. The Pauline wishes are for grace, peace, and mercy from God the Father and the Lord Jesus Christ, but not the Spirit. The Spirit *is* the grace, peace, and mercy.[152]

This subsistence of the mutual love between the Father and the Son is a distinct and personal agent.

> That I think the Scripture does sufficiently reveal the Holy Spirit as a proper Divine Person; and thus we ought to look upon Him as a distinct personal agent. He is often spoken of as a person, revealed under personal characters and in personal acts, and it speaks of His being acted on as a person, and the Scripture plainly ascribes every thing to Him that properly denotes a distinct person; and though the word person be rarely used in the Scriptures, yet I believe that we have no word in the English language that does so naturally represent what the Scripture reveals of the distinction of the Eternal Three,---Father, Son, and Holy Ghost,---as to say they are one God but three persons.[153]

The logic of Edwards is purely analogous. When one takes this imperfect and vague notion that we experience in human love and infinitely multiply it in the context of the divine, we can approach in some small measure how infinite divine love can be personified in the Holy Spirit.

---

150. Edwards, "Misc. 334," *WJE* 13:411.

151. Edwards, "Misc. 336," *WJE* 13:412.

152. Edwards, "Discourse on the Trinity," *WJE* 21:125; Edwards, "Treatise on Grace," *WJE* 21:185.

153. Edwards, "Treatise on Grace," *WJE* 21:181.

If the Holy Spirit is a person that has understanding and will (Edwards's definition of *persona*), then how can this love be said to have understanding if the Son is the divine understanding and is a distinct person from the Spirit? Edwards answers this objection by reference to the doctrine of *circumincession* or *perichoresis*:

> There is such a wonderful union between [the three] that they are after an ineffable and inconceivable manner one in another; so that one hath another, and they have communion in one another, and are as it were predicable one of another . . . So the Holy Ghost, or the divine essence subsisting in divine love, understands because the Son, the divine idea, is in him . . . The understanding is so in the Spirit, that the Spirit may be said to know, as the Spirit of God is truly and properly said to know and to "search all things, even the deep things of God" [1 Cor. 2:10].[154]

Through their interpenetration of one another, the one divine understanding and love subsists in its entirety in each of the three persons. There are three distinct persons, but there are not three wills, minds, or deities.[155]

---

154. Edwards, "Discourse on the Trinity," *WJE* 21:133–34.

155. There is certainly an Augustinian "flavor" to Edwards's approach to the Trinity. As Stephen Holmes notes, Edwards's "approach [to the Trinity] is clearly that of a child of Augustine: The Trinity of the mind, the mind knowing itself/God and the mind loving itself/God is straight from the master's work." Holmes, *God of Grace*, 69. Augustine reflects on this understanding of the Divine mind, its understanding, and the mutual love of mind and understanding in *The Trinity*: "How are they are all in all of them we have already shown above; it is when the mind loves all itself and knows all itself and knows all its love and loves all its knowledge, when these three are complete with reference to themselves. In a wonderful way therefore these three are inseparable from each other, and yet each one of them is substance, and all together they are one substance or being, while they are also posited with reference to one another." Augustine, *Trinity*, 275.

It must be remembered that Edwards employs the language of social themes within the context of a broadly Augustinian trinitarian framework. When Edwards speaks about the immanent Trinity as a family or society he always has in mind the society of the Father and the Son who fellowship *in* the Spirit. The Spirit is not strictly a consenting person alongside of the Father and the Son. He *is* the personal consent between them. Edwards, "The Mind," *WJE* 6:364; Edwards, "Misc. 517," *WJE* 18:110. While Edwards does speak of the "society of the three persons of the Godhead," he is referencing only the Father and the Son and the elect as the communing persons. The Spirit is he *in whom* they all have communion. Hence, when Amy Plantinga Pauw and William Danaher cite Edwards use of social and familial terms such as "society" or "family" of three for the interpersonal nature of the Trinity, they cannot account

Edwards maintains that there is no *temporal* distinction within the Trinity; it is an *eternal* mutual love (otherwise there would be no eternally consenting perfection in the Godhead). However, there is a logical order ("there is such a thing as prior and latter in order") that does not infer a temporal distinction between the Lover and the Beloved and does not contain or suggest any notion of inferiority (subordination) in the Godhead. There are no varying degrees of dignity or excellency. All three persons of the Trinity are equally the same God, sharing the same substance and the same divine essence. All the divine perfections, dignity, and excellency that belong to the Godhead belong equally to the Father, the Son, and the Spirit: "though one proceeds from another, yet one is not inferior to another."[156] There was never a time when God did not think of himself, nor love himself. God has from eternity existed as triune. Edwards expresses the relationship as, "The Son is the Deity generated by God's understanding, or having an idea of himself; the Holy Ghost is the divine essence flowing out, or breathed forth, in infinite love and delight. Or, which is the same, the Son is God's idea of himself, and the Spirit is God's love to and delight in himself."[157] It is a logical unfolding, not a temporal one. Edwards also uses an analogy to the sun. He likened the sun to the Father. The light of the sun he likened to the Son, who is the brightness and glory of the Father. The Spirit, then, is the warmth derived from the sun, providing the heat and being a continually emitted influence upon the world, warming, enlivening, and comforting. Each is distinct yet they are one.[158]

The identification of the Spirit with divine love entails several important implications for understanding the covenant structure in Edwards's theology. First, the Holy Spirit is most properly responsible for the dynamic activity (love) of the Godhead. "Though all the divine perfections are to be attributed to each person of the Trinity, yet the Holy

---

for the interpersonal relations of love among the three persons of the Trinity nor can they provide an account for the order and manifestations of God's triune creation and redemption of the world through the mission of the Son and the Spirit. Pauw, *Supreme Harmony*; Danaher, *Trinitarian Ethics*; Studebaker, "Edwards's Social Augustinian Trinitarianism," 268–85; Studebaker and Caldwell, *Trinitarian*.

156. Edwards, "Misc. 1062," *WJE* 20:430; Edwards, "Threefold Work of the Holy Ghost," *WJE* 14:379.

157. Edwards, "Misc. 405," *WJE* 13:468.

158. Edwards, "Misc. 362," *WJE* 13:434–35; Edwards, "Misc. 370," *WJE* 13:441–42; Edwards, "Christ the Light of the World," *WJE* 10:535–46.

Ghost is in a peculiar manner called by the name of love *agape*."[159] Love is the only means of generating union between intelligent spirits: "the holiness of God consist[s] in his love, especially in the perfect and intimate union and love there is between the Father and the Son. But the Spirit that proceeds from the Father and the Son is the bond of this union."[160]

If the infinite intratrinitarian act of love is the rationale for the Spirit's subsistence in the Trinity, then the Spirit must proceed from both the Father and the Son. This is Edwards's apology for the Western concept of *filoque* (dual procession): "[S]o the Holy Spirit does in some ineffable and inconceivable manner proceed and is breathed forth both from the Father and Son, by the divine essence being wholly poured and flowing out in that infinitely intense, holy and pure love and delight that continually and unchangeably breathes forth from the Father and the Son, primarily towards each other and secondarily towards the creature."[161] Unlike Eastern Orthodox theology, there is no division between the Spirit's immanent procession and economic mission. There is a high degree of continuity between the Spirit's inner-trinitarian life and economic work.

Within the immanent Trinity also resides the theme of the "hiddenness" of the Spirit. Love, by its nature, highlights the object of its gaze and does not call attention to itself. The Holy Spirit "highlights" God the Father's beloved (the Son), as well as the Son's beloved (the Father):

> Hence 'tis to be accounted for, that though we often read in Scripture of the Father loving the Son, and the Son loving the Father, yet we never once read either of the Father or the Son loving the Holy Spirit, and the Spirit loving either of them. It is because the Holy Spirit is the divine love itself, the love of the Father and the Son. Hence also it is to be accounted for, that we very often read of the love both of the Father and the Son to men, and particularly their love to the saints; but we never read of the Holy Ghost loving them, for the Holy Ghost is that love of God and Christ that is breathed forth primarily towards each other, and flows out secondarily towards the creature. This also will well account for it, that the apostle Paul so often wishes

159. Edwards, "Treatise on Grace," *WJE* 21:181.

160. Edwards, "Treatise on Grace," *WJE* 21:186. See also Edwards, "Misc. 398," *WJE* 13:463.

161. Edwards, "Treatise on Grace," *WJE* 21: 185–86. See also Edwards, "Misc. 143," *WJE* 13: 298–99; Edwards, "Charity and Its Fruits," *WJE* 8:373; Edwards, "Discourse on the Trinity," *WJE* 21:121, 135.

> grace, mercy and peace from God the Father, and from the Lord Jesus Christ, in the beginning of his epistles, without even mentioning the Holy Ghost, because the Holy Ghost is himself the love and grace of God the Father and the Lord Jesus Christ. He is the Deity wholly breathed forth in infinite, substantial, intelligent love: from the Father and Son first towards each other, and secondarily freely flowing out to the creature, and so standing forth a distinct personal subsistence.[162]

Edwards perceives continuity between God's inner trinitarian life and the new life experience by the redeemed. While he maintains a sharp distinction between God and his people (Creator-creation distinction), at the same time the redeemed know and love God much in the same way, albeit analogically or ectypally, that God knows and loves himself.

A New Arrangement between the Father and the Son

The Covenant of Redemption is a special new arrangement that exists only between the Father and the Son.

> Though the Father, merely by virtue of his economical prerogative as Head of the Trinity, is the first mover and beginner in the affair of our redemption and determines that a redemption shall be admitted, and for whom, and proposes the matter first to his Son, and offers him authority for the office, yet it is not merely by virtue of his economical prerogative that he orders, determines and prescribes all that he does order and prescribe relating to it. But he does many things that he does in the work of redemption in the exercise of a new right that he acquires by a new establishment, a free covenant entered into between him and his Son, in entering into which covenant the Son (though he acts on the proposal of the Father) yet acts as one wholly in his own right, as much as the Father, being not under subjection or prescription in his consenting to what is proposed to him, but acting as of himself. Otherwise there would have been no need of the Father and Son's entering into covenant one with another, in order to the Son's coming into subjection and obligation to the Father with respect to any thing appertaining to this affair. The whole tenor of the gospel holds this forth: that the Son acts altogether freely, and as in his own right, in undertaking the great and difficult and self-abasing work of our redemption,

---

162. Edwards, "Treatise on Grace," *WJE* 21:186.

and that he becomes obliged to the Father with respect to it by voluntary covenant engagements, and not by any establishment prior thereto; so that he merits infinitely of the Father in entering into and fulfilling these engagements. The Father, merely by his economical prerogative, can direct and prescribe to the other persons of the Trinity in all things not below their economical character. But all those things that imply something below the infinite majesty and glory of divine persons, and which they can't do without as it were laying aside the divine glory, and stooping infinitely below the height of that glory, those things are below their oeconomical divine character, and therefore the Father can't prescribe to other persons anything of this nature, without a new establishment by free covenant empowering him so to do.[163]

The Covenant of Redemption is not "new" in any temporal sense, nor does it imply a change in God. Rather, it is the recognition by Edwards that the Covenant of Redemption (as well as everything associated with creation) is not *necessary* to God's being. The Father, by virtue of his "economical prerogative as Head of the Trinity," is the first mover and initiates the plan of redemption, proposing a plan of redemption, and proposes that plan to the Son. Yet all else with regards to the Father's ordering, determining, and prescribing with regards to the work of redemption is undertaken by virtue of the "new" order the comes into existence by the Son willingly entering into this new covenant arrangement with the Father. The Father acquires a new right of headship and authority over the Son, one that is not inherent within the Trinity outside of the freely entered into covenant agreement. The Father has a covenantal authority to prescribe the Son what is needed to glorify himself through the difficult task of human redemption.[164] The Father also undertakes a new obligation, which is to enable and provide for the success of the Son's mission.

Within the parties of the covenant there is free mutuality and consent. In an undated sermon on Hos 13:9, Edwards says, "Though we read that he was sent by the Father and that he received commandments of the Father, yet the Father did not command him to undertake it. But when he had of his own accord undertaken it in the covenant of redemption, he thereby became a mediator and as such he was subject to

---

163. Edwards, "Misc. 1062," *WJE* 20:436.
164. Edwards, "Misc. 1062," *WJE* 20:437.

God and was commanded by him."[165] In his treatise *Justification by Faith Alone*, Edwards answers the question as to why Christ's obedience should be accepted on our account if he was not obliged to obey for himself:

> Christ was not obliged on his own account, to undertake to obey. Christ in his original circumstances, was in no subjection to the Father, being altogether equal with him: he was under no obligation to put himself in man's stead, and under man's law, or to put himself into any state of subjection to God whatsoever. There was a transaction between the Father and the Son, that was antecedent to Christ's becoming man, and being made under the law wherein he undertook to put himself under the law, and both to obey and to suffer.[166]

By this covenant agreement the Son willingly takes on his mediatorial office as the "second Adam." He puts himself voluntarily under the law, the Covenant of Works, both to obey and to suffer for the sake of those whom the Father gives him. Christ, as the Second Person of the Trinity, was "under no manner of obligation, either to obey the law, or to suffer the penalty of it." After this transaction, Christ was equally under obligation to both for "henceforth he stood as our surety or representative." What the first Adam (and his posterity with him) failed to accomplish, Christ as the second Adam stands in his stead, both in terms of accepting the curse of the first covenant as well as the obligations for perfect obedience.[167]

165. Edwards, *Blessings of God*, 214.
166. Edwards, "Justification by Faith Alone," *WJE* 19:192.
167. Robert Letham argues that by describing the intratrinitarian arrangement in terms of a covenant, or to affirm that there is a need for them to enter into covenant, even contractual, arrangements opens the door to heresy. "The will of the Trinity is one; the works of the Trinity are indivisible. For all the good intentions of those who proposed it, the construal of the relations of the three persons of the Trinity in covenantal terms is a departure from classic Trinitarian orthodoxy." Letham, quoted in Allen and Swain, *Christian Dogmatics*, 117. This objection is not new and was well known, and handled, by federal theologians. For instance, Wilhelmus à Brakel: "This raises a question: Since the Father and the Son are one in essence and thus have one will and one objective, how can there possibly be a covenant transaction between the two, as such a transaction requires the mutual involvement of two wills? Are we then not separating the Persons of the Godhead too much? To this I replay that as far as Personhood is concerned the Father is not the Son and the Son is not the Father. From this consideration the one divine will can be viewed from a twofold perspective. It is the Father's will to redeem by the agency of the second Person as Surety, and it is the will of the Son to redeem by His own agency as Surety." Brakel, *Christian's Reasonable Service*, 252.

Besides a new obligation, through the covenant agreement the Son receives a new kind of rule and authority which is foreign (new) to his position in the economy of the immanent Trinity. The Son assumes a position as supreme ruler and head of the universe. The Son also receives the Father's "own divine treasure, the Holy Spirit," to dispense of it as he pleases to the redeemed.[168] As the Son is Lord of creation and redemption, he is also the progress of redemption, and is Lord over the Third Person of the Trinity having the authority to administer the Spirit to the elect as he pleases.

In a corollary to *Misc. 1062*, Edwards argues against those who would suppose that the sonship of the Second Person in the Trinity consists solely in the relationship he bears to the Father in his mediatorial character as redeemer in the Covenant of Redemption. While the Son was "begotten" as part of the covenant arrangement (Heb 1:5), the Son's generation or proceeding from the Father as a Son does not consist only in his being "appointed, constituted and authorized of the Father to the office of a mediator." For Edwards, there is a priority of the Father to the Son "in the order of nature" prior to the Covenant of Redemption.[169]

The Role of the Holy Spirit

Within the Covenant of Redemption, the Holy Spirit is also intimately involved, but not as a covenant partner. Edwards did not view the Holy Spirit as the mere agent who applied the gifts of redemption earned by Christ but was the actual gift itself that was purchased. By this formulation of the role of the Holy Spirit, Edwards maintained the co-equality and unity in the Trinity in the work of redemption.

In orthodox formulations of covenant theology, the Spirit was understood to be the agent who applied the benefits purchased for the redeemed through the death of the Son. Edwards, however, felt that this way of stating the role of the Holy Spirit implied a subordination of the agent of application to the purchaser of the benefit (salvation), also implying a subordination within the immanent Trinity itself. Edwards resolved this perceived problem by maintaining the equality of excellency and the absence of any notion of subordination with the immanent Trinity. At the same time, he asserted that there is a subordination observable in the

---

168. Edwards, "Misc. 1062," *WJE* 20:439.
169. Edwards, "Misc. 1062," *WJE* 20:443.

economic Trinity, that is, in the divine work of redemption. The Spirit is to regard the Son as he regards the Father in the immanent Trinity. He is "put under the Son, or given to him and committed to his disposal and dispensation as the Father's vicegerent . . . the Son will have the disposal of the Spirit in the name of the Father, or as ruling with his authority." This relationship terminates at the consummation of the history of redemption after Christ returns in judgment. At that point, the Son hands back over all authority and dominion to the Father, so that God may be all in all, and that all things will thenceforth be dispensed "only according to the order of the economy of the Trinity."[170]

The Spirit becomes subject to the Son, not only as the Second Person of the Trinity, but as the God-man and "husband" who is the head of the church. This relation is eternal and is never abrogated. Just as Christ the God-man continues for all eternity to be the "vital head and husband" of the Church, so too is the bond of union between the two covenant persons in the Covenant of Grace and the ground of their mutual consent and agreement which is the Holy Spirit:

> The Spirit was the inheritance that Christ as God-man purchased for himself and his church, or for Christ mystical, and it was the inheritance that he, as God-man, received of the Father at his ascension for himself and them. But the inheritance he purchased and received is an eternal inheritance. It is, in this regard, with the authority Christ was invested with at his ascension with respect to the Spirit, as 'tis with the authority he then received over the world. He then was invested with a twofold dominion over the world: one vicarious, or as the Father's vicegerent, which shall be resigned at the end of the world; the other as Christ God-man, and head and husband of the church. And in this latter respect he will never resign his dominion, but will reign forever and ever, as is said of the saints in the new Jerusalem, after the end of the world, Rev. 22:5[171]

These new relations are not technically part of the Covenant of Redemption. While these new relations involve a subjection of the Spirit to the Son in a "new and diverse" way from that which flows from the economic Trinity, it is only "circumstantially" new. It is not properly a

---

170. Edwards, "Misc. 1062," *WJE* 20:440; cf. 1 Cor 15:28 (ESV): "When all things are subjected to him, then the Son himself will also be subjected to him who put all things in subjection under him, that God may be all in all."

171. Edwards, "Misc. 1062," *WJE* 20:440.

new kind of subjection in that it does not involve any extraordinary self-abasement or emptying of dignity like the Son's humiliation or abasement in being made under the law.[172] This subjection "implies no abasement" of the Spirit by any special covenant arrangement, but is by the gift of the Father, "exercising his prerogative as Head of the Trinity." Christ as God-man is given no less honor and is accorded no less worship then he has as the Second Person of the Trinity.

By viewing the Spirit as the actual benefit purchased by Christ, Edwards maintains the co-equality of the Father, Son, and Spirit in the work of redemption. At the same time, there is subordination within the economic Trinity. But this subordination is with regards to the way each person acts in the work of redemption, not in their respective involvement. The Spirit is subordinated to the Son, "that Christ might [have] the whole work of salvation in his hands."[173] This subordination does not imply inequality. According to Weber:

> Just as there is a logical order (*taxis*) in the immanent Trinity in regard to the underived Father, the Son (begotten of the Father), and the Spirit (proceeding from both the Father and the Son) without a notion of inequality in excellency between the three persons, so also is there a logical manner of acting in the divine economy in which the Father determines the work to be done, the Son acts in obedience to the Father as representative, and the Spirit acts in subordination to the Son in applying the benefits purchased."[174]

God the Father determines whether there should be any redemption of sinners. It is his "majesty and authority as supreme rector, legislator and judge," "he is the person who is especially injured by sin . . . the person whose wrath is enkindled, and whose justice and vengeance is to be executed and must be satisfied."[175] The determination *that* a redemption shall be allowed precedes the covenant agreement of the persons of the Trinity relating to the *particular manner and means* of it. The economy, by which the Father acts in this capacity, is prior to the covenant. For Edwards this is not mere metaphysical speculation, for he says that, "nothing is more plain from Scripture [than] that the Father chooses the

---

172. Edwards, "Misc. 1062," *WJE* 20:440.
173. Edwards, "Three Fold Work of the Holy Spirit," *WJE* 14:381.
174. Weber, "Trinitarian Theology," 316–17.
175. Edwards, "Misc. 1062," *WJE* 20:433.

person that shall be the redeemer and appoints him, and that the Son has his authority in this office wholly from him, which makes evident that the economy, by which the Father is head of the Trinity, is prior to the covenant of redemption."[176]

A Work of the Whole Trinity

Edwards would agree with John Owen that "the agent in, and chief author of, this great work of our redemption is the whole blessed Trinity; for all the works which outwardly are of the Deity are undivided and belong equally to each person, their distinct manner of subsistence and order being observed."[177] For Edwards, the "affair of our redemption" was "concerted" among all three persons of the Trinity, and determined by their perfect consent. "[T]here was a consultation among the three persons about it, as much doubtless as about the creating of man (for the work of redemption is a work wherein the distinct concern of each person is infinitely greater than in the work of creation), and so that there was a joint agreement of all, but not properly a covenant between 'em all."[178]

In a sermon on John 16:8 "The Threefold Work of the Holy Ghost" preached in April 1729, predating his *Essay on the Trinity* of 1730, Edwards says, "All the three persons are concerned in the salvation of man, as they were in his creation. When man was first created, there was a consultation among the persons of the Trinity. God said, 'Come and let us make man in our image, after our likeness' [Gen 1:26]. So it is in the work of redemption . . . The persons of the Trinity, they consulted from all eternity about it as being the main work of divine wisdom."[179] In *The History of the Work of Redemption*, he explains, "The persons of the Trinity were as it were confederated in a design and a covenant of redemption."[180] All three persons of the Trinity are equally concerned in the whole work of redemption, including the Covenant of Redemption, and, in the end, it was toward the honor and glory of all the persons of the Trinity.

---

176. Edwards, "Misc. 1062," *WJE* 20:433.
177. Owen, *Works*, 10:163.
178. Edwards, "Misc. 1062," *WJE* 20:442.
179. Edwards, "Threefold Work of the Holy Ghost," *WJE* 14:410.
180. Edwards, "History of the Work of Redemption," *WJE* 9:118.

There is no inequality in involvement or honor in Edwards's Covenant of Redemption. The subordination that exists is a voluntary subordination that completely maintains the equal divinity of the subordinate one and the one who appoints him to subordination. The Son was appointed by command only after the covenant had been made to do so.[181] The economy of the Trinity precedes the Covenant of Redemption and remains after the work of redemption is finished, at which time it will become more visible and conspicuous.[182]

Edwards's model of the intratrinitarian relations follows the Reformed dogma that all essential acts of the Godhead are acts of the three persons operating as the one God. These acts nonetheless terminate on one of the divine persons, as is evident in incarnation and sanctification. Muller has ably demonstrated how early Reformed articulations of the *ad intra-ad extra* movement correlates the divine decree and the subordination of the Mediator to his own divinely decreed work. This *ad intra-ad extra* movement or pattern (which Muller argues is a fundamental architectonic device in older Reformed theology) is key to understanding the Reformed approach to questions regarding divine absoluteness and divine relationality. Imbedded in the prolegomena of Reformed orthodox writings in the seventeenth century was the distinction between archetypal and ectypal theology.[183] This distinction differentiated between the *ad intra* absolute and necessary knowledge that only God can know about creation, providence, and salvation, and the relative and accommodated *ad extra* knowledge of those divine works as revealed to and as accessible to God's creatures. Muller notes that the distinction was important not only to differentiate between what is *ad intra* to God and what is *ad extra*, but also to establish a "fundamental and positive relation" between what is *ad intra* and *ad extra*.[184] True theology must be ectypal, a finite reflection and articulation of the divine archetypal theology, grounded in God's own self-revelation of his own working in the archetype itself, thus establishing a fundamental pattern of relationality between the absolute God and his rational creatures. This *ad intra-ad extra* movement or pattern (motif) points to an essential foundation in God that provides an

---

181. Edwards, "Sacrifice of Christ Acceptable," *WJE* 14:440–57.
182. Edwards, "Misc. 1062," *WJE* 20:434. Edwards cites 1 Cor 14:24–28 in support.
183. Asselt, "Fundamental Meaning of Theology," 319–35.
184. Muller, "God as Absolute and Relative," 56–73, 57.

ontically absolute and therefore constant and dependable ground for all that God brings about in the works of creation and redemption.

The Eternal Decrees

In Edwards, as well as in Reformed covenant theology, the Covenant of Redemption is founded upon the eternal decrees of the Godhead. The *ad intra-ad extra* provides the basis by which God's absoluteness in terms of the eternal decrees forms the pattern for God's relationality in the covenants and how this plays out in Reformed theology. Edwards gives an extended treatment of the decrees in his *Miscellanies* and sermons and maintains that the Covenant of Redemption is nothing more than the means by which God decrees to carry out what he has committed himself to do.

According to Muller, the Reformed writers of the seventeenth century "correlate a view of the *ad intra opera personalia* with an interpretation of the *ad extra opera appropriate*, in a version of the *ad intra-ad extra* pattern."[185] This *ad intra-ad extra* pattern serves to underscore and provide the metaphysical basis for the Reformed understanding that the absoluteness of the divine decrees (or in terms of Gods attributes, the simplicity and immutability of the divine being) serve not to exclude but rather to define the nature of the divine relationality, to assure its constancy, and to undergird its radical freedom.[186] Barth's critique of the German Reformed theologian Amandus Polanus's (1561–1610) definition of God as immutable and immobile, as if it meant that God, "confined . . . by his simplicity, infinite and absolute perfection" would therefore be incapable of "any relationship between Himself and a reality distinct from Himself" other than a "relation of pure mutual negativity" lacking any "concern for this other reality," is totally unfounded and misguided.[187] For Polanus, the "unmoved" nature of God is the very foundation for declaring that God

---

185. Muller, "God as Absolute and Relative," 61. See also Muller, *Christ and the Decree*, 150–52, 156–59; Muller, "Toward the *Pactum Salutis*," 62–63; Muller, *Post-Reformation Reformed Dogmatics*, 4:257–74.

186. Muller, "God as Absolute and Relative," 60. Muller cites Richard Baxter, *The Divine Life in Three Treatises* (1664).

187. Barth, *Church Dogmatics*, 2/1:494. Barth's misreading of Polanus is repeated by Christopher R. J. Holmes. Holmes, "Theological Foundation," 206–23. See also the misinterpretations in Weber, *Foundations of Dogmatics*, 1:439; Brunner, *The Christian Doctrine of God*, 306, 312, 317.

is the source of all movement in all things. God's absoluteness *ad intra* is the very foundation for his relationality *ad extra*.

For Edwards, as much as it was for early Reformed theology, covenant theology and its conditions were not an alternative to or in opposition to a theology of the absolute divine decrees. The absolute nature of the divine decrees served not only as the basis for the covenants, but the *ad intra-ad extra* movement served to establish the divine promises inherent in the covenant conditions. As Muller puts it, "Just as the decree is understood as both necessary and free, so also is it understood to be both absolute and relative, as unconditioned but willed with conditions."[188] In Reformed writings, the conditions established in the decree itself and the decree meeting those conditions in its execution frequently stood side-by-side. The Reformed doctrine allowed language of relation, relative willing, and conditionality along with formulations that maintained the absoluteness or simplicity of the divine decree.[189] Johannes Wollebius (1589–1629) said, "Predestination is an absolute decree and it is not (*praedestinatio est decretum absolutum et non est*)." He goes on to explain, "It is absolute with respect to its impulsive efficient cause, which is neither faith in the elect nor sin in the reprobate, but the most free will of God," but "it is not however absolute with respect to the materials, namely the objects and means, through which the decree is executed."[190] From the infralapsarian perspective of Wollebius (as well as Edwards), the decree must be relative inasmuch as human beings are not considered absolutely in election and reprobation, but as fallen. Muller also cites John (not Jonathan) Edwards (1637–1716), who states that "the Decree depends not on Conditions, yet there are many Conditions belonging to those things which are decreed, and that even by an Absolute Decree," and, with reference to election, "The Decree of Election is not so Absolute as to put a Force upon any of the Persons that are Elected. God hath so purpos'd and ordain'd all things

---

188. Muller, "God as Absolute and Relative," 66.

189. This is not unique or original to Reformed thought but has roots in medieval scholastic thought. While Aristotle denied divine providence because of his stance on the contingency of human actions, Thomas Aquinas accounted for both God's providence and the contingency of man's acts. Aquinas conceived God as a transcendent intellect, will, and source of operation. See *De Veritate*, q. 23, a.5 and the *Contra Gentiles*, III, c. 94, where God is shown as a universal transcendent cause, completely outside the mundane orders of contingency and necessity. The transcendent operation follows as a corollary from the divine knowledge and will.

190. Muller, "God as Absolute and Relative," 66, citing Wollebius, *Compendium theologiae chritianae* (1657).

which relate to them, that they act Freely, notwithstanding his Decree."[191] The underlying assumption of the Reformed doctrine of the decrees is that the eternal will of God, resting only on God's own unconditional nature, ordains both absolutely and freely and, through divine *concursus*, a world order in which events occur contingently and the will of rational creatures operate freely in accordance with accomplishing the divine will.

Edwards gives an extended treatment of his views of God's absolute decrees in *Misc. 704*.[192] God's ultimate and highest end, which is not a means to anything higher, is "the shining forth of God's glory, and the communication of his goodness." But there are also other decrees that follow, or are "posterior," or "inferior." To say that one decree can be "prior" or "posterior" is not to say that one is before another in the order of time. The ordering of the decrees is rather a logical ordering or, as Edwards phrases it, out of respect to another, the ground of another, or because of another. A logical ordering occurs when one is the end of another, such as when the good is prior to the means of obtaining it. It may also occur when one is the ground of another, or in Edwards's terms, the foundation of the capableness or fitness. For example, as sinfulness is the ground for God's glorifying himself in his justice in the punishment of sinners, so both sin (as the ground) and the glory of divine justice (the end) are prior to the decree of damning the reprobate.

Edwards reiterates the classic Reformed doctrine when he asserts that all the decrees of God are unconditional. But this assertion, he insists, needs careful qualifying as to not occasion "difficulty in controversies about the decrees."[193] The eternal decrees do not depend on things, or certain conditions, that are as yet un-decreed. Yet decrees may in another manner be "conditions" of other decrees in that one decree may follow upon another. Edwards recognizes the difficulty of speaking of such subjects: "I acknowledge to say God decrees a thing 'because' is an improper way of speaking, but not more improper than all our other ways of speaking about God. God decrees the latter even because of the former, no more than he decrees the former because of the latter."[194] God not only decrees the ends but decrees the means to those ends and so

191. Muller, "God as Absolute and Relative," 67, citing John Edwards, *Veritas redux* (1707).

192. Edwards, "Misc. 704," *WJE* 18:314–21. See also Edwards, "Misc. 29," *WJE* 13:216–17; Edwards, "Misc. 1062," *WJE* 20:430–43.

193. Edwards's main attack is against the Arminian doctrine of foreknowledge.

194. Edwards, "Misc. 29," *WJE* 13:216.

forth. When God decrees to provide the blessing of rain, he decrees the prayers of his people. When he decrees the prayers of his people, he very commonly decrees rain, etc. It is not so much that a decree is a condition of another, as there is a harmony and "natural fitness" to the eternal decrees as they are enacted in time. In *Misc.* 29 Edwards says that, "all the decrees of God are harmonious; and this is all that can be said for or against absolute or conditional decrees. But this I say, it's improper to make one decree a condition of another, [any] more than [the] other a condition of that; but there is a harmony between both."[195] His 1737 sermon on Rom 8:29 emphasized this point with its title, "The things which God doth for the salvation and blessedness of the saints are like an inviolable chain reaching from a duration without beginning to a duration without end."[196] Likewise, "God has regard to conditions in his decrees," and he in his wisdom decreed an order and connection to that "one part of the wise system of events would not have been decreed, unless the other parts had been decreed."[197] Hence, in terms of redemption, God decrees conformity to his Son as well as effectual calling. And when he decrees calling, he decrees justification, and when he decrees justification, he decrees everlasting glory.

In terms of reprobation, God's vindictive justice (God's glorifying his justice in punishing sin) is not to be considered a "mere" or ultimate end, but as a means to an end. It is not a distinct attribute to be glorified, but a certain way and means for the glorifying an attribute (justice, or God's holiness and greatness). Not recognizing this distinction, warns Edwards, leads to great "misrepresentations and undue and unhappy expressions" about the decree of reprobation. "Hence, the glorifying of God's vindictive justice on such particular persons has been considered as altogether prior to the decree to their sinfulness; yea, [to] their very beings."[198] The decree of eternal damnation of the reprobate is not prior to the fall and not prior to the very being of persons, but follows (logically) upon the fall (as grounds) as in view of all mankind as fallen sinners, having broken the first covenant with Adam.

The decree of eternal glory for the elect is different. The goodness of God (his ultimate end and decree) gives the *being* as well as the *happiness*

---

195. Edwards, "Misc. 29," *WJE* 13:216.
196. Edwards, "Sermon on Rom. 8:29–30," *WJEO* 54, L. 2r.
197. Edwards, "Misc. 415," *WJE* 13:474–75.
198. Edwards, "Misc. 704," *WJE* 18:316.

of the creature and doesn't presuppose it, while the decree of glorifying God's mercy and grace considers man as being created and fallen. The decree of God to glorify his love and communicate his goodness, and to glorify his greatness and holiness is logically (to be considered as) prior to the creation and fall of man, because the glory of God's love and the communication of his goodness necessarily implies the happiness of the creature and gives both their being and happiness and presupposes neither. The decree of reprobation (as it pertains to particular subjects), on the other hand, is consequent on the decree of their being (their creation), and permission of their fall. Edwards here makes another careful distinction, in that the actual execution of election in time, which he equates with effectual calling, is considered consequent on the decrees of creation and fall, the elect being actually and effectually "called" from a presupposed fallen state. So in one sense God's election (as it related to the glory of his love and the communication of his goodness) precedes and gives being to the elect, in another sense follows creation and the permission of the fall in the effectual calling of the elect.[199]

In the Father's covenanting with the Son in eternity past, he chooses those united to Christ. God in "foreowning" certain persons chooses them "to be actually his . . . by being in Christ, or being members of his Son." In foreknowledge he gives certain persons to Christ, and then predestines them "to be conformed to the image of his Son, both in his holiness and blessedness."[200] Edwards continues: "For God having in foreknowledge given us to Christ, he thenceforward beheld us as members or parts of him; and so ordaining the head to glory, he therein ordained the members to glory. Or, in destining Christ to eternal life, he destined all parts of Christ to it also, so that we are appointed to eternal life in Christ,

---

199. Gerstner explains that while the elect are certainly chosen from eternity, they are not admitted to the new covenant until the moment they accept Jesus Christ as their redeemer. "When God gave Christ to die for the elect, He looked on them as they are in themselves (fallen); but in actually bestowing eternal life, he does not look on them as they are in themselves, but as they are in Christ." Gerstner, *Rational Biblical Theology,* 2:111. In covenant terms, Edwards would say that the elect in the Covenant of Redemption are looked upon as fallen and as such are given to Christ for redemption. But when they enter the benefits of the new covenant, they enter into Christ, and are viewed by the Father as in him, and receive the salvation he obtained as their covenant head. See Edwards unpublished sermon on Gal. 3:16 (no. 810) preached February 1746, "In the divine transactions and dispensations relating to man's salvation, Christ and believers are considered as it were as one mystical person." Yale University Library Beinecke Rare Book and manuscript Library, Box 110, Folder 766.

200. Edwards, "Misc. 769," *WJE* 18:418. Edwards cites Eph 1:4.

being in Christ his members from eternity. In his being appointed to life, we are appointed."²⁰¹ Therefore, Christ's election is the foundation of each individual believer's election, as much as his justification and glorification are the foundation of each elect believer's justification and glorification. And just as God's eternal (pre-covenantal) and benevolent love toward the elect was particular to specific individuals, so also God's love is particular to those made beneficiaries of the Covenant of Redemption by being united to Christ from all eternity. "The love of Christ to you was no new thing . . . it was a thing of old standing when the foundation of the heavens and the earth were laid. Christ had a book written, the Lamb's Book of Life, wherein your names had been written from all eternity. God the Father and the Son did as it were consult together from the days of eternity about the redemption of lost men and made a covenant together, and then was your name mentioned as one of those that should be redeemed."²⁰²

The Covenant of Redemption is nothing more than how God decrees to carry out what he has committed himself to do. In a sermon on Rom 8:29, Edwards explains that it is the elect whom the Father gives to the Son in the Covenant of Redemption: "And this eternal foreknowledge implies three things: 1. God the Father's choosing them and 2. His giving them to the Son to be his as he did in the covenant of redemption. Christ speaks of those that the Father had given him, John 6:37. 3. It implies the Son's accepting them and looking on them as his from eternity."²⁰³ The love of God to the elect precedes creation and the existence of the elect in the created world. "The Father has given all believers to Jesus Christ before they come to him," for "every particular believer was given to Christ in that eternal Covenant of Redemption.²⁰⁴

The covenant in no sense "relieves" the doctrine of the decrees. As Gerstner puts it, God "is already bound by His decree; this covenant can bind Him no tighter. It binds Him more specifically. That is, it binds Him

---

201. Edwards, "Misc. 769," *WJE* 18:418.

202. Edwards, "Sermon on Gal. 2:20," *WJEO* 43, L. 2v. Edwards cites John 6:37, 17:2, 17:9, 10:16, 2 Tim 1:9, 2:19, Rom 8:29, and Rev 21:27.

203. Edwards, "Sermon on Rom. 8:29–30," *WJEO* 54, L. 5r (my transcription of Edwards's sermon notes). Edwards's original manuscript reads: "& this Eternal foreknowl. Implies 1. God the Fa-thers Choosing them and ~~also~~ 2 his Giving them to the son to be his as he did in the Cov. of Redemption X ~~of~~ speaks of those that the F. had given him Joh. 6. 37. 3 It implies the sons accepting them & Looking on them as his from Et."

204 Edwards, "Sermon on Rom. 8:29–30," *WJEO* 54, L. 2v.

with respect to a particular plan, which He has imposed upon Himself."[205] For Edwards, there was no inconsistency or contradiction between his Reformed predestinarian Calvinism and his covenant theology. In the Covenant of Redemption, the Son would become the mediator of the elect, and the Covenant of Grace was the revelation and outworking in history of that covenant.

Relation to the Covenant of Works

It was common for Reformed writers to sharply contrast the differences between the Covenant of Works (the Old Covenant) and the Covenant of Redemption (the New Covenant). But Edwards also notes the similarities between the two covenants and their implications. First, both covenants were made between God and a representative, not between God and all individuals concerned. In the first covenant (of works), it was made with Adam as mankind's representative. In the second covenant (of redemption), it was made with Christ representing his "bride" or "mystical body," the elect.

> The covenant of redemption, which is the new covenant, the covenant with the second Adam, that which takes effect in the second place (though entered into first, in the order of time), after the covenant with the first Adam was broken, was made only between God the Lawgiver and man's surety and representative, as the first covenant, that was made with the first Adam, was. The covenant of redemption was the covenant in which God the Father made over an eternal reward to Christ mystical, and therefore was made only to Christ, the head of that body.[206]

In neither was a covenant made particularly to individual men or women. Both the covenant promises and blessings are mediated through a covenant head, either Adam or Christ.

Second, the conditions of the two covenants were the same: perfect complete obedience. Eternal life or death was offered in the Covenant of Works based on Adam's works, his obedience to the covenant stipulations. Likewise, in the Covenant of Redemption life is promised on the basis of Christ's own perfect and complete obedience.[207] A corollary to

---

205. Gerstner, *Rational Biblical Theology*, 2:112.
206. Edwards, "Misc. 1062," *WJE* 20:442.
207. The law to which the Christ and Adam were both subjected was not identical,

this is that the Covenant of Works implied that Adam's posterity would not have had to undergo the same trial of works (not eating of the Tree of the Knowledge of Good and Evil) as Adam had to undergo, but would have inherited eternal life by no other means than their "being born."[208] "[I]f Adam had stood and got the victory, all his posterity would have had a right to the reward without another trial . . . his posterity were not properly to perform any condition. Their being born was only their existing; merely by existing they could not be said properly to perform a condition."[209] The blessings and curses stipulated by the first covenant come by one man's obedience or disobedience and, through him, are imputed to his posterity by mere physical birth (without proper conditions). Likewise, in the Covenant of Redemption, the obedience of one man (the God-man Christ) brings life to his spiritual posterity by a spiritual re-birth through faith[210] and the blessings are imputed to them. "[S]o, seeing Christ has done the work in which Adam failed and has gotten the victory, all his children have a right to the reward . . . in Christ's posterity nothing else is required but their being born again, in order to their being entitled to happiness . . . the new birth is but existing . . . by the new creation, or new birth, we reexist."[211] In both cases, there are no other covenant stipulations that apply to receiving eternal life or death other than those taken on by the covenant mediator (Adam or Christ), and those conditions, perfect and complete obedience to God's law, are the same.

There are also notable differences between the two covenants noted by Edwards. For instance, the subjects of the two covenants did not entail the same persons. That is, every human being was an heir of the Covenant of Works, but only some human beings are heirs of the Covenant of Grace. Not all who were in the Covenant of Works under Adam were in the covenant with Christ. Edwards taught repeatedly that only few,

---

but they were equivalent. "There was wanting the precept about the forbidden fruit, and there was added the ceremonial law. Thine thing required was perfect obedience. It is no matter whether the positive precepts were the same, if they were equivalent." Edwards, "Justification by Faith Alone," *WJE* 19:196.

208. Edwards, "Misc. 171," *WJE* 12:322.

209. Edwards, "Misc. 171," *WJE* 12:322.

210. In *Misc. 1280* Edwards says that faith is not a condition because Christ is the ultimate condition. Edwards, "Misc. 1280," *WJE* 23:226. Edwards's use of the term "condition" and faith as a "condition" or "instrument" will be explored in the penultimate chapter.

211. Edwards, "Misc. 171," *WJE* 12:322.

relatively speaking, would be saved as heirs of the second covenant. To put it another way, all the non-elect were in the Covenant of Works alone, while only the elect were of concern in the Covenant of Redemption.

Implications for Evangelical Obedience

Edwards's theology of the Covenant of Redemption necessitates two conclusions regarding the role of "works" in the Christian life. First, Edwards's formulation of his covenant theology categorically rules-out any consideration that "works" (obedience to God's law) can contribute, either before conversion (in terms of Edwards's doctrine of preparation) or after conversion (in terms of evangelical obedience), to fulfilling the covenant obligations for eternal life and blessing. Covenant considerations, as articulated by Edwards is his biblical narrative of redemptive history, and as applied to individual salvation in the *ordo salutis*, maintain a strict law-gospel distinction. While both covenants are ultimately covenants of works, the "works" of individual believers do not play any role whatsoever in terms of covenant fulfillment apart from their relationship to the covenant mediators.

Second, evangelical obedience, or "good works," do have a role, indeed are "necessary," in the application of the Covenant of Redemption in time to individual elect believers. This necessity of evangelical obedience, on the other hand, is not "meritorious," nor does it introduce any form of strict conditionality on man's part into the second covenant. The second covenant always remains gracious. This does not imply that the first Covenant of Works, as explained earlier, did not contain a gracious element (in terms of goodness and condescension). As Edwards explains in an unpublished sermon on Rom 4:16:

> The goodness of God appeared in the first covenant which proposed justification by works, it was an act of God's goodness and condescension towards man to enter into any covenant at all with him, and that he would become engaged to give eternal life to him upon his perfect obedience. But the second covenant that God has entered into with us since we broke the first may by way of distinction by called the covenant of grace. The free and sovereign and rich grace of God appears in it in a manner very distinguishing and the grace of God in it appears immanently in this that it proposes justification by faith alone.[212]

212. Edwards, "4:16," *WJEO* 45, L. 2r (my transcription of Edwards's original

Edwards's unique formulation of the relationship of the Covenant of Grace to the Covenant of Redemption bears this out. These twin aspects of "works" in relation to Edwards's law-gospel distinction will be worked out more fully in subsequent chapters.

Conclusion

The Covenant of Redemption in Jonathan Edwards's theology is rooted in his doctrine of the Trinity and represents the gracious ground of the plan of salvation. Edwards formulated a doctrine of the Covenant of Redemption that was consistent with the broader Reformed tradition, albeit not without Edwards's own unique exposition. As with his doctrine of the Trinity, Edwards remained orthodox while being creative, constructing his own articulation of these doctrines in ways he thought would improve upon the deficiencies in traditional Reformed writings and confessions. Even when engaging topics that remained highly speculative, such as the eternal intratrinitarian *pactum salutis* and the immanent intratrinitarian relationships, Edwards, as a biblical Reformed pastor-theologian, always anchored his more philosophical discussions in Scriptural exegesis, prioritizing spiritual knowledge in the service of Christian practice.[213]

In terms of the trinitarian background to his covenant theology, Edwards's philosophical principles of God's self-communicating nature,

---

notes). Edwards's original manuscript reads: "The Goodness of G. appeared in the first Coven. Which Proposed Justif by works. it was an act of Gods Good-ness ~~towards men to Enter into an~~ & Condescension to-wards man to Enter into any Cov at all to with him. & that he would become Engaged to Give Eternal life to him upon his Perfect Obed. But the second Cov that G. has Entered into with us since we broke the first ~~tho~~ may by way of distinction be Called ~~an~~ the Cov. of Grace. The free ~~G~~ & sovereign & Rich Grace of G. appears in it in a manner very dis-tinguishing and the Grace of G. in it appears Emi-nently in this that it Proposes Justification by faith alone."

213. "Divinity is commonly defined, *the doctrine of living to God*; and by some who seem to be more accurate, *the doctrine of living to God by Christ*. It comprehends all Christian doctrines as they are in Jesus, and all Christian rules directing us in living to God by Christ. There is nothing in divinity, no one doctrine, no promise, no rule, but what some way or other relates to the Christian and divine life, or our living to God by Christ. They all relate to this, in two respects, viz. as they tend to promote our living to God here in this world, in a life of faith and holiness, and also as they tend to bring us to a life of perfect holiness and happiness, in the full enjoyment of God hereafter." Edwards, "The Importance and Advantage of a Thorough Knowledge of Divine Truth," *WJE* 22:86.

idealism, and aesthetics converged on his biblical centrism. At times this resulted in expressing fundamental doctrines in ways diverse and sometimes foreign to the usual Puritan and Reformed expressions. However, in almost all cases Edwards can be seen as saying the same thing in a different way.[214] In particular, Edwards's own covenant formulation involved the Holy Spirit to a greater degree, even if not as a covenant partner *per se*, and emphasized in a more consistent manner the work of the "whole" Trinity in the affair of redemption. It is also clear in Edwards that covenant theology and the doctrine of the eternal decrees go hand-in-hand, a much needed correction to the historiography of Edwards and the Puritans that is just now coming out from under the long shadow of Perry Miller's seminal and influential early scholarship.

Comparing and contrasting the Covenant of Works with the Covenant of Redemption, Edwards highlights the works principle that remains at the heart of the covenant obligations for both Adam and Christ. Edwards can even say that the two are simply one covenant with two distinct covenant mediators. The following chapter will show how Edwards construed the Covenant of Grace as the revelation and outworking of the Covenant of Redemption in history and its application to the salvation of individual believers in time. The works principle of covenant fulfillment, especially in terms of the imputation of the active righteousness of Christ to the individual believer, is a central theme that unites these covenants in Edwards.

---

214. A good example of this is comparing Edwards to Richard Sibbes (1577–1635), an English Puritan of the century preceding Edwards. Sibbes explains how Christ is beloved of God. He says that Christ is the engraven image of his Father, so is the *primum amiabile*, the first lovely thing that ever was. When the Father loves him, he loves himself in him, so he loves him as God, as the Second Person of the Trinity, as his own image and character. Sibbes, "Description of Christ," 11. Compare this to Edwards: "The image of God which God infinitely loves and has His chief delight in, is the perfect idea of God. It has always been said that God's infinite delight consists in reflecting on himself and viewing his own perfections or, which is the same thing, in His own perfect idea of himself, so that 'tis acknowledged that God's infinite love is to and his infinite delight [is] in the perfect image of Himself. But the Scriptures tell us that the Son of God is that image. Edwards, "Misc. 94," *WJE* 13:259. Sibbes speaks of the Son of God as existing and being the image of God; Edwards sees the Son of God existing as idea in the mind of God. Edwards will go on to prove that this is one and the same thing. While not readily apparent, it is arguable that Sibbes and Edwards are saying the same thing but not in the same way.

4

Jonathan Edwards on the Covenant of Grace

Introduction

JONATHAN EDWARDS HAD A unique conceptualization of the Covenant of Grace, especially in terms of its relationship to the Covenant of Redemption. While this conceptualization was unique in terms of its formulation and terminology, it remained essentially the same in substance and in continuity with traditional Reformed theological understandings. Edwards's formulation was addressed to correct perceived deficiencies in accurately describing and distinguishing the covenants, deficiencies which he thought gave an opening to the errors of Arminianism and neonomianism. Edwards believed his covenant distinctions reconciled differences expressed by other Reformed writers, including whether the Covenants of Redemption and Grace were one or two separate covenants, as well as whether the promises of the Covenant of Grace were conditional or unconditional. The distinction between the Covenant of Redemption between God the Father and the Son, as mediator and surety for the elect, and the marriage covenant between Christ and believers ensured the distinction between law and gospel in Edwards's theology.

I will begin by summarizing how representative Reformed theologians prior to Edwards formulated the relationship between the Covenants of Redemption and Grace, focusing on Herman Witsius, Francis Turretin, and Peter Bulkeley, along with the perspectives of later theologians, including Charles Hodge (1797–1878), William G. T. Shedd (1820–1894), and Herman Bavinck (1854–1921). In terms of

Edwards's own formulations, two recent scholars, Michael McClymond and Gerald McDermott, propose that Edwards held three separate views of the Covenant of Grace during three different periods of his writings. I will present my own view defending a greater unity and continuity in Edwards, describing what I think is a more coherent view of Edwards's mature covenant structure involving the relationship between the Covenants of Redemption and Grace, and argue that Edwards's views are consistent from his earliest *Miscellanies* through his later writings. This is not to say there was not development or increased nuance in Edwards's views, but it is to argue that all the substantive elements of Edwards's theology are present in at least germinal form from his earliest writings.

The Covenant of Grace in Reformed Theology

The relationship between the Covenant of Grace to the Covenant of Redemption and whether they were in fact one single covenant or two distinct covenants was one particular aspect of covenant theology on which Reformed theologians took varying positions. In this section I will look at several representative views as a means of defining the questions and placing Edwards in historical and theological perspective.

Discussions on the origins of the Covenant of Grace in Reformed theology center on its purpose of maintaining the essential unity of the Old and New Testaments. In keeping with the biblical insight that the relationship between God and Adam (and his posterity) before the fall was covenantal (specifically of works), Reformed theologians were led to the parallel biblical insight that the Covenant of Grace, as made with Christ, was also essentially a covenant of works. A further distinction was made between the covenant made with Christ from eternity (*pactum salutis*) and the actual implementation of that covenant in history with believers. Subsequently this distinction was blurred or voided. On this history Herman Bavinck observes:

> The covenant of grace and the counsel of peace were now viewed as being essentially identical; the covenant of grace itself was shifted to eternity as being made there with Christ and in him with all his own. This last point, the identification of the counsel of peace with the covenant of grace, was first developed in England in the work of Robert Rollock, John Preston, Thomas Blake (?1597–1657), and the *Longer Westminster Catechism*,

and was later take over from the English by Alexander Comrie (1707–1774), Jan Jacob Brahe (1726–1776), and others. Many Reformed theologians, however, continued to object to this identification and to insist on the difference between the two.[1]

For instance, Witsius emphasizes the distinction between the covenants:

> In order the more thoroughly to understand the nature of the covenant of grace, two things are above all to be distinctly considered. 1st. The covenant which intervenes between God the Father and Christ the Mediator. 2nd. That testamentary disposition, by which God bestows by immutable covenant, eternal salvation, and everything relative thereto, upon the elect. The former agreement is between God and the Mediator: the latter, between God and the elect. The last pre-supposes the first, and is founded upon it.[2]

Turretin also explains this nuanced nature of distinguishing but not separating the covenants:

> And it seems superfluous to inquire here whether this covenant was made with Christ as one of the contracting parties and in him with all his seed (as the first covenant had been made with Adam and in Adam with his whole posterity—which pleases many because the promises are said to have been made to him [Gal. 3:16] and because, as the head and prince of his people, he holds the first place among all, so that nothing can be obtained except in him and from him); or whether the covenant was made in Christ with all the seed so that he does not so much hold the relation of a contracting party as of Mediator, who stands between those at variance for the purpose of reconciling them (as seems to others more appropriate). It is superfluous, I say, to dispute about this because it amounts to the same thing. It is certain that a twofold pact must be attended to here or the two parts and degrees of one and the same pact. The former is the agreement between the Father and the Son to carry out the work of redemption. The latter is that which God makes with the elect in Christ, to save them by and on account of Christ under the conditions of faith and repentance. The former was made with the surety and head for the salvation of the members; the latter was made with the members in the head and surety.[3]

---

1. Bavinck, *Reformed Dogmatics*, 3:227 n. 66.
2. Witsius, *Economy of the Covenants*, 1:165.
3. Turretin, *Institutes*, 2:177.

Referring to Turretin, Charles Hodge notes, "There is no doctrinal difference between those who prefer the one statement and those who prefer the other; between those who comprise all the facts of Scripture relating to the subject under one covenant between God and Christ as the representative of His people, and those who distribute them under two."[4] Later, Hodge notes: "This confusion [reconciling the *Westminster Standards* on the parties of the covenant] is avoided by distinguishing between the covenant of redemption between the Father and the Son, and the covenant of grace between God and his people. The latter supposes the former, and is founded upon it. The two, however, ought not to be confounded, as both are clearly revealed in Scripture, and moreover they differ as to the parties, as to the promises, and as to the conditions."[5] In his *Dogmatic Theology*, William Shedd asserts, "Though this distinction [between the Covenant of Redemption and the Covenant of Grace] is favored by Scripture statements, it does not follow that there are two separate and independent covenants antithetic to the Covenant of Works. The covenant of grace and redemption are two modes or phases of the one evangelical covenant of mercy."[6]

Peter Bulkeley, as another example, argues for a three-covenant model, consisting in the Covenant of Works, the eternal covenant between the Father and the Son, and the Covenant of Grace (as opposed to a two-covenant model consisting in the Covenant of Works and a Covenant of Grace in eternity to which human beings are not a party). For Bulkeley, denying that there is a covenant between God and human beings not only goes against the text of Scripture, but undermines the sacraments, leads to the conclusion that infidelity and unbelief in us is not considered sinful, and tends to condone licentiousness (antinomianism).[7]

Covenant Distinctions in Jonathan Edwards

Discontinuity in Edwards

Is the Covenant of Redemption to be distinguished from a Covenant of Grace in Edwards's writings and, if so, how are they to be distinguished? In

---

4. Hodge, *Systematic Theology*, 2:358.
5. Hodge, *Systematic Theology*, 2:359.
6. Shedd, *Dogmatic Theology*, 679.
7. Bulkeley, *Gospel Covenant*, 31–36.

their study of Edwards's view of the covenants, McClymond and McDermott propose that the development of Jonathan Edwards's views on the relationship of the Covenants of Grace and Redemption was influenced by the different polemical discussion he was engaged in at the time.[8] They propose that Edwards underwent three phases of development in his view of covenant theology which he inherited from his own Reformed scholastic tradition. They locate the first period of his development beginning in or around 1723. This period is characterized, according to McClymond and McDermott, by warnings against a distinction between the Covenant of Redemption and the Covenant of Grace. Edwards was evidently concerned during this period with the dangers of Arminianism. By distinguishing the Covenant of Grace from the Covenant of Redemption, according to Edwards, one was more apt to view faith as a condition for entering into the Covenant of Grace. The only true condition, in Edwards's understanding of the biblical view of redemption, is perfect obedience to the law. In the Covenant of Redemption the perfect obedience is (and can only be) performed by Christ. Edwards was supposedly reticent about referring to faith as a condition during this period and this reticence influenced his discussion on the relationship between the Covenants of Redemption and Grace.

McClymond and McDermott look specifically towards Edwards's earliest *Miscellanies*, which he began during this period,[9] to justify their position. Although Edwards uses the idea of covenant and covenant language throughout all his works, his most systematic discussions occur in a series of long *Miscellanies*. Several *Miscellanies* entries in 1723 form the background for their description of the first period of Edwards thought. There Edwards supposedly warns against theologians distinguishing the Covenant of Redemption from the Covenant of Grace, for then the Covenant of Grace functions as a covenant between God and humanity. In reality, counters Edwards, "God never made but one [covenant] with man, to wit, the Covenant of Works"[10] wherein God promised eternal life to Adam as humankind's representative on condition of Adam's perfect obedience.

---

8. McClymond and McDermott, *Theology of Jonathan Edwards*, 324–26.

9. Schafer, "Editor's Introduction," *WJE* 13:1–112, especially Table 2: "The *Miscellanies* and Chronological Parallels: May 1719-August 1731," 91–109.

10. Edwards, "Misc. 30," *WJE* 13:217.

In God's offer of grace to humankind, it is customary to speak of faith as a condition, writes Edwards. But this "tends to make us apt to depend on our own righteousness." The proper alternative, Edwards urges, is to realize "there have never been two covenants, in strictness of speech, but only two ways constituted of performing of this [one] covenant [i.e., the Covenant of Works]."[11] Edwards also notes that the Covenant of Works "never yet was abrogated, but is a covenant stands in full force to all eternity without the failing of one tittle." The only other covenant enacted by God was the Covenant of Redemption, which was the intratrinitarian plan for the Son to fulfill the condition of the Covenant of Works for the sake of redeemed humanity (Christ's mystical body). McClymond and McDermott interpret Edwards as saying that "the covenant of grace is not really a covenant—for there was no agreement between believers and the Father—but simply a 'free offer of life.'"[12] Edwards, because he was concerned that all talk of "conditions" (including faith) fulfilled by believers reinforces Arminian presumptions of moral worthiness as well as an incipient neonomianism, to distinguish between a Covenant of Redemption and a Covenant of Grace was dangerous. Edwards seems to confirm this when he writes, "The covenant of grace is not another covenant made with man upon the abrogation of this [the Covenant of Works], but a covenant made with Christ to fulfill it."[13] Therefore, in this first phase of Edwards's reflection on the covenants, he did not distinguish between the Covenant of Redemption and the Covenant of Grace.

A decade later, in 1733, Edwards writes in *Misc. 617, Covenant of Grace*:

> It seems to me there arises considerable confusion from not rightly distinguishing between the covenant that God makes with Christ and with his church or believers in him, and the covenant between Christ and his church or between Christ and men. There is doubtless a difference between the covenant that God makes with Christ and his people, considered as one, and the covenant of Christ and his people between themselves.[14]

Here it seems, according to McClymond and McDermott, Edwards reverses his opinion regarding the distinction between the Covenant of

---

11. Edwards, "Misc. 35," *WJE* 13:219.
12. McClymond and McDermott, *Theology of Jonathan Edwards*, 325.
13. Edwards, "Misc. 30," *WJE* 13:217.
14. Edwards, "Misc. 617," *WJE* 18:138.

Redemption and the Covenant of Grace. They note how remarkable this is since he does not refer to his former position, as he often refers to other entries in his *Miscellanies* and sometimes explicitly deals with points he made in those earlier entries.[15] At this juncture, Edwards appears to be disturbed not so much by Arminian self-confidence as by antinomian laxity. Given this background, they see it as logical that Edwards is now more willing to speak about a personal Covenant of Grace between Christ and believers and speaks without restraint about faith as a condition of entering into the covenant.

A third period of Edwards's development is marked by McClymond and McDermott around 1739 in which they mention Thomas Boston's denial of the distinction between the Covenants of Redemption and Grace. At the end of a letter to Jonathan Edwards regarding his book *The Religious Affections*, the Scottish minister Thomas Gillespie asks, "Are the works of great Mr. Boston known in your country, viz. the Fourfold state of Man, View of the Covenant of Grace, and a Discourse on afflictions, and Church communion, etc.? If not, inform me by your letter. I have now need to own my fault in troubling you with so long a letter, and so I shall end."[16] On September 4, 1747, Edwards replies, "As to Mr. Boston's view of the covenant of grace, I have had some opportunity with it, and I confess I did not understand his scheme delivered in that book. I have read his *Fourfold State of Man*, and liked it exceeding well. I think he herein shows himself to be a truly great divine."[17] This is also the period that Edwards pens his own mature thoughts about the relationship between the Covenant of Redemption and the Covenant of Grace. Presumably, Edwards did not understand Boston in a literal sense, in that he did not comprehend Boston, but because his mature tricovenantal scheme differed from Boston's own bicovenantal scheme.[18] McClymond and McDermott conclude that by the 1740s Edwards had distinguished four different covenants having to do with salvation: the Covenant of Works, the Covenant of Redemption, the Covenant of Grace (with Christ as mediator between the Father and believers), and the marriage covenant between Christ and believers. They see Edwards's view of

---

15. Rather than being "remarkable," this actually may be a clue that they have misinterpreted Edwards on this point.

16. Edwards, "Religious Affections," *WJE* 2:477.

17. Edwards, "Religious Affections," *WJE* 2:489.

18. It would seem difficult to arrive at any firm conclusion from a single remark in a letter exchange.

the Covenant of Grace as a "renewal" of the Covenant of Redemption, much as the Mosaic covenant was a renewal of the Abrahamic covenant. "The Covenant of Grace was different but not distinct from the Covenant of Redemption."[19] Because such a development would be a major influence on the interpretation of Edwards's thought, it is important to see if these divisions in Edwards's thought in McClymond and McDermott's chapter really hold up.

In a closer analysis of Edwards's works, Cornelis van Der Knijff presents a critique of this division and modifies it with a more nuanced proposal of his own.[20] He maintains, along with McClymond and McDermott, that Edwards initially held to a two-covenant scheme and later, around 1733, changed his view to a three-covenant scheme in which the Covenant of Grace was distinguished from the Covenant of Redemption. However, he accuses McClymond and McDermott of placing too heavy an emphasis on Edwards's remarks to Gillespie in 1747 regarding Edwards's not understanding Boston's scheme[21] and disagrees with them also in ascribing to Edwards another second transition in his thought regarding the covenants. Knijff focuses more on Edwards's movement from a concern with faith as a condition to explicating the differences between the Covenants of Redemption and Grace. He notes that Edwards's writings from 1733 onwards contain both an acceptance of conditionality in the covenant as well as a distinction between the two covenants. Since most of the covenant elements of the latter period are contained in some form in *Misc. 617* of 1733, the second period, while certainly displaying some development, is more a development of details and nuances than a development of content and it is therefore more convenient to view it as a single period.

---

19. McClymond and McDermott, *Theology of Jonathan Edwards*, 326.

20. Knijff, "Development," 269–81.

21. Given the methodological difficulties in making any specific interpretations on exactly why Edwards did not understand Thomas Boston based on only a brief parenthetical remark in a single piece of correspondence, Knijff and Vlastuin justify their interpretation as "the most obvious" given the specific context and the non-polemical tone of the letters. They also raise the danger of comparing two views, one based on a single book in which the topic is explained systematically (Boston) and the other based on a collection of complete works, wherein the topic is never discussed systematically (Edwards). Knijff and Vlastuin, "Why Edwards Did Not Understand," 44–56, especially 45 n. 4.

Continuity in Edwards

While these studies offer valuable insights into Edwards's view of the covenants, I will argue that they are both mistaken regarding the historical development of Edwards's views and the specifics of why his views differed from Thomas Boston's. A closer reading of Edwards, from his earliest remarks on, will show precisely what Edwards meant by a "wrong distinction" (*Misc.* 2, 1723) of the covenants and "not rightly distinguishing" between the covenants (*Misc.* 617, 1733). This understanding will indicate a greater continuity in Edwards's views than is appreciated by the above studies. Edwards was not discussing whether there was a distinction between the two Covenants (of Redemption and Grace), but rather the "proper" distinction between the two as located in the proper understanding of the parties to each.

Edwards's lack of understanding of Thomas Boston may be due to Boston's confounding the two covenants (Covenant of Redemption and Covenant of Grace) when he writes, "The Covenant of Redemption and the Covenant of Grace are not two distinct covenants, but one and the same."[22] Edwards warns against this. While Edwards in one sense maintains the unity (inseparability) of the two covenants, he also maintains the importance of "rightly" distinguishing them. Donald MacLeod observes that Boston's view in effect "resolves everything into the Covenant of Redemption and virtually obliterates the covenant between God and the believer."[23] He notes how this view has contributed historically to the hyper-Calvinist leanings of several of the covenanter and Dutch denominations that held to Boston's view.[24]

Edwards may also be reacting to Boston's view of the condition of the Covenant of Grace: "Receiving is not the thing, upon which the buyer's right and title to the commodity, or the hireling's right and title to the reward, is founded: therefore, though it may be called a condition of connexion in the respective covenants, yet it cannot, in any propriety

---

22. Boston, *View of the Covenant of Grace*, 32.

23. Macleod, "Covenant Theology," 216.

24. Supporters of the distinction between the Covenant of Redemption and the Covenant of Grace during the seventeenth century included Samuel Rutherford, David Dickson, Patrick Gillespie (1617–1675), Hermann Witsius, and Wilhelmus à Brakel. Those that followed Thomas Boston after his treatise was published in 1734 included Adam Gib (1714–1788), John Dick (1764–1833), and the Secession Church that broke off from the Church of Scotland near the end of Boston's life. Vos, "Doctrine of the Covenant," 234–70.

of speech, be called the condition of them."[25] For Boston, Christ is the condition of the Covenant of Grace, "The condition of the covenant of Grace, properly so called, is Christ in the form of a bond-servant, as last Adam."[26] Defining Christ and his work as the condition of the Covenant of Grace would make no sense to Edwards because, for Edwards, Christ is one of the covenanting parties with believers in the Covenant of Grace. Making Christ the condition as well as one of the covenanting parties would be illogical, even though Edwards views Christ's *work* as the condition of the Covenant of Redemption.

Edwards's "not understanding" Boston may also be traced to Edwards's increasing focus on the historic unfolding of the Covenant of Redemption, which made him critical towards the absence of this historical aspect in Boston's covenant view. This development in Edwards focused on both the relationship and the distinction between the eternal Covenant of Redemption between God the Father and God the Son on the one hand, and on the temporal application of God's eternal covenant in redemptive history as the functioning of the Covenant of Grace on the other hand.[27] The distinction is between a covenant made in eternity with eternal parties (the Father and the Son), and another covenant with parties that are not eternal (Christ and individual elect believers, i.e., the Church) in which individual believers, who have a beginning in time, consent to the covenant terms. While Edwards could say that the Covenant of Grace was everlasting in that it was founded upon and inseparable from the eternal Covenant of Redemption, this does not make the Covenant of Grace a-temporal as the Covenant of Redemption is. In Boston's view, the eternal and the temporal were conflated.

Edwards's distinction between the two covenants, a subtle but important difference from most Reformed Puritan formulations of the covenants, is important for several reasons. First, Edwards is careful to observe as first principle that God cannot deal directly, even by way of covenant, with postlapsarian (i.e., sinful) mankind. Second, Edwards's preserves the notion that all covenants contain obligations and blessings, while at the same time maintaining the unconditionality of the covenant promises. This is reflected in Edwards's view of faith, perseverance, and evangelical obedience, and why a proper understanding of his covenant

---

25. Boston, *View of the Covenant of Grace*, 84.
26. Boston, *View of the Covenant of Grace*, 84.
27. Knijff and Vlastuin, "Why Edwards Did Not Understand," 44–56.

theology in its redemptive-historical context is essential for understanding Edwards on these issues.

In his earliest *Miscellany* touching on the covenants, Edwards begins by noting the difficulties arising from talking about being saved "upon the account" of faith, or faith "being the condition" upon which God has promised salvation.[28] He wants his readers to understand how this way of thinking about faith makes faith a "particular grace and virtue"[29] by (for) which men are saved. According to this error, Edwards concludes that the difference between the covenant with Adam and this view of the Covenant of Grace becomes only one of degree: Adam being saved "upon the account of" possessing all virtues, and mankind since Adam's fall of possessing only one virtue or grace, that of "faith." Hence both covenants boil down to covenants of works, and this leads, per Edwards, to the foundation of Arminianism and neonomianism by making Adam's fallen progeny value themselves for their own righteousness.

Edwards goes on to explain how this confusion arises from "the wrong distinction men make between the covenant of grace and the covenant of redemption." This phrase, coupled with the last phrase in this *Miscellany* ("If we would leave off distinguishing the covenant of grace and the covenant of redemption, we should leave all these matters plain and unperplexed.") could certainly lead one to understand that Edwards is expounding a bicovenantal model, conflating the Covenant of Redemption and the Covenant of Grace. But this is not necessarily the case. Anticipating further arguments in later *Miscellanies*, Edwards wants to make a proper distinction between the covenants, based on the proper parties involved, as well as the specific promises and conditions specific to the individual parties in each covenant. Edwards is well aware of the difficulties in theological nomenclature inherent in discussions of the covenants: "But I must confess after all, that if men will call this free offer and exhibition a covenant, they may . . . But I believe it is much the more hard to think right, for speaking so wrong."[30] In this early *Miscellany*, he is disputing the idea that God has made a covenant with Christ as our Mediator (the Covenant of Redemption) and a separate covenant

---

28. Edwards, "Misc. 2," *WJE* 13:197.

29. By "grace," Edwards is not referring to the free unmerited love and favor of God, nor the application of Christ's righteousness to the sinner, but rather the virtuous or religious affection or disposition of excellence, i.e., the original righteousness of Adam's prelapsarian state.

30. Edwards, "Misc. 2," *WJE* 13:199.

with men (a so-called Covenant of Grace), which is distinct from man as incorporated in the mystical body of Christ (or "public Christ") as the mediator and federal head.

> But it seems to me, all this confusion arises from the wrong distinction men make between the covenant of grace and the covenant of redemption. It seems to me to be true, that as the first covenant was made with the first Adam, so the second covenant was made with the second Adam; as the first covenant was made with the seed of the first Adam no otherwise than as it was made with them in him, so the second covenant is not made with the seed of the second Adam any otherwise than as it was made with them in him. It was not one covenant that was made with Adam, and another, that he had nothing to do with, that was made with his seed; so neither was it one covenant that was made with Christ, and another, that Christ had nothing to do with, with believers. But then, in all respects wherein Adam was a common head and representative of men, so Christ is a common head and representative of believers; as Adam was only the first created of men, so Christ is the eldest brother of believers.[31]

In the taxonomy of Edwards's covenant theology, God did not make a separate covenant with fallen humans outside of Christ, nor could he. The continuity in Edwards's thought is evident here as it anticipates remarks made in a later *Miscellany* that, "God the Father makes no covenant and enters into no treaty with fallen men distinctly, by themselves. He will transact with them, in such a friendly way, no other way than by and in Christ Jesus, as members and as it were parts of him."[32] This is reiterated in the second sermon of his *History of the Work of Redemption*: "For when man had sinned, God the Father would have no more to do with man immediately. He would no more have any immediate concern with this world of mankind that had apostatized from him and rebelled against him. He would henceforward have no concern with man, but only through a mediator, either in teaching men or in governing or bestowing any benefits on them."[33] Consistent with this statement, Edwards goes on to say that in the record of sacred history when we read what God did for his church and people, when he spoke to them and revealed himself

---

31. Edwards, "Misc. 2," *WJE* 13:198.
32. Edwards, "Misc. 1091," *WJE* 20:477.
33. Edwards, "History of the Work of Redemption," *WJE* 9:131.

to them, we are to understand it as referring to the Second Person of the Trinity in his role as covenant mediator.[34]

To further add to his argument, Edwards goes on to distinguish between a "covenant" and "a free offer." The free offer of the gospel can in no way be termed a "covenant," which is bound by conditions and promises. To confuse the gospel as the free offer of salvation with a covenant, Edwards argues, is to confound definitions and open one up to viewing "faith" as a condition, in the strict sense, of salvation. To attach conditions to a "free offer" would be an apparent contradiction and has led to much confusion of equating "that which is commonly called covenant of grace" with "Christ's open and free offer of life ... without any condition."[35] Faith is not condition, but a receiving itself; Christ holds out and believers receive. "There is no covenant made, or agreement upon something that must be done, before they might receive."[36]

As outlined in the previous two chapters, the condition of the first covenant (Covenant of Works) was Adam's standing in righteousness. The condition of the second covenant (Covenant of Redemption) is Christ's standing and his performance of the conditions of the New Covenant which, Edwards maintains, is essentially no different in terms of its conditions (perfect and complete obedience) than the first (they are, in essence, one with different mediators). There is no other covenant condition imposed on sinful men and women to fulfill that is not already fulfilled in Christ: "There is nothing more to be done; all is done already. We have nothing to do, upon the account of which we are to be saved; we are to do nothing but only to receive Christ and what he has done already. Salvation is not offered to us upon any condition, but freely and for nothing. We are to do nothing for it, we are only to take it."[37] Faith is the taking and receiving. For Adam, it was certainly, "Do this and you will inherit the blessing of eternal life." This remains true for Adam's posterity as well (in terms of judgment, not ability to fulfill), but now salvation is also offered freely and unconditionally through Christ: "'Come and

---

34. Edwards, "History of the Work of Redemption," *WJE* 9:131. Edwards cites John 1:18, "No man [hath seen God at any time; the only begotten Son . . . hath declared him]." By this he also means that Christ often appeared in "an human form."

35. Edwards, "Misc. 2," *WJE* 13:199.

36. Edwards, "Misc. 2," *WJE* 13:199-98.

37. Edwards, "Misc. 2," *WJE* 13:198.

take it; whosoever will, let him come' [Rev 22:17]"[38] As Edwards explains clearly in *Misc. 30*:

> With reference to what has been before spoken of the covenant [No. 2]. Covenant is taken very variously in Scripture, sometimes for a divine promise, sometimes for a divine promise on conditions. But if we speak of the covenant God has made with man stating the condition of eternal life, God never made but one with man to wit, the Covenant of Works; which never yet was abrogated, but is a covenant stands in full force to all eternity without the failing of one tittle. The covenant of grace is not another covenant made with man upon the abrogation of this, but a covenant made with Christ to fulfill it. And for this end came Christ into the world, to fulfill the law, or Covenant of Works, for all that receive him.[39]

This does not contradict what Edwards says in *Misc. 717*, where he states that, "though the obligation thereof, as a law, distinct from a covenant, and the curse, arising from the sanction thereof, remains still in force against fallen man; yet, as a covenant, in which life was promised," on condition of obedience, "it was from that time, abrogated."[40] It is abrogated in the sense that the matter of man's obedience is already decided; obedience was what man had already failed of under Adam.[41] So in one sense, "we are indeed now under the Covenant of Works so, that if we are perfectly righteous we can challenge salvation."[42] The "we" in this context refers to both Old Testament and New Testament saints who are both also under the Covenant of Grace. The purpose of Edwards's insistence is not so much to express a hypothetical conditional as it is pedagogical, to establish and maintain the works principle inherent in Christ's obedience to the Covenant of Redemption, and that perfect and complete obedience which continues as the sole condition for eternal life and blessing. Edwards makes this explicit in sermon fifteen of *History of the Work of Redemption*:

> Every command that Christ obeyed may be reduced to that great and everlasting law of God that is contained in the Covenant

38. Edwards, "Misc. 2," *WJE* 13:198.
39. Edwards, "Misc. 30," *WJE* 13:217.
40. Edwards, "Misc. 717," *WJE* 18:348.
41. Edwards, "Misc. 717," *WJE* 18:348.
42. Edwards, "Misc. 250," *WJE* 13:362.

of Works, that eternal rule of righteousness that God had established between himself and mankind. Christ came into the world to fulfill and answer the Covenant of Works, that is the covenant that is to stand forever as a rule of judgment, and that is the covenant that we had broken, and that was the covenant that must be fulfilled.[43]

In the same *Miscellany*, Edwards can maintain the impossibility of obtaining life by that covenant because it was only made with Adam, which already imputes the guilt of that first covenant failure on his posterity. The resulting actual sin of Adam's posterity experientially negates any possibility of covenant fulfillment requiring "perfect and absolute" obedience. As I will explore in more detail in the following chapter, the Covenant of Works functions in at least three ways. First, it serves a condemning function, reminding of the curse entailed by Adam's failure. Second, it serves a pedagogical function to lead one away from one's own righteousness and towards the promises of the New Covenant. It breaks any thought of meeting the covenant demands by one's own inherent righteousness. Third, it establishes the need for an alien imputed righteousness obtained by Christ as the fulfillment of the Covenant of Redemption as our "second Adam." The Covenant of Works as pertaining to Adam's prosperity cannot be fulfilled, but nevertheless remains in force, in so far as its conditions, sanctions, and blessings, for Christ to fulfill. This distinction between the continuing obligation and the impossibility of fulfillment except by a mediator or surety is the foundation for the law-gospel distinction in Edwards's theology.

There is nothing in the first of Edwards's *Miscellanies* dealing with the covenants that is inconsistent or requires positing a major shift or discontinuity in Edwards's thinking. Everything Edwards goes on to develop in further discussions is found here in germinal form. To say that Edwards sees a wrong distinction between the Covenant of Redemption and the "so-called" Covenant of Grace as expounded in the various formulations in his day and within Reformed scholasticism, does not simply mean that he held to a bicovenantal structure during this early period and then changed his mind later. Certainly, the matter of terminology is problematic and confusing, as is recognized by Edwards. But he will go on to show how the covenants can be rightly distinguished, focusing on the parties of the covenants, the Covenant of Redemption between God

43. Edwards, "History of the Work of Redemption," *WJE* 9:308–9.

the Father and Christ, and the marriage covenant between Christ and the Church (the elect).

Misc. 617, dated 1733, is purported by both McClymond and McDermott and by Knijff as marking a shift from Edwards's supposed early bicovenantal view to a tricovenantal view. The focus is on Edwards's opening sentence: "It seems to me there arises considerable confusion from not rightly distinguishing between the covenant that God makes with Christ and with his church or believers in him, and the covenant between Christ and his church or between Christ and men."[44] But if one takes into account the specific arguments and distinctions Edwards was making in his earlier *Miscellanies*, then these later *Miscellanies* show considerable continuity, if not complete agreement, with Edwards's earlier views as he further develops his covenant theology. To say there is development in Edwards's covenant theology in terms of greater clarification and precision in language and definition is not to say there was any major change in the essential structure. Edwards's heading notation for *Misc. 617* links it to *Misc. 825, 919*, and *1091*. Even though these *Miscellanies* may have been written over the course of 14 years (1733–1747), they can be considered as a single group in Edwards's development, just as Edwards linked them together in his notations.[45] With these caveats in mind, a more coherent view of Edwards's doctrine of the Covenant of Grace can be constructed.

Jonathan Edwards on the Covenant of Grace

Edwards used the term "Covenant of Grace" in two ways: first, in unity with the Covenant of Redemption as the historic revelation and outworking of the Covenant of Redemption in history and in the life of individual believers, and second in distinction from the Covenant of Redemption

---

44. Edwards, "Misc. 617," *WJE* 18:148.

45. Ava Chamberlain dates *Misc. 612* to no earlier than Jan. 1733 and *Misc. 625* to no earlier than June 1733, which would bracket *Misc. 617* between those dates. Chamberlain dates *Misc. 807* to no earlier than Aug. 1739 and *Misc. 832* to winter 1739–1740, which would bracket *Misc. 825* between those dates. Chamberlain, "Editor's Introduction," *WJE* 18:1–48, and Table 2, 48. Pauw dates *Misc. 901* to no earlier than mid-1743 and *Misc. 1021* to after 1742, positioning *Misc. 919* between those dates. Amy Plantinga Pauw also dates *Misc. 1069* to c.1744 and *Misc. 1101* to no earlier than summer 1748, which would bracket *Misc. 1091* between those dates. Pauw, "Editor's Introduction," *WJE* 20:1–39, and Table 1, 38.

in terms of the covenant parties. The relationship between the Covenant of Grace and the eternal Covenant of Redemption has important implications for the law-gospel distinction in Edwards. Edwards viewed the Covenant of Grace as a "marriage" covenant between Christ and believers. It was a true covenant with conditional promises. Edwards intimately relates the two covenants in their mutual and interrelated conditions and promises, and this forms the foundation of the law-gospel distinction in his theology.

Covenant Terminology in Edwards

The first interpretive hurdle to overcome is nomenclature, and the various meanings Edwards gives to the term "Covenant of Grace." In *Misc. 919*, Edwards delineates the different understandings of what is commonly termed the "Covenant of Grace":

> [I]f by the covenant of grace, we understand the covenant between God the Father and men, [at this point Edwards strikes out "believers" and inserts "men"] [it] is no other than a revelation of part of the covenant of redemption to men, even that part of [it] that contains promises of blessings to men, renewing the same promises to believers as in Christ and as it were parts of him, that had before been made to Christ for them; if it be understood as the covenant between Christ and believers, 'tis the marriage covenant. The covenant between God the Father and believers is, in some respect, the same with the covenant of redemption between the Father and the Son—as much as the covenant God made with Abraham, when he bid him depart out of his own country, etc., and made him such promises concerning himself and his seed, was the same with the covenant that God made afterwards in the wilderness with Abraham's seed. 'Tis no more than a revelation of part of a covenant made already, and renewing of the same promises over again.[46]

In *Misc. 30*, supposedly written as early as July–August 1723,[47] after maintaining the non-abrogation of the Covenant of Works and its standing in full force to all eternity, Edwards says that the Covenant of Grace "is not another covenant made with man" that supposedly replaces

46. Edwards, "Misc. 919," *WJE* 20:167.
47. Schafer, "Editor's Introduction," *WJE* 13:92.

an abrogated Covenant of Works (as was being preached and taught by certain antinomian and neonomian theologians), but "a covenant made with Christ to fulfill it." It is also significant that Edwards ties this *Miscellany* into his earlier entry *Misc. 2*.

So according to Edwards, the term "Covenant of Grace" may refer to a progressive revelation of the Covenant of Redemption in history. This is one of the major themes of Edwards's *History of the Work of Redemption*.[48] The covenant blessings and promises made to Christ in the Covenant of Redemption are made to Christ and to his "mystical body" or bride, but not to them directly or as individuals. These eternal promises and blessings are reiterated and renewed in time as the work of redemption unfolds from the fall until the consummation. Edwards uses the illustration of Abraham and Moses in their respective roles as "typical" mediators of covenant promises. When those same promises were made to Abraham's "seed" or Israel under Moses, it was not a different covenant but the same covenant and promises now communicated to those whom Abraham and Moses represented. The Covenant of Grace in this specific sense is the successive temporal revelation of and fulfillment in history of the eternal Covenant of Redemption made to Christ as it is now communicated to "men" (all mankind, men and women). *Misc. 30*, then, is consistent in that it speaks about the Covenant of Grace in terms of temporal fulfillment: "And for this end came Christ into the world, to fulfill the law, or Covenant of Works, for all that receive him." So there is both a unity and distinction between the Covenant of Redemption and Covenant of Grace exhibited in this definition.

This is entirely consistent with Edwards's exposition in one of his later *Miscellanies*, no. 1091, that Pauw dates to sometime after 1744.[49] Here Edwards reiterates that "there are promises of God the Father made to believers, and not only made to Christ for them, before the world was. And yet it will not follow there is a distinct Covenant of Grace between God the Father and believers, besides the eternal Covenant of Redemption that God made with is Son."[50] Edwards is worth quoting at length:

> The promises that God, in the covenant of redemption, made to his Son of benefits to be given to him and his people jointly, such as justification, the privileges and benefits of his children, the

---

48. Edwards, "History of the Work of Redemption," *WJE* 9:117–18.
49. Pauw, "Editor's Introduction," *WJE* 20:38.
50. Edwards, "Misc. 1091," *WJE* 20:475.

eternal inheritance and kingdom, were properly made to Christ mystical. For they were made to Christ as a public person, as virtually containing the whole future church that he had taken as it were into himself, having taken their names on his heart, and having undertaken to stand as representing them all. And therefore the promises are in effect not only made to Christ, but his members. For they were made to the whole mystical Christ, and though the whole of Christ mystical was not yet in being, only the head of the body as yet is in being, and the members only existing in God's decree. And as in process of time the members, one after another, come into being, and then the same promises that were virtually made to 'em before are expressly revealed to 'em, and directed to 'em. Yet this does not make the promises, as revealed and directly made to the members, a different covenant from the promises that were before made to the head, that existed before 'em and stood for 'em. If the members had all then been existing in union with their head, when God the Father made a covenant with their head for them, and gave promises pertaining to the whole mystical body, head and members, then doubtless it would have been proper that the promises should be directed to the head and members both, as united; for the promises are the same, and both head and members are concerned in them. And then surely the promises, as made to the head, would not have been one covenant, and another, as declared to the members; out the promises, as declared to the whole and every part, would have been but one covenant. And the promises are not the less the same, nor the covenant the less one, for being declared and explicitly directed to the several parts successively, as they come into being.[51]

Edwards compares the relationship as to a father who makes a promise or covenant with his son concerning him and his future spouse, giving promises to both and considering them both as one even though his son has not yet obtained a spouse. When a spouse is obtained and is united to him in marriage, the son brings all those covenant promises in his hand as it were, and delivers them to her from his father just as if those promises were made to them jointly. For Edwards, this doesn't make it now another covenant "anymore than if Christ's spouse had actually been with Christ when the covenant was first made."[52] Edwards concludes that "there is a covenant that God the Father makes with believers, of which

---

51. Edwards, "Misc. 1091," *WJE* 20:475.
52. Edwards, "Misc. 1091," *WJE* 20:476.

Jesus Christ is the Mediator, yet this covenant is in no wise properly a distinct covenant from the covenant God makes with Christ himself, as the believers' head and surety, and that he made with him before the world was."[53]

What is clear in Edwards, a point that needs repeated emphasis if we are to understand Edwards correctly, is his reticence to refer to the Covenant of Grace as between God and sinful men and women, i.e., God and individual unredeemed sinners as covenanting parties, as is usually formulated in Reformed covenant language:

> God the Father makes no covenant and enters into no treaty with fallen men distinctly, by themselves. He will transact with them, in such a friendly way, no other way than by and in Christ Jesus, as members and as it were parts of him. The friendliness and favor shall not be to them in their own name, but it shall all be to Christ, and all acts of friendship and favor shall be to him, and all promises made to him, and the fulfillment of promises also shall be to him, and to believers only as being in him, and under the covert of his name, and as being beheld and reckoned as parts of him.[54]

In Edwards's estimation, the use of covenant language that refers to the Covenant of Grace as between God and postlapsarian mankind circumvents or short-circuits the mediatorial role of Christ as their covenant surety and contributes to the confusion and controversies that exist with regards to faith, works, and justification.

This covenant distinction has consequences on how to properly understand Edwards's theological language of evangelical obedience as both necessary and non-meritorious. To be sure, when Reformed theologians such as Turretin and Witsius refer to the Covenant of Grace as between God and man, they are quick to qualify this language as including the central mediatorial role of Christ. But for Edwards, "it is much the more hard to think right, for speaking so wrong."

In a sermon on Heb 13:8 dated April 1738 entitled, "Jesus Christ, the Same Yesterday, Today, and Forever,"[55] Edwards can speak of the "covenant of grace which God established with man." But it is obvious in this sermon that Edwards is not positing a separate covenant (he does

---

53. Edwards, "Misc. 1091," *WJE* 20:477.
54. Edwards, "Misc. 1091," *WJE* 20:477.
55. Edwards, "Jesus Christ the Same," *JE* 2:949–54.

speak of it as "two-fold"), but rather a covenant "not essentially different from the covenant of redemption." It is but an "expression of it," "only that covenant of redemption partly revealed to mankind for their encouragement, faith, and comfort."[56] The context of this section of the sermon is Christ in his mediatorial office, specifically with regard to its inviolable execution. The promises made to Christ in the Covenant of Redemption are inviolable, and as such are inviolably made to elect believers as "in Christ" or as part of his "mystical body" as well. The one Covenant of Redemption is a "covenant that God the Father makes with Christ . . . wherein believers are looked upon as in Christ."[57] The important sermon "Application" that Edwards makes is that Christ's promises (as well as warnings) to those "that have entered into the bonds of the Christian covenant" are just as inviolable and trustworthy. In another unpublished sermon on 2 Sam 23:5, Edwards notes that "the covenant of grace is in every way so ordered as is needful in order to its being made firm and sure." The basis of this is "the covenant of redemption, which God made with Christ from all eternity . . . surely God will fulfill the engagements that he from all eternity entered into with his own Son."[58]

In an unpublished sermon on John 1:16, Edwards says that in "covenanting with the Father to be for us and in our stead . . . [Christ] . . . made himself one with us by his own voluntary act from all eternity." In so doing he "assume[d] mankind into an union with himself," such that the covenant with Christ is a covenant with his bride, as if "they were all but one person."[59]

From his earliest writings Edwards is consistent in his conviction that the Covenant of Redemption and the Covenant of Grace, in this specific use of the term, are essentially one, yet distinguishable. This is evident as early as *Misc. 2* (c. 1723) and remains essentially unchanged through his later *Miscellanies* two decades later. As Carl Bogue concludes, "While Edwards apparently sees in the historical manifestation of God's plan of salvation a necessity to distinguish the two covenants, he prefers the divine perspective in which there is really only one covenant."[60] The comfort of the historical revelation of the Covenant of Grace is anchored

56. Edwards, "Jesus Christ the Same," *JE* 2:950.
57. Edwards, "Misc. 825," *WJE* 18: 536-37.
58. Edwards, "Sermon on II Sam. 23:5," *WJEO* 44.
59. Edwards, "Sermon on John 1:16," *WJEO* 45, L. 3v.
60. Bogue, *Jonathan Edwards*, 96.

in the eternal Covenant of Redemption. As far as sinners are concerned, the Covenant of Redemption is the eternal basis for the Covenant of Grace. This is not to say that Edwards did not appear to struggle with the nomenclature of his received Reformed tradition. For instance, in one of his earliest discussions on the Covenant of Grace, he grapples with the common use of the term as it relates to the free gospel offer of salvation, an offer free of conditions. He objects to this free offer of the gospel being termed a "covenant." All covenants have conditions and, therefore, "It is not proper, when a man holds out his gift to a beggar that he may take it without any manner of preliminary conditions, [to say] that he makes a covenant with the beggar. No more proper is it to say, that Christ's holding forth life in his hand to us that we may receive it, is making a covenant with us."[61]

Covenant Conditions

The conditionality of the covenants is a major concern of Edwards in his writings. In the early *Miscellanies*, his emphasis is on the unconditionality of the New Covenant as it involves elect believers. As discussed before, the foundation of the New Covenant is the Covenant of Redemption, a conditional covenant made only with Christ directly on the basis of his own obedience. With respect to the believer's interest in the covenant, it is unconditional. The "covenant" signifies an absolute promise to believers.[62] It is curious to note that Edwards encloses the word "covenant" with quotation marks in this passage, which is unusual and not seen anywhere else. While it is pure conjecture as to why he chose to do so in this single instance, and any conclusion based on this single passage is necessarily tenuous, it would be consistent with his thought that he is equivocating on the use of the term "covenant" in the absence of any condition (although he does speak of "covenants" based on absolute promise). What he may be insinuating by this grammatical mark is that the conditional Covenant of Redemption with respect to Christ's obedience takes the form of an absolute unconditional promise in relation to believers. Another possibility is that he is using the term "covenant" as it was used in other Reformed writings to refer to the "covenant" between God and mankind. This usage he deems inappropriate in the strict sense because

61. Edwards, "Misc. 2," *WJE* 13:199.
62. Edwards, "Misc. 165," *WJE* 13:321.

it implied an unmediated covenant between God and postlapsarian mankind, yet he also understands the qualifications and nuances of how many Reformed writers used the term, whereby the mediatorial role of Christ was not directly stated but implied.

Despite the unconditionality of the Covenant of Redemption, Edwards can also talk about the Covenant of Grace containing conditions. How is this possible without contradiction? To do so requires a consistent synthesis of Edwards's covenant language, especially with regards to the Covenant of Grace. Considering the entire corpus of Edwards's writings, a complex and rich picture emerges, but one that does not fit the usual formulations present in Reformed covenant theology (although it can be found in some writings). For Edwards, the eternal Covenant of Redemption includes and is the foundation for the Covenant of Grace, which in one sense is merely the temporal progressive revelation and outworking of the Covenant of Redemption in history. The revelatory aspect of the Covenant of Grace is the gospel announcement. The gospel is not by definition a covenant, but only an announcement or revelation of the promises of God that are contained in the covenant. It is a free offer or invitation. The temporal aspect of the Covenant of Grace contains the entire preparatory work of redemption from the fall until the incarnation (Christ's life, death, and resurrection) and the application of the promises and rewards made to Christ to individual elect believers. While the Covenant of Grace can refer in one sense to the entire history of the work of redemption, Edwards refines and focuses his later writings on the more specific sense of the covenant with regards to its application to individual believers. This is his famous analogy of the marriage covenant.

The Marriage Covenant between Christ and Believers

The Covenant of Grace as a marriage covenant between Christ and believers is central to Edwards's covenant thinking. Edwards's introduction of the "marriage covenant" as a separate covenant is not necessarily evidence of a change in his overall covenant structure other than reflecting a more nuanced refinement and distinction. The interrelationships and distinctions between the covenants in some ways defy simple bi- or tri-covenantal classification in Edwards. The "marriage covenant," which he prefers to equate with the Covenant of Grace in his later writings, is still the temporal outworking of the Covenant of Redemption. It is how the promises of the Father to the Son in the Covenant of Redemption are applied and come to fruition from the period of the fall until Christ's return. While the distinct parties of the two covenants distinguish the Covenant of Redemption from the Covenant of Grace, they are still intimately tied together as promise is to fulfillment, as redemption accomplished and applied. It is also no coincidence that Edwards begins his discussions on this "marriage covenant" in *Misc. 617* at or about the time of the half-way covenant controversies in his parish at Northampton (a controversy which would eventually lead to his dismissal) as it specifically deals with the conditional requirements for entering into the covenant. Edwards uses the marriage covenant analogy frequently in his discussions of the half-way covenant controversy. But this does not require positing any essential change in the overall structure or nature of Edwards's covenant views.

Beginning in *Misc. 617*, Edwards distinguishes two covenants based on their respective covenanting parties: the covenant that God makes with Christ (and with his church or elect believers in him considered as one, i.e., his "mystical body") and the covenant between Christ and individual elect believers.

> There is doubtless a difference between the covenant that God makes with Christ and his people, considered as one, and the covenant of Christ and his people between themselves. The covenant that a father makes between a son and his wife, under one or considered as one, must be looked upon different from the marriage covenant or the covenant of the son and his wife between themselves. The father is concerned in this covenant only— as a parent in a child's marriage— directing, consenting and ratifying.[63]

It is a marriage covenant between "Christ and the soul," the covenant of "union" whereby the soul becomes united to Christ. It is equivalent to the soul's conversion whereby the soul has an interest in Christ and his benefits. "In marriage, or in the soul's conversion, it becomes a proper covenant. This is what is called the Covenant of Grace, in distinction from the covenant of redemption."[64] The uniting is faith itself. Faith is the consenting to the covenant agreements or, more specifically, a closing and adhering to Christ with one's entire soul.

63. Edwards, "Misc. 617," *WJE* 18:148.
64. Edwards, "Misc. 825," *WJE* 18:537.

In so defining the Covenant of Grace as the marriage covenant, it becomes a true covenant in which there are conditional promises. "To suppose that there are any promises of the covenant of grace, or any covenant promises, that are not conditional promise," says Edwards, "Seems an absurdity and contradiction."[65] By structuring the covenants in this manner, Edwards finds a way to "reconcile the difference between those divines that think [the Covenant of Redemption] and the covenant of grace the same, and those that think 'em different."[66] He is explains it this way:

> The covenant that God the Father makes with believers is indeed the very same with the covenant of redemption made with Christ before the foundation of the world, or at least is entirely included in it. And this covenant has a mediator, or is "ordained in the hand of a mediator" [Gal 3:19]. But the covenant by which Christ himself and believers are united, one with another, is properly a different covenant than that, and is not made by a mediator. There is a mediator between sinners and the Father to bring about a covenant union between them, but there is no mediator between Christ and sinners to bring about a marriage union between Christ and their souls.[67]

Edwards also finds this as a means "to reconcile the difference between those divines that [think] the covenant of grace is not conditional as to us or that the promises of it are without any proper conditions to be performed by us, and those that think that faith is the proper condition of the covenant of grace."[68] The two-fold understanding of the Covenant of Grace in Edwards is the key to this conundrum. When the term "Covenant of Grace" is used to refer to the revelation and outworking in history of the Covenant of Redemption, that is the covenant between God the Father and believers *in Christ*, the covenant that he "ordains in the hand of [a] mediator" and the promises given us *in him*, it is indeed in this respect unconditional for the elect believer.

> [The covenant of grace] is indeed without any proper conditions to be performed by us. Faith is not properly the condition of this covenant, but the righteousness of Christ. Faith is no

---

65. Edwards, "Misc. 617," *WJE* 18:148.
66. Edwards, "Misc. 1091," *WJE* 20:477.
67. Edwards, "Misc. 1091," *WJE* 20:477-88.
68. Edwards, "Misc. 1091," *WJE* 20:478.

more properly the condition of this covenant made with the second Adam, for himself and believers in him, than a coming into being by descent from Adam would properly have been the condition of the covenant God made with Adam, and the promises made to his posterity in him. Adam's righteousness was the alone proper condition, not only of Adam's eternal life but of his posterity's, according to the tenor of that covenant. So Christ's righteousness is the alone proper condition of eternal life to the second Adam and his spiritual seed, according to the tenor of the new covenant made with him.[69]

Edwards contrasts this with his use of the "Covenant of Grace" in its second sense, as the marriage covenant between Christ and "his church or his members." In this sense it is indeed conditional. Edwards compares and contrasts the two covenants in terms of conditionality and in terms of the distinct parties in this manner:

[T]he proper condition of it [the marriage covenant with Christ], which is a yielding to Christ's wooings and accepting his offers and closing with him as a redeemer and spiritual husband, is to be performed by us. A proper condition of a covenant is that qualification or act of the party with whom the covenant is made by which, according [to] the tenor of the covenant, the party is interested in the benefits therein promised. But the party with whom God the Father, as supreme Lord, ruler and disposer of all, makes his covenant in favor of fallen men is Christ mystical, containing both head and members, and will have nothing to do in any such friendly transaction with fallen men any otherwise but as in and under Christ, and considered as one party with him. But that in this party by which alone, according to the tenor of the covenant, the party, both head and members, is interested in eternal life is Christ's righteousness. But in the covenant between Christ and his members or spouse, she is by herself a party in the covenant, and that in this party by which alone, according to the tenor of the covenant, she is interested in the benefit of union and propriety in Christ (which is the benefit directly conveyed in this covenant) is her believing in Christ, or her soul's active union with him.[70]

Understanding which sense of the "Covenant of Grace" Edwards is using avoids misunderstandings of his theology on several points.

---

69. Edwards, "Misc. 1091," *WJE* 20:478.
70. Edwards, "Misc. 1091," *WJE* 20:478–79.

Edwards goes on to delineate the respective conditions and promises of each of the covenants, and in so doing elucidates how "it appears that many of the things promised in both these covenants are the same, but in some things different. So that those things that are promises in one of these covenants, are conditions in another."[71] The interrelationship of the conditions and promises of the two covenants both unites them and distinguishes them: "The promises of the former of these covenants being revealed, do become the promises of the Father to believers. These are the promises that are given us in Christ; that is, they are promises made to us by the Father as being in Christ, being parts of Christ and so having a right to the same blessing that are promised to Christ himself, our head."[72] Not properly distinguishing these covenants is for Edwards at the root of many of the controversies regarding the nature of the covenants, especially regarding the nature of faith and obedience in justification, and the confusion of law and gospel.

Edwards finds support for his distinction of the Covenant of Grace, based on the parties covenanting (Christ and his church), on the biblical use of the word "testament" when referring to this covenant. Testament refers to a will that is confirmed by the death of the testator. Since the testator that died was Christ, and not the Father, and the Covenant of Grace is seen as his last will and testament to his church, then it requires that Christ and the church (Christ's spiritual spouse) are the parties involved. He points to Luke 22:29 ("I do by covenant dispose unto you a kingdom, as my father by covenant disposed unto me."), noting that the word *diatithemai* signifies "to covenant, or make a contract or testament, or to appoint or dispose by covenant or testament." He points to its parallel use in Acts 3:25 and Heb 8:10.

Edwards also appeals to Old Testament passages in support of his marriage analogy. In the context of the Northampton half-way covenant controversy and his defense of his views on the nature of an adult person's profession of piety, Edwards draws on passages from Deuteronomy and Isaiah:

> To own this covenant, is to profess the consent of our hearts to it; and that is the sum and substance of true piety. 'Tis not only a professing the assent of our understandings, that we understand

---

71. Edwards, "Misc. 617," *WJE* 20:149.
72. Edwards, "Misc. 617," *WJE* 20:150.

there is such a covenant, or that we understand we are obliged to comply with it; but 'tis to profess the consent of our wills, it is to manifest that we do comply with it. There is mutual profession in this affair, a profession on Christ's part, and a profession on our part; as it is in marriage. And 'tis the same sort of profession that is made on both sides, in this respect, that each professes a consent of heart: Christ in his Word declares an entire consent of heart as to what he offers; and the visible Christian, in the answer that he makes to it in his Christian profession, declares a consent and compliance of heart to his proposal. Owning the covenant is professing to make the transaction of that covenant our own. The transaction of that covenant is that of espousals to Christ; on our part, it is giving our souls to Christ as his spouse: there is no one thing, that the covenant of grace is so often compared to in Scripture, as the marriage covenant; and the visible transaction, or mutual profession there is between Christ and the visible church, is abundantly compared to the mutual profession there is in marriage. In marriage the bride professes to yield to the bridegroom's suit, and to take him for her husband, renouncing all others, and to give up herself to him to be entirely and forever possessed by him as his wife. But he that professes this towards Christ, professes saving faith. They that openly covenanted with God according to the tenor of the institution (Deuteronomy 10:20), they visibly united themselves to God in the union of that covenant: they professed on their parts the union of the covenant of God, which was the covenant of grace. It is said in the institution, "Thou shalt cleave to the Lord and swear by his name"; or as the words more literally are, "Thou shalt unite into the Lord, and swear into his name." So in Isaiah 56:6 'tis called a "joining themselves to the Lord." But the union, cleaving, or joining of that covenant is saving faith the grand condition of the covenant of Christ, by which we are in Christ: this is what brings us into the Lord. For a person explicitly or professedly to enter into the union or relation of the covenant of grace with Christ, is the same as professedly to do that which on our part is the uniting act, and that is the act of faith. To profess the covenant of grace is to profess the covenant, not as a spectator, but as one immediately concerned in the affair, as a party in the covenant professed; and this is to profess that in the covenant which belongs to us as a party or to profess our part in the covenant; and that is the soul's believing acceptance of the Savior. Christ's part is salvation, our part is a saving faith in him; not a feigned, but unfeigned faith; not a common, but special and saving faith; no other faith than this is the condition of the covenant of grace.[73]

Edwards's marriage analogy of the Covenant of Grace is not his own, but is one drawn from the pages of Scripture.

Covenant Promises

The intimate relationship between the Covenants of Redemption and Grace is evident when comparing the conditions and promises in each (see Table 4.1). The condition of the covenant between God and Jesus Christ as a public person is all that Christ has done and suffered to procure redemption. It includes all of Christ's works of obedience to the Covenant of Works, as well as his active obedience unto death[74] as taking on the curse of the Covenant of Works wrought by Adam's disobedience. The condition of the marriage covenant between Christ and a believer is that they should "close with him and adhere to him," which is faith. The nature of faith as a "condition" will be discussed in a subsequent chapter. For the moment, suffice it say that faith is the sole non-meritorious condition that unites the elect believer to Christ as in a marriage union. It is the illocutionary "I do" of the marriage vows which brings about a new relationship whereby all that belongs to Christ now belongs equally to his

---

73. Edwards, "Humble Inquiry," *WJE* 12:205–6.

74. Reformed theologians usually consider Christ's sufferings and death as part of his "passive" obedience. Edwards understands Christ's death as part of his active obedience. He explains this in his sermon, "The Threefold Work of the Holy Ghost": "I would observe that Christ's sufferings themselves may be considered as part of Christ's active obedience and positive righteousness. Christ, by dying, did not only procure for us negative righteousness or mere freedom from guilt as an expiatory sacrifice, but it was also part of his obedience and positive righteousness which he performed. He had received this command of the Father, that he should lay down his life. John 10:17–18, 'Therefore doth my Father love me, because I lay down my life, that I might take it again. No man taketh it from me, but I lay it down of myself. I have power to lay it down, and I have power to take it again. This commandment have I received of my Father.'" Edwards, "Threefold Work of the Holy Ghost," *WJE* 14:400. The distinction in Reformed theology was asserted to maintain the unity and merit of Christ's obedience in life and death as opposed to interpretations rendering Christ's life of obedience as merely an example of piety, separate from the substitutionary nature of his death. While Edwards rejects the terminology of "passive" and "active" obedience, he is still affirming the original intent of the distinction, namely, the unity of the redemptive and substitutionary nature of Christ's obedience in both life and death. For a helpful discussion, see Berkouwer, *Work of Christ*.

bride, the church, in that covenant union. The sole meritorious condition for justification is Christ's obedience (to the Covenant of Works), a justification that comes to believers by way of being united (declaratively and covenantally, not ontologically) to Christ in his justification. The promises of the Covenant of Grace "is the enjoyment of himself and communion with him in the benefits he himself has obtained of the Father by what he has done and suffered."[75] Just as in a marriage covenant, the espoused give themselves and all they have to each other:

> The sum of all that Christ promises in his covenant with his people, is that he will give himself to them. In marriage the persons covenanting, giving themselves to each other, do give what they have to each; the union which they mutually consent to infers [and] confers communion. This promise of the covenant of Christ with his people, implies eternal life of both soul and body. The happiness of eternal life, it consists in the enjoyment of Christ and in communion with him or partaking with him in the happiness and glory of his reward, who is rewarded with the eternal life and glory of both soul and body.[76]

This union also involves a sharing of the guilt sinners have incurred from Adam's disobedience. Just as Christ gives himself to his people, he must also represent them. The justice due them as sinners takes hold of Christ now as well, and all the sinners' obligations lie upon Christ. "These things necessarily follow from Christ's making himself one with them" in the marriage covenant or Covenant of Grace. In addition, the promise of Christ's incarnation, death and suffering is included in these promises "before these things were actually accomplished." Edwards unites the entire history of redemption and the *ordo salutis* with respect to the salvation of Old Testament saints who were saved in the same manner under the Covenant of Grace as New Testament saints. They were made partakers of eternal life by way of promise, a promise inherent in the covenant itself. In this manner they are saved in the same way as New Testament believers, but in the order of promise of future fulfillment rather than actual fulfillment. I will explore more about the Covenant of Grace under the Old Testament and Mosaic dispensation in the following chapter.

The promise of the Father's covenant with the Son, according to Edwards, includes eternal life, perseverance, and justification, along with

---

75. Edwards, "Misc. 617," *WJE* 18:148.
76. Edwards, "Misc. 617," *WJE* 18:148–49.

regeneration or conversion.[77] It includes the giving of faith as well as "all thing necessary in order to faith." By this Edwards includes all the means of grace, God's Word and ordinances. Edwards notes the reciprocity between the covenant promises and conditions. "Hence it appears that many of the things promised in both these covenants are the same, but in some things different. So that those things that are promises in one of these covenants, are conditions in another."[78] Thus regeneration and closing with Christ (conversion and faith) are conditions of the marriage covenant with Christ and at the same time are promises to Christ on the condition of his perfect covenant obedience, "what [Christ] has done and suffered and are parts of his reward."[79] And since regeneration, faith, sanctification, and perseverance are all gifts of the indwelling of the Holy Spirit, it is another way of saying that the Holy Spirit *is* the blessing and promise of Christ's obedience. *All* the conditions for the marriage covenant are *given* through the Holy Spirit, who is given *as* Christ's reward. The Holy Spirit as gift unites the believer with Christ in those promises that he has obtained through his perfect obedience. As Edwards concludes: "As the Holy Spirit is the infinite riches and fullness of the Godhead to be communicated in the work of redemption, so he is the great good covenanted for, and the end of the covenant."[80]

---

77. Edwards speaks little about "adoption," but when he does it is always in the context of justification. Being "married" into covenant fellowship with the triune family and being "adopted" into sonship are both parallel and apt analogies that bring together the concepts of the legal and the familial, both being loving relationships based on legally binding realities. Edwards preferred metaphor of "marriage" seems to overshadow "adoption," even though both are present in Edwards's writings, particularly his sermons regarding the peace we have with the Father through adoption. Examples are Edwards, "Misc. 1353," *WJE* 20:492 ("And the saints were made partakers of the same benefits, the same effectual calling by the Spirit of God, the same justification, adoption and sanctification, and obtained the same eternal glory in heaven."), and Edwards, "The Peace Which Christ Gives His True Followers," *WJE* 25:542 ("This Christ has procured for his followers and laid a foundation for their enjoyment of, in that he has procured for them the other two, viz.: peace with God, and one with another. He has procured for them peace and reconciliation with God, and his favor and friendship, in that he satisfied for their sins, and laid a foundation for the perfect removal of the guilt of sin, and the forgiveness of all their trespasses, and wrought out for them a perfect and glorious righteousness, most acceptable to God and sufficient to recommend them to God's full acceptance and to the adoption of children, and to the eternal fruits of his fatherly kindness.").

78. Edwards, "Misc. 617," *WJE* 18:149.

79. Edwards, "Misc. 617," *WJE* 18:149.

80. Edwards, "Misc. 1062," *WJE* 20:443.

There are also promises that are the same in both covenants. "The promises of a new heart, and a right spirit, and of writing God's law on our heart, etc."[81] are in different respects promises of both covenants.

> These promises, as they respect the first regeneration, belong to God's covenant with his Son. As they respect what is done in the work of sanctification after conversion, they belong also to Christ's covenant with his people. As they denote the public prosperity and glory of the church, they likewise belong to both covenants. For the conversion of sinners to Christ is one thing wherein the church's glory consists, and what every saint looks upon as part of his prosperity, and so is part of that prosperity that Christ has promised to his people for their comfort.[82]

Both covenants come by means of revelation and for consolation and elect believers are concerned in both. They are concerned in the Covenant of Redemption, not as a sole covenant party but only as they are "in Christ" or "as being parts of Christ" with Christ acting as a "public person." He is the "surety" of the covenant taking over the obligations of the Covenant of Works on behalf of the elect.

Edwards can say that in the Covenant of Redemption believers are "one of the parties contracting," but only in terms of the promises involved in the covenant in the way Christ's bride (the Church) is both rewarded and promised in the Father's covenant with his Son. In terms of the Covenant of Grace as the marriage covenant, believers "are concerned as being distinctly" by themselves "one of the parties contracting... The promises of the former of these covenants being revealed, do become the promises of the Father to believers. These are the promises that are given us in Christ; that is, they are promises made to us by the Father as being in Christ, being parts of Christ and so having a right to the same blessing that are promised to Christ himself, our head."[83] For Edwards, this was a comforting doctrine of assurance that he used in many of his sermons. For instance, in his sermon on Heb 13:8 he preaches that the Covenant of Grace "is only that covenant of redemption partly revealed to mankind for their encouragement, faith, and comfort." He then adds that Christ "will never depart from the covenant of grace; for all that was promised to men in the covenant of grace, was agreed on between the Father and

---

81. Edwards, "Misc. 617," *WJE* 18:150.
82. Edwards, "Misc. 617," *WJE* 18:150.
83. Edwards, "Misc. 617," *WJE* 18:150.

the Son in the covenant of redemption."[84] The covenant "being revealed" is the historic progressive revelation of the Covenant of Redemption. The promises and blessings of the Father to believers in Christ come by way of the marriage covenant whereby believers are united in Christ and the Father's promises to both him and his bride.

Edwards's way of formulating these covenant distinctions builds an impenetrable wall between law and gospel. The entire obligation of covenant fulfillment for eternal life comes only through Christ's obedience. The condition of entering into the marriage covenant is not a condition of obedience to the "eternal rule of righteousness which is never abrogated," but a consent to and uniting with (faith) Christ as surety. According to Edwards, even this faith (in regeneration, conversion, etc.), as the gift of the Holy Spirit, is given as part of the promises to Christ for his covenant obedience. Any meritorious virtue on the part of the believer's faith is categorically ruled-out on the basis of this covenant relationship.

That God both establishes the conditions and then fulfills them, that the conditions of one covenant are the promises of the other, are reflected in Augustine's profound statement: "Let God give what he commands, and command what he will."[85] It is also reflected in Calvin's exegetical study of how the "three classes of precepts" show that without grace we can do nothing:

> Oftentimes both in the Law and in the Prophets the Lord commands us to be converted to him [Joel 2:12; Ezek. 18:30–32; Hos. 14:2 f.]. On the other hand, the prophet answers: "Convert me, O Lord, and I will be converted . . . for after thou didst convert me I repented," etc. [Jer. 31:18–19, Vg.]. He bids us circumcise the foreskin of our heart [Deut. 10:16; cf. Jer. 4:4]. But through Moses he declares that this circumcision is done by His own hand [Deut. 30:6]. In some places he requires newness of heart [Ezek. 18:31], but elsewhere he testifies that it is given by him [Ezek. 11:19; 36:26]. "But what God promises," as Augustine says, "we ourselves do not do through choice of nature; but he himself does through grace." This observation he lists in fifth place among the rules of Tychonius: we must distinguish carefully between the law and the promises, or between the commandments and grace. Now away with those who infer from the precepts that man is perhaps capable of obedience, in

---

84. Edwards, *Sermons of Jonathan Edwards*, 248; also Edwards, *JE* 2:950.
85. Augustine, "Confessions," *NPNF* 1/1:153.

order to destroy God's grace through which the commandments themselves are fulfilled.[86]

The distinction between the law and promises, or law and gospel, in Augustine and Calvin finds systematic expression in the covenant theology of Edwards. The righteousness of Christ, as the infinite satisfaction of God's eternal and unalterable rule of righteousness, becomes the righteousness of the believer through covenant union.[87]

So great is the redemption obtained through the infinite merit of Christ that Edwards dares to assert that the rewards of the Covenant of Grace are infinitely better than those promised to Adam. In his *Controversies Notebook* section on justification, Edwards argues for the greater righteousness believers obtained through grace in Christ than they would have obtained by virtue of their own righteousness: "And besides, divine holiness is exhibited to us in the gospel salvation in a far more endearing light than in the law; God's moral excellency therein so much appears in the riches of his grace towards us. That righteousness which is set forth as our great example, which is infinitely more transcendent, wonderful and amiable than would have been the righteousness of the law performed by us in our own names, is the righteousness by which we are saved."[88] Contrary to the majority of Reformed writers,[89] Edwards did not think

---

86. Calvin, *Institutes*, 2:325.

87. For an extended and comprehensive study of Edwards on this theme that corroborates many of the conclusions of this chapter, see Biehl, *The Infinite Merit*.

88. Edwards, "'Controversies' Notebook: Justification," *WJE* 21:353.

89. Turretin frames the question, "Whether Adam had the promise of eternal and heavenly life so that (his course of obedience being finished) he would have been carried to heaven." Turretin, *Institutes* 1:583. He claims his was "the received opinion among the orthodox...that the promise given to Adam was not only of a happy life to be continued in paradise, but of a heavenly and eternal life . . . " He argues that the promises of God are not "regulated according to the proportion of the merit. On the contrary, they depend upon God's will and goodness (*avoluntate bonitate Dei*)." Turretin, *Institutes* 1:583; cf. 1:578. Rowland Ward maintains that there was no consensus regarding the nature of life promised to Adam at the time of the Westminster Assembly in 1647. Ward, *God and Adam*, 108. Thomas Boston, Thomas Ridgley (1667–1734), and John Brown (1722–1787) concur with Turretin, along with Heinrich Heppe who characterized the Reformed position as being a consensus on this question. See Boston, *Complete Works*, 8:17; Ridgley, *Body of Divinity*, 2:85; Brown, *Compendious View*, 200; Heppe, *Reformed Dogmatics*, 294–95. Heppe cites Heidegger as well as Canon VIII of the *Formula Consensus Helvetica* to support his position. John Gill (1697–1771) and Thomas Goodwin (1600–1680) both agreed with Edwards as the minority opinion. Gill, *Complete Body*, 222, and Goodwin, *Works*, 7:49. Goodwin says, "the reward, the

that Adam was promised a heavenly reward apart from eternal happiness in this "earthly" life. "There is not a word tending to lead Adam to a thought of another unseen world. And if God did not by anything he said lead him to expect it, then it is certain that he did not promise it and make it over to him by covenant." The believer's union with Christ brings about a new and more glorious "spiritual" existence.

> The first Adam was earthy and of the earth in respect to the place of the habitation of his person, in the world he was of and belonged to, as well as in the habitation of his soul, or the body that [he] dwelt in; and in both we should have been conformed to him. And so in both Christ's posterity are conformed to him. He is from heaven and is heavenly in both these respects. He dwells in an heavenly body, and heaven is his proper country and dwelling place; and in both these respects his posterity shall be conformed to him. They shall have spiritual heavenly bodies, and shall dwell in heaven; and they would have had neither of these had it not been for the redemption of Jesus Christ. New bodies and the new world are both of them [to] be by the redemption of Jesus Christ (see No. 806). The new sort of bodies which the saints will have, viz. their spiritual and heavenly bodies, whereby they are fitted to dwell in heaven, which they will have by the resurrection or that change that passed on the bodies of the living, this change of the body shall be only by the second Adam in distinction from the first, as the Apostle is very express and full, 1 Corinthians 15:22, and 1 Corinthians 15:44–52. But if Adam and his posterity would have been translated to heaven for his perfect obedience, then doubtless their natural bodies must have passed under this change, and made spiritual and heavenly: for as the Apostle says, 1 Corinthians 15:50, "Flesh and blood shall not inherit the kingdom of God"; and then this would have been by the first Adam, which is quite contrary to the doctrine of the Apostle. And the new world, or the new heavens and new earth, is as much by the redemption of Jesus Christ as the new body (see No. 806). But this—so far as a place of habitation is meant—is heaven. This world don't pass away but by a dissolution occasioned by the fall. And therefore, mankind would not have ascended and left this world, for if they had so done, this world would have passed away without a

---

promised life and happiness that he should have had for doing and obeying, was but the continuance of the same happy life which he enjoyed in paradise, together with God's favour towards him ... not the translating him, in the end, unto that spiritual life in heaven, which the angels have, and which the saints shall have."

fall. One reason why heaven is bestowed is because this world is ruined by the fall, and is to be destroyed; therefore, Christ will come and take away his elect to another world, a better world than this is, or ever was.[90]

Edwards's point is that the happiness secured by Christ's obedience and righteousness for the elect is "vastly HIGHER and more glorious [Edwards's emphasis]" than that which Adam would have obtained, and so much so that the new heavens and new earth are required for such enjoyment, the old heavens and earth having passed away. Heaven is not one of the promises of the first covenant but is of the second.

Conclusion

Edwards's view of the Covenant of Grace focuses on the covenant parties and conditions. Edwards discusses the single Covenant of Grace in two senses, which he uses interchangeably throughout his writings. The Covenant of Grace is the revelation and outworking of the eternal Covenant of Redemption in history. It is also the marriage covenant between Christ and believers. The distinguishing feature is the two parties involved in the covenant. The parties of the Covenant of Redemption are the Father and Son. The elect have an interest in this covenant only in that they are included as the Son's "mystical body." Christ is the surety, representative, or mediator of the elect. The elect are not specific parties to the covenant in any other way than through Christ. Elect believers are, however, direct parties in the marriage covenant with Christ. It is by way of this covenant that the promises and blessings achieved through Christ's obedience to the covenant demands are possessed by believers. Edwards can then discuss the covenants as being both conditional and unconditional. In terms of the Covenant of Redemption and promises given to believers in Christ as their mediator and representative, salvation is unconditional. In terms of the marriage covenant it is conditional. Yet even the conditions of the marriage covenant are given "unconditionally" in the promises to Christ in the Covenant of Redemption. God's sovereignty in election and covenant salvation are not antithetical. God's sovereignty in election is the ground of his covenants, and his covenants are the means to accomplish his sovereign purposes in election.

---

90. Edwards, "Misc. 809," *WJE* 18:514–15.

I have argued that Edwards's formulation was unique but not inconsistent with Reformed orthodoxy. He saw dangers in the implications of not "rightly" distinguishing the covenants with regards to the parties involved, particularly the twin errors of Arminianism and neonomianism. According to Edwards, God makes no covenant directly with postlapsarian man in any other way than through a mediator. Formulations of the Covenant of Grace as between "God and man" confuse the issue, leading to a view of faith as a virtue or "work," blurring the distinction between law and gospel. I argue that Edwards's (re)formulation of the nature of the Covenant of Grace built an impenetrable wall between law and gospel. Justification comes only by way of the obedience of Christ in the Covenant of Redemption. The obedience of believers, even the obedience of faith, does not and cannot justify. To be "justified by faith" is only shorthand for justification through Christ's obedience. Because faith is the uniting to Christ and all his benefits in the marriage covenant (Covenant of Grace) it has no justifying virtue of its own. It has no covenant reference to fulfilling the obligations of the Covenant of Works, the only covenant that God gave to man directly for obtaining eternal life. Interpreting and understanding Edwards's views on the relationship between faith and obedience in justification cannot ignore this central concept.

In the following chapter I will explore Edwards's view of the Mosaic covenant, a topic that has been the source of much discussion and debate within Reformed theology. How Edwards views the Mosaic covenant in relationship to the Covenant of Works and grace in the Christian Old Testament not only contributes to understanding Edwards's overall covenant theology, but also provides insight into his theology of the nature of faith and works. It is in this context that the law-gospel distinction is most clearly revealed.

TABLE 4.1. The Structure of Jonathan Edwards's Covenant Theology

	Covenant of Works	Covenant of Redemption	Covenant of Grace
Parties	God and Adam	God the Father and the Son, along with the Son's "mystical body" (i.e., elect believers)	Christ and elect believers
Conditions	Adam's obedience (works)	The Son's obedience (to the Covenant of Works)	Closing with Christ in faith
Promises	Eternal life	The Holy Spirit, encompassing for the church (i.e., elect believers): Regeneration Giving of faith Justification Sanctification Perseverance	The incarnation, death, and sufferings of Christ Enjoyment of Christ and communion with him in the benefits he himself has obtained by his Father

5

Jonathan Edwards on the Mosaic Covenant

Introduction

THE RELATIONSHIP BETWEEN THE law and ordinances delivered to Israel at Mt. Sinai, referred to as the Mosaic covenant, and the Covenant of Grace in redemptive history has been a focus of discussion and debate among theologians throughout the Christian era. Not only is it important for understanding the Christian relationship between the Old and New Testaments but is also central for developing a coherent biblical theology of the role of works in the Christian life. Reformed covenant theology provides a powerful and theologically rich framework for navigating the biblical landscape, and yet it has also been the source of countless controversies and disputes. Referring to the Mosaic law and its place within a comprehensive covenant theology, Anthony Burgess famously remarked that, "I do not find in any point of Divinity, learned men so confused and perplexed (being like Abraham's Ram, hung in a bush of briars and brambles by the head) as here."[1]

In this chapter I will present Edwards's view of the role of the Mosaic covenant and the law in redemptive history. As with the previous chapters on the Covenants of Redemption, Works, and Grace, I will begin with a brief overview of the subject as found in historic Reformed theology to provide a context for Edwards's own views and to place him within the context and continuity of the Reformed tradition as a whole. At the end of the chapter I will show how Edwards viewed the relationship between faith and obedience to the law in the context of the Mosaic covenant. This

---

1. Burgess, *Vindiciae Legis*, 229.

will serve as a prelude to the following chapter on Edwards's theology of faith and works in justification.

Interpretations of the role of the Mosaic covenant in the context of a comprehensive biblical theology are fraught with a multitude of nuances, definitions, seeming contradictions, and paradoxes. Charting a coherent course through various interpretations can be challenging. In order to provide a more systematic understanding of how Reformed theologians have addressed various concerns related to the Mosaic covenant within covenant theology, I will use a helpful taxonomy of Brenton Ferry, taken from a recent collection of essays addressing different aspects of the role of works and grace in the Mosaic covenant.[2]

The Mosaic Covenant in Reformed Theology

From the inception of the early Christian church, the question of how the Old Testament relates to the New Testament was of utmost importance. In the New Testament, the question was part of Christ's revelation of his person and work after his resurrection (Luke 24:44–47) and was approached in the New Testament writings from the perspective of evangelism (Acts 8:30), apologetics (Rom 3:9), as a pastoral warning (Rom 9:6), and as central to the Christian life (Rom 4 and 1 Cor 10).[3] The question was a part of the early Church's polemical debates, including Irenaeus's polemics against Marcion's denial of the unity of the two testaments, Justin Martyr's defense against the rejection of the New Testament by Trypho, and Augustine's arguments against the rejection of the Old Testament by Faustus.[4]

During the seventeenth century in England, in the century preceding Edwards, the role of the Mosaic covenant was an important point of discussion and debate. Three major theological controversies catalyzed this reflection and discussion on the role of the Mosaic law: Amyraldianism, Arminianism, and antinomianism. The Arminian and antinomian controversies centered on the place of the law in the Christian life. Van Dixhoorn characterizes these debates as ranging between the "far left," in which antinomians opposed the need to even confess sin, to the "far

---

2. Ferry, "Works," 76–108.
3. Ferry, "Works," 76–77.
4. Irenaeus, "Against Heresies," *ANF* 1:462–525; Martyr, *"Dialogue," ANF* 1:199–208; Augustine, "Reply to Faustus," *NPNF* 1/4: 161–75.

right" Saturday-Sabbatarian's who argued for the necessity of circumcision, observation of the Mosaic law, including sacrifices, the rebuilding of the temple at Jerusalem, and the possession of the land of Canaan.[5]

Debates on the relationship between the Testaments of Christian Scripture, and particularly on the role of the Mosaic law under the "old dispensation," have continued to the present day. Within Reformed theology, an intramural discussion has recently ensued in this regard, centering on the law-gospel antithesis which, according to Mark Karlberg, is resulting in a "radical reinterpretation of Reformation theology."[6] Of central concern in these debates is the interpretation of the Mosaic covenant, chiefly on whether the Mosaic covenant is to be viewed in some sense as a covenant or works or not and, if it is, how it is related to the Covenant of Grace. The particulars of these debates, both within and beyond Reformed confessional orthodoxy, is not of immediate concern in this chapter. However, the study of Edwards's views on this topic is germane to current discussions by providing historical arguments of continuity and discontinuity within the Reformed tradition. In recent surveys of the historical development of Reformed theology with respect to the Mosaic dispensation in relation to the Covenant of Grace, Edwards is conspicuously absent.[7] Given his key historic position between the culmination of late protestant orthodoxy and the rising ascendency of Enlightenment modernity's assaults on classic Christian confessional doctrines, Edwards's own contribution to this historic and ongoing discussion is important and can provide a vital link for assessing the continuities and discontinuities of Reformed thought between the *Westminster Standards* in England and nineteenth-century American Presbyterianism.[8]

Brenton Ferry, in his chapter in *The Law is Not of Faith: Essays on Works and Grace in the Mosaic Covenant*, provides a helpful and

5. Dixhoorn, "Reforming the Reformation," 3.1.90r.

6. Karlberg, "Reformed Interpretation," 3. See also Karlberg, "Mosaic Covenant."

7. For instance, Karlberg's survey moves directly from the *Westminster Standards* to Robert L. Dabney and the Princetonian Hodges.

8. "Late orthodoxy" is classified by Muller as that period, roughly after 1725, as "theologies clinging to the definitions of orthodoxy and standing in the tradition of the confessional dogmatics of the high orthodox era, but no longer as closely bound by the confessions of the church. In some of its forms, late orthodoxy was increasingly influenced by various schools of rationalist philosophy—in others it moved away from overt recourse to philosophical categories. In all forms, it was beset by the tides of historical critical exegesis." Muller, *Post-Reformation Reformed Dogmatics*, 1:82.

systematic taxonomy of views in Reformed thought on the relationship between the Old and New Testament and the role of the Mosaic covenant.[9] Ferry distinguishes three distinct sets of questions or issues that have focused discussion in this area. First is the question of the relationship of the Mosaic covenant to the New Covenant. This is a "forward looking" approach which he distinguishes as the question of "discontinuity" or "antithesis." Second is the question of the relationship of the Mosaic covenant to the original Covenant of Works with Adam. This is a "backward looking" approach that involves the question of whether the Mosaic covenant was a "republication" of the Covenant of Works and, if so, in what sense. Third is the question of the relationship of the Mosaic covenant to the Covenant of Grace. In the remainder of this section I will summarize Ferry's taxonomy as it applies to Reformed covenant theology as a helpful way to understand and contextualize Edwards's own position as taken from his writings.

The Question of Antithesis

There are two seemingly competing views of covenant transition between the Old and New Testaments. This transition is sometimes couched in terms of a law-gospel contrast. John 1:17 provides the exegetical context: "The law was given through Moses; grace and truth came through Jesus Christ" (ESV). This verse seems to imply that the redemptive-historical transition from Moses to Christ reflected the systematic-theological law-gospel distinction. In contrast, salvation has always been understood as a matter of grace received through faith. How these seemingly competing perspectives can both be true is what Ferry refers to as the "problem of antithesis."[10] The *Westminster Confession* illustrates this problem of antithesis in chapter VII when it speaks of the one Covenant of Grace administered diachronically across periods distinguished by law and gospel: "This Covenant [of Grace] was differently administered in the time of the Law, and the time of the Gospel."[11] The problem of antithesis is how to account for law-gospel contrast between Moses and Christ, while at the same time preserving the continuity of the Covenant of Grace.[12] Ferry

---

9. Ferry, "Works," 76–108.
10. Ferry, "Works," 81.
11. WCF 7.5.
12. Murray holds the view that "covenant" and "works" are *antithetical* concepts.

categorizes eight general approaches used by Reformed theologians to account for this "antithesis."[13]

Substance and Accidents

The first approach uses the categories of substance and accidents, most evident in David Dickson's *Therapeutica Sacra* (1664). In this approach the Mosaic covenant is described as having two levels: an essential level (substance) and an administrative level (accidents). Discontinuities between the Old (Mosaic) and New Covenant is only at the level of the administrative. Ferry cites John Owen as representing the contrary position. Owen argues that such an "antithetical discontinuity" requires the Mosaic covenant to be "extracted" from the stream of the Covenant of Grace and conceived as a separate covenant altogether.[14]

Ceremonial, Civil, and Moral Law

A second means of addressing the "antithesis" question was in the common Reformed distinction between the ceremonial, civil, and moral laws given at Mt. Sinai. The ceremonial, as typical of Christ's atoning sacrifice, and the civil, as only pertaining to the nation of Israel, were abrogated with the coming of Christ, thus accounting for the discontinuity. The moral law, as an eternal rule for the Christian life, was not abrogated, thus accounting for the continuity.

Different Emphases

A further way to navigate the question was to view the antithesis in terms of different emphases. In the Old Covenant the "law" aspect was emphasized to a greater degree in its "legal, discontinuous accidentals."

Karlberg calls this "a novel proposal in the history of federalism." Karlberg, "Reformed Interpretation," 49. There is no "problem of antithesis for Murray" in that the Mosaic covenant was exclusively a covenant of grace without any works principle. See, for example, Murray, "The Adamic Administration," 50.

13. With regards to terminology, the "Old Covenant" in Ferry's chapter is what I generally refer to as the Mosaic dispensation of the Covenant of Grace. The "New Covenant" is the Covenant of Grace in the gospel era of the New Testament.

14. Owen, *Hebrews*, 6:74.

In the New Covenant the gospel overshadows the law. The "free and gracious character" of the Mosaic covenant is "somewhat eclipsed by all kinds of external ceremonies and forms which, in connection with the theocratic life of Israel, placed the demands of the law prominently in the foreground."[15] This is illustrated in the *Westminster Confession*: "Under the new testament, the liberty of Christians is further enlarged, in their freedom from the yoke of the ceremonial law, to which the Jewish church was subjected."[16] The emphasis could also be expressed in terms of the relative difference in the activity of the Holy Spirit in the Old Covenant "and in greater boldness of access to the throne of grace, and in fuller communications of the free Spirit of God, than believers, under the Law, did ordinarily partake of."[17]

National Covenant

The presence of a national principle of works inheritance under the Mosaic covenant that only pertained to the nation of Israel and the earthly inheritance of Canaan is another way of accounting for discontinuity. Different Reformed theologians held different opinions as to whether this was or was not a separate national covenant. For instance, Louis Berkhof and Charles Hodge did not view it as a separate covenant.[18] Those who held to the view that it was indeed a separate covenant, neither of works or grace, differed on whether it promised spiritual blessings along with the earthly blessings, e.g., Witsius,[19] or a covenant of merely external and carnal affairs, e.g., Robert Bolton (1572–1631) and John Owen.[20]

Historical Relative Contrast

Vos appeals to the perspective of redemptive history, whereby the Apostle Paul in the New Testament (Gal 3:23, 3:25) makes "a historically

---

15. Berkhof, *Systematic Theology*, 297–98. See also John Ball's comment: "Most Divines hold the old and new Covenants to be one in substance and kind, to differ only in degree." Ball, *Treatise of the Covenant*, 95.
16. *WCF* 20.1.
17. *WCF* 20.1.
18. Berkhof, *Systematic Theology*, 297–99; Hodge, *Systematic Theology*, 2:375.
19. Witsius, *Economy of the Covenants*, 2:186.
20. Ferry, "Works," 86–87. Cf. Bolton, *True Bounds*, 99; Owen, *Hebrews*, 6:90.

relative contrast in absolute terms."[21] The same perspective is also present in Hodge's *Systematic Theology*: "When viewed in relation to the state of the Church after the advent, it [the Mosaic covenant] is declared to be obsolete. It is represented as a lifeless husk from which the living kernel and germ have been extracted, a body from which the soul has departed."[22] This does not mean that the Old Covenant was purely a legal dispensation of works-righteousness devoid of the grace of the gospel. Geerhardus Vos and Charles Hodge merely take the Apostle Paul's statements to be exaggerating the "obedience" aspects of the Old Covenant from the perspective of the "grace" of the new.

Principle of Abstraction

The law in the Old Covenant can also be viewed from an "absolute perspective" in terms of a law-gospel antithesis when it is "abstracted and compared" to the New Covenant. Ferry terms this the "principle of abstraction" and cites its appropriation by John Murray concerning Paul's use of Lev 18:5 in Rom 10.[23] According to Murray, in the original setting of Lev 18:5 "it does not appear to have any reference to legal righteousness as opposed to that of grace." In Rom 10 the Apostle Paul "appropriates" the verse "as one suited to express the principle of law righteousness."[24]

Promise-Fulfilment

Ferry also presents what he calls the "softer contrast" approach. He cites Dabney and Murray as representative examples who proposed a promise-fulfilment paradigm in place of a law-gospel paradigm (noting the theme of promise-fulfillment was not absent from other approaches).[25] According to Murray, the covenant "is not contrasted with the old because the old has law and the new does not. The superiority of the new does not consist in the abrogation of that law but in its being brought into . . . more

---

21. Ferry, "Works," 87. Cf. Vos, *Biblical Theology*, 128–29.
22. Hodge, *Systematic Theology*, 2:376.
23. Ferry, "Works," 87–88.
24. Murray, *Epistle to the Romans*, 2:51.
25. Ferry, "Works," 88–89. See also Dabney, *Systematic Theology*, 458–59; Murray, *Covenant of Grace*, 29.

effective fulfillment in us." The New Covenant is the "richest and fullest expression" of the Covenant of Grace.[26]

Misinterpretation

Connected with a "softer contrast" approach is the misinterpretation theory. According to this theory, the Apostle Paul is not contrasting the Old and New Covenants in terms of law and gospel but contrasting the New Covenant with its legalistic misinterpretation. In other words, the Apostle Paul is in polemic with the Pharisees and their legalism rather than what the Old and New Covenants actually claimed. Ferry specifically cites Dabney as a proponent of this *argumentum ad hominem* approach. Norman Shepherd also supports this approach when he says, "Paul uses an *ad hominem* argument by quoting Scriptures according to the sense in which his opponents understood it."[27] Like the promise-fulfillment paradigm, Reformed writers who maintain the systematic distinction of law-gospel, including Berkhof, Calvin, Turretin, and Witsius,[28] do not deny a "misinterpretation" element in their approach to Paul's statements. The difference is that they do not elevate it to systematic status to explain away the antithesis between the Old and New Covenants.

The Principle of Republication

The second major question in Ferry's taxonomy involves the relationship of the Mosaic covenant to the Covenant of Works. The Reformed tradition appreciated a connection between the Covenant of Works and the Mosaic covenant in that they are somehow similar, or that one explains the other.[29] Reformed writers evidence a multitude of ways to express this

---

26. Murray, *Covenant of Grace*, 29.

27. Ferry, "Works," 89–90. See also Dabney, *Systematic Theology*, 458; Shepherd, *Call of Grace*, 37.

28. Berkhof, *Systematic Theology*, 297, 300; Calvin, *Institutes*, 1:456; Turretin, *Institutes*, 2:234, 267–68; and Witsius, *Economy of the Covenants*, 2:184–85.

29. Beginning with Murray, this is not universally the case. Murray did not view the old dispensation as anything other than the Covenant of Grace and "distinctly redemptive in character." Neither did he hold to the "Adamic administration" as one characterized by a Covenant of Works (although he does speak of it in terms of covenant). Because there was no "Covenant of Works," there can be no "republication." Murray claims, "The view that in the Mosaic covenant there was a repetition of the

relationship. The common exegetical touchstone is Lev 18:5 ("Do this and live"), where Moses is talking about the Mosaic covenant, and the Apostle Paul's comments in Gal 3:12 and Rom 10:5. According to Karlberg, "The Mosaic Covenant is to be viewed in some sense as a Covenant of Works." The discussion under this category involves the questions, "In what sense is the Mosaic covenant a Covenant of Works?" and, "What is the nature of the continuity between them?"

Material Republication

Ferry defines what is meant by "republication" under two headings: material republication (as the moral law) and formal republication (as a Covenant of Works). Almost all reformed writers that reject a formal republication accept some form of material republication. Conversely, most Reformed writers who hold to a formal republication also include a material republication aspect as well. The two are not mutually exclusive. Material republication recognizes in the Mosaic covenant the precepts of the law as a "rule of life," a moral law that is in continuity with the prelapsarian covenant. Ferry characterizes this when he says, "It extracts any sense of a covenant function or intent from the likeness between Adam and Moses, admitting only a moral continuity."[30] This moral continuity is not restricted to the Mosaic dispensation but applies to "every historical dispensation" from Adam to the Parousia.

Formal Republication

Conversely, formal republication means that the Mosaic dispensation was a republication of the Covenant of Works as a rule and a covenant.

---

so-called covenant of works, current among covenant theologians, is a grave misconception and involves an erroneous construction of the Mosaic covenant, as well as fails to assess the uniqueness of the Adamic administration. The Mosaic covenant was distinctly redemptive in character and was continuous with and extensive of the Abrahamic covenants." Murray, "Adamic Administration," 50. With regards to Murray's last point, that the Mosaic covenant was continuous with and extensive of the Abrahamic covenants, all Reformed covenant theologians (including Edwards) would agree. The substance of the Covenant of Grace (which included the Mosaic covenant) remains the same. The question is how to explain the peculiar law-function in the Mosaic dispensation.

30. Ferry, "Works," 92.

This is usually attended with the important qualification that the Mosaic law, as a republication of the Covenant of Works, was never intended as a means of justification or a viable alternative to the Covenant of Grace. The Mosaic law was more than merely the moral law *redivivus*, yet not the Covenant of Works fully re-established. Still, it was still in the "form" of the Covenant of Works properly speaking. How it takes this "form" is expressed in different ways in Reformed writings.

Relative to Grace

One way this is expressed is represented by the *Westminster Larger Catechism* Q.96 and Q.97. The Mosaic covenant is a Covenant of Works relative to the state of the individual, whether in the state of grace or not. To those in the state of grace the Mosaic covenant is a form of the Covenant of Grace, to those outside the state of grace it is in the form of the Covenant of Works. *Westminster Larger Catechism* Q.96 explains how the law functions as a Covenant of Works relative to the unregenerate: "Question 96: What particular use is there of the moral law to unregenerate men? Answer: The moral law is of use to unregenerate men, to awaken their consciences to flee from wrath to come, and to drive them to Christ; or, upon their continuance in the estate and way of sin, to leave them inexcusable, and under the curse thereof."[31] Relative to the regenerate, the law no longer functions as a Covenant of Works. They are neither justified nor condemned by it:

> Question 97: What special use is there of the moral law to the regenerate? Answer: Although they that are regenerate, and believe in Christ, be delivered from the moral law as a Covenant of Works, so as thereby they are neither justified nor condemned; yet, besides the general uses thereof common to them with all men, it is of special use, to show them: How much they are bound to Christ for his fulfilling it, and enduring the curse thereof in their stead, and for their good; and thereby to provoke them to more thankfulness, and to express the same in their greater care to conform themselves thereunto as the rule of their obedience.[32]

---

31. *WLC*, Q. 96.
32. *WLC*, Q. 97.

The law is further described "as a rule of their obedience" or as a moral guide that is common to all. The law has a "two-fold servitude," one that condemns those who seek to establish their own righteousness and another as a "tutor to Christ." It also serves as a rule for godly living for those who trust exclusively in Christ.[33] The *Westminster Larger Catechism* exhibits elements of both material and formal republication.

Pedagogical

The Mosaic covenant can serve a pedagogical function. In this expression of the formal principle the Mosaic covenant serves to teach the Israelites at Sinai about the Covenant of Works, specifically as a trial of their obedience to show how impossible it is to fulfill. It does not serve strictly as a covenant for them to fulfill. While the law serves to teach the Covenant of Works directly (albeit in a negative way), it also points towards the Covenant of Grace indirectly. The function is taken from Gal 3:24: "The Law has become our tutor to lead us to Christ" (NASB). The Greek word translated as "tutor," *paidagōgos*, is also translated as "schoolmaster" (KJV and the GB).

Hypothetical Covenant

In addition to the pedagogical function (and in many instances complementing it), some Reformed divines proposed that the Covenant of Works is "hypothetically" republished.[34] Ball explains how this clarifies the administrative differences between the Old and New Testaments: "The old testament doth promise life eternall plainly under the condition of orall obedience perfect, that is under condition altogether impossible, together with an heavy burden of legal rites and a yoke of most strict pollicie, but covertly under the condition of repentance and faith."[35]

---

33. Ball, *Treatise of the Covenant*, 141–42, 135.

34. Ferry helpfully distinguishes the use of the term "hypothetical" in this context from the way it is used by Obadiah Sedgwick. Sedgwick speaks of absolute covenants and hypothetical covenants. The former are monergistic, unconditional covenants, which require no reciprocal response from man (the covenant with Noah is an example). The latter is a conditional covenant, requiring a response from man, either of works or faith. Ferry, "Works," 95 n. 77.

35. Ball, *Treatise on the Covenant*, 96. See also Vos, "Doctrine of the Covenant," 254–55.

While the Covenant of Works as a "hypothetical" offer of salvation is peculiar to the Old Testament and is not found in the New Testament,[36] it does reflect a specific use of the law, the so-called "second use of the law."[37] However, this "second use of the law" in Reformed writings is meant to convey what is continuous about the moral law in every age, not what is distinctive and unique about the Mosaic, legal economy.

Typological

The works principle can also be explained in a typological fashion, as a figure, type, or foreshadowing of Jesus, born under the law to fulfill the law by his active righteousness on behalf of sinners. God's covenant with Israel was really placed on Christ. Bolton explains this as one of the positions held by divines of his day: "Another interpretation is this: that 'Do this and live', though it was spoken to the people of Israel in person, did not terminate with them, but through them was spoken to Christ, who has fulfilled all righteousness for us, and purchased life by His own obedience."[38] Just as the sacrificial system foreshadowed Christ's passive obedience in suffering the curse of the law, the works principle ("Do this and live") foreshadowed his active, perfect, and complete obedience in keeping the precepts of the whole law (the Covenant of Works). Ferry cites Vos and Kline as modern examples of the use of this approach.[39]

---

36. It is sometimes claimed that this "hypothetical covenant" is evident in the response of Christ to the question of the rich young ruler (Luke 18:18–30, also in Matt 19:16–30 and Mark 10:17–31) where Christ responds with the impossible offer of salvation by works to humble him. The difference, according to Ferry, is that the Old Covenant hypothetical offer was an actual accessory of the covenant administration. See John Calvin's and Thomas Boston's commentary on this passage. Calvin, *Commentaries*, 16:392–95, and Fisher, *Marrow of Modern Divinity*, 205.

37. The pedagogical use of the law is referred to as the *usus spiritualis* or *theologicus* (the theological use of the law). Reformed theologians distinguish two other uses, the *tertius usus legis* (third use of the law) or *usus in renatis*. Another use of the law, the civil or political, is characterized as a guide to society in promoting civic righteousness and, as such, belongs to God's general revelation. Berkhof, *Systematic Theology*, 614.

38. Bolton, *True Bounds*, 105.

39. Ferry, "Works," 97. Cf. Vos, *Biblical Theology*, 127; Kline, *Treaty*, 65, 124–25.

Complex Formal

Thomas Boston is presented by Ferry as representing what he terms the "complex, formal republication" approach. Boston proposes a double republication view whereby the Covenant of Works and the Covenant of Grace were republished simultaneously at Mt. Sinai: "I conceive the two covenants to have been both delivered on Mount Sinai to the Israelites. First, the Covenant of Grace made with Abraham . . . Secondly, the Covenant of Works made with Adam."[40] The Decalogue was not "simply" a republication of the Covenant of Works, but a mixed, complex republication of the Covenant of Works and Grace simultaneously.

Ferry concludes that the Reformed tradition recognized a "material and/or a formal" relationship of the Mosaic covenant to the Covenant of Works. It was a republication "in some sense." In terms of a material relationship, the precepts are the same. As formal the covenant is "revived" but modified in function as subservient to the Covenant of Grace. It functions to this effect by several non-exclusive and frequently overlapping and complimentary means, including "to reveal those who are in Adam (the relative principle), to teach them about their moral ineptitude (the pedagogical principle), by presenting an impossible offer of salvation by works (the hypothetical principle), which only Christ has fulfilled (the typological principle), coupled with the relief and offer of grace and forgiveness by Christ's mediation (the complex principle)."[41] All these views appear complementary, but according to Ferry's historical review few Reformed theologians have attempted to incorporate all of these principles into a single position. As I turn to Edwards's complex view later in this chapter, I will demonstrate that Edwards incorporates, at least to some extent, each of these principles in his writings.

The Mosaic Covenant and the Covenant of Grace

A third distinct question is how the Mosaic covenant is related to the Covenant of Grace. Ferry identifies two general categories in his typology: the Mosaic covenant as an organically integrated administrative part

---

40. Boston, "Marrow," 197.
41. Ferry, "Works," 98.

of the Covenant of Grace or is a separate and distinct covenant which nevertheless serves the purposes of the Covenant of Grace.[42]

Different Administrations

The majority position in the seventeenth century among Reformed writers appears to be the administrative view.[43] This position recognizes the differences between the Old and New Covenants as administrative rather than substantive, differing only in "accidentals" and administration. In substance there was only the single Covenant of Grace (in the postlapsarian period). This position is not incompatible, however, with the Mosaic law being a republication of the Covenant of Works "in some sense," as some held.[44]

Separate and Distinct

The minority position held that the Mosaic covenant was organically distinct from the Covenant of Grace and the New Covenant. This was expressed in several different ways, but all agreed that the Mosaic covenant and the Covenant of Grace differed "substantively." The Mosaic covenant was not an internal administration of the Covenant of Grace, but another distinct covenant in its own right. It could take the form of a Covenant of Works, a Covenant of Grace, or a mixed Covenant of Works and Grace. The second option, the Mosaic covenant as another Covenant of Grace, is the one view that seems to be ruled out by the *Westminster Confession*: "There are not therefore two covenants of grace, differing in substance, but one and the same, under various dispensations."[45]

Alternatively, it may have no relation to either the Covenants of Grace or Works, but pertain exclusively to the national covenant with Israel. Witsius appears to promote this view because of the imperfect nature of the obedience required of Israel, requiring grace to achieve the promised reward. The reward for obedience, important for Witsius's view,

---

42. Ferry, "Works," 98.

43. Ferry cites the testimony of Ball, Bolton, and Owen in support. Ball, *Treatise of the Covenant*, 95; Bolton, *True Bounds*, 99; Owen, *Hebrews*, 6:71.

44 Calvin and Turretin are two examples. See Calvin, *Commentaries*, 19:386–87; Turretin, *Institutes*, 2:227.

45. WCF 7.6. The implication was that there would be two methods of salvation.

is both temporal and spiritual, received in this life and the next (it is not "purely" temporal or carnal).[46] This distinguishes his view from Bolton who prefers to view the Mosaic covenant as a subservient covenant. While reflecting the influence of the Covenants of Works and Grace, the rewards of the national covenant remained "this worldly," limited to the temporal sphere and having respect to the inheritance of the land of Canaan and not heaven. It is subservient because it pedagogically serves the soteric nature of the Covenant of Grace.[47]

Ferry's taxonomy is a helpful guide to the various understandings and perplexities found in Reformed writings. As with any taxonomy it can suffer from "pigeon-holing" specific writers into categories, glossing over the nuances and complexities of a given interpretation. Ferry is sensitive to this limitation in his chapter. While useful for sorting through the kinds of questions being asked, one needs to exercise a degree of caution when applied to this complex issue. Such caution will be even more important when attempting to understand the nuances of Edwards's own views.

Jonathan Edwards on the Mosaic Covenant

During the Northampton Half-Way Covenant controversy, Edwards responds to his detractors who are attempting to use Old Testament covenant analogies to support their case. In response, Edwards disparages their misappropriation of the Old Covenant in this particular polemical context, reflecting on the complexities and dangers of using it for this purpose:

> There is perhaps no part of divinity attended with so much intricacy, and wherein orthodox divines do so much differ, as the stating the precise agreement and difference between the two dispensations of Moses and of Christ. And probably the reason

---

46. Witsius, *Economy of the Covenants*, 2:186.

47. Bolton, *True Bounds*, 99. John Owen also promotes this position. Owen, *Hebrews*, 6:85. Ferry also identifies another view which he calls the "bastard" covenant. This view differs from all others in that it was a covenant established by the Israelites at Mt. Sinai and not by God. This was a view held by David Dickson which he calls a "counterfeit, bastard covenant of works." While God called the Israelites to a covenant of grace, they turned it around and sought their own justification through external, ceremonial obedience. Dickson sees this "bastard" covenant in the New Testament among the false apostles in Galatia. Ferry, "Works," 102. See also Ward, *God and Adam*, 138–39.

> why God has left it so intricate, is, because our understanding the ancient dispensation and God's design in it is not of so great importance, or does so nearly concern us. Since God uses great plainness of speech in the New Testament, which is as it were the charter and municipal law of the Christian church, what need we run back to the ceremonial and typical institutions of an antiquated dispensation, wherein God's declared design was, to deliver divine things in comparative obscurity, hid under a veil, and involved in clouds?[48]

This statement of Edwards reflects not so much his lack of concern or interest in the Mosaic dispensation as it related to the new dispensation and Christ, but rather his own understanding of that relationship. The relationship between the Covenant of Grace in the old dispensation and the Mosaic covenant was one of revelation through "contraries." It was a revealing under shadows, figures, and types that obscured the true meaning of the gospel to those who were unenlightened and self-righteous. Nevertheless, it was a true revelation of the Covenant of Grace, a revelation more clearly revealed with the coming of the New Testament in Christ. His point was that the far greater clarity of the New Testament writings should be preferred in addressing the controversy over the more obscure and shadowy revelations, however true, of the Old Testament. In this statement Edwards recognizes the "intricacy" of this topic "wherein orthodox divines so much differ."

In the previous chapter, I discussed the view of McClymond and McDermott who suggested that Edwards developed or modified his views regarding the Covenant of Grace over time. They also take this approach in their view of Edwards regarding the Mosaic dispensation. They note Edwards's early explicit reference to the covenant with Israel as a further revelation of the Covenant of Works[49] and in his later writings referring to it as a mixed Covenant of Works and Grace.[50] In his *Notes on Scripture*, Edwards suggests, according to their reading, that the first giving of the law was part of the Covenant of Works and the second, after the Israelites apostasy by worshipping and sacrificing to a golden calf (Exod 32 and

---

48. Edwards, "Humble Inquiry," *WJE* 12:279.

49. Edwards, "Misc. 250," *WJE* 13:362; Edwards, "Misc. 439," *WJE* 13:487.

50. Edwards, "Misc. 1353," *WJE* 23:500. According to Bogue, Edwards held that both the Covenant of Grace and the Covenant of Works were renewed at Mt. Sinai, the Mosaic period being a legal dispensation of the covenant of grace. Bogue, *Jonathan Edwards*, 96.

Deut 9), was part of the Covenant of Grace.[51] McClymond and McDermott are correct to see all these themes in Edwards, but not correct to insinuate, as I think they are doing, that Edwards held to different views at different times. All these themes are found in federal theology prior to Edwards. Edwards's complex, multifaceted, and nuanced approach to the role of "law" in the Mosaic dispensation of the Covenant of Grace is easily reconciled with these individual snapshots.

Although he touches on this subject in numerous *Miscellanies*, sermons, and his *Notes on Scripture*, not to mention as an embedded framework for his redemptive-historical narrative in *History of the Work of Redemption*, his most extensive and systematic reflections on this topic occur in *Miscellanies 250, 439, 874,1 352, 1353, 1354*, and his *Controversies Notebook*. It is on these later *Miscellanies* and *Notebook* that I will focus, as they likely represent his most systematic and mature writings on the subject.

Continuity in Substance

Edwards discusses how the two dispensations or testaments of the one Covenant of Grace, that under Moses and that under Christ, are in agreement as to substance or essence. In *Misc. 1353* he lists eight specific ways of agreement.[52] First, both dispensations provide in substance for the same salvation. Sinners under both dispensations are by nature "children of wrath" and justly deserved the same eternal damnation. Under both dispensations the remedy required is the same, effected by the same effectual calling by the Holy Spirit, the same justification by faith, adoption and sanctification, and each obtaining the same eternal glory of heaven.

Second, both dispensations agree in terms of "the grand medium of salvation." By this Edwards means the same Mediator, Christ. The benefits obtained under both dispensations of the Covenant of Grace are obtained by the same mediatorial work of Christ by his incarnation, suffering, satisfaction, righteousness, and intercession. In the old dispensation this came by way of promise, in the new by way of fulfillment. Edwards is clear to emphasize the law-gospel distinction when he notes that it is

---

51. Edwards, "Misc. 441," *WJE* 15:522–24.
52. Edwards, "Misc. 1353," *WJE* 23:492–95. See also Edwards, "Misc. 874," *WJE* 20: 115–18.

"not at all by their own righteousness or by the mediation, sacrifice or righteousness of any other mediation."[53]

Third, the Holy Spirit is the divine person applying Christ's redemption. As discussed in the chapter on Edwards's view of the Covenant of Redemption, he understands this to mean that the Holy Spirit does not merely apply Christ's benefits, but is the benefit itself. Edwards characterizes the Holy Spirit's work as "enlightening the mind, renewing the heart, etc. acting herein especially as the Spirit of Christ."[54]

Fourth, the method of bestowing eternal salvation is the same in substance. The "grand qualification" for justification is faith, and this remains the same under both dispensations. While it is the same spirit of faith, it differs in terms of how that faith is exercised and exhibited as to the "opportunity and occasion" afforded by different degrees of revelation of the Covenant of Grace in the two dispensations. Edwards defines the common aspect of faith under both dispensations as the "active uniting of the heart to Christ," accompanied by repentance and conviction of sin.[55]

Fifth, the external means of application are in substance the same. These are the word of God and the ordinances of worship. Not in their specific details, but in their substance appropriate to the degree of revelation available at the time. The substance of the worship ordinances common to each dispensation include prayer, praise, the hearing of God's word, and sacraments (circumcision and the Passover in the old dispensation replaced by baptism and the Lord's Supper in the new dispensation).

The sixth and seventh ways the two agree was that the "grand benefits" of the Covenant of Grace is exhibited, represented, and to some degree actually made known and revealed in both. In the old dispensation they were revealed and represented under the cover of typical observances of Israel's law and worship, the purpose of which was to lead to a "gospel temper of mind," ultimately leading to a more explicit faith in Christ and his satisfaction, righteousness, and redemption when such "greater light" of revelation appeared. The "grand benefits" were more fully revealed in the wilderness wanderings and at Mt. Sinai when God revealed that he would be "their" God and they would be "his" people, their sins should be forgiven, they would have God's Spirit given them, and their hearts

---

53. Edwards, "Misc. 1353," *WJE* 23:492.
54. Edwards, "Misc. 1353," *WJE* 23:493.
55. Edwards, "Misc. 1353," *WJE* 23:493.

sanctified on their repenting and turning to God (citing Exod 34:5–7, Lev 26:12, 42–46, Deut 39:1–6, 3–15, and 30:19).

Finally, the same eschatological blessings of a future state are in some degree revealed and promised. According to Edwards's reasoning, God's promises to them on Mt. Sinai implied a happiness that could not be fulfilled by the things of this world. "The promises of life so often made to the righteous in the Old Testament, as a blessing by which they should be distinguished, plainly implied future life . . . imply a promise of eternal life."[56]

In summary, Edwards demonstrates significant continuity between the old and new dispensations. There is only one single Covenant of Grace and only one means of salvation, from the fall until the eschaton, encompassing both dispensations. Edwards proves this continuity by demonstrating that both dispensations are characterized by the same eschatological salvation, the same medium of salvation (Christ), the same application of salvation (the Holy Spirit), the same qualification for salvation (faith alone), the same means of salvation (word, sacrament, and worship), and the same revelation of salvation and eternal blessings. While "substance" of salvation is the same in both dispensations, Edwards also notes the discontinuities between the dispensations, specifically by way of law and gospel contrast. Edwards presents a multifaceted approach to the Mosaic covenant in reconciling this "antithesis," particularly in his use of "contraries" that both hide and reveal the Covenant of Grace in the old dispensation.

Antithesis and Discontinuity

For however much the Mosaic dispensation agreed to and served the ongoing revelation of the one Covenant of Grace in substance, it differed in the "accidents" or the "manner and circumstances" of the revelation it provided.[57] First, it was an indirect revelation, being "diverse from the things aimed at." In the Mosaic covenant God made use of "contraries" to obtain his ends. Edwards used the picture of "covering" or "veiling" in the way the Mosaic covenant served to reveal the substance of the Covenant of Grace in being "diverse" to it. And yet it could be seen as a revelation of the gospel revealed "no more plainly and fully." As a Covenant of Works,

---

56. Edwards, "Misc. 1353," *WJE* 23:494–95.
57. Edwards, "Misc. 439," *WJE* 13:487–90.

it served as a "subordinate constitution" with respect to the Covenant of Grace.

Edwards distinguishes two aspects or "covenants" of the Mosaic dispensation that served to "cover" the Covenant of Grace: The Covenant of Works as exhibited in the Mosaic law and the national covenant with Israel. Both covenants acted as "coverings" for the Covenant of Grace. They do not void or act as alternatives to the one Covenant of Grace during this dispensation, but act in subservient roles to "reveal" through "covering." Various word pictures, or pictorial representations, are used to describe the relationship between these Mosaic covenants and the Covenant of Grace. The Mosaic covenants are as a "cortex" to the "medulla" of the Covenant of Grace, or as the putamen is to the nucleus, or as the shell is to the kernel. The Covenant of Grace is hidden and obscured in its revelation, yet it is also revealed through this hiddenness, albeit indirectly and "diversely." In contrast, the gospel is revealed "more simply and directly" in the new dispensation of the Covenant of Grace. The gospel is all uncovered as the "essence" of the thing itself is exhibited in its simplicity. All is "simple and homogenous" in the New Testament as opposed to the "heterogenous" nature of the Old Testament.

Edwards refers to this hidden-revealed dialectic as a distinction between the "letter" and the "spirit." This is not a reference to the essential role of the Holy Spirit in regeneration and empowering Old Testament believers (which was in essence the same), but rather concerns two hermeneutical principles of understanding "law" passages. They can be either understood in a "carnal" sense of advocating works righteousness or as illuminating the need for another righteousness that comes through the mediatorial work of Christ.[58]

> The legal sense was most obvious, and that which would occur first to a cursory view, and would be most easily and plainly seen by such as were not spiritually enlightened, and by all such as were chiefly under the influence of a carnal and legal, self-righteous disposition. The gospel, or covenant of grace, was really and sufficiently implied, and signified, and properly established by the words, yet was not so obvious, but more hidden; though when the words with their circumstances were duly considered, it was evident the real intent and design of them was

---

58. For an example of this confusion, see Karlberg's critique of Sailhamer in Karlberg, "Recovering the Mosaic Covenant," 233–50; Sailhamer, *The Meaning of the Pentateuch*.

> to establish the covenant of grace, and that only. Yet in order to discern that, there was need of diligently attending to the words and thoroughly considering them, and there was also need of a truly humble, penitent and pious mind well to discern this secret design and grand aim of the revelation. It being thus, that the gospel was a covenant of grace, being the true design of the Spirit of God in them, and the design and meaning which men were enabled rightly to discern and apply to themselves only by the gracious influences of that Spirit, and so to taste and be nourished by the kernel: hence this nucleus is called "the spirit" and the other is called "the letter," because the words in their more obvious meaning, and to them who viewed only the letter with a carnal eye, saw no more contained in them than the law. These are the letter that "kills," and the spirit that "gives life" (2 Corinthians 3:6).[59]

The same words can be taken as the "letter" or the "spirit," depending on whether one saw in the same revelation a need for perfect obedience (the "letter") or the sincere obedience of faith ("the spirit"). The difference depended on the state of one's spiritual illumination. It was through the Holy Spirit enlightening the mind that the gospel promises contained in the law became manifest. The way to salvation by faith (compliance and acceptance of God offering his fullness to us) was revealed through the contrary of law. While hidden from the self-righteous as law, it was revealed to the humble and repentant as gospel. Edwards discusses the two senses of "law," the "letter" of the law and the "spirit" of the law, in *Misc.* 1353:

> Such words are used as in their proper signification may be applied to signify that perfect obedience which is the condition of the Covenant of Works, and that sincere obedience of faith which is the great qualification of the covenant of grace. The thing revealed and applied is holiness and obedience, and in such words that they may be understood either of holiness, or our offering to God as it is considered in the Covenant of Works, or as it [is] the compliance and acceptance of God offering his fullness to us, as it is to be considered in the covenant of grace.[60]

Edwards establishes the continuity of the Covenant of Grace across both dispensations, and also provides for the way that continuity is

---

59. Edwards, "Misc. 1353," *WJE* 23:498–99.
60. Edwards, "Misc. 1353," *WJE* 23:497–98.

both "hidden" and "revealed" by way of law-gospel antithesis in the promulgation of the Mosaic covenants.

Covenant of Works in the Mosaic Law

The two covenants that form the outer cortex or putamen are the Covenant of Works and the national covenant with Israel. Both covenants act as "coverings" for the Covenant of Grace. They do not void or act as alternatives to the one Covenant of Grace during this dispensation, but act in subservient roles to "reveal" through "covering." They may either act as the "letter" in their carnal interpretation obscuring the grace of the gospel, or as the "spirit" leading one to grace and revealing the gospel.

Edwards is quite clear that he believes the Mosaic covenant was in some sense the Covenant of Works. In *Misc. 250* he says from the start, "I think really that the covenant that God made with the children of Israel was the Covenant of Works. He still held them under that covenant."[61] And again in *Misc. 439* he says, "God proposed a covenant to them that was essentially and entirely different, which was the Covenant of Works."[62] That this was not a "new" covenant but the old Covenant of Works as made with Adam (re)exhibited or republished is evident when he continues that God "promulgated the moral law to them, together with many positive precepts of the ceremonial and judicial law, that answered to the prohibition of eating the forbidden fruit; which God proposed to them with the threatening of death, and the curse affixed to the least defect in obedience." The law (moral-ceremonial-judicial) as a (re)exhibition of the Covenant of Works is a covenant "entirely diverse and opposite" to the Covenant of Grace, says Edwards. It acts in subordination to and in independence of the Covenant of Grace.

Hypothetical Covenant

This covenant is exhibited and proposed, but it is not "established."[63] The word "proposed" is used by Edwards in contradistinction from

---

61. Edwards, "Misc. 250," *WJE* 13:362. See also Edwards, "Misc. 337," *WJE* 13:412: "The covenant that God made with the children of Israel with respect to outward blessings was entirely legal, a covenant of works."

62. Edwards, "Misc. 436," *WJE* 13:487.

63. In the New Testament, with the completion of Christ's work, the Covenant of

"established" to convey that it was impossible, as a covenant, for them to be saved by it. Its purpose was not to provide a legal means of obtaining eternal life. "But in the old testament, the Covenant of Works was no covenant that God established or entered into with his people as the designed, immediate method of his favor. 'Twas not proposed with a command to men that they should seek and hope for life in this way, not proposed as anything that they were necessitated personally to fulfill as the only method of justification. Both the law and the gospel were proposed, but the gospel only was established."[64] In this context Edwards uses the traditional Reformed distinction between the moral, ceremonial, and civil laws. While all three were part of the Mosaic covenant, only the moral law remains as a rule for the Christian life under the new dispensation (the other laws in their typological function having been fulfilled by Christ as the antitype). The law in this sense is still "exhibited" in that it still teaches of the need for salvation through Christ's own righteousness and fulfillment of the law, but is no longer "proposed" in its condemning function as a covenant "in force." According to Edwards, the Covenant of Works with Adam was both proposed and established. Under the old Mosaic dispensation of the New Covenant, the Covenant of Works was exhibited and proposed, but not established. Under the New Covenant's new dispensation in Christ, the Covenant of Works is still exhibited, but neither established nor proposed (see Table 5.1).

TABLE 5.1.

The Relationship of the Covenant of Works (Moral Law) to the Old and New Covenants according to Jonathan Edwards

Old Covenant with Adam	New Covenant of Grace	
	Mosaic Dispensation	New Dispensation in Christ
Proposed and established	Proposed and exhibited, but not established	Exhibited, but not proposed or established

Works is still "exhibited," but neither proposed nor established.

64. Edwards, "Misc. 436," *WJE* 13:497.

In an earlier *Miscellany* Edwards emphasized that the Covenant of Works has no justifying power. It was proposed "hypothetically" as a trial to bring them to despair of any self-righteousness.

> Although it was as much impossible for them to be saved by it as it is for us, yet it was really proposed to them as a covenant for them, for their trial (Exod 20:20), that they might this way be brought to despair of obtaining life by this covenant, and might see their necessity of free grace and a Mediator. God chose this way to convince them, by Proposing the Covenant of Works to them, as though he expected they should seek and obtain life in this way, that everyone, when he came to apply it to himself, might see its impracticableness; as being a way of conviction to that ignorant and infantile state of the church.[65]

Edwards illustrates this from the New Testament in one of his favorite lessons in the way Christ dealt with the rich young ruler (Matt 19:16–30; Mark 10:17–31; Luke 18:18–30). When the rich young ruler inquired of Jesus what he should do to inherit eternal life, Jesus bid him to keep the commandments. The law was used in this fashion to draw the young ruler away from his own self-righteousness and to seek a righteousness from another (Christ). In this narrative the law "covered" the gospel message while simultaneously revealing it to the young ruler who could not see past the "letter" into the "spirit" (evidently Jesus' disciples were similarly blinded at this time as well).[66]

On the other hand, it is "proposed," not as antiquated and out-of-date (abrogated), but as a covenant still "in force" and of the greatest importance. While no longer a covenant with the possibility of fulfillment, the judgments incurred by Adam's disobedience remain. By exhibiting

---

65. Edwards, "Misc. 439," *WJE* 13:487–89.

66. Thomas Boston also uses the illustration from the New Testament of the rich young ruler. The purpose of the "hypothetical offer" was to meet and break down pride. "But God knew well enough that the Israelites were never able to yield such an obedience; and yet he saw it meet to propound eternal life to them upon these terms; that so he might speak to them in their own humour, as indeed it was meet: for they swelled with mad assurance in themselves, saying, 'All that the Lord commandeth we will do,' and be obedience, Exod. xix.8. Well, said the Lord, if you will needs be doing, why here is a law to be kept; and if you can fully observe the righteousness of it, you shall be saved: sending them of purpose to the law, to awaken and convince them, to sentence and humble them, and to make them see their own folly in seeking for life that way; in short, to make them see the terms under which they stood, that so they might be brought out of themselves, and expect nothing from the law, in relation to life, but all from Christ." Boston, "Marrow," 205–6.

this covenant, the same as given to Adam, and proposing it as a trial of obedience, it served the purposes of the Covenant of Grace in revealing that "supreme and unalterable rule of righteousness between God and man, that must someway or other be fulfilled."[67] As such it served as a "schoolmaster" to drive one to Christ and to reveal the method of Christ's redemption. The Covenant of Grace, says Edwards, was established as the *immediate* rule of God's bestowment of favor and salvation to believers. The Covenant of Works was the *mediate* rule of God's favor and salvation and the *immediate* rule of God's justice in punishing sinners, but was not the *immediate* method of God's favor.[68] This is what Edwards means when he says that "both the law and the gospel were proposed, but the gospel only established."

Pedagogical Use

The Mosaic covenant as a Covenant of Works was subservient to or served the purpose of driving the Israelites to the realization that they needed a second mediator who could fulfill the obligations for them in the Covenant of Grace. Edwards argues from Gal 3:17 that because the covenant with Abraham (a further revelation of the Covenant of Grace)[69] could not be annulled, the giving of the law at Mt. Sinai as a Covenant of Works was not meant as "establishing that law as a rule of justification."[70] The Mosaic covenant does not annul the Covenant of Grace or serve as a parallel covenant, but is subservient as a particular dispensation of the Covenant of Grace. As a "new work" of God in the history of redemption, it is a further revelation of the Covenant of Grace, especially in terms of serving to reveal more fully the law-gospel distinction. Edwards explains:

---

67. Edwards, "Misc. 1353," *WJE* 23:497.

68. The Covenant of Works is, however, the *immediate* rule of God's favor in terms of Christ's work according to the covenant of redemption. As the Puritan Samuel Petto (1624–1711) notes, "If he [Christ] had not been born under the very Law, as a covenant of works, he should not have satisfied it, by answering the penalty or fulfilling the righteousness of it, but had only done and suffered something in lieu and stead thereof, it would not have been the *idem* for us; and this sheweth how exceedingly necessary the Sinai Covenant was." Petto, *Difference*, 125.

69. This was the Covenant of Redemption revealed in time as the Covenant of Grace.

70. Edwards, "Justification by Faith Alone," *WJE* 19:171–72.

> The next thing that I shall take notice of here that was done towards the Work [of] Redemption was God's giving the moral law in so awful a manner at Mount Sinai. This was another new thing that God did, a new step taken in this great affair, Deuteronomy 4:33, "Did ever a people hear the voice of God speaking out of the midst of the fire, as thou hast heard, and live?" And it was a great thing that God did towards this work, and that whether we consider it as delivered as a new exhibition of the Covenant of Works or given as a rule of life.
>
> The Covenant of Works was here exhibited to be as a schoolmaster to lead to Christ, not only for the use of that nation in the ages of the Old Testament, but for the use of God's church throughout all ages to the end of the world, as an instrument that the great Redeemer makes use of to convince men of their sin and misery and helplessness and God's awful and tremendous majesty and justice as a lawgiver, and so to make men sensible of the necessity of Christ as a savior. The Work of Redemption in its saving effect in men's souls in all the progress of it to the end of it, is not carried on without the use of this law that was now delivered at Sinai.[71]

The law not only serves a pedagogical function, to lead one to the grace of Christ, but also as a "rule of life" for living under the Covenant of Grace.

Ordo Salutis and Historia Salutis

The law serves this pedagogical function not only in reference to the objective history of redemption, but also in the subjective order of salvation in the individual believer. One can see this especially in the third sermon of Edwards's *History*:

> And here by the way I would observe that the increase of gospel light and the carrying on the Work of Redemption as it respects the elect church in general, from the first erecting of the church to the end of the world, is very much after the same manner as the carrying on of the same work and the same light in a particular soul from the time of its conversion till it is perfected and crowned in glory. The work in a particular soul has its ups and downs. Sometimes the light shines brighter, and sometimes 'tis a dark time. Sometimes grace seems to prevail; at other times it seems to languish for a great while together and corruption

---

71. Edwards, "History of the Work of Redemption," *WJE* 9:180.

prevails and then grace revives again. But in the general grace is growing from its first infusion till it is perfected in glory; the kingdom of Christ is building up in the soul. So it is with respect to the great affair in general as it relates to the universal subject of it, as 'tis carried on from the first beginning of it after the fall till it is perfected at the end of the world, as will more fully appear by a particular view of this affair from beginning to end in the prosecution of this subject, if God gives opportunity to carry it through as I propose.[72]

William Scheick notes this element in Edwards's *History*. He proposes "that Edwards thought of his study as innovative because in it he treats history as an allegory of the conversion experience. History, in his view, merely manifests in large the experiences of the individual soul undergoing the regenerative process." Edwards was possessed by the "vision of merging the notions of nature, of history, and of the saint's private self into one theological tract."[73] Scheick wants to see a direct link between the imagery of the Edwards's *History* with the Puritan tradition of delineating the subjective stages of conversion and redemption.

John Wilson disagrees with Scheick's approach and interpretation. For Wilson, Edwards's point was not to show a direct parallel between the stages of salvation in the soul and in creation, but rather to show that the progress of redemption in both is fundamental and secure. The *Redemption Discourse* was not "concerned with the effect of redemption upon the soul of the saint . . . the objective side was the focus, that is, the divine Work of Redemption. For him, if there was an analogy, it was from the greater redemption of creation to its pale shadow in the soul, not vice versa."[74] Wilson argues that Scheick is making too much of Edwards's analogy, reading into it notions of nineteenth-century Romanticism.

I believe Scheick recognizes something important in Edwards's presentation. Wilson, while offering a helpful criticism of Scheick's presuppositions, makes a similar error to that which he accuses Scheick. Both are interpreting Edwards from a rhetorical and literary perspective and thereby miss the profound theological point he is making. Edwards is not drawing a direct parallel between God's working in the history of

---

72. Edwards, "History of the Work of Redemption," *WJE* 9:144–45. See also Edwards's sermon on Rev. 14:14–20, Edwards, "Seasons of Ingathering," *WJE* 22:476–89.

73. Scheick, "Grand Design," 300–14.

74. Wilson, "Editor's Introduction," *WJE* 9:99–100.

redemption to specific subjective stages in a believer's conversion. Nor is he saying that the transition from the old dispensation to the new dispensation is one from pure law to pure gospel (the law-gospel distinction is a principle that operates within each dispensation, albeit by different means). Rather, he is making the general claim regarding the centrality of the law-gospel distinction in redemption, evident in both God's revelation of the Covenant of Grace in the objective history of the work of redemption and also in the normal subjective order of revelation (logical, not necessarily temporal) in the individual believer. Edwards links these two explicitly in terms of law and gospel in *Misc. 337*:

> This being the method God takes with the world, first to make a revelation of his dreadful majesty and justice before he reveals his grace, as in this instance—and so he first revealed the law with thunders and lightnings from Mount Sinai before the full revelation of his grace by Jesus Christ, to prepare the more for the reception of that grace, and so in the destruction of Jerusalem before the preaching the gospel to the Gentile world, and the dreadful destruction of Antichrist before the full revealing his grace to the whole world; many instances the Scripture history is full of—so 'tis but reasonable to suppose that this is his common method with particular persons, first to awaken them to a sense of the dreadful justice of God and his displeasure against sin, and then to give them a sense of his grace. And as there are generally these legal awakenings before grace is bestowed, so very commonly after a principle of grace is infused, repentance is generally first in exercise (or at least this is first in a very sensible exercise) before the plain exercise of faith in Jesus Christ; as John the Baptist was sent to preach repentance to prepare the way for Christ. There generally precedes the sinner's humble sense of his exceeding sinfulness, of his unworthiness of God's mercy and desert of his wrath; if not precedes, yet always accompanies.[75]

Edwards is identifying the law-gospel distinction in both its objective and subjective revelations by showing how the objective historical is recapitulated in the subjective individual. He is not using this parallel to delineate a temporal subjective experience that follows universally (albeit a "common method in particular persons") or projecting a puritanical subjective conversion scheme onto history. He is promoting a logical and theological law-gospel distinction that drives both biblical and historical

75. Edwards, "Misc. 337," *WJE* 13:412–13.

hermeneutics (*historia salutis*) as well as the systematic theological *ordo salutis*. There is no dichotomy of *historia salutis* and *ordo salutis* in Edwards. This principle of salvation, centered as it is in the works principle, is revealed in history as the Covenant of Grace in the same manner as it is applied to individual believers in the marriage covenant. They are both grounded in the works principle of the Covenants of Works and Redemption. An understanding of Edwards's covenant theology is the key to Edwards's synthesis. It also serves as the key for how Edwards conceptualized the role of the Mosaic covenant in redemptive history, including the relationship between the old and new dispensations of the Covenant of Grace.

The Decalogue

Edwards believed that the Decalogue, given to Israel at Mt. Sinai, contained both the Covenant of Works and Grace. As a Covenant of Works, it was exhibited in its pedagogical function to convince Israel of their sin and need for a second mediator. This was not only for Israel but for the use of God's church throughout all ages to the end of the world. "The Work of Redemption in its saving effect in men's souls in all the progress of it to the end of it, is not carried on without the use of this law that was now delivered at Sinai."[76]

The Decalogue also contained the Covenant of Grace. Edwards cites the preface to the Ten Commandments as confirming the Covenant of Grace when it not only declares that God is their God and Redeemer but also how they should behave towards him as Jehovah, their covenant God and Redeemer. The Commandments were an instruction to them of how to receive him, cleave to him, and trust in him as their Redeemer. Edwards ties in the preface with the first commandment or "word." According to Edwards, "This first word comprehended the whole."[77] All the other commandments were "particular explications" of how they should "cleave to Jehovah and trust in him as their only and all-sufficient, living Redeemer."[78] The words annexed to the second commandment ("showing mercy to thousands of them that love me, and keep my commandments" Exod 20:6) evidenced the elements of mercy and grace embedded

---

76. Edwards, "History of the Work of Redemption," *WJE* 9:180–82.
77. Edwards, "Misc. 1353," *WJE* 23:505.
78. Edwards, "Misc. 1353," *WJE* 23:505.

in the Decalogue as delivered to Israel. Finally, Edwards looked to how the words which God delivered at Mt. Sinai, including the Decalogue and all that were annexed to them, were sealed with the "blood of the sacrifice" (Exod 24:5–8, compared with Heb 9:18–23) which "typified the blood of Christ."[79] The moral law contained in the Decalogue also served as a "rule of life," as a "directory" for God's church "to show them the way in which they must walk, as they would go to heaven."[80]

The National Covenant with Israel

There is another covenant that Edwards calls the covenant of God with Israel in the flesh. This is not to be confused with and must be distinguished from the covenant between the Father and the "mystical church" that pertains solely to the eternal Covenant of Redemption. This is a "national" covenant made with an "external" temporal society that is characterized by its "this worldly" orientation. As external and carnal, it is solely concerned with Israel's outward safety (from foreign invasion and captivity) and prosperity, having nothing to do with the internal salvation of individual believers. The blessings were external and carnal, involving the inheritance and life of Israel in Canaan and only pertained to Israel as a nation during this particular historic period. The stipulations of this covenant, in keeping with its external and carnal orientation, involved an outward and external conformity to the law of God to the moral law as well as to the external and carnal laws embodied in the ceremonial and judicial law, along with an external and carnal worship. The pardon and sanctification promised by that covenant were also external. Pardon meant freedom from guilt as exclusion from external privileges and sanctification meant, among other things, to be separated from carnal pollutions ("uncleanliness") and qualifying for carnal privileges.[81]

Edwards concludes that this covenant was a "mixed" covenant, containing both elements of law and gospel, partaking of the nature of both the Covenant of Works and of Grace. It took on the works principle in its requirement of perfect, legal purity in every aspect. In that

79. Edwards, "Misc. 1353," *WJE* 23:506.

80. Edwards, "History of the Work of Redemption," *WJE* 9:181. It is important to note that Edwards says in this sense the law shows the way sincere believers must walk "*as* they would go" and not "*so that* they would go" to heaven (emphasis mine). The difference is crucial.

81. Edwards, "Misc. 1352," *WJE* 23:499.

it required an offering of each individual to God to procure his favor, it "savers more of the first covenant" of works. It resembled the Covenant of Works "because it was given as an additament and appendage to the Covenant of Works as it was delivered and proposed to them for the trial of their obedience."[82] The main law or rule in the Covenant of Works is to be obedient to all God's positive commands, and just as the positive precept of not eating the forbidden fruit was added to the Covenant of Works in the Garden, God added to the moral law "a great number of positive precepts." In many areas it provided no means of reconciliation.

In another sense, it resembled the Covenant of Grace in that it admitted of confession, sacrifice, and reconciliation in other things. It resembled the Covenant of Grace "because it was given on purpose to be a type and representation of that covenant and things belonging to it."[83] The national covenant served in a typological fashion in that under shadows and types it revealed both the Covenant of Works and the Covenant of Grace in Israel's "earthly" recapitulation of redemptive history.

In summary, Edwards proposes that under the old dispensation of the Covenant of Grace, the "kernel" of the gospel was delivered or revealed under a twofold shell: the law or Covenant of Works (the moral, ceremonial, and judicial laws) and the symbolic "carnal" national covenant. As "shells," considered in and of themselves, they hid the gospel they served by their "heterogenous" and "diverse" nature as a Covenant of Works, in terms of law as opposed to grace. In the symbolical and carnal national covenant with Israel the spiritual (heavenly, internal) nature of the Covenant of Grace was hid under the carnal (earthly, external). As coverings or veils they could be interpreted in reference to either the letter or spirit. Interpreted as letter they hid the gospel from carnal, unconvinced sinners, blinding their minds on occasion of their own self-righteousness. Interpreted as spirit (and by the Spirit) they were means to bring God's elect to partake of the gospel "kernel." Both acted in a pedagogical function as a "schoolmaster" to bring the Israel to the need of a second mediator to fulfill the Covenant of Works on their behalf, to bring the church to Christ.

---

82. Edwards, "Misc. 1353," *WJE* 23:500.
83. Edwards, "Misc. 1353," *WJE* 23:500–1.

Implications for Faith and Obedience

Edwards's covenant theology has several implications for the relationship between faith and obedience. Because the one Covenant of Grace was present in the old dispensation, salvation was by faith and not works in the same manner as it is in the new evangelical dispensation. The promises to Abraham, promises that were received by Abraham through faith, were not annulled. The substance of faith was the same. But there is a difference "circumstantially." Edwards means by "circumstantially" that the faith of the Old Testament saints was answerable to the differences in the revelation they received. Since the revelation of Christ and his salvation was not exhibited to the clarity and degree as it is in the New Testament, an explicit act of faith with respect to Christ and the gospel doctrines was not as necessary as it is now. Edwards did not mean that Israel's faith had nothing to do with Christ, that in substance it did not directly relate to Christ's person and work, or that the revelation to Israel did not reveal Christ and his work in some sense. Israel was not merely instructed in the way of faith "in general," but the revelation they received was to faith specifically in "the second person in the Godhead as their Mediator and advocate, and in the Messiah as their great high priest and sacrifice."[84]

On this matter Edwards delves extensively and specifically in his *Controversies Notebook* under the essay, "Question: In What Sense Did the Saints under the Old Testament Believe in Christ to Justification?"[85] His answer is, "A great deal." Nevertheless, in the Mosaic dispensation there was a greater emphasis on the "subordinate condition," that is the fruit of faith, than under the new dispensation.

> The spirit or principle of faith in the heart was the same; and the person who is the object of faith is the same, viz. the Son of God, as Mediator. The same spirit of repentance and humiliation belonged to it then as does now. But not exactly the same exercises of faith were then required as are now, but there was a difference, answerable to the difference of the revelation in which the Mediator and his salvation is exhibited. As the revelation now is much more plain, particular and full, so a more particular and explicit regard to the Mediator, with respect to the things revealed, is required.[86]

---

84. Edwards, "Misc. 1354," *WJE* 23:540.
85. Edwards, "'Controversies' Notebook: Justification," *WJE* 21:372–408.
86. Edwards, "Misc. 1353," *WJE* 23: 502–3.

Under the Mosaic dispensation the general nature of the covenant conditions was the same as under the gospel dispensation: "Exercise of the same spirit of true holiness, and gracious respect to God in faith, and a sincere and universal obedience."[87]

It is also the same Holy Spirit that is given in both dispensations, but there was a "circumstantial" difference in the spiritual blessings bestowed, not in terms of the eternal blessings of life and communion with God, but in terms of the spiritual blessings bestowed on the church "in this world." Old Testament saints did not enjoy the revealed nearness to God as the adapted children or spouse as was revealed in the greater revelation of the New Testament. "That exalted union and communion of the saints with God, which is brought to light by the gospel, was comparatively but little of it known under the old. And therefore their grace was less manifested in love and joy, and more in fear. The Spirit of God was not so much given as a Spirit of adoption as it is now, and not so much as an earnest of the future inheritance, giving foretastes of heavenly joy and glory."[88] Christ's ascension brings a new age of the Holy Spirit with greater blessings. Edwards speculates that not the earthly blessings, but the heavenly happiness itself, differs between that experienced by the Old Testament saints who ascended into heaven from the New Testament saints who ascended after Christ's ascension (presumably both now enjoy the same). Christ's ascension brings not only greater earthly blessings to his church through "the Spirit of the Risen Christ," but also greater heavenly blessings, a "world of light, of love, and joy, and glory" immensely more than it was before Christ's ascension.[89]

Objections Answered

In *Miscellany 1354* Edwards addresses the objection of how justification by faith alone[90] can be the main qualification and the same in substance

---

87. Edwards, "Misc. 439," *WJE* 13:488. See also Edwards, "Misc. 1052," *WJE* 21:503.

88. Edwards, "Misc. 1353," *WJE* 23:503.

89. Edwards, "Misc. 1353," *WJE* 23:503.

90. In this section Edwards gives one of his most comprehensive and clearest definitions of what is meant by being justified by faith alone: "[T]hat we are justified (i.e. accepted of God as free from guilt, wrath and the punishment of sin, and as now righteous and so the objects of favor, and as properly entitled to the rewards of righteousness), not by any righteousness of ours, any virtue in us as recommending us to such a privilege by its moral beauty or value in the sight of God, considering us as

under the old and new dispensations, when from all appearances the overwhelming focus in the Old Testament is on "obedience to God, loving God, doing that which is good in his sight, etc.?"⁹¹ Edwards proceeds with a four-page litany of Old Testament biblical passages that seem to affirm obedience, as opposed to faith, as the "grand qualification" of salvation in the Old Testament, and in which it appears that the moral value of Israel's obedience was the price of God's favor. By this he means that obedience appears not only as a thing "consequentially necessary" or as a "secondary condition" of the covenant, but as the "main thing" required, the "grand condition," of God's mercy, favor, blessing, and life. Edwards takes on this objection under several headings: 1) Edwards distinguishes between the "obedience" required in these texts as they apply to the Covenant of Works exhibited and "proposed" as a trial and the "obedience" required in the Covenant of Works as "established" in the original covenant with Adam. 2) Obedience as evidence of the proper condition of the Covenant of Grace, which is the hearing and yielding to the voice of God (faith). 3) Obedience as the distinguishing character of faith. 4) Obedience as the fruit and distinguishing mark of faith. 5) The obedience discussed in these passages is at times confused with the obedience required in the national covenant with Israel. 6) There is no moral value of the obedience demanded that would recommend one to God's mercy. I will discuss each of Edwards's answers in turn.

First, the terms of the Covenant of Works as exhibited and proposed as a trial to lead to Christ were by design couched in the terms of strict and perfect obedience. The proposed legal terms promulgated at Mt. Sinai under Moses were never meant as a means for justification or directed to that end, but rather as a trial to demonstrate that Israel could not fulfill them. "It was signified to the people, at the same time that these legal terms were proposed to 'em, that they could not fulfill them."⁹² In response to Israel's promise to fulfill the demands of the law, it was

---

we are in ourselves, but only by faith in Christ, or our cordial reception of Christ and active unition with him as our atoning and righteous Mediator; and that though faith be indeed an excellent virtue, yet in this affair it is not the virtuousness or value of its moral excellency that is the thing considered, but only its relation to Christ, as making one with him and so interesting the believer in his satisfaction and righteousness; and that it was always thus with regard to the justification of fallen man, the main qualification and condition of justification being the same in substance under the old testament as under the new." Edwards, "Misc. 1354," *WJE* 23:506–7.

91. Edwards, "Misc. 1354," *WJE* 23:507.
92. Edwards, "Misc. 1354," *WJE* 23:512. Edwards cites Deut 5:29.

plainly revealed to them that the "holiness strictness and perfection of God's law is such that they can never answer the demands of it, and that the forwardness of their profession and promises arose from ignorance of themselves."[93] Nevertheless, the law and covenant was left with them for their conviction (citing Deut 5:29 and Josh 24:19–27). This was also expressly declared in Exod 20:20 when Moses said, "God is come to prove you."

Edwards demonstrates how the demands of the law *in toto* do not comport with the Mosaic dispensation being a means of justification in the same manner as the Covenant of Works. The demands of the Mosaic dispensation spoke only of future obedience, assuming past sins. The terms of the Covenant of Works require perfect and complete obedience "at all times."[94] Any sin in the past would have nullified the covenant immediately and for the future. Furthermore, the Mosaic dispensation speaks of repentance and turning from sin (citing the prophet Ezekiel in chapter 33, a passage brought up earlier as evidence that the obedience required was of the nature of the Covenant of Works), which are entirely alien from the Covenant of Works. The benefits promised for repentance, according to "the Prophet" (Ezekiel), is pardon of sin, which is also "inconsistent" with the Covenant of Works and is plainly "peculiar" to the Covenant of Grace. Edwards summarizes this point:

> It must be considered that God never proposed the Covenant of Works in the whole of it, and in its true and complete nature, including both past and future fulfillment. Nor was this necessary to God's end, which was not the bringing men to eternal life and happiness in that way, but only a conviction of their sinfulness and impotence. When God is pleased to take this method with men for their conviction, viz. to put 'em on endeavors of their souls, that they may be convinced by experiment, it would not have been proper for him to put them on endeavors to alter what was past, to endeavor that their past lives might be perfectly innocent and holy. That would have [been] absurd. Therefore, God is pleased to put 'em on future trial, and to promise life to 'em if they will perfectly obey for the future, which implies a forgetting all that is past—though merely their future obedience

---

93. Edwards, "Misc. 1354," *WJE* 23:512.

94. Edwards, "Misc. 1354," *WJE* 23:515. Edwards uses the term "Covenant of Grace" at this point in his manuscript, where he obviously means "Covenant of Works."

would make no atonement for past disobedience, and so could not have at all answered the eternal rule or Covenant of Works.[95]

The proposal of "such impossible terms" had a "proper tendency" to answer that which was truly God's end, to convict Israel of their sin and need for another means of redemption.

Second, Edwards represents obedience as the "most proper condition of the covenant of grace" or "that qualification in us" by which we come to be accepted and justified is "nothing against the doctrine of justification by faith alone."[96] By this Edwards uses an argument and definition that is central to many of his writings on the relationship of obedience to faith. The substance or essence of true evangelical obedience is, for Edwards, a "hearing and yielding to the voice of God." This is the substance of both the response of faith in effectual calling as well as to the faithful response in complying with the precepts of pure law. Obedience is not so much the proper condition as it is evidence of the proper condition of the Covenant of Grace, which is the hearing and yielding to the voice of God (i.e., faith).

Third, the requirement of "keeping the commandments of the Lord" can be taken in two senses. It can mean a yielding to the authority of a "mere Lawgiver" for *his* own sake, demanding what is due him for his pleasure and honor. This is what Edwards means by the "letter" of the law. But it can also mean an attending to the directions of a Redeemer and spiritual head and husband, obeying his word of command for deliverance from one's enemies. The law is not given for *his* sake, but for *our* sake, and obedience is a manifestation or evidence of trust in him. "Trust" properly signifies "willing and hearkening," which is the nature of obedience in this sense.[97] The obedience to these commands, therefore, "was the condition of life, not as the price of life and happiness, but as an accepting it, a closing with it and an embracing it, as the gift of the love of a spiritual Father, Savior and husband . . ."[98] Edwards is not confusing obedience and faith, but is distinguishing two types of obedience, a legal one of servitude that looks to the moral value of obedience itself as proper condition and as something done for the sake of the master, and an

---

95. Edwards, "Misc. 1354," *WJE* 23:515.

96. Edwards, "Misc. 1354," *WJE* 23:517.

97. Edwards, "Misc. 1354," *WJE* 23:517. Edwards interprets the "willing and obedience (*shama*)" in Isa 1:19 as "willing and hearkening."

98. Edwards, "Misc. 1354," *WJE* 23:521.

evangelical one that is evidence of the reality of repentance and evidence of accepting the way of life, "embracing the methods of grace which bestows eternal life." There is no moral value or virtue in obedience that would merit God's blessing. Obedience is only the inseparable evidence of trusting and fearing God, which is the substance of faith.[99]

Fourth, obedience is not only evidence of the proper condition but is a distinguishing character of the proper condition. It is a sign or "distinguishing character and mark" of that faith which is the more primary condition of acceptance. It is a fruit of faith by which faith is outwardly observable and made known. Edwards compares it to a person's proper name as their distinguishing character. So, when the question is asked, "Who has a title to salvation?" and the response is: "He that walketh righteously (Isa 33:15–16)," Edwards equates this with simply calling a person by their proper name: "If the answer had been given by mentioning the names of the persons, nobody would have taken it that the name was the thing that first recommended the person to a title to the benefit." As a distinguishing character, "walking righteously" is not the thing that recommends a person, nor that which qualifies for a title to salvation. "But only that the persons who were accepted to a title might be known by it. And no more can be argued, when the answer is made, by mentioning the distinguishing character instead of the name."[100] "Walking righteously" is the outward distinguishing mark by which the faithful are known and identified.

The law's positive evidentiary role and its negative convicting role are brought together in Edwards's sermon on Deut 10:13:

> III. The goodness of God appears in requiring obedience of us in order to eternal life. Under the first covenant perfect obedience was required in order to eternal life, as the price of eternal life, as righteousness that procured a title. And under the second covenant our own obedience be not the righteousness that is the price of eternity. Yet a sincere and universal obedience is required as an evidence of faith in Christ (Matthew 7:21). So that none that live another kind of life that is not a life of obedience can have any title to heaven (Matthew 7:26) . . . 1. As [the strictness of God's commands] tends to make us sensible of the necessity of a Mediator, tis profitable for us to have so strict a law enjoined upon us to convince us of the impossibility of salvation

---

99. Edwards, "Misc. 1354," *WJE* 23:524.
100. Edwards, "Misc. 1354," *WJE* 23:526.

by the works of the law and to convince us of our own guilt and misery and so to prepare us to come to Christ. As God's mercy appears in providing us a Savior so it appears in providing suitable means to bring us to that Savior (Galatians 3:23–24).[101]

The law is merciful in driving the sinner away from his own righteousness to Christ's righteousness. The obedience to the law is the necessary, yet non-meritorious, evidence of, fruit of, or demonstration of the true character of the believer's faith in Christ. Faith and obedience are inseparably linked. One is not given without the other. But it is only faith that justifies, however much the evidence of such faith is necessarily displayed, exhibited, and emphasized in terms of obedience.

Fifth, Edwards additionally cautions how the obedience required under the Mosaic dispensation of the Covenant of Grace can be confused with the truly legal, yet merely temporal, national covenant with Israel. Edwards reminds his readers of this other covenant and how passages referring to the obedient requirements, as fully legal in the context of this "established" covenant, can be confused with the "obedience" required under the Mosaic dispensation of the Covenant of Grace. These are truly legal requirements, pertaining strictly to the "letter," whereby the moral value of outward obedience is what recommends to God his blessings and rewards as proper conditions. But the blessings and rewards under this covenant have nothing to do with the "spiritual" rewards and blessings of fellowship with God and eternal life. It is completely diverse from the Covenant of Grace. It remains "carnal" and "external," pertaining solely to Israel's inheritance and prosperity in the land of Canaan. "We have as good warrant from the Word of God to suppose the whole ceremonial law to be given in order to a figurative representing and signifying spiritual and evangelical things to mankind, as we have to suppose that prophetical representations are to represent and signify the events designed by them, and therefore as good reason to endeavor to interpret them."[102] It serves the purpose of leading Israel to the Covenant of Grace through its symbolism and types, but it is not to be confused with it.

Sixth, and finally, the evangelical obedience required in both the old and new dispensations of the Covenant of Grace has an "agreeableness" to the holy nature and will of God. As such it is in "some

---

101. Edwards, "Deut 10:13," *WJEO* 48, L. 7r, and L. 8r, 8v (my transcription of Edwards's sermon notes).

102. Edwards, "Types of the Messiah," *WJE* 11:324. Edwards was fascinated with "types" throughout all redemptive history.

respect" a positive ground in being the "appointed term" or condition of justification. Edwards's use of these terms ("positive ground," "appointed term," or "condition") in speaking of the role of obedience in justification has caused no small amount of confusion in interpreting Edwards and questioning whether he was truly orthodox in terms of justification by faith alone. What Edwards means by "positive ground" needs to be carefully qualified: "[T]he holiness of faith and evangelical compliance with the Savior is not [that] which recommends the person to a justified state, and in itself considered is not sufficient to do anything towards it."[103] It does not contribute by way of any intrinsic moral value, but merely as an appointed means of "agreement." God as "infinitely holy and wise" would not contrive any other way or appoint any terms of salvation that did not secure and promote holiness or an agreement with "the infinitely holy heart of God." There is a moral value in the obedience of believers, but this arises from their relation to Christ and is a "secondary recommendation." By "secondary recommendation" Edwards does not mean it *contributes* in any manner towards justification but is *consequent* on justification.

Hidden and Revealed

While it is true that under the old dispensation the evangelical doctrines of justification by faith alone, doctrines revealed "above the light [of nature]," were "less clearly revealed" than in the New Testament, Edwards insists that they were nonetheless "truly revealed." They were revealed under cover of the "terribleness" of Sinai in revealing the people's utter hopelessness in their own righteousness. They were also revealed in the provisions of sacrifices, especially in the varied and perpetual nature which tended to lead them by their typical representations "to suppose that their own moral value" was not sufficient.

> Those sacrifices were offered as atonement for sin, which taught 'em that their own righteousness made no satisfaction, but [they] were put in mind that, notwithstanding all their righteousness, they deserved the most terrible punishment. They saw the image of what their guilt exposed 'em to. They saw the creature's blood shed, and its dying struggles, and its very vitals—its inward, vital parts, or the fat about them, and the

---

103. Edwards, "Misc. 1354," *WJE* 23:532.

> blood—burnt, scorched and consumed in the fire. And by this also they were put in mind of the necessity of a satisfaction to be made, that death should be suffered and God's threatening of wrath some way fulfilled, and justice in some respect satisfied, that they might not think that for the sake of value in them God abated of his threatenings, relinquished the honor of his majesty and authority. For they must conceive of this terrible suffering of the creature as the effect of the wrath of God against their sin.[104]

Not only did the ceremonial law convey the nature of God's hatred of sin and judgment, they also conveyed the way of redemption and atonement by acting as types of Christ.

> These sacrifices also were offered as a sweet savor to recommend 'em to God, which intimated to 'em that their own righteousness was not sufficient to recommend. 'Tis very evident from God's own word that he made use of personal types of Christ to that end, that they might not trust in their own righteousness, turning the people's eyes off from their own righteousness to those personal types. Deuteronomy 9:5, "Not for thy righteousness... but to perform the word which the Lord sware unto thy fathers." So there is all reason to think that the real types were made use [of] for the same end.[105]

God manifested himself as graciously disposed to pardon and accept them as a patient and waiting father, not "waiting for a compensation or satisfaction for sin from them" but as having no pleasure in the death of sinners. When God offers his pardon on their repentance "he does it in such a manner as not at all to lead sinners to suppose that it was on account of the valuableness of their repentance, or because it made any compensation so as in its own nature, as it were, to abolish and destroy the transgression."[106] The removing and abolishing of guilt is represented as God's own and free act, of his "mere motion and great grace." Through his active and passive obedience, the Second Person of the Trinity bears the burden of this guilt and fulfills the righteousness that the original Covenant of Works required.

While the way of justification by faith was truly revealed, it was proposed to the children of Israel in a "legal manner in the books of Moses" for their trial. The way of faith was not so fully revealed "till after the

---

104. Edwards, "Misc. 1354," *WJE* 23:536.
105. Edwards, "Misc. 1354," *WJE* 23:536.
106. Edwards, "Misc. 1354," *WJE* 23:537.

nation had had some ages' experience of their utter inability to obtain justification in the way of the law." Edwards is keen to show that Israel was not only instructed in the way of faith "in general," but that the revelation they received was to faith specifically in "the second person in the Godhead as their Mediator and advocate, and in the Messiah as their great high priest and sacrifice."[107]

Edwards devotes an entire section in his *Controversies Notebook* to the topic of how the Old Testament saints were justified through faith in Christ. Edwards's approach is framed in his doctrine of the Trinity and God's atoning work in Christ. He argues that the Israelites knew that the "Lord on earth," who redeemed them from their bondage in Egypt and guided them through the wilderness was "a different person from him in heaven that sustained the dignity and maintained the rights of the Godhead, and acted as first and head and chief in the affairs of God's kingdom."[108] This power that the Israelites experienced in their history was referred to as, "the angel of the Lord," "the presence of the Lord," "the name of the Lord," "the strength of the Lord," "the glory of the Lord," and "the son of God." These names did not refer to mere divinely-derived power, but to their God and "object of worship."[109] The Israelites came to understand that the God in heaven was somehow distinct from the God who was with them in the wilderness and "dwelt in the Holy of Holies." These were not different Gods, but the same God. Edwards's trinitarian theology comes through when he explains that "to prevent the Jews having any notion of two Gods, and to lead 'em to conceive of the infinitely near relation between that person and more immediately dwelt among them and the first person in the Godhead, as being in him and as having one nature and one substance, called him his 'name,' . . . signifying the relation that there is between him and his idea."[110] Edwards contends that the Second Person of the Trinity was sent to be the Mediator between them and God and was the one through whom the atoning of their sinfulness was made possible.[111] According to Edwards, the saints in Israel knew that their sacrifices were acceptable to God "not on account of the value of their offerings as in themselves, but through that person

---

107. Edwards, "Misc. 1354," *WJE* 23:540.
108. Edwards, "'Controversies' Notebook: Justification," *WJE* 21:372.
109. Edwards, "'Controversies' Notebook: Justification," *WJE* 21:376.
110. Edwards, "'Controversies' Notebook: Justification," *WJE* 21:378.
111. Edwards, "'Controversies' Notebook: Justification," *WJE* 21:386–87.

called God's name" who dwelt on the mercy seat in the Holy of Holies "as their Mediator, and through his worthiness ... did as it were cover the nakedness and deformity of the people, and recommend them by his excellency and beauty."[112]

Although the saints in Israel experienced atonement and justification through the divine Mediator, they also knew that the "true, complete and final atonement" was yet to be revealed more fully in the future through God's own Son.[113] This true experience of salvation came by way of types. Types for Edwards were not simply symbolic reflections, but true representations that "participated in a scheme of adumbrations and fulfillment."[114] They not only pointed to something else but also participate in the reality to which they point. For example, when Abraham offered up his son Isaac, he received Christ "in a figure, or *en parabole*, as it is in the original [Heb 11:19]; i.e., he received the antitype of Christ slain and risen in that type of his son Isaac." Edwards makes the connection that, "[I]f Abraham by faith received Christ and his sacrifice in that type, 'tis likely that the saints received him in the type of the legal sacrifices."[115] While the revelation given to Israel was a less complete revelation than the New Testament saints had through the incarnate Messiah, it was still a real and true participation in the complete and final atonement that would come; it was "a real atonement and peace with God."[116] Edwards concludes:

> And if any [think] that the revelations of the way of justification in the Old Testament are too obscure to lead the people to seek and depend upon justification in this way, it may be considered that 'tis certain and beyond dispute that there were many things of an evangelical nature that the church of God under the old testament were fully established in the belief of, and express and plain in their profession of, that the Old Testament itself was no more express and full in than in this way of justification. Thus they were full in the belief of the immortality of the soul, as the heathen philosophers were, and so in their belief of the resurrection of the dead, as is evident by the New Testament and by the ancient Jewish writings. By these it is plain those doctrines

112. Edwards, "'Controversies' Notebook: Justification," *WJE* 21:389–90.
113. Edwards, "'Controversies' Notebook: Justification," *WJE* 21:398.
114. Lowance, "Editor's Introduction," *WJE* 11:166.
115. Edwards, "'Controversies' Notebook: Justification," *WJE* 21:406.
116. Edwards, "'Controversies' Notebook: Justification," *WJE* 21:394.

were esteemed as great and main articles of their faith. And thus I suppose the saints under the old testament trusted in Christ and were justified by faith in him.[117]

The "cortex" of the law, as both the Covenant of Works exhibited and proposed and the external national covenant established with Israel, functioned both to hide from the self-righteous and to reveal to the saints the Covenant of Grace in its shadows and types.

Conclusion

How should we characterize Edwards's view of the Mosaic covenant in terms of Ferry's typology? It should be evident that Edwards presents a view that touches on many of the perspectives outlined by Ferry that were present in other Reformed covenant theologians. But was Edwards able to construct a more comprehensive integration of these perspectives? I would argue that he does.

Edwards is clear that the substance of the old and new dispensations were identical, but differed only in the accidentals of its administration. He further accounts for the law-gospel contrast (the question of antithesis) by presenting a dialectic of "hidden" and "revealed" in which the Mosaic law both hides the Covenant of Grace and reveals it. Central to his interpretation is picturing the Mosaic covenants (the Covenant of Works and the national covenant) as "covering" the Covenant of Grace, as a "cortex" to the "medulla." In doing so he integrates to some extent nearly all of Ferry's categories. The use of the substance-abstract distinction, the identification of a national covenant with Israel, a principle of abstraction, and the themes of historical relative contrast and promise-fulfillment are all discernible aspects of Edwards's dialectic. Edwards uses the distinction between the ceremonial, civil, and moral laws in contrasting the old and new dispensations. The theme of "emphasis" is also present in Edwards's explanation of how the fruit and evidence of faith, i.e., obedience, receives greater emphasis under the Old Covenant administration in view of the differing degrees of revelation between the covenants. Even the misinterpretation theory is given theological grounding in his "letter" and "spirit" distinction.

In terms of Ferry's principle of republication, or the relationship of the Mosaic covenant to the Covenant of Works, Edwards has a

---

117. Edwards, "'Controversies' Notebook: Justification," *WJE* 21:407–8.

multi-perspectival approach that appears to coordinate most, if not all, of Ferry's categories. Edwards argues a formal republication of the Covenant of Works (also respecting a material element) in being exhibited and proposed. It is not established, however, as a means of justification. The Covenant of Works is subservient to the Covenant of Grace in its pedagogical function, in its typological revelation, and in its hermeneutics of "letter" and "spirit" that reveals or hides the nature of the Covenant of Grace relative to one's state of spiritual enlightenment. The relationship exhibits a complex nature whereby the Covenant of Grace is revealed through the "contrary" of law and obedience (the Covenant of Works).

The Mosaic covenant was not a distinct and separate covenant, offering another way of salvation in opposition to the Covenant of Grace. It performed an administrative or subservient role to the Covenant of Grace. Indeed, it was part of the revelation of the Covenant of Redemption in history, a "new work of God" that ultimately furthered the work of redemption. Though clouded and obscured in its revelation of the gospel as compared to the New Covenant administration, it nevertheless truly revealed the works principle and the requirement of obedience that can only be met by a second covenant mediator. The Mosaic covenant laid the historical and covenant context for Christ. It highlighted the need for and the provision of the imputation of Christ's righteousness in the Covenant of Grace.

As a biblical theologian, Edwards's understanding of the Mosaic covenant's relation to the Covenant of Grace informed his theology of faith, works, and justification. In the last chapter, I argued that Edwards's distinction between the Covenant of Grace as the revelation of the Covenant of Redemption in time and the marriage covenant between Christ and his church builds an impenetrable wall between law and gospel. Edwards's view of the Mosaic covenant, with its emphasis on obedience, provides a deeper understanding of the role of obedience in relation to faith. In the next chapter I will begin to bring Edwards's covenant theology to bear on faith and justification, demonstrating how Edwards's more controversial statements are best understood and clarified from this covenant perspective, as opposed to prioritizing aspects of his more philosophical speculations.

6

Jonathan Edwards on Justification and Faith

Introduction

EDWARDS SELF-CONSCIOUSLY CONSIDERED HIMSELF a defender of the Reformed faith against its Arminian and antinomian detractors. He was even not above identifying the office of the Pope and the papacy as the "Antichrist" in his polemic with Roman Catholicism.[1] So, it becomes surprising that scholars could read Edwards as having practically undermined the Reformed doctrine of justification. According to Sweeney, Edwards's doctrine of justification has become "one of the most important interpretive conversations in the field."[2] In this section I will address and critique several studies that have been critical of Edwards regarding his formulations of justification and that have read into Edwards a more Roman Catholic understanding of the relationship between justification and works. I will argue for a different reading of Edwards that will center on his understanding of justification in the context of his covenant theology. I will argue that these studies have either not understood Edwards adequately in this context or have begun with false assumptions regarding Edwards' metaphysical philosophy.

---

1. "He arrogates to himself the power and prerogatives of God, opposing and exalting himself above all that is called God, or that is worshiped, so that he as God sitteth in the temple of God, shewing himself that he is God. [He] pretends to the same power over the church as Jesus Christ hath." Edwards, "Apocalypse Series," *WJE* 5:125. See also, Edwards, "They Sing a New Song," *WJE* 22:227; Edwards, "Misc. 340," *WJE* 13:415.

2. Sweeney, "Justification by Faith Alone?," 130.

I will summarize the arguments of three scholars: Thomas Schafer, George Hunsinger, and Anri Morimoto. Each of these scholars advances a common thesis that Edwards's language and formulations opened the door to a theology that more closely represented Roman Catholic understandings of justification, particularly on the relationship between faith and works. They each read Edwards from the perspective of an "ontological soteriology," whereby there is something inherent within the believer that merits or earns the blessing of justification. I will argue that reading Edwards from a covenant perspective avoids these mistaken interpretations. Aside from misrepresenting Edwards either contextually or by proceeding from theoretical premises that are not essentially compatible with his covenant-based soteriology, the conclusions these interpreters reach presents an Edwards that appears grossly incongruous when seen in light of his biblical and pastoral teaching.

In the last section of this chapter, I will take a closer look at three specific areas where Edwards's language has been challenged for being more consistent with Roman Catholicism than Reformed Protestantism. These areas include his language of "infusion," his language of "union with Christ," and his distinction between the natural and moral fitness of faith. I will defend the position that Edwards, when read from a covenant perspective, is well within the bounds of historic orthodox Reformed theology.

Jonathan Edwards on Justification: Critiques

As I argued earlier, it is important for any reading of Edwards to privilege him primarily as a pastor-theologian in the Reformed tradition, one who prioritized the authority and centrality of Scripture over philosophical speculation in his theology. This is especially important with regards to the "ethics" of Edwards, by which I limit to the role of and motive for "good works" in the life of the redeemed believer or, as Edwards preferred, evangelical obedience.

Interpreting difficult and ambiguous passages in Edwards in such a way that sets him in significant opposition to central tenets of the Reformed tradition needs to be explained. By this I do not mean that we should not be critical in reading Edwards, merely assuming he is orthodox and "eisogetically" reading a traditional Reformed interpretation into his writings. Edwards himself admits to not being above critiquing his own tradition. Conversely, theologians have also pointed out problematic areas in Edwards's thought which possibly conflict with the mainstream of Reformed confessional theology. Rather, what I mean is that if we interpret Edwards, as some have done, in ways that place him outside a tradition of theology that he himself clearly saw himself as part of and staunch defender of (e.g., interpreting him as a universalist, neonomian, antinomian, or holding to a view of justification more in line with Roman Catholicism) it should at least give one pause to reconsider what presuppositions have been made in our interpretation and question whether we have read Edwards correctly and as he would have intended. I contend that because a covenant hermeneutic was so central to Reformed theology one must read Edwards within this context. Understanding Edwards's doctrine of evangelical obedience, the non-meritorious necessity of good works as they relate to justification and the Christian life, can be adequately understood only after situating him within the bounds of his covenant theology.

Thomas Schafer: "Ambiguous and somewhat precarious"

In 1951 Thomas Schafer wrote a learned and insightful article on Edwards's theology of justification by faith.[3] In his article, Schafer admits that Edwards's discourse on justification in his *Masters Questio* and later lectures and treatise in 1734/1738 was "unequivocal enough" in that it affirmed justification only by faith in Christ and not by any manner of virtue or goodness in the believer. Justification is thus not merely the remission of sins (an Arminian position) but a status of positive righteousness in God's sight. Christ's satisfaction of God's justice and the righteousness of his active obedience constitute the only meritorious cause of justification, becoming the believer's only by imputation. However, Schafer contends that in the last twenty years of Edwards's works

---

3. Schafer, "Jonathan Edwards," 55–67. For responses to Schafer that give different readings, see Waddington, "Jonathan Edwards's Ambiguous," 357–72, Kang, "Justified by Faith," 106; Bombaro, "Beautiful Beings"; Bombaro, *Jonathan Edwards's Vision*; Bombaro, "Dispositional Peculiarity," 121–58. While John Bombaro situates Edwards more in his "particularistic" Reformed tradition, he changes the focus of Edwards's goals in justification away from individual salvation to an eschatological/apocalyptic driven vision. For Bombaro justification in Edwards is foremost concerned with eschatology and the expansion of a worldwide community of justified believers hastening the establishment of Christ's kingdom on earth and consequently his *parousia* and bodily reign.

there is an "almost total lack of emphasis on the doctrine" and that there were important elements in Edwards's religious thought which caused his doctrine of justification to "occupy an ambiguous and somewhat precarious place in his theology."[4]

Schafer highlights three specific elements in Edwards's thought to support his claim. First, Edwards grounded the legal imputation of Christ's righteousness to the believer in the believer's real (ontological) union with Christ. Second, Edwards placed sanctification prior to justification. Third, Edwards used the notion of formed faith, a notion more amendable to the Roman Catholic doctrine of *fides caritate formata* than to the Protestant *sola fide*.

Schafer's first concern is based on Edwards's statement that "what is real in the union between Christ and his people, is the foundation of what is legal, that is, it is something really in them, and between them, uniting them, that is the ground of the suitableness of their being accounted as one by the Judge."[5] Schafer says that "the natural creates the legal, not vice versa; something really existing in the soul precedes the external imputation . . . Justification from this point of view is but the restatement in forensic terms of a *fait accompli*, for faith is the union, and the union effects the justification."[6] For Schafer, grounding justification in union with Christ is somehow incompatible with the external and forensic nature of righteousness. Schafer is either reading Edwards's "union" as ontological (a co-mingling with Christ or divinization) and/or involving an innate or intrinsic virtue of holiness. Another possibility is that he is equating the "real" with the transformational aspect of union with Christ, i.e., sanctification, in Edwards's soteriology.

Reading Edwards from a covenant perspective on union with Christ involves none of these scenarios. While the Holy Spirit (the Spirit of Christ) acts in the soul of the believer in regeneration, there is no ontological merging. Neither is justification based on something innate or intrinsic in the soul. While the Holy Spirit is the ground of the transformative, Edwards, along with other Reformed orthodox theologians, did not entertain any necessary antithesis between the forensic (the external) and the transformative (the internal). Both are the *duplex gratia*, the twin blessings of a believer's union with Christ. Justification and sanctification

---

4. Schafer, "Jonathan Edwards," 57.
5. Edwards, "Justification by Faith Alone," *WJE* 19:158.
6. Schafer, "Jonathan Edwards," 58.

are both works of the Holy Spirit and they are never separate, even as they are to be distinguished.

Schafer also claims that Edwards compromised the Reformed doctrine of justification by placing sanctification before justification.[7] Conrad Cherry summarizes the concern: "The upshot of the argument appears to be an abandonment of the traditional Calvinist position that sanctification is a progressive struggle for holiness that *grows out of* faith, and the adoption of a view repugnant to the thrust of Reformation Protestantism, the view that faith is based upon man's becoming sanctified or holy-in-himself."[8] Schafer presents as evidence Edwards's statement: "There must be the principle before there can be the action, in all cases . . . Yea, there must be the principle of holiness before there can be the action, in all cases."[9] On the surface this would appear to make Edwards saying that the exercise of faith by the believer rests upon some innate virtue or "principle of holiness."

One of the problems with Schafer's interpretation of Edwards is that he confuses how the terms sanctification and regeneration are being used. In the Reformed tradition, regeneration precedes faith and repentance (and therefore, justification) in the typical *ordo salutis*.[10] The terminology used in the Reformed tradition can be fluid, in that sanctification can refer to both the growth in grace that follows justification and conversion and to regeneration proper. Similarly, regeneration is used in the broad sense of sanctification and the entire renovative process in the Christian life and, in a more narrow sense, pertaining to the initial vivifying work of the Holy Spirit in effectual calling. When Edwards uses the words "holiness" and "sanctification" in the passage quoted by Schafer, he is clearly talking about regeneration in the narrow sense as used in Reformed writings.[11] Cherry explains:

> It is perhaps best to call this action of the Holy Spirit, which is the foundation of faith, a *kind* of sanctification. Traditionally Reformed theologians held to "progressive" sanctification: it

---

7. Schafer, "Jonathan Edwards," 59.
8. Cherry, *Theology of Jonathan Edwards*, 41.
9. Edwards, "Misc. 77," *WJE* 13: 244–45.
10. According to John Calvin, "Christ cannot be known apart from the sanctification of the Spirit. It follows that faith can in no wise be separated from a divine disposition." Calvin, *Institutes*, 1:552–53.
11. For Edwards's most complete discussion on the technical or theological use of the term "regeneration" or "conversion," see Edwards, "Misc. 847," *WJE* 20: 68–74.

was the activity of God's Spirit in man's inward parts whereby regeneration, initiate by vocation, was continued and gradually completed as man struggled in the race of life and as the Spirit more and more cleansed man of his sin. Sometimes the term "regeneration" was virtually identical with "sanctification" embracing the whole work of the Spirit in man. At other times "regeneration" designated the new birth of man in conversion which does not admit of degrees, while "sanctification" referred to the progressive cleansing of the Holy Spirit. Although Edwards applied "sanctification" to the gift of the principle that awakens the act of faith, and although he is not careful at all times to distinguish sanctification from regeneration and calling, he by no means fell away from his Reformed tradition in meaning.[12]

The technical use of these terms in their narrow sense is frequently confused and can be a source of misreading. Edwards is simply affirming the Reformed *ordo salutis* of regeneration preceding (logically, not temporally) conversion.

Furthermore, there is no "inherent state" or quality of the soul that is the ground for justification. Regeneration is the act of the Holy Spirit and the disposition to exercise faith is a gift wrought by the immediate work of the Holy Spirit (the "new sense," "the sense of the heart," "spiritual understanding," or a "relish for God and the things of God"). Edwards is concerned to stress the *immediacy* of God's sovereign action on the soul in distinction from the Arminian view of *mediate* "moral suasion." Edwards's argument is that if faith is caused by the immediate (effective and irresistible) influence of the Spirit (by the Word), then there is no possibility for human merit. Faith is a gift from God: "'Tis of God that we receive faith to close with him."[13] The Holy Spirit communicates a "divine light" without which saving faith is impossible: "[T]his light, and this only, will bring the soul to a saving close with Christ. It conforms the heart to the gospel . . . it causes the heart to embrace the joyful tidings . . . it effectually disposes the soul to give itself entirely to Christ."[14] I will discuss these issues in more detail later.

In covenant context, the Holy Spirit is the blessing achieved for believers in the Covenant of Redemption. Faith (or any regenerative/sanctifying holiness preceding faith) does not in any way merit justification

---

12. Cherry, *Theology of Jonathan Edwards*, 42–43.
13. Edwards, "God Glorified in Man's Dependence," *WJE* 17:202.
14. Edwards, "Divine and Supernatural Light," *WJE* 17:424.

in Edwards's theology. Faith is the "condition" for justification as an act of union that is naturally, not morally, fitting for God's accounting the believer "in Christ." Edwards explicitly denies that faith has a "merit of congruity; or indeed any moral congruity at all" to either union with Christ or his benefits.[15] Any holiness in the believer "is looked upon as nothing, until the man is justified." Edwards upholds the priority of justification over sanctification.[16]

Finally, Schafer accuses Edwards of accepting in some form the notion of formed faith, traditionally a Roman Catholic doctrine: "According to the Catholic theologians, it is love which makes faith saving and meritorious, changing it from mere 'informal' assent to 'formal' and living faith."[17] Schafer recognizes that love (or consent or affiance) is central in Edwards's soteriology.

> Here is the center of Edwards' piety: a direct intuitive apprehension, a "sight," a "sense," a "taste" of God's majestic beauty, a love of God simply because he is God, an exultant affirmation of all God's way. This, to Edwards, is the meaning of faith. Upon this experience Edwards builds his doctrine of the "divine and supernatural light," which confers and is this new sight and taste of the essential loveliness of God and divine things. Spiritual light does not reveal new articles of faith; it suffuses the familiar gospel with a glow that irresistibly draws the soul. True faith is its essence and fruit.[18]

Schafer is equating the presence of love that characterizes true faith, which Edwards acknowledges, with the meritorious nature of love in the Roman Catholic doctrine of formed faith, which Edwards denies.

Edwards does not separate love and faith as both are the expressions of the same divine disposition in the believer. "There is implied in believing in Christ not only and merely that exercise of mind which arises from a sense of his excellency and reality as a Savior, but also with that, what arises from the consideration of his relation to us and our concerns in

---

15. Edwards, "Justification by Faith Alone," *WJE* 19:159.

16. Cf. *WSC* Q.3: "How doth the Spirit apply to us the redemption purchased by Christ? A. The Spirit applieth to us the redemption purchased by Christ, by working faith in us, and thereby uniting us to Christ in our effectual calling." The "thereby" in the catechism seems to signal that Spirit-wrought faith and not regeneration *per se* is the "instrument" of union with Christ in the application of redemption.

17. Schafer, "Jonathan Edwards," 59.

18. Schafer, "Jonathan Edwards," 61.

him, his being a Savior for such as we, for sinful men, and a Savior that is offered with his benefits to us."[19] The act of loving and sensing God's beauty for what he is and does, considered in itself, and the act of faith in God for what God has done for us, are inseparable.[20]

Edwards is rejecting the kind of piety that loves God merely and only out of private interests, which "don't sincerely and really accept anything that is divine." In the Roman Catholic doctrine "unformed faith" is true faith. It becomes a meritorious faith by the addition of love and obedience. For Edwards (and Protestant theology as a whole), "unformed faith" is not faith at all. True salvific faith is evidenced by love and obedience. Jeffrey Waddington explains:

> Love is neither the form for faith nor is it meritorious for Edwards as it is for Roman Catholic doctrine. For Edwards, in order for his stress on love to be the virtual equivalent of formed faith, he would have to have a notion of *true* faith that is both true and unaccompanied by love *per se* (which given Edwards's grounding of faith in regeneration or the 'new sense" seems impossible) *and* he would have to hold some idea of love as meritorious so that this formed faith (true faith plus meritorious love) is what merits justification.[21]

Edwards maintains that even faith "as any goodness or loveliness of the believer, follows justification; the goodness is on the fore-mentioned account justly looked upon as nothing, until the man is justified."[22] Schafer has it backwards. For Edwards it is not loving obedience that gives faith its (meritorious) form, it is (unmeritorious) faith that forms love and obedience, uniting (or *as* the uniting) the believer to Christ and his benefits.

Schafer's reading of Edwards cannot take into account Edwards's doctrine of imputation. Justification involves the imputation of both the positive and negative righteousness of Christ. For a sinner to have his "sins being removed by Christ's atonement, is not sufficient for his justification; for a justifying a man . . . is not merely pronouncing him innocent or without guilt, but standing right, with regard to the rule he is under, and righteous unto life."[23] Christ's righteousness is imputed

---

19. Edwards, "Faith," *WJE* 21:434.
20. Lee, "Editor's Introduction," *WJE* 21:102.
21. Waddington, "Jonathan Edwards's Ambiguous," 370.
22. Edwards, "Justification by Faith Alone," *WJE* 19:194–95.
23. Edwards, "Justification by Faith Alone," *WJE* 19:190–91.

to the unrighteous so that the sinner is looked upon as having obeyed God's law perfectly as well. Edwards approvingly quotes Richard Rawlin (1687–1757) on imputation in his *"Controversies" Notebook: Justification*:

> God mercifully and graciously imputes and reckons [Christ's] righteousness to the soul in believing, and so we come, according to the tenor and constitution of the new covenant, to have a real and pleadable interest in it. Not that he reckons we have wrought it out in our own persons, so that the individual obedience and sufferings of Christ are judged to be our obedience and sufferings; this destroys the imputation of that which is done by another for us, and is not according to the judgment of truth: nor that he takes it from Christ, and transposes it into us, so that we become the seat and subject of it by way of inherency, and this righteousness an inherent quality in us; that is impossible in the nature of things. But the meaning is, that he graciously accepts it for our pardon and justification, as if we had personally wrought it out ourselves; and as it was performed in our room and stead, by a proper substitution of Christ to bear the guilt and punishment of our sins, as such he considers it in his law, and deals with us accordingly, and all the benefit and advantage of it, by the constitution of the new covenant, redound to us. This is what we mean by imputation.[24]

Positive imputation continues for the regenerate believer even after initial justification, in that the value of a Christian's good works "is founded in, and derived from Christ's righteousness and worthiness."[25] As Sang Hyun Lee reminds us, "A positive imputation of Christ's perfect righteousness is an idea that belongs to the forensic doctrine of justification."[26] *Contra* Schafer's reading of Edwards, believers are not justified by what is in them but rather by what Christ has earned for them in the Covenant of

---

24. Edwards, "'Controversies' Notebook: Justification," *WJE* 21:342. Edwards is quoting Richard Rawlin, *Christ the Righteousness of His People: Or, The Doctrine of Justification by Faith in Him* (1741).

25. Edwards, "Justification by Faith Alone," *WJE* 19:215. Aquinas discusses the "negative role" of imputation in justification in that it "proceeds from the Divine love, that sin is not imputed to a man by God." The positive imputation of Christ's righteousness plays no role in Aquinas's theology. Justification for Aquinas involves an actual change, or "transmutation," that proceeds from the infusion of grace that results in an inherent righteousness. Aquinas, *Summa Theologica*, 1–2.113.2.

26. Lee, "Editor's Introduction," *WJE* 21:75.

Redemption and applied in the Covenant of Grace. Everything is "outside us."[27]

George Hunsinger: "An American tragedy"

George Hunsinger argues that Edwards's doctrine of justification, at least in its "more technical, complex, and subtle account," opened the door to concepts that were opposed to core and foundational Reformation teachings, especially in terms of the relation between justification and works, and concludes that Edwards's doctrine ultimately was more Catholic than Protestant.[28] He calls this "an American tragedy" in a popularized summary of his article.[29] Much of his reading of Edwards parallels Schafer's and is addressed above. I will begin by summarizing his arguments and then offer a constructive critique and defense of Edwards's view of justification as falling well within Reformed orthodoxy.

Hunsinger makes two points in his reading of Edwards: 1) Edwards makes faith out to be a secondary but real ground for the believer's acceptance by God in addition to Christ, and 2) Edwards blurs the traditional Reformed contrast between the declaratory and contributory aspect of works or obedience in justification. First, Edwards says that faith is a "secondary reason" why believers should be accepted by God (the "primary reason" being Christ). Hunsinger questions this language on several counts. For one, it seems to contradict the inherent versus imputed contrast that is so central to Protestantism, which affirmed that justification was grounded solely on the merits of Christ's righteousness and not in any inherent righteousness, holiness, or virtue in the believer. Justification is totally passive; Christ's ground is solely and only sufficient (not merely "primarily" sufficient) and does not need to be supplemented by anything "secondary."[30] For Edwards there is "something" really in believers that justifies them. Hunsinger reads Edwards as saying faith is more than a necessary "condition," but "as a positive qualification it

---

27. "*Extra nos*" is an expression used by Martin Luther to describe the external righteousness that is not one's own. Luther, "Lectures on Galatians," *LW* 26:233–34.

28. Hunsinger, "Dispositional Soteriology," 107–20. For a different reading and perspective on Edwards, see Lee, "Grace and Justification," 130–46. See also the critique by Bombaro, "Jonathan Edwards's Vision," 45–67.

29. Hunsinger, "American Tragedy," 18–21.

30. On the passive nature of justification, Hunsinger quotes Luther in his commentary on Ps 51:6; cf. Luther, "Ps 51," *LW* 12:368.

functions as a secondary and *ex post facto* ground" of justification.[31] He also reads Edwards as giving insufficient weight to Calvin's view of union with Christ. While Edwards describes a "legal" union, which is more formal and external, this is far from Calvin's more relational union and "communion." Quoting Calvin, Hunsinger says that Christ does not give his benefits without giving himself.[32] He summarizes these points by arguing, "The idea of faith as a pleasing disposition that God would reward then opened the door to themes that the reformation had excluded. Inherent as opposed to alien holiness, active as opposed to passive righteousness, and Christ's righteousness as a benefit de-coupled from his person."[33]

In support of his argument, Hunsinger examines Edwards's exegesis of Jas 3:14–26 and the question of how the Epistle understands the relationship between faith and works, "What good is it, my brothers, if someone says he has faith but does not have works? Can that faith save him? . . . You see that a person is justified by works and not by faith alone" (ESV), and how this can be reconciled with Paul's statement in Rom 3:28, "For we hold that one is justified by faith apart from works of the law" (ESV). He claims that Edwards departs from standard Reformed interpretations, or at least as presented by Turretin, in three significant ways. First, Edwards claims that the word "faith" is used differently in Rom 3:28 and Jas 3:14, whereas Turretin maintains that it is the word "justified" that has different meanings in each passage. Second, that Edwards makes good works essential to the definition of faith. Hunsinger makes the (erroneous) conclusion that this makes works an essential contribution to salvation and justification: "Faith alone [for Edwards] is not enough . . . what is inward is not sufficient for salvation . . . only the inward in conjunction with the outward is sufficient."[34] Third, that for Edwards, faith must be expressed or "completed" by works in order to be efficacious.

Hunsinger reads Edwards as implicitly operating with a category that is more fundamental than either faith or works in terms of his use of "dispositional soteriology." In *Misc. 27b*, Edwards talks about the role of dispositions in salvation, particularly how a regenerate "disposition" is expressed as faith, hope, love, and obedience. If these are all mere

---

31. Hunsinger, "Dispositional Soteriology," 114.
32. See Calvin, *Institutes*, 1:736–37.
33. Hunsinger, "Dispositional Soteriology," 113.
34. Hunsinger, "Dispositional Soteriology," 117.

"expressions" of a single disposition, Hunsinger reasons, then *ergo* there is no real distinction between them. Edwards is better represented as saying a believer is justified by "disposition alone" rather than by "faith alone."

There are several contextual problems with Hunsinger's reading of Edwards. Hunsinger concentrates almost solely on Edwards's treatise *Justification by Faith Alone*. There is little interaction with later (and more extensive) writings of Edwards, such as his later *Miscellanies*, sermons, and the extensive treatment of justification in his *Controversies Notebook*. Michael McClenahan provides extensive evidence and argument that Edwards's 1738 treatise had a more limited design than to present a complete doctrine of justification. It was an extended scholastic disputation directed at the theology of Archbishop John Tillotson (1630–1694) and the rising threat of Arminianism in New England.[35] Because of the nature of Edwards's disputation, Edwards exploits aspects of the traditional teaching that particularly support his own polemical agenda (such as union with Christ) without presenting his complete view on the subject. The narrow and limited nature of the text in the course of his concentrated arguments do not do justice to his broader contributions exhibited in his later writings, particularly in terms of the historical turn in Edwards and situating his theology within a covenant framework. McClenahan has demonstrated how this limited reading has led to misinterpretations of Edwards's early writings on justification. If reading Edwards, on this and other vital texts, is informed by a self-conscious reliance on the Reformed faith (as was Edwards's own self-conscious position), then "the balance of probability seems to indicate that Edwards' soteriology is less innovative than the secondary literature suggests."[36]

Hunsinger's comment that Edwards is deficient in describing the union with Christ as a mere formal and external "legal" union is hard to reconcile with Edwards's extensive writings on the centrality of union with Christ in justification and salvation, which would be consistent with the limited focus of his paper. As I have demonstrated, union with Christ is a central motif for Edwards in his covenant theology, and this union begins in eternity in the Covenant of Redemption. For Edwards,

---

35. McClenahan, *Jonathan Edwards*. The elements of a scholastic disputation, including presentation of the question, indication of the subjects, objections, and answers (proofs) are all present in his *Master's Quaestio* and the far more developed 1738 discourse. Tillotson's arguments are cited in Tillotson, *Works*.

36. McClenahan, *Jonathan Edwards*, 195.

while the unity of the believer with Christ never involves any mixture of essence of being (there is no divinization or theosis), there is also no antithesis between the "external" and forensic nature of justification in a believer's union with Christ and the rich "internal" communion believers have with Christ. Edwards's likening the Covenant of Grace to a marriage covenant is telling in this regard. Marriage is certainly a legal union, an external declaration, between two distinct parties that remain distinct, but it is also a perlocutionary act of unition that initiates a deeply rich and personal relationship. In the Covenant of Grace, it is the giving of the Holy Spirit which is the perlocutionary act of effectual calling in the believer that unites the believer to Christ. The Holy Spirit *is* the blessing obtained by Christ in the Covenant of Redemption (that brings justification, sanctification, perseverance, etc.). In the covenant relationship Christ is never separated from his blessings. There certainly is "something" really in believers that justifies them, and that "something" is precisely the "someone" who is the Holy Spirit, the very Spirit of Christ.

Hunsinger also misreads Edwards when he suggests that Edwards allows works to function as a "qualification" for justification (secondary or *ex post facto* ground). In his reading Hunsinger fails to distinguish between the role of faith in justification and the role of works in external rewards. Edwards's discussion in the section quoted by Hunsinger is about the latter. Hunsinger cites the texts out of context and distorts Edwards's view by applying it to justification. To say that a "person's acceptance by God (justification) thus rests not only on the relation, but also remarkably, on the 'inherent holiness' of faith itself"[37] is to negate precisely what Edwards is arguing. Edwards takes exactly the opposite position. On the same page (as Hunsinger's citation) Edwards says, "'Tis no way impossible that God may bestow heaven's glory wholly out of respect to Christ's righteousness, and yet in reward for man's inherent holiness, in different respects, and different ways. It may be only Christ's righteousness, that God has respect to, for its own sake, the independent acceptableness, and dignity of it being sufficient of itself, to recommend all that believe in Christ, to a title to this glory."[38] It is in consequence of justification, says Edwards, that good works (and faith) become rewardable with spiritual and eternal rewards. This is the reverse of any "Catholic" notion of justification and works. Justification is predicated on union with Christ, so

---

37. Hunsinger, "Dispositional Soteriology," 114.
38. Edwards, "Justification by Faith Alone," *WJE* 19:215.

the acts of a believer are only appropriately assessed as believers are in covenant union with Christ or "in Christ." "This is the very foundation of our virtues."[39] Hunsinger, just as Schafer, gets it backwards. It is not works that form faith, but faith (as shorthand for the union with Christ that justifies) that forms works in Edwards's theology.

In terms of Edwards's interpretation of James's epistle, McClenahan notes that "Hunsinger misreads Edwards at this stage because he does not place the discussion of Paul and James in the context of Tillotson's sermons."[40] In its appropriate context Edwards does not blur the declaratory and contributory aspects of works. In fact, reading Edwards in the proper context shows that his exact point is just the opposite. "To be justified is to be approved and accepted," writes Edwards, "but a man may be said to be approved and accepted in two respects; the one is to be approved really, and the other to be approved and accepted declaratively."[41] James is using the term in this second sense. Edwards goes on to explain: "'Tis evident by the Apostle's reasoning, that the necessity of works that he speaks of, is not as having a parallel concern in our salvation with faith; but he speaks of works only as related to faith, and expressive of it; which after all leaves faith the alone fundamental condition, without anything else having a parallel concern with it in this affair, and the other things conditions, only as several expressions, and evidences of it."[42] Faith alone, as an internal state, cannot be the sole requirement for this type of justification, which is external and declarative. This "manifestative justification" comes by no other way than the visible manifestation of the fruit of faith. This is no different from Turretin who said that this manifestation "can be gathered from no other source more certain than by works as its effects and indubitable proofs."[43] As I argued in the previous chapter on the Mosaic covenant, Edwards used this very argument when he maintained that even the emphasis on the obedience of faith under the old dispensation did not negate that Old Testament saints were saved by faith alone. A covenant context makes this clear in Edwards.

It was an Arminian assertion that the word faith was used differently in Romans and James. "[W]e on the other hand," counters Edwards,

---

39. Edwards, "Justification by Faith Alone," *WJE* 19:211.
40. McClenahan, *Jonathan Edwards*, 174.
41. Edwards, "Justification by Faith Alone," *WJE* 19:233.
42. Edwards, "Justification by Faith Alone," *WJE* 19:235.
43. Turretin, *Institutes*, 2:676.

"suppose that the word justify is to be understood in a different sense from the apostle Paul."[44] Edwards argues that this is not only at least as plausible as the Arminian interpretation ("as fair for one scheme as the other"), but is also in agreement with the "current" of Scripture. It is only in the concluding part of his discussion that he concedes that some may wish to take the word justify, "precisely as we do in Paul's epistles."[45] McClenahan is helpful in clarifying what Edwards meant in the context of his polemics with Tillotson: "[Edwards] is not (theoretically) agreeing with Tillotson that it is the word 'faith' that must have a different meaning. Edwards says that in this case the phrase 'works' refers to the 'acts or expressions of faith,' and these are not [to] be excluded from justification, but are evidence of a true and lively faith."[46] McClenahan also reminds the reader of the polemical nature of Edwards's discourse, which was aimed directly at Tillotson in defense of the Reformed position of *sola fide*. Hunsinger completely misreads Edwards on this point when he states that Edwards diverges from "Turretin and the Reformation" because they "had concluded that Paul and James use the word faith differently."[47] This conclusion is further evidenced when Edwards approvingly cites Turretin on his understanding of the relationship between Paul and James in his *Controversies Notebook* on justification.[48]

Hunsinger also contrasts Edwards with Turretin when he states that Edwards insists that good works are "necessary to salvation." Yet Turretin argues the exact same point as Edwards in his description of *sola fide*: "Although the other virtues do not justify with faith, still faith cannot justify in their absence . . . which if they do not contribute to justification, still contribute to the existence and life of faith . . . [works] are adduced as arguments and testimonies indubitable *a posteriori*, from which the truth of their faith could be proved."[49] Turretin devotes an entire section to the question, "Are good works necessary to salvation?" His answer is, "We

---

44. Edwards, "Justification by Faith Alone," *WJE* 19:231.

45. Edwards, "Justification by Faith Alone," *WJE* 19:234–35.

46. McClenahan, *Jonathan Edwards*, 176.

47. Hunsinger, "Dispositional Soteriology," 116.

48. Edwards, "'Controversies' Notebook: Justification," *WJE* 21:344. See also the broader context of Edwards's view of the Epistle of James in Cherry, *Theology of Jonathan Edwards*, 133–42, as well as Edwards's discussion in "Misc. 996," *WJE* 20:324–25.

49. Turretin, *Institutes*, 2:680–81.

affirm" for "obtaining glory."⁵⁰ "Everyone sees that there is the highest and an indispensable necessity of good works for obtaining glory. It is so great that it cannot be reached without them."⁵¹ There is a distinction between justification and the broader context of salvation in both Edwards and Turretin that Hunsinger misses. Reformed theologians can use the term "salvation" to describe the experience of justification or the fuller salvation granted at the point of eschatological glorification. McClenahan explains, "The first act of faith marks the moment of final justification because faith brings the sinner into a spiritual union with the eschatologically justified Christ. Yet this does not remove the possibility of distinguishing between justification and ultimate salvation."⁵² He further clarifies that, "Edwards did not believe he needed to address the issue of the necessity of works for salvation—that would be like asking him to affirm the doctrine of the Trinity. The disputed point is the exact role of works in justification. This distinction is of central importance and the point is frequently overlooked."⁵³

Hunsinger misinterprets Edwards on several fundamental issues by not reading him in context, both in terms of the immediate context of the *Justification* discourse as well as in the larger context of Edwards's writings. Two important aspects of justification that are relevant to these discussions, the working of grace in the soul and the nature of saving faith, are reserved for Edwards's other writings and sermons.⁵⁴ Edwards's Reformed soteriology does not need to be relegated to a "dispositional

---

50. Turretin, *Institutes*, 2:702.

51. Turretin, *Institutes*, 2:705.

52. McClenahan, *Jonathan Edwards*, 149.

53. McClenahan, *Jonathan Edwards*, 148 n. 78. McClenahan acutely observes that on page 117 of Hunsinger's article the second paragraph begins with the term "justification" and ends with the term "sanctification."

54. McClenahan argues that two earlier sermons of Edwards that preceded the 1738 justification discourse, entitled *God Glorified in Man's Dependence* (1731) and *A Divine and Supernatural Light* (1734), were part of Edwards's continued pulpit campaign in addition to the press in refuting Tillotson's Arminian theology, and "only when these are placed in the context of the ongoing response to Tillotson can they be accurately interpreted." McLenahan, *Jonathan Edwards*, 177. It appears that Edwards had also planned to use these sermons in conjunction with his *Justification* discourse, along with other *Miscellanies* and notes, in a planned comprehensive treatise on justification, in which he intended to "explain the nature of JUSTIFICATION, the Scripture notion of it, and then SECONDLY the nature of FAITH. Explain this form the Scripture, then how 'tis BY FAITH." Edwards, "'Controversies' Notebook: Justification," *WJE* 21:342.

ontology." A covenant context for understanding Edwards's defense of *sola fide* is sufficient.

Anri Morimoto: "Dispositional Ontology"

Anri Morimoto likewise reads Edwards as less Reformed and more Catholic in his soteriology in his influential book, *Jonathan Edwards and the Catholic Vision of Salvation*.[55] I will not offer a comprehensive response to Morimoto's extensive work, but will only make some brief general comments summarizing where I think he has also misread Edwards.[56]

Central to Morimoto's interpretation is his view of Edwards's metaphysics. According to Morimoto, Edwards rejected Aristotelian substance ontology in favor of a dispositional ontology. Much of Morimoto's discussion is dependent on Sang Hyun Lee's seminal study of Edwards's ontology of "dispositions" in *The Philosophical Theology of Jonathan Edwards*. In Lee's study, Edwards is described as paving a middle way between scholastic Aristotelian ontology and the empiricism of John Locke and David Hume.[57] For Aristotle, man is comprised of substance, habits, and acts. Habits, or dispositions, exist on the "accident" side of the substance/accident dichotomy and are described to be real virtues (powers or skills). Empiricists, on the other hand, reduced habits to mere customs, having no reality of their own.[58] According to Lee, Edwards accepts a realist (as opposed to nominalist) and relational view of dispositions, but unlike Aristotle he combined the concepts of substance and disposition, which for Aristotle were two distinct things. This definition is realistic in that dispositions are not mere customs or regularities of events but are ontologically abiding powers that possess a mode of realness even when they are not being exercised. A disposition is a relational

---

55. Morimoto, *Jonathan Edwards*. His arguments are summarized in Morimoto, "Salvation as Fulfillment," 13–23.

56. Waddington provides a response to Morimoto, defending Edwards's Protestant and Reformed views of justification. According to Waddington, Morimoto misreads Edwards by "failing to understand him within his own Reformed tradition and context," and that "Morimoto's ecumenism and inclusivism have led him to try and make Jonathan Edwards resemble a John Hick or Karl Rahner born out of time." Waddington, "Must We Believe?," 11–21. See also Bombaro, "Jonathan Edwards's Vision," 45–67; Yazawa, *Covenant of Redemption*, 113–18.

57. Lee, *Philosophical Theology*, 17–46.

58. Lee, *Philosophical Theology*, 25.

principle in that it is a general law that governs the manner or character of actual actions and events.

Morimoto embraces the dispositional ontology of Edwards as interpreted by Lee and uses it as a lens to read Edwards. Because a person can possess a disposition or habit even if it never actualized, he interprets Edwards as believing that a person can possess a holy disposition (to believe in God), apart from its exercise, and that this is the only thing necessary for salvation.[59] He applies this to the case of infants (who can possess a holy disposition and be saved even when they die in infancy) as well as to the salvation of Old Testament saints (who could not have explicit faith in Christ, since he was yet to be incarnate).[60] In both cases the disposition alone is sufficient for salvation and is that which God accepts as the only necessary ground. It is not the actual exercise of that disposition in explicit belief in or profession of Christ. The disposition is "real" whether it is actualized or not. One is not saved by faith alone, but by disposition alone. Morimoto speculates that this could well be the case with those outside the visible church as well and makes the speculative leap that all are born with a "holy disposition," even if few exercise it. Morimoto does not suggest that this was actually Edwards's belief. He is rather pointing to "suggestions" in Edwards's theology (much in the way Schafer and Hunsinger did) that would move beyond Reformed exclusivism and into a more Barthian inclusivism where unbelievers just have to be shown that God has already saved them in the work of Christ, especially in the incarnation.

Whether or not Lee's interpretation of Edwards's dispositional ontology as appropriated by Morimoto is correct or fair,[61] two main issues arise with Morimoto's use of the dispositional model. First, Edwards's dispositional ontology was teleological, a point glossed over by Morimoto. While dispositional properties could be possessed and never exercised, an ontological disposition always tends toward a goal or *telos* in that it needs to be exercised. This is ably demonstrated in John Bombaro's study.[62] Second, Morimoto confuses ontological

---

59. Morimoto presents as evidence his reading of Edwards's *Miscellany. 27b*; cf. Edwards, "Misc. 27b," *WJE* 13:213–14.

60. Morimoto, *Jonathan Edwards*, 31–33.

61. Stephen Holmes and Oliver Crisp have questioned whether Lee presents an accurate and fair reading of Edwards's ontology. See Holmes, "Does Jonathan Edwards Use," 99–113, and Crisp, "Jonathan Edwards's Ontology," 1–20.

62. Bombaro, *Beautiful Beings*, 274–76.

dispositions with dispositional properties. Edwards did not think of the holy disposition in terms of a dispositional property that might or might not get exercised. Rather, he thought in terms of ontological dispositions which *had to* exercise themselves. An agent cannot be said to possess a given ontological disposition unless it is exercised. Bomarao helpfully explains that

> such dispositions must manifest *at least* an initiatory exercise or else it is "of no manner of use"; that is, they are not constitutive of that agent's ontic structure because there lacks consciousness of it as its own "ideal-existence." Which is to say, an ontic-mental disposition without an initiatory exercise must be classified not as one with a virtual mode of reality, but as non-existent. Consequently, in Edwards, there is a difference between constitutive ontological dispositions that define human being and nature as such and dispositional properties exemplifying personal propensities, characteristics, and traits. One could be dispositionally courageous without ever having the opportunity to express it, but one could not possess an ontic disposition of holy consent to God without an initiatory exercise of it . . . It is the difference between *actually* being a certain category of human being and not. In Edwards' soteriology, real dispositional union is crucial for justification, for "What is real in the union between Christ and his people, is the foundation for what is legal." By equating the two distinct kinds of dispositions within Edwards' philosophical-theology, Morimoto builds his thesis not upon dormant dispositions but defunct dispositions.[63]

The opening sentence of *Misc. 27b*, a *Miscellany* that is used to support a form of salvation by disposition alone, is usually truncated. The first sentence reads: "'Tis most certain, both from Scripture and reason, that there must be a reception of Christ with the faculties of the soul in order to salvation by him, and that in this reception there is a believing of what we are taught in the gospel concerning him and salvation by him, and that it must be a consent of the will or an agreeableness between the disposition of the soul and those doctrines."[64] Faith, word, and Spirit work in a unified *concursus* of divinely ordained providence. Furthermore, *Misc. 27b*, *393*, and *849*, all quoted by Morimoto to support his thesis, must be taken together in their context. The subject of these *Miscellanies* is not justification *per se*, but the appearance of a "principle of faith" to the agent

---

63. Bombaro, *Beautiful Beings*, 275.
64. Edwards, "Misc. 27b," *WJE* 13:213.

by its exercises. Or, as Edwards puts it, "a discovery of the mercy of God in Christ, whereby [a person] becomes justified in his own conscience, and acquires a sense of his own justification."[65] While regeneration and conversion are simultaneous and instantaneous (Morimoto splits them asunder), a person's awareness or subjective apprehension of the effects of regeneration and conversion may not be. These *Miscellanies* are not about the objective order of saving activities but the subjective awareness of each. Edwards is not saying anything different from what the Puritan tradition said in their examinations of "cases of conscience"—the pastoral concern to assure troubled parishioners of their justified status.[66]

When Morimoto reads Edwards's dictum, "What is real is the foundation of what is legal," he interprets this as "something more than legal and forensic justification." For Morimoto, "His [Edwards's] effort to furnish the legal transaction with an ontological basis" was a necessary move to defend the reality of justification from a forensic fiction. In other words, "Edwards's theories of infused grace exhibit a balanced combination of Protestant and Catholic concerns in one form."[67] Moreover, Morimoto finds this thought already extant in Luther, Calvin, Ames, and Mastricht, such that "Edwards was only reiterating what was readily available in [the] tradition."[68] Perry Miller, a generation before, also interpreted Edwards's dictum as an intentional move away from "seventeenth-century legalism" to "eighteenth-century physics."[69] Schafer similarly interpreted Edwards's dictum ontologically when he said, "The natural creates the legal, not vice versa; something really existing in the soul precedes the external imputation."[70]

The precedent for an ontological soteriology does not appear in Calvin or later Reformed federal theologians, but rather in the Lutheran theologian Andreas Osiander (1498-1552). Osiander also tried to safeguard justification from the charge of "legal fiction" by arguing

---

65. Edwards, "Misc. 393," *WJE* 3:458.
66. Bombaro, *Beautiful Beings*, 267. For an example, see Perkins, *Works*, 2:1-152.
67. Morimoto, *Jonathan Edwards*, 68.
68. Morimoto, *Jonathan Edwards*, 58.
69. Miller, *Jonathan Edwards*, 77-78. For Miller, the legal becomes subordinate and secondary to the ontological, and he sees in this a clear refutation in Edwards of New England federal theology. Miller understands the "real" as the "experience of regeneration," which he interprets as a move from logic to experience in Edwards's theology.
70. Schafer, "Jonathan Edwards," 58.

that imputation had to be based on something "real" since it would be insulting to God and contrary to his nature that he should justify those who actually remained wicked. Union with Christ, which was a prerequisite reality for imputation, established the ontological reality by which the divine attributes, particularly righteousness, would be ontologically shared with man. Calvin reacted strongly: "Indeed, he accumulates many testimonies of Scripture by which to prove that Christ is one with us, and we, in turn, with him—a fact that needs no proof. But because he does not observe *the bond of this unity*, he deceives himself . . . . He says that we are one with Christ. We agree. But we deny that Christ's essence is mixed with our own."[71] Calvin argued that this ontological union of *essence* was a serious threat to the gospel, which presented the covenant reality. Justification is "not according to his divine nature,"[72] but according to the redemptive-historical work that Christ undertook in his humanity. Turretin also rejects Osiander's "essential" righteousness: "By the righteousness of Christ we do not understand here the 'essential righteousness of God' dwelling in us (as Osiander with Schwenkfeld dreamed, opposing himself to Stancar his colleague, who acknowledge Christ as Mediator only according to his human nature—which error was exploded and perished with its author). The righteousness could not be communicated to us subjectively and formally which is an essential attribute of God without our becoming gods also."[73] Morimoto does not go so far as to claim that Edwards taught that believers are united with Christ's deity on the order of Osiander, but his ontological view of Edwards, as with Osiander, does not capture the covenant dynamic and reality of justification that Edwards (along with Calvin, Turretin, Ames, and Mastricht) espoused.

Schafer, Hunsinger, and Morimoto all read Edwards, and in many instances the whole of the Reformation tradition, through the lens of an ontological soteriology of one form or the other rather than through a covenant and redemptive-historical model.[74] In an ontological soteriol-

---

71. Calvin, *Institutes*, 1:730.
72. Calvin, *Institutes*, 1:735.
73. Turretin, *Institutes*, 2:650.

74. One might also include the reading of Edwards by Gerald McDermott. McDermott takes a different approach, using Edwards's idea of the *prisca theologia* to show that the "heathen" have a plethora of natural revelation available to them that combined with the powers of reasoning allow for the possibility of those without special revelation, and without having to explicitly trust in Jesus Christ for salvation,

ogy the Reformed place and order of justification is challenged and even takes on a different meaning. It can become merely God's rewarding of "the inherent good" or as Paul Tillich's "to accept the acceptance."[75] Likewise, justification becomes the due recognition of "God's crowning of his own gift," in Morimoto (borrowing a phrase from Augustine), that is "nothing but a delightful recognition of the fact that they are already accepted."[76] Morimoto ends up questioning whether "there is in his [Edwards's] system a place for justification at all," or a "role of forensic declaration of righteousness in Christ,"[77] and Schafer can only express frustration with Edwards's doctrine of justification because it seems to "occupy an ambiguous and somewhat precarious place in his theology."[78] None of this seems to resemble the Edwards that one gleams from even a casual glance of his sermons or in his treatises as the staunch defender of the Reformed faith against his Arminian, antinomian, neonomian, and Roman Catholic detractors. Aside from misrepresenting Edwards either contextually or by proceeding from theoretical premises that are not essentially compatible with his covenant-based soteriology, the conclusions these interpreters reach presents an Edwards that appears grossly incongruous when seen in light of his biblical and pastoral teaching. They fail to appreciate and read Edwards in the context of his covenant and redemptive-historical context and are therefore unable to deal with Edwards's forensic justification within the covenant reality of a believer's union with Christ. In light of this covenant reality, Edwards does not abandon the *ordo salutis*, but puts it in the context of the *historia salutis*. Edwards's redemptive-historical approach centered on his covenant theology is a more useful, and I would argue more faithful, lens with which to read Edwards.

---

a means to exercise their "faith" for their justification. McDermott, *Jonathan Edwards Confronts the Gods*. See also Studebaker, *Trinitarian Vision*; Studebaker, "Jonathan Edwards' Pneumatological Concept," 324–29.

75. Tillich, *Courage to Be*, 164–67.
76. Morimoto, *Jonathan Edwards*, 118–19.
77. Morimoto, *Jonathan Edwards*, 73–74.
78. Schafer, *Jonathan Edwards*, 57.

Jonathan Edwards on Justification: A Defense

In this section I will consider three areas that Edwards is accused of being more Catholic than Protestant. First, his use of "infusion" language appears to conflict with the Protestant use of "imputation." Second, Edwards's view of the believer's ontological union with Christ is sometimes confused for a kind of *theosis* or hypostatic union that would justify a meritorious "reality" inherent in the believer. Third, his use of "fitness" to describe faith's role in justifying the believer is simply another way of saying that faith is in some way "meritorious." While a superficial reading of his language can appear to raise questions about his conformity with Reformed Protestant theology, I will show that Edwards uses this language in a manner that is inconsistent with Catholicism and in line with his own Reformed tradition. Edwards must be read in the context of his covenant theology and in terms of his historical-redemptive approach to the Bible, rather than through an ontological-dispositional lens.

Infusion Language

Roman Catholicism has traditionally held that justification occurs by the infusion of Christ's righteousness into the heart of a saint.[79] Justification is looked upon as a continuous event or process in which this infused divine grace enables good works that increasingly merit God's acceptance. A sinner is actually transformed, becoming righteous due to an inherent righteousness. Infusion in this sense correlates with an ontological reality of righteousness. The Reformed (and Lutherans) maintained use of the term "imputation" in justification in distinction from the Catholic exclusive use of infusion or impartation in the polemical context of the Reformation.[80] Imputation represented the covenant reality of a believer's being "accounted righteous" on behalf of Christ's righteousness. The imputation/infusion divide is considered one of the distinguishing marks that separate Reformed and Catholic views of justification. For that reason, it is surprising to some scholars that Edwards uses the

---

79. "The Grace of Christ is the gratuitous gift that God makes to us of his own life, infused by the Holy Spirit into our soul to heal it of sin and to sanctify it." *Catechism of the Catholic Church*, Part 3, Section 1, Chapter 3, Article II.

80. "Those whom God effectually calleth he also freely justifieth; not by infuring righteousness into them, but by pardoning their sins . . . [and] by imputing the obedience and satisfaction of Christ unto them." *WCF*, 11.1.

term "infusion" in his discussions on justification. For Hunsinger, this infusion language of Edwards was enough to open the doors to a more Catholic interpretation of Edwards on justification. For Morimoto, Edwards's language was compatible with Lee's disposition ontology and was sufficient to account for an ontological-dispositional model of union with Christ in salvation.[81]

Edwards uses the term "infusion" or "physical infusion" throughout his writings, but not in the sense of the Catholic theological meaning of the term. He uses a number of terms besides "infusion," including "principle," "habit," and "disposition," that are theologically and philosophically charged and need to be read carefully in the context of Edwards's overall theology. These terms are more "discursive" than technical and are expressions that Edwards uses to represent the Spirit's indwelling the believer. In the majority of cases they are not meant to be precise, analytical, and scholastic definitions.[82] Rather, these terms were used to describe the harmony and mystery of the Holy Spirit's operation in the creaturely domain, not any ontological change in the believer. Cherry says that, "the 'physical' in Edwards is not about 'a naturalizing of the supernatural' or reducing grace to an ontological potentiality."[83] So when Edwards says that, "if there be any immediate influence or action of the Spirit of God at all on any created beings, in any part of the universe, since the days of the apostles, it is physical,"[84] he is referencing the mystery and miracle of the Holy Spirit's immediate work in the heart of the believer. The covenant reality of salvation in the temporal sphere involves both human and divine participation. The supernatural character of grace and the natural human faculties are both involved, while neither is compromised or overshadowed. Grace is not a created quality nor do human beings have to be deified through an ontological change. In *Religious Affections*,

---

81. Morimoto argues that this also proves that infusion has a place in Protestant theology. Morimoto's narrative links the ontological theology of Thomas Aquinas to Edwards "physical infusion" by way of Turretin. He further argues that Calvin held the "moral suasion" view of regeneration, whereas subsequent federal theologians held to a "physical infusion" view. Morimoto aligns Edwards with Calvin's followers in opposition to Calvin. Edwards's holistic view of man represented in terms of his "heart language" was supposedly more in agreement with "physical infusion" than "moral suasion." Morimoto, *Jonathan Edwards*, 13–22.

82. Kang, "Justified by Faith," 316. For examples in Edwards, see Edwards, "Concerning Efficacious Grace," *JE* 2: 551–52; Edwards, "Misc. p," *WJE* 13:171.

83. Cherry, *Theology of Jonathan Edwards*, 37.

84. Edwards, "Remarks on Important Theological Controversies," *JE* 2:553.

Edwards says: "Not that the saints are made partakers of the essence of God, and so are 'Godded' with God, and 'Christed' with Christ, according to the abominable and blasphemous language and notions of some heretics; but, to use the Scripture phrase, they are made partakers of God's fullness."[85] In his sermon on John 16:8 entitled *The Threefold Work of the Holy Ghost*, Edwards says, "Believers are united to Christ, and in a sense are partakers of the his nature, in that they are partakers of his Spirit."[86] "Partaking" is a keyword for union and imputation in the context of the sermon. It is the partaking of the Holy Spirit from the believer's vantage. Partaking of Christ's "nature" is not an ontological union of essence but is referencing the redemptive-historical work of Christ in his incarnation (as explained below). Paul Ramsey notes that infusion language denoting the Spirit's presence and operation in the creaturely context of regeneration has "deep family resemblances" to Calvin.[87] Ramsey is referencing Calvin's statement: "For in such a way does the Lord Christ share his righteousness with us that, in some wonderful manner, *he pours into us* enough of his power to meet the judgment of God."[88] This "infusion language" occurs in a section on the imputation of Christ's righteousness apart from any inherent righteousness. Infusion language and the Reformed insistence on imputation are not necessarily opposed in Calvin, if read in context.

Close attention to the context of Edwards's writings will show that this language was directed at his Pelagian, Socinian, and Arminian opponents who rejected the immediate and "arbitrary influence" of the Holy Spirit in regeneration.[89] Mastricht also argued for the "physical" operation of the Holy Spirit to stress the immediate effect of the Spirit in regeneration as opposed to mediate and external moral "suasion."[90] Turretin uses the term immediate in the context of several debates in church history, including the fifth-century Pelagian controversy and the seventeenth-century Calvinist and Arminian controversy.[91] Reformed scholastics used the term "infusion" to express either the work of the

---

85. Edwards, "Religious Affections," *WJE* 2:203.
86. Edwards, "Threefold Work of the Holy Ghost," *WJE* 14:403.
87. Ramsey, "Infused Virtues," *WJE* 8:750.
88. Calvin, *Institutes*, 1:753 (emphasis mine).
89. Edwards, "Treatise on Grace," *WJE* 21:177.
90. Mastricht, *Treatise on Regeneration*, 17–22, 37–46.
91. Turretin, *Institutes*, 2:526–28.

Holy Spirit in regeneration or in effectual calling. Turretin says, "The Spirit in effectual calling . . . acts immediately with the word on the soul, so that the calling necessarily produces its effect."[92]

Edwards talks of the Spirit of God influencing the soul as a vital indwelling principle, creating within the soul new and holy principles of life and action. In *Religious Affections* he says: "The Spirit of God in his spiritual influences on the hearts of his saints operates by infusing or exercising new divine and supernatural principles; principles which are indeed a new and supernatural nature, and principles vastly more noble and excellent than all that is in natural men."[93] In *A Divine and Supernatural Light*, he says, "[God] imparts this knowledge immediately not making use of any intermediate natural causes, as he does in other knowledge."[94] For Edwards, "natural" is means that operates by its own power or natural force. God makes use of these means (such the Word of God, i.e., Scripture or preaching) but not as mediate causes to produce the effect. The immediacy of divine causality is meant to underscore the human dependence on divine grace, not only in the first act of grace, but in all subsequent gracious acts of the soul.[95]

In all of this Edwards is careful to maintain the integrity of the human person, making clear that regeneration works in harmony with the rational faculties.[96] Edwards distinguishes the indwelling of the Holy Spirit from the new foundation laid in the soul by the Holy Spirit. In other words, the new "indwelling vital principle" is distinguished from

---

92. Turretin, *Institutes*, 2:526–28.

93. Edwards, "Religious Affections," *WJE* 2:207.

94. Edwards, "Divine and Supernatural Light," *WJE* 17:415–16. On the "natural means" Edwards says, "The Word of God is no proper cause of this effect: it don't operate by any natural force in it. The Word of God is only made use of to convey to the mind the subject matter of this saving instruction: and this indeed it doth convey to us by natural force or influence. It conveys to our minds these and those doctrines; it is the cause of the notion of them in our heads, but not of the sense of the divine excellency of them in our hearts. Indeed a person can't have spiritual light without the Word. But that don't argue, that the Word properly causes that light. The mind can't see the excellency of any doctrine, unless that doctrine be first in the mind; but the seeing the excellency of the doctrine may be immediately from the Spirit of God." Edwards, "Divine and Supernatural Light," *WJE*: 17:116.

95. Edwards, "Misc. 629," *WJE* 18:157.

96. Edwards, "Divine and Supernatural Light," *WJE* 17:416.

the new holy principles and gracious dispositions which exist because of the rebirth in regeneration.[97]

> This new spiritual sense, and the new dispositions that attend it, are no new *faculties*, but are new *principles* of nature. I use the word "principles," for want of a word of a more determinate signification. By a *principle of nature* in this place, I mean that foundation which is laid in nature, either old or new, for any particular manner or kind of exercise of the faculties of the soul; or a natural habit or foundation for action, giving a person ability and disposition to exert the faculties in exercises of such a certain kind; so that to exert the faculties in that kind of exercises, may be said to be his nature. So this new spiritual sense is not a new faculty of understanding, but it is a new foundation laid in the nature of the soul, for a new kind of exercises of the same faculty of understanding. So that new holy disposition of heart that attends this new sense, is not a new faculty of will, but a foundation laid in the nature of the soul, for a new kind of exercises of the same faculty of will.[98]

The new principles of nature are infused habits of grace which provide the (new) foundation for gracious acts. Edwards illustrates one aspect of this infusion of grace in his sermon *A Divine and Supernatural Light*: "There is such a thing, as a spiritual and divine light, immediately imparted to the soul by God, of a different nature from any that is obtained by natural means."[99] This divine light that illuminates the understanding is not the indwelling Spirit or a new faculty created in the soul, but is the effect of the Spirit's regenerative effect on human understanding. Its result is " a real sense and apprehension of the divine excellency of things revealed in the Word of God."[100] It is "this light, and this only, will bring the soul to a saving close with Christ."[101]

---

97. Jeffrey Waddington says that, "the new disposition is the Holy Spirit himself." Waddington, "Jonathan Edwards's Ambiguous," 367. Conrad Cherry claims that "Edwards is not beyond referring to the divine principle as a 'disposition' of the human soul." Cherry, *Theology of Jonathan Edwards*, 42. Thomas Atchison maintains that, "the indwelling Holy Spirit is a new disposition." Atchison, "Towards Developing a Theology," 197. According to McClenahan, "If this is in fact Edwards' view, it is very difficult to see how he can retain the integrity of the human person." McClehahan, *Jonathan Edwards*, 187.

98. Edwards, "Religious Affections," *WJE* 2:206.

99. Edwards, "Divine and Supernatural Light," *WJE* 17:410.

100. Edwards, "Divine and Supernatural Light," *WJE* 17:413.

101. Edwards, "Divine and Supernatural Light," *WJE* 17:424. In *Misc. 782* Edwards

Edwards's believed that true faith is only possible when human understanding is enlightened by divine power and revelation. It is caused by the immediate (effective and irresistible) influence of the Holy Spirit, in conjunction with the Word, on the faculties of the soul. Hence, there is no possibility for merit, even the merit of faith itself. Edwards's use of infusion language is not meant to connote the same technical significance of the Catholic understanding, nor does it have any relation to Morimoto's dispositional ontology.

Ontological Union

In his sermon on John 16, Edwards says, "In order to a sinner's being thus accepted with God, there must be some real righteousness that must be the sinner's. God don't look upon sinners as righteous for nothing."[102] Imputation makes Christ's righteousness the believer's reality, though it does not create a hypostatic union. The righteousness imputed to the elect believer really constitutes the believer's righteousness so that God sees them as righteous. This is their justification. In Edwards, as in Reformed theology since Calvin, the forensic and the real are not antithetical notions. Justification is not based on a "legal fiction," as a mere pretension of "as if," but is based on a real ground. That real ground is the covenant reality of the believer's union with Christ.

Edwards brings his trinitarian covenant theology to bear when he says, "Now the foundation of the propriety of this imputation of righteousness seems to lie in these two things: in Christ's union with God, and his union with men. It would not be proper that the righteousness of any person should be accepted by God for another, but a person that was one with God; nor would it [be] proper that it should be accepted for any person, but only a person that he is one with."[103] "Union" or "oneness" is necessary for God to view one person's righteousness for another's. Christ has that union with God due to his divine nature and his infinite divine love. As he is infinitely near and perfectly united to the Father in nature, he is also in love. The Father loves the Son infinitely in "the same love wherewith God loves himself." In Edwards's covenant accounting,

---

links this "new sense" to the "[s]aving conviction of divine truth." Edwards, "Misc. 782," *WJE* 18:465.

    102. Edwards, "Threefold Work of the Holy Ghost," *WJE* 14:395.
    103. Edwards, "Threefold Work of the Holy Ghost," *WJE* 14:401.

this infinite love and union gives an infinite value to Christ's suffering and positive righteousness in the believer's stead under the Covenant of Redemption. Christ, in his voluntary submission to be under the law in his incarnation as a man, which he was not under by virtue of his divine nature, provided the means to fulfill the Covenant of Works in man's stead. Christ's ontological equality with the Father in his infinite excellency and worthiness demonstrates that it is God alone who can restore divine justice.

This righteousness becomes the elect believer's through a union with Christ, in which they are so nearly united that they may be looked upon as one. This union between Christ and the elect believer, just as between the Son and the Father, also consists both in a unition of nature and love. The unition of nature, as already discussed, is not an ontological or hypostatic union of the believer with Christ's essence, but refers to Christ's own hypostatic union, taking on human nature in the incarnation, under the law, to perform the works of the law. By taking on human nature, and voluntarily placing himself under the Covenant of Works in the Covenant of Redemption, he becomes a fit "head" of human nature, the head of all the elect. "He sufficiently in the sight of God and in the sight of angels assumed the elect part of mankind into a union with himself, and was justly looked upon as their head."[104] He is a fit covenant Mediator for both parties in their reconciliation because of his union with both parties. Believers are united to Christ, "in a sense, partakers of his nature" in that they partake of his Spirit. Just as the Spirit is the love between the Father and the Son in the intratrinitarian relationship, so the Spirit of Christ is the love that unites the believer to Christ. "Christ is united to us in love. Christ loves the elect with so great and strong a love, they are so near to him, that God looks upon them as it were as parts of him."[105] The trinitarian fellowship is the foundation for the assurance of the elect. Through the marriage covenant, the Father's infinite love for the Son extends to his bride as well.

> Surely if God loves and accepts the head for its holiness and amiableness, he won't separate head and members; but he will accept of and delight in the members for the sake of the excellency of the head. That is our great encouragement, that God has declared from heaven that Christ is his beloved Son, in whom he is well pleased; and we have confidence that seeing it is so,

---

104. Edwards, "Threefold Work of the Holy Ghost," *WJE* 14:403.
105. Edwards, "Threefold Work of the Holy Ghost," *WJE* 14:403.

and we are in him, that he will be well pleased with us for his excellency's and righteousness' sake. I think we are plainly taught this doctrine, *Ephesians 1:6*, "He hath made us accepted in the Beloved," where we are plainly taught this, that we are accepted and beloved because we are in him who is beloved. Christ is more than our head, he is as the whole body; and we are not only joined to him as the members to the head, but he covers us all over; he is as clothing to us; we are commanded to put him on, so that our deformity don't appear. Seeing we are clothed with him who is so beautiful, and for his beauty with which we are clothed, are we accepted and loved.[106]

In the Covenant of Redemption, the Father sees the bride (the elect, Christ's mystical body) as one with Christ the groom and his love for his Son spills over to his Son's bride.

John Bombaro reminds us that this union takes place in eternity as it is grounded in the eternal Covenant of Redemption. Ultimately, the foundation of justification does not take place in the temporal sphere as "there is no infusion of grace logically prior to a declaration of righteousness." In the eternal confederation God constitutes the union with Christ and his Church, and this is the basis for an "antecedent declaration of righteousness," which, in a certain sense, "provides the efficient cause of the temporal union via regeneration."[107] God, as it were, regards the Spirit "purchased" by the Son *as* the mutual consent or actual union between the sinner and the Son, and therefore imputes righteousness to the sinner on account of what the Son has procured for them, i.e., the Spirit. When Christ "purchases" the Spirit for his bride in the Covenant of Redemption, he also "purchased saving faith and converting grace for such as shall be saved."[108] Faith and conversion are the effects and fruits of the Spirit. For Edwards, the *ordo salutis* is based on the eternal covenant arrangement, as well as the logical ordering of temporal application. This is simply a corollary to Edwards's covenant relationships, whereby the Covenant of Grace, in one sense, is the historical-redemptive outworking and revelation of the eternal Covenant of Redemption in history and in the life of individual elect believers.

The atoning work of Christ is a necessary part of this loving union. Christ's love is so great for his bride (the elect) that he is moved to fulfill

---

106. Edwards, "Misc. 385," *WJE* 13:453.
107. Bombaro, "Beautiful Beings," 279.
108. Edwards, "Misc. 1159," *WJE* 23:72.

God's justice by assuming her just suffering and death. Love and justice are both consummated in Edwards's covenant framework of union. The satisfaction of Christ, performed out of love, restores divine justice completely.

> Christ does as it were hereby bring their guilt upon himself, but not in any blameable sense. It was not esteemed a fit thing for Christ thus by love to unite himself to such guilty ones, unless he had manifested a readiness to bear their guilt himself and suffer their punishment. It would have been a greatly countenancing of their wickedness; it would be a kind of taking their part against God. But now he shows that he does not countenance it; he acknowledges its infinite evil and ill desert, by his appearing ready to suffer the punishment deserved, himself. It was but fair, and what justice required, that seeing Christ would so unite himself by love to sinners that had deserved wrath, that they might be partakers of the Father's love to him and so they be screened and sheltered, that he himself should receive the Father's wrath to them. That love of Christ which united him to sinners, assumed their guilt upon himself. So that Christ's death and sufferings were absolutely necessary, in order [to] our being delivered from destruction for the sake of Christ's worthiness and excellency, and through the love of God to him that loved us.[109]

Christ takes his bride's guilt and deserved punishment upon himself, yet without becoming guilty or sinful himself.

That Christ's righteousness truly becomes the believer's is, according to Edwards, consistent with "the law." By "law" is understood the principle of works: "Do this and live." It is "the fixed and established rule of all transactions between God and us that all mankind are under."[110] Edwards clearly means the original Covenant of Works with Adam when he summarizes "the law" as, "If though eatest, thou shalt surely die. [Gen. 2:17]," drawing together the imputation of sin and the imputation of righteousness under the rubric of divine law whereby the Covenants of Works, Grace, and Redemption find their harmony. Because Adam's progeny are guilty of his one act through the imputation of his mediatorial disobedience, it holds equally true by divine constitution that Christ's

---

109. Edwards, "Misc. 483," *WJE* 13:524-27. See also Edwards, "Misc. 398," *WJE* 13:463-64; Edwards, "Misc. b," *WJE* 13:164-65.

110. Edwards, "Threefold Work of the Holy Ghost," *WJE* 14:404.

obedience as the new mediator can be imputed to the elect in Christ.[111] The imputation of Christ's righteousness is a constitutive reality while not being ontological. Believers obtain a real righteousness in Christ that is more than a mere legal and external transfer of accounts or a fictional pretense. A person is actually constituted with Christ's righteousness in the reality of the covenant union.

Edwards understood that "the sin of the apostasy is not theirs, merely because God imputes it to them; but it is truly and properly theirs, and on that ground, God imputes it to them."[112] This is one of the more controversial points in Edwards's view of original sin, but it underscores the nature of the "real" in imputation. What Edwards is saying is that the constitutive reality is established through union (federal headship) before imputation. The headship of Adam goes back to the first act of sin. Traditional views begin the headship with the consequence of sinning. The implication in Edwards is that Adam's posterity was united with him in the very moment of sinning.

> *The first being* of an evil disposition in a child of Adam, whereby he is disposed to *approve* the sin of his first father, as fully as he himself approved of it when he committed it, or so far as to imply a full and perfect consent of heart to it, I think, is not to

---

111. Obviously, the issue of original sin is raised and the question of how the sin of one person (Adam) can become someone else's (his progeny's) sin. Edwards addresses this question in *The Great Christian Doctrine of Original Sin Defended* (1757) in polemic with John Taylor's (1694-1761) *The Scripture-Doctrine of Original Sin, Proposed to Free and Candid Examination*. Edwards agrees with Taylor in accepting that someone cannot be charged with something they had not done themselves. But in Edwards's covenant theology it is *not* someone else's sin but one's own. The question becomes how to define this solidarity/union between Adam and his posterity. While this is important to the present discussion of the constitutive character of imputation, it is beyond the scope of this chapter to fully evaluate Edwards's metaphysics of personal identity in this regard. I defer to Charles Hodge's summary. Even though he was uncomfortable with Edwards's way of explaining identity in terms of the "arbitrary constitution of God," Hodge does end up distinguishing "realism" (which Edwards did not affirm) from a true constitutive reality (which Edwards did affirm) in Edwards's concept of union/solidarity. More recently, Gerstner famously concluded, "Edwards ... argued that God *identified Adam with his posterity* so that *his* choice and act was *their* act and choice. That is federal representationism with a vengeance." For further discussion on this topic, see Kang, "Justified by Faith in Christ," 159; Logan, "Review of *Tragedy*," 26-52; Otto, "Solidarity of Mankind," 205-21; Hodge, *Systematic Theology*, 2:207-20; Murray, *Imputation*; Crisp, *Jonathan Edwards and the Metaphysics of Sin*; Gerstner, *Rational Biblical Theology*, 2:323-34.

112. Edwards, "Original Sin," WJE 3:408.

be looked upon as a consequence of the imputation of that first sin, any more than the full consent of Adam's own heart in the act of sinning; which was not consequent on the imputation, but rather *prior* to it in the order of nature. Indeed the derivation of the evil disposition to Adam's posterity, or rather the *coexistence* of the evil disposition, implied in Adam's first rebellion, in the root and branches, is a consequence of the union, that the wise Author of the world has established between Adam and his posterity: but not properly a consequence of the *imputation* of his sin; nay, rather *antecedent* to it, as it was in Adam himself. The first depravity of heart, and the imputation of that sin, are both the consequences of that established union: but yet in such order, that the evil disposition is *first*, and the charge of guilt *consequent*; as it was in the case of Adam himself.[113]

Adam's guilt is not imputed to his progeny without their being a logically prior ground for their guilt. They are not accounted guilty because of Adam's sinful act. It was actually their act "in Adam" that accounted them guilty. In a *Miscellany* written before his *Original Sin* treatise Edwards writes:

But a man is guilty before God as soon as he is born, upon the account of the corruption of his nature, as it is the *continuation* of the first apostasy . . . and as by it the soul of the infant does consent to it, and as it were act and commit it, 'tis imputed as being the same poison then in act, and now remaining in habit. This seems to be evident, by considering how it must be supposed to be with Adam himself: the corruption of Adam's nature began with the act of sin; the corruption of nature began in exercise.[114]

For Edwards, there exists a constitutive reality (rather than realism) that supplies the ground for the guilty pronouncement.[115]

Just as with Adam, so it is with Christ. In order for there to be a forensic justification of the believer there must first be a union between the believer and Christ. "There is no *peccatum alienum* or *iustitia aliena* in Edwards. The alien notion is not compatible with Edwards' federal

---

113. Edwards, "Original Sin," *WJE* 3:391.

114. Edwards, "Misc. 384," *WJE* 13:452–53.

115. Edwards's constitutive reality distinguishes his theory from mediate imputation theories. Adam's guilt is not an alien guilt, but it is also not a proper guilt as in realism.

theology, let alone his understanding of constitutive reality."[116] The "forensic" and "real" are not antithetical categories, with regards to either Adam or Christ, in Edwards's covenant theology. Ava Chamberlain misreads this aspect when she sets these two (the real and the forensic) in opposition. In the "Editor's Introduction," she writes that "the primary focus of Edwards' analysis of the doctrine of justification is not the forensic transaction that occurs by means of justification but the ontological transformation that occurs by means of union with Christ."[117] She concludes that "the limitations of the doctrine of justification became increasingly evident, a second model of conversion, which operates exclusively on this 'real' or ontological level, displaces justification as the central organizing concept of Edwards' soteriology."[118] But this is to oppose two aspects of union with Christ that were never separated in Edwards, or Reformed theology in general, and that is the relationship between justification and sanctification. Both are dependent upon the elect believer's union and relation to Christ. In reference to the Reformed scholastic tradition as a whole, Muller defines the orthodox position:

> In relation to the *ordo salutis*, or order of salvation, the Protestant scholastics distinguish the initial *unitio*, or uniting, or the *unio mysticai*, which is the basis of the imputation of Christ's righteousness to the believer and which corresponds with adoption of the believer, and the ongoing *unio*, or union, of the *unio mystica*, which continues concurrent with sanctification throughout the life of the believer.[119]

Justification and sanctification are the *duplex gratia* of union with Christ and, while they are both simultaneous, they are also distinguished in Edwards's theology.[120]

---

116. Kang, "*Justified by Faith*," 165. While Luther stressed an *iustitia aliena*, he did not preclude the "in Christ" (*unio cum Christo*) context altogether. He simply meant to emphasize Christ's righteousness in rejection of all human righteousness as the ground of justification, for he had found Augustine's "made-righteous" notion of justification unsatisfactory. For Luther, the core of the matter is the meaning of Baptism, i.e., the death of sin and the resurrection of the new person becoming effective in the baptized person because God unites himself with the sinner both through the sacramental act and through faith. Luther, "Against Latomus," *LW* 32:232–33.

117. Chamberlain, "Editor's Introduction," *WJE* 18:39.

118. Chamberlain, "Editor's Introduction," *WJE* 18:39.

119. Muller, *Dictionary of Latin and Greek*, 314–15.

120. Calvin is an example when he writes, "But if the brightness of the sun cannot be separated from its heat, shall we therefore say that the earth is warmed by its light,

Nor is the forensic a "bare legal" pronouncement, devoid of any relational aspect. It is grounded in the infinite intratrinitarian love between the Son and the Father. It is that love spilling over to Christ's bride that is the bond of union and forms the loving relationship that characterizes the Covenant of Grace. By virtue of the believer's union with Christ by the Spirit, something real in eternity is realized in time as the elect believer comes to possess all the righteousness, holiness, faith, and love of Christ.

Natural and Moral Fitness

Edwards argues that this "relation or union to Christ, whereby Christians are said to be in Christ (whatever it be), is the ground of their right to his benefits," and that "faith is that qualification in any person, that renders it meet in the sight of God that he should be looked upon as having Christ's satisfaction and righteousness belonging to him."[121] Something must be done on the part of the unregenerate elect to bring them into this union with Christ. According to Edwards, "In order to an union's being established between two intelligent active beings or persons, so that they should be looked upon as one, there should be the mutual act of both."[122] This is explained in more detail:

> God, in requiring this (a mutual act of both) in order to an union with Christ as one of his people, treats men as reasonable creatures, capable of act and choice; and hence sees it fit that they only, that are one with Christ by their own act, should be looked upon as one in law. What is real in the union between Christ and his people, is the foundation of what is legal; that is, it is something really in them, and between them, uniting them, that is the ground of the suitableness of their being accounted as one by the Judge.[123]

In his 1732 lectures, Edwards is particularly clear that what is real, "on their part," is faith.[124] The act of faith is an act of "uniting" with Christ.

---

or lighted by its heat? . . . The sun, by its heat, quickens and fructifies the earth, by its beams brightens and illumines it. Here is a mutual and indivisible connection. Yet reason itself forbids us to transfer the peculiar qualities of the one to the other." Calvin, *Institutes*, 1:732.

121. Edwards, "Justification by Faith Alone," *WJE* 19:155–56.
122. Edwards, "Justification by Faith Alone," *WJE* 19:158.
123. Edwards, "Justification by Faith Alone," *WJE* 19:158.
124. Edwards, "Justification by Faith Alone," *WJE* 19:158.

Faith constitutes a "union" with Christ in that it is a movement of the heart or an affectional response. Edwards uses a multitude of expressions to convey this including "closing with," "heartily joining," and "consenting." In the context of Edwards's covenant theology, faith is the "I do!" of the marriage covenant, whereby the elect believer consents with the terms of Christ's covenant and accepts the gracious terms of salvation. "[T]he heart must close with the new covenant by dependence upon it, and by love and desire."[125] This consent is not merely "affectional," but includes the understanding. "Heart," for Edwards, is to be understood as the affectional response of the understanding mind. Faith's uniting includes assenting and trusting in the true (real) knowledge of Christ. In Edwards's broader covenant picture, this mutual consent, or love, the "greatest and highest excellency" between two spirits, *is* the Holy Spirit, purchased as the gift in the Covenant of Redemption. The faith that unites the elect believer to Christ in the moment of their salvation is a communication or manifestation of the Spirit of Christ.[126] Faith is both a condition of consent to the Covenant of Grace, as well as the gift purchased by Christ.

Working through a precise subjective anthropology of salvation is not Edwards's concern, and his explanations can be fluid. For instance, he can say that faith is "the Christian's uniting act, or that which is done towards this union or relation" with Christ. He can also say that faith "is itself the very act of unition on their part," or that faith is what on the believer's part "makes up this union between him and Christ."[127] Edwards admits to great mystery in the experience of salvation. His main concern is not to make a "comprehensive synthetic statement about the nature of this union."[128] This is probably best summed up by Robert Caldwell: "God's natural regard for the unity of faith, union with Christ, and justification, and not his love for the moral excellency of faith in the believer, leads him to justify the sinner who in faith has joined herself to Christ. Because the believer's own act of faith is the product of the Spirit's union to the soul's faculties, the whole affair, from the widest possible angle, is ultimately and entirely of God."[129]

125. Edwards, "Faith," *WJE* 21:423.

126. Edwards can affirm that, "Every motion and action of grace is Christ living in us, and nothing else." Edwards, "Misc. 66," *WJE* 13:235.

127. Edwards, "Justification by Faith Alone," *WJE* 19:156–58.

128. McClenahan reminds us of the limited polemical context of Edwards's treatise on justification. McClenahan, *Jonathan Edwards*, 117.

129. Caldwell, *Communion in the Spirit*, 185.

Edwards's central purpose is to show that it is the believer's union with Christ that is the ground for the sharing in his benefits, and not the goodness, holiness, or meritorious nature of faith, whether faith is identical with the union or brings about that union. Edwards distinguishes between "moral fitness" and "natural fitness." Faith, if it were a morally fit act, meaning that it has a moral excellency which would commend itself, then justification would be rightly given as a reward. But it is not. There is only a "suitableness" or "natural fitness" in the act of faith. "There is a wide difference between its being looked on it suitable, that Christ's satisfaction and righteousness should be theirs, than believing because an interest in Christ's satisfaction and righteousness is but a suitable reward of faith, or a suitable testimony of God's respect to the amiableness and excellency of their faith."[130] There is a natural fitness when "it appears meet and condecent that he should be in such a state or circumstances, only from the natural concord or agreeableness there is between such a qualification and such circumstances; not because the qualifications are lovely or unlovely, but only because the qualifications and circumstances are like one another."[131] It is only because God has a love of order that he has regard to "the beauty of that order that there is in uniting those things that have a natural agreement, and congruity, and union of the one with the other."[132] This aesthetic argument of beauty and loveliness is a common theme in Edwards, which he employs "as a structural analytic concept for the interpretation of the full range of the moral life rather than simply as a term of praise for only the highest form of virtue."[133] It is God's love of order that he looks upon the act of faith as constituting being in Christ, and not out of any love to the act because of its moral fitness. Faith is "a suitable and appropriate act" which brings union with Christ and his blessings.

Faith is a naturally fitting act for Edwards because it is agreeable to the salvation that Christ has earned through his righteousness. "Christ will not receive those as the objects of his salvation who trust to themselves, their own strength or worthiness, but those alone who entirely rely on him. The reason of this is very natural and easy."[134] In other words, it

130. Edwards, "Misc. 568," *WJE* 18:105.
131. Edwards, "Justification by Faith Alone," *WJE* 19:159.
132. Edwards, "Justification by Faith Alone," *WJE* 19:159.
133. Delattre, *Beauty and Sensibility*, 191.
134. Edwards, "Misc. 37," *WJE* 12:219–21.

would not be "meet and proper" for Christ to receive those who rely on their own strength and worthiness, because this would not be a consenting to the terms of Christ's covenant whereby his righteous obedience is the only means of fulfilling the terms of justification.

> In every covenant there is required the consent of both parties ... This consent of theirs, whereby with their souls they accept of the second covenant to be performed by Christ, is justifying faith. Consenting to a covenant is consenting to the terms of it; therefore consenting to the second covenant is with the heart consenting to Christ's working out a perfect righteousness by his obedience and suffering for them, for this is the terms of the second covenant. The reason is very plain why it is faith that is required, because consent to a covenant is necessary to the very being in that covenant; a man can't be in any covenant till he consents to it. There is nothing else to do but consent to the terms of the new covenant, which Christ has fulfilled.[135]

To rely on one's own worthiness would be a repudiation of Christ's work and the very opposite of faith. Faith is a "voluntary delegation" of Christ to act as representative and "a hearty choosing of him as Mediator."[136] Faith is fitting, appropriate, natural, conforming, convenient, agreeable, suitable, etc. but none of these terms has the connotation of "deserving" or "earning" or anything that would put a claim on Christ. To do so would not be conforming to Christ's covenant offer in the gospel. It would be the exact opposite.

In *Misc. 507*, Edwards says that faith is the active "suitableness" or "suiting" of the receiver with Christ and his redemption, under the notion and quality of a free gift. It is a "suiting with the way wherein it is procured and made ours," that righteousness *having already been fulfilled*. Edwards strains for similes to express this relationship. He calls it "the mind's receiving like the body's open hand," "as the socket for the jewel that is set in it," and "as transparent bodies admit light, when opaque bodies refuse it."[137] The point is that the believer is purely passive, yet properly receptive in his or her passivity. "Why should there be a declared belonging of Christ's salvation to that soul that disagrees and refuses and wars against it?"[138] In his *Controversies* notebook on justification, he says

---

135. Edwards, "Misc. 299," *WJE* 13:386.
136. Edwards, "Misc. 33," *WJE* 13:218.
137. Edwards, "Misc. 507," *WJE* 18:53.
138. Edwards, "Misc. 507," *WJE* 18:53–54.

that "natural fitness" is not properly a fitness of the subject to be in Christ as the fitness of God's act in looking on such as one being in Christ. "The moral fitness in this case is not in the act of faith but in the act of God with respect to the believer . . . a determination of the act of God's goodness to an object with certain qualifications to answer some wise design of his own."[139] This is to be distinguished from the merit of the object of God's favor, or a moral qualification of the object attracting that favor and recommending God to it.

There are two reasons that the first act of saving faith can have no moral fitness or merit. First, disobedience to the moral law (sin, or "the nature of things") is an infinitely sinful act such that there is no possibility of moral goodness. The sinner is under infinite guilt in God's sight and nothing in the sinner can be suitable until they are actually justified, or that "God should by any act testify pleasedness with, or acceptance of, anything as excellency or amiableness of his person, or indeed have any acceptance of him, or pleasedness with him to testify."[140] Second, mankind is already condemned under the Covenant of Works in Adam. The "divine constitution" stands in the way in that God cannot reward faith (as morally fit) because it would be inconsistent with the "honor of the majesty of the King of Heaven and Earth, to accept of anything from a condemned malefactor."[141]

The origin of Edwards's "natural" and "moral" distinction is not clear. Fiering argues that the language of fitness comes from Samuel Clarke's influence, which is entirely based on Clarke's use of the language of fitness. But Clarke's use of fitness is more general and the distinction between "natural" and "moral" is not present. Cherry argues that Edward's distinction has echoes of medieval congruent and condign merit, while disavowing the Scholastic *meritum de congruo*.[142] More plausible is McClenahan's conclusion that Edwards's distinction came neither from English philosophy nor medieval scholasticism, but was merely the language of the Puritan tradition. McClenahan cites as an example Thomas Manton's (1620–1677) sermon on Ps 119, where he speaks of moral unfitness and natural unfitness. Manton also describes faith as specially "fit" for the role it is assigned in justification: "Faith is the grand and primary

---

139. Edwards, "'Controversies' Notebook: Justification," *WJE* 21:339–40.
140. Edwards, "Justification by Faith Alone," *WJE* 19:151.
141. Edwards, "Justification by Faith Alone," *WJE* 19:165.
142. Cherry, *Theology of Jonathan Edwards*, 95.

Condition of the Gospel. If you ask why Faith is appointed? We might look no further than the Will of the free Donor: But faith has a special aptitude and fitness for this Work."[143] Edwards was familiar with Manton's sermons, and the quote is from a sermon on justification by faith that Edwards copied into his notes on salvation.[144] This language and its distinctions were characteristic of Reformed methodology.

Edwards uses this terminology throughout his *corpus* but does not appear to invest much significance in the actual terms. At most he wants to say that, "there is a two-fold fitness to a state," but "I know not how to give them distinguishing names otherwise than by calling the one a *moral* and the other a *natural* fitness."[145] Edwards uses these terms, the best he sees as available, to explain his conclusions about the act of faith. Because man is a condemned sinner, no act is received by God as morally fit or worthy. Because faith is in some sense a virtue (at least as consenting and trusting in God's word of promise), there is a natural suitableness in God looking upon the believer as "one with Christ." To use Edwards's analogy of the marriage union, it may be a virtuous act for one to say, "I do" in consenting to a marriage union for various reasons (promise keeping, pledge of faithfulness, etc.), and the act of saying, "I do" is a perlocutionary act of union. But the act of saying, "I do" does not bring about the marriage union on the ground that it is virtuous. Rather, it brings about the union because it is only naturally fitting in the eyes of the state (or church) that a man and woman be married by mutual consent.

Conclusion

In this chapter I reviewed ways in which certain scholars have (mis) read Edwards, questioning whether he was more Roman Catholic than Protestant, or even more universal than particularistic, in his soteriology. These scholars have either not understood Edwards's language in its proper context or have begun with false assumptions regarding Edwards's metaphysical philosophy. Reading Edwards through the lens of an ontological soteriology rather than through his own covenant and redemptive-historical biblical centrism leads to misrepresenting his

---

143. McClenahan, *Jonathan Edwards*, 124. The quotation from Manton is taken from *A Fifth Volume of Sermons* (London, 1701), 277.

144. Edwards, "Misc. 1130[a]," *WJE* 20:508–9.

145. Edwards, "Justification by Faith Alone," *WJE* 19:165 (emphasis in the original).

views on justification. The theological portrait of Edwards presented by these scholars is a far cry from the Puritan pastor who would preach the following sentiments in a sermon entitled, "God Glorified in Man's Dependence":

> Hence those doctrines and schemes of divinity that are in any respects opposite to such an absolute and universal dependence on God, do derogate from God's glory, and thwart the design of the contrivance for our redemption. Those schemes that put the creature in God's stead, in any of the mentioned respects, that exalt man into the place of either Father, Son, or Holy Ghost, in anything pertaining to our redemption; that however they may allow of a dependence of the redeemed on God, yet deny a dependence that is so absolute and universal; that own an entire dependence on God for some things, but not for others; that own that we depend on God for the gift and acceptance of a redeemer, but deny so absolute a dependence on him for the obtaining of an interest in the Redeemer; that own an absolute dependence on the Father for giving his Son, and on the Son for working out redemption, but not so entire a dependence on the Holy Ghost for conversion, and a being in Christ, and so coming to a title to his benefits; that own a dependence on God for means of grace, but not absolutely for the benefit and success of those means; that own a partial dependence on the power of God, for the obtaining and exercising holiness, but not a mere dependence on the arbitrary and sovereign grace of God; that own a dependence on the free grace of God for a reception into his favor, so far that it is without any proper merit, but not as it is without being attracted, or moved with any excellency; that own a partial dependence on Christ, as he through whom we have life, as having purchased new terms of life, but still hold that the righteousness through which we have life is inherent in ourselves, as it was under the first covenant; and whatever other way any scheme is inconsistent with our entire dependence on God for all, and in each of those ways, of having all *of* him, *through* him, and *in* him, it is repugnant to the design and tenor of the gospel, and robs it of that which God accounts its luster and glory.[146]

Edwards was certainly creative in his language and formulations in ways he thought contributed to shoring up areas of weakness in his own tradition. Even so, he stayed well within the bounds of orthodox

---

146. Edwards, "God Glorified in Man's Dependence," *WJE* 17:212–13.

and confessional Reformed theology, as several other studies have also concluded.[147] As Stout understands, "[Edwards] was every bit the federal theologian that his Puritan predecessors were."[148] My own conclusion is that a proper understanding of Edwards's covenant theology helps to put his language of faith, obedience, and justification in its proper perspective and can prevent reading this great New England apologist for Calvinism in ways he would have certainly repudiated.

The theme of this chapter might be called the "negative" view of evangelical obedience. It is about what works "do not do" in Edwards's covenant theology. Works do not contribute in any meritorious fashion to justification. There is no prior meritorious holiness or virtue in the unbeliever prior to the believer's union with Christ in his justification. It is truly the unjustifiable that are justified. Even faith, while virtuous in some sense, is only a "fitting" response of the believer by which God views the believer as united with Christ, having no inherent meritorious virtue of its own. The only "works" that bear directly on justification, as having any merit or interest in justification, are Christ's alone which are imputed to the believer through their covenant union with Christ. Justification is ultimately through works, but only through a mediatorial fulfillment of the covenant requirements imputed to elect believers as they are looked upon as Christ's bride. Edwards's covenant theology forms an unbridgeable divide between the law and gospel. The next and final chapter will examine the "positive" role of evangelical obedience in covenant perspective and explain the necessity, albeit a non-meritorious necessity, of works in the Christian life.

---

147. Recent examples would include Biehl, *Infinite Merit*; Moody, *Jonathan Edwards*; Cho, *Jonathan Edwards on Justification*; Strobel, *Jonathan Edwards's Theology*; and Strobel, "By Word and Spirit," 45–70. See also in the same volume, Logan, "Justification and Evangelical Obedience," 95–128; Sweeney, "Justification by Faith Alone?," 129–45.

148. Harry S. Stout, "Puritans and Edwards," 143.

7

Jonathan Edwards on Evangelical Obedience

Introduction

IN THIS FINAL CHAPTER I will look at the "positive" role of evangelical obedience in Edwards's theology. Edwards maintained the necessity, albeit non-meritorious necessity, of works in the Christian life. Much of Edwards's emphasis and language about the role of works in salvation has been subject to criticism, especially from conservative Reformed theologians who have questioned his orthodoxy in terms of justification by faith alone. Some scholars have seen in Edwards's writing a shift from a firm defense of the Reformed doctrine of *sola fide* in his earlier writings to a more Roman Catholic view of the relationship between works and justification in his later writings. In this chapter I will provide a defense of Edwards's Reformed view of the role of works in salvation and argue that he is frequently misread, taken out of context, or interpreted through the lens of secondary sources. Edwards's language can be confusing at times and prone to misinterpretations. A closer reading of Edwards, especially in the context of his covenant theology, will mitigate many of the concerns that he deviated significantly from the Reformed orthodox position with regards to evangelical works and justification.

I will begin by looking at what Edwards means when he says that works are necessary for salvation, or even that works contribute to justification. Statements like these can be fraught with interpretive difficulties. I will examine several examples of how Edwards has been misread and provide a closer reading of Edwards, particularly with respect to the covenant context of these statements. Edwards always maintained that works were evidences or manifestations of saving faith, but the close and necessary connection between the two allowed Edwards to say that works were necessary to salvation, without straying from the bounds of Reformed orthodoxy. In fact, his more controversial statements, when read in context, merely reflect in sometimes different terms positions articulated by previous Reformed theologians. I will then discuss Edwards's theology of perseverance and the declarative nature of persevering faith and obedience in eschatological justification. I will finally look at Edwards's defense and explanation of heavenly rewards for earthly evangelical obedience, along with his reflections on how works reflect the believer's love for God's holiness and plan of redemption. I will conclude that reading Edwards in the context of his covenant theology helps to understand and to put into proper context his theology of evangelical obedience.

The Necessity of Good Works

Edwards is adamant that the inherent good works of the elect and regenerate believer in no way contribute to their justification. As he preached in a sermon on Matt 15:23 entitled "Profitable Hearers of the Word" (June 1756), "We should not mingle the righteousness of Christ with our own righteousness . . . or go about to cover ourselves partly with his righteousness and partly with our own, as though the garment of Christ's righteousness was no sufficient of itself to cover us and adorn us without being patched with our righteousness to eke it out."[1] And yet Edwards could also say with equal adamancy that works are necessary for salvation. For instance, "Universal and persevering obedience is as directly proposed to be sought and endeavored by us, in Scripture, as necessary to salvation [and] as the condition of our salvation, as faith in Jesus Christ."[2] How these seemingly conflicting statements can be reconciled in Edwards is the subject of this section.

---

1. Edwards, "Profitable Hearers of the Word," *WJE* 14:256. Edwards, in a previous sermon on Luke 14:16, "The Spiritual Blessings of the Gospel Represented by a Feast," exhorted his congregation to, "Labor to get your soul clothed with Christ's righteousness. At the day of judgment, none will be admitted but those that shall be found having on Christ's righteousness. All others, that cloth themselves with their own righteousness, shall be stripped naked, and they shall see their shame." Edwards, "Spiritual Blessings of the Gospel," *WJE* 14:280.

2. Edwards, "Misc. 412," *WJE* 13:532.

Edwards's viewed the nature of saving faith as a persevering and working faith. So closely tied is the nature of faith to its persevering quality and its outworking in acts of loving obedience, that perseverance and evangelical obedience can be viewed as "secondary conditions" of justification in that they witness to or evidence the nature of that faith which alone saves. While good works have no direct interest in a believer's justification (other than as evidence of saving faith), a regenerate believer's works are rewarded with further degrees of glory in heaven. Edwards held to a doctrine of the degrees of glory and countered several objections to this doctrine. Edwards also held that evangelical obedience expresses a love for God's holiness in the context of the work of redemption.

Works and the Nature of Justifying Faith

Several commentators on Edwards's works have proposed that Edwards shifted toward a more Catholic understanding of the role of works in salvation in his later writings. Amy Plantinga Pauw reads Edwards in this manner when she says that Edwards's "view of the redemptive work of the Holy Spirit tilted away from a conventionally Protestant emphasis on God's sovereign grace in saving sinners towards a typically Catholic stress on the abiding reality of salvation in human persons."[3] She sees this specifically in Edwards's response to George Whitefield's (1714–1770) message of the immediate experience of spiritual rebirth that was sweeping the New England countryside, including his own congregation. Edwards preached to his congregation that whereas regeneration, "the first work" of the Holy Spirit, infused a new sense of the sweetness of God's loving mercy in Christ, there must be a continuing growth in true virtue. "The whole work of sanctification" should be considered part of God's regeneration of the sinner, "and therefore the new birth is not finished till the soul is fully restored, and till the corruption and death that came by Adam and the first birth is wholly removed."[4] Likewise, Ava Chamberlain alludes to this supposed shift in Edwards as he became "increasingly aware of the importance of persevering Christian practice in the religious

---

3. Pauw, *Supreme Harmony*, 167. See also Pauw, "Editor's Introduction," *WJE* 20:25. See also Sweeney's rebuttal in Sweeny, "Jonathan Edwards and Justification," 151–73.

4. Edwards, "Misc. 847," *WJE* 20:71. This *Miscellany* was written shortly after Whitefield's visit to Northampton in 1740.

life."[5] According to Chamberlain, the "miscellanies from the 1730's reveal how Edwards arrived only gradually at a recognition of the importance of Christian practice."[6] Both these editors of volumes in the Yale edition of *The Works of Jonathan Edwards* read into Edwards a shift from his earlier works on justification in his *Master's Quaestio* of 1723, sermons, and early *Miscellanies* to a greater accommodation, at least in emphasis, for the role of works in justification.

This reading of Edwards is misguided for several reasons. First, Edwards preached numerous sermons in his early years (prior to the 1730s *Miscellanies*) on the necessity of good works. For example, in his sermon on Gal 2:17 he preached against the notion that the doctrine of justification by faith alone "makes Christ the author of sin." Imploring his congregation that the "Gospel is no encouragement to sin," Edwards said that those who do not see the connection between the gospel and good works are guilty of "gross misunderstanding."[7] Second, McClenahan notes that Edwards's specific context of the 1730s *Miscellanies* was the preparation of his 1734 lectures for publication, and therefore had a specific focus.[8] In other sermons and *Miscellanies* Edwards would address the "twin heresy" of Arminianism and antinomianism. Third, and most importantly, this reductionist reading of Edwards ignores the Reformed orthodox position, which Edwards is merely echoing.

The Reformed tradition does not neglect the inherent holiness and the continued growth in holiness in the elect believer. During the Reformation, Roman Catholic theologians, including the Jesuit cardinal Robert Bellarmine (1542–1621), often asserted that Reformed theologians denied any inherent righteousness and accused Protestants of teaching a "demon" or "devil's" faith (Jas 2:18).[9] The *Westminster Confession*, however, speaks of the inherent transformation that occurs under sanctification:

> They, who are once effectually called, and regenerated, having a new heart, and a new spirit created in them, are further sanctified, really and personally, through the virtue of Christ's death

---

5. Chamberlain, "Editor's Introduction," *WJE* 18:38–39.
6. Chamberlain, "Editor's Introduction," *WJE* 18:20.
7. Edwards, "Gal. 2:17," *WJEO* 47, L. 1v.
8. McClenahan, *Jonathan Edwards*, 89–126.
9. Sweeny, *Edwards the Exegete*, 210, 369–70. Cf. Turretin, *Institutes*, 2:560. Edwards directly addresses this accusation in a sermon on Jas 2:19, "True Grace, Distinguished from the Experience of Devils," *WJE* 25:608–42, esp. 617.

and resurrection, by his Word and Spirit dwelling in them: the dominion of the whole body of sin is destroyed, and the several lusts thereof are more and more weakened and mortified; and they more and more quickened and strengthened in all saving graces, to the practice of true holiness, *without which no man shall see the Lord.*[10]

Turretin argued that good works are necessary to salvation "so that no one can be saved without them—that thus our religion may be freed from those most foul calumnies everywhere cast most unjustly upon it by the Romanists."[11] Turretin is representative of the Reformed federal tradition in that he does not pose any antithesis between forensic imputation and the Spirit's internal infusion of moral virtues. The imputation of Christ's righteousness and the Spirit-wrought inherent righteousness of the regenerate believer represent the *duplex gratia* of union with Christ, the one never received without the other. Yet it is only the imputation of Christ's righteousness that bears on justification. So Turretin:

> Just as Christ sustains a twofold relation (*schesin*) to us, of surety and head (of surety, to take away the guilt of sin by a payment made for it; of head, to take away its power and corruption by the efficacy of the Spirit), so in a twofold way Christ imparts his blessings to us, by a forensic imputation, and a moral and internal infusion. The former flows from Christ as surety and is the foundation of our justification. The latter depends upon him as head, and is the principle of justification. The latter depends upon him as head, and is the principle of sanctification. For on this account God justifies us, because the righteousness of our surety, Christ, is imputed to us. And on this account we are renewed, because we derive the spirit from our head, Christ, who renews us after the image of Christ, and bestows upon us inherent righteousness.[12]

Likewise, Mastricht discusses infusion in his *A Treatise on Regeneration*:

> For regeneration, strictly so called, finds man spiritually dead (Ephesians 2:2, 5), into whom it infuses the first act of principle of the spiritual life, by which he has a power or ability to perform spiritual exercises. Therefore, without this, he can neither see the kingdom of God—that is, mentally, since he is blind,

---

10. WCF 13.1 (emphasis mine).
11. Turretin, *Institutes*, 2:703.
12. Turretin, *Institutes*, 2:647.

and perceiveth not the things of the Spirit of God, for they are foolishness unto him, neither can he know them, because they are spiritually discerned (1 Corinthians 2:14)—nor, if he could see, could he enter into the kingdom of God, since he is not subject to the law of God, neither indeed can be (Romans 8:7). Of himself, he is not sufficient to think anything spiritually good (2 Corinthians 3:5), and therefore stands in absolute need of illumination by regeneration in order to see the kingdom of heaven, and of a renovation of his will, in order to be willing to enter into it.[13]

Later in his treatise Mastricht describes regeneration as a "physical act powerfully infusing spiritual life in the soul."[14] Paul Ramsey, in his appendix to Edwards's *Ethical Writings*, discusses Edwards's use of "infused virtues" in its Calvinistic context, showing how Calvin's doctrine of *duplex gratia* set forth the rule, "that we must be made holy because our God is holy . . . that, infused with his holiness, we may follow whither he calls."[15] In conversion God justifies sinners by imputing the perfect righteousness of Christ to their accounts, and simultaneously and with the same regenerative act of the Holy Spirit that binds sinners to Christ, infuses righteousness, redirects their affections (attuning them to God), and begins a life of bearing fruit.

Even a cursory reading of Edwards's *Charity and Its Fruits*, his *On the Nature of True Virtue*, or even his *Miscellanies* on the "gracious" affections, evidences his doctrine of infused righteousness alongside a doctrine of Christ's imputed righteousness. His doctrine of the Christian moral life is one of progressive sanctification grounded on a doctrine of infused moral virtues. When Edwards speaks of being remade in the "spiritual image of God," he is speaking of the Spirit becoming "an indwelling vital principle in the soul,"[16] and the subject becoming "a spiritual being." This

13. Mastricht, *Treatise on Regeneration*, 7–8.

14. Mastricht, *Treatise on Regeneration*, 17. By "physical" Mastrich, as with Edwards, does not mean that the Holy Spirit bestows a new natural faculty (such as the understanding, will, or affections), but simply in opposition to "moral." A moral operation is the effecting of something by moral suasion or by the laying of argument and inducement before the mind. "Physical" implies a positive, immediate act of the divine spirit on the soul, infusing a new principle of spiritual and divine life whereby the soul is enabled or qualified to exercise its natural powers and faculties in a new spiritual manner.

15. Calvin, *Institutes*, 1:685–86.

16. Edwards, "Charity and Its Fruits," *WJE* 8:157–158. See also Edwards, "Religious Affections," *WJE* 2:201–208 for Edwards's discussion of the meaning of "spiritual."

is to be distinguished from having been made in the "natural image of God," by which he means of natural birth to the "mortal part" of creation.

An active (justifying) faith is a faith that changes a person's entire being. In his sermon on Rom 4:16, Edwards says that saving faith is a "sense and conviction of the Reality & excellency of [Christ] as savior," a new spiritual sense that "Entirely Inclines & unites the heart to him." It involves "the whole soul . . . every faculty entirely Embracing and acquiescing in the Gospel."[17] In a sermon on Hab 2:4, Edwards preaches that "faith is acquiescence of the whole soul to Christ and the gospel."[18] In another sermon Edwards distinguishes saving faith from common faith: "Saving faith differs from . . . common faith in its nature, kind, and essence . . . [In] him that is in a state of salvation faith produces another effect; it works another way: it produces a settled determination of mind to walk in a way of universal and preserving obedience."[19] Godly love is implied in saving faith. It is not a condition that obtains, merits, or has an interest in justification before God, but a condition without which one does not have genuine faith. The new spiritual sense is evidence of a justifying, Spirit-wrought faith.

In his *Justification by Faith Alone* sermon, Edwards defines several uses of the word "condition" as it applies to faith, justification, and salvation:

> Christ alone performs the condition of our justification and salvation; in another sense, faith is the condition of justification; in another sense, other qualifications and acts are conditions of salvation and justification too: there seems to be a great deal of ambiguity in such expressions as are commonly used (which yet we are forced to use), such as "condition of salvation"; "what is required in order to salvation or justification"; "the terms of the covenant," and the like; and I believe they are understood in very different senses by different persons. And besides as the word *condition* is very often understood in the common use of language, faith is not the only thing, in us, that is the condition of justification; for by the word *condition*, as 'tis very often (and perhaps most commonly), used; we mean anything that may have the place of a condition in a conditional proposition, and as such is truly connected with the consequent, especially if the proposition holds both in the affirmative and negative, as the

---

17. Edwards, "Rom 4:16," *WJEO* 45, L. 3r–v.
18. Edwards, "Hab 2:4," *WJEO* 44, L. 2v–3r.
19. Edwards, "Saving Faith and Christian Obedience," *WJE* 25:498–508.

condition is either affirmed or denied; if it be that with which, or which being supposed, a thing shall be, and without which, or it being denied, a thing shall not be, we in such a case call it a condition of that thing: but in this sense faith is not the only condition of salvation or justification, for there are many things that accompany and flow from faith, that are things with which justification shall be, and without which it will not be, and therefore are found to be put in Scripture in conditional propositions with justification and salvation in multitudes of places: such are "love to God," and "love to our brethren," "forgiving men their trespasses," and many other good qualifications and acts. And there are many other things besides faith which are directly proposed to us, to be pursued or performed by us, in order to eternal life, as those which, if they are done or obtained, we shall have eternal life, and if not done or not obtained, we shall surely perish.[20]

Universal and persevering obedience necessarily follows saving faith. It is this necessary and immutable connection that allows Edwards to use the term "condition" with reference to obedience as well as faith in salvation. Obedience is a condition of salvation in that it evidences or is the expression of the true nature of saving faith, while faith alone is properly the condition of justification: "But 'tis not obedience and good works, which is that which God has any primary respect to in any man, that makes it appear to him a suitable thing so to look upon him as in Christ, and so to impute to him Christ's righteousness."[21] Evangelical works necessarily evidence saving faith, and without which there can be no saving faith. Saving faith is the proper condition of justification. *Ergo*, evangelical works are also a condition of justification in that without them, there is no saving faith.[22] The issue is the nature of working faith, a faith that is exercised in receiving Christ and producing evangelical works, which are the fruit of that union. As Edwards addressed it in his *Master's Quaestio*:

---

20. Edwards, "Justification by Faith Alone," *WJE* 19:152. See also Edwards, "Misc. 412," *WJE* 13:471–74; Edwards, "Misc. 416," *WJE* 13:475–76; Edwards, "Misc. 670," *WJE* 18:222–23; Edwards, "Misc. 808," *WJE* 18:510–12; Edwards, "Misc. 859," *WJE* 20:84–85; Edwards, "Misc. 996," *WJE* 20:324–25.

21. Edwards, "Misc. 412," *WJE* 13:472.

22. When Edwards says that works or perseverance is a "secondary" condition, this is not meant in any contributory sense, but only in the sense that they manifest, evidence, or declare the true nature of the "primary" condition.

> We are not even asking whether or not we are justified by this evangelical obedience, but whether we are justified by this evangelical obedience because of its intrinsic goodness, or merely because it is only by evangelical obedience that Christ is received. For every part of evangelical obedience is an implicit reception of Christ and an act of justifying faith. We assert, therefore, that a sinner is justified in the sight of God neither totally nor in part because of the goodness of such obedience, or of any works at all, but only on account of what Christ did and suffered, received by faith.[23]

Edwards expresses his frustration: "Tis a hundred pities that men don't think what the question is about what they dispute."[24]

Misc. 856 is provocatively titled, "Justification. How Works Justify, or How a Christian Life and Practice Justifies." This *Miscellany* is linked with five others, *859, 861, 876, 996,* and *1030*. In this series of *Miscellanies* Edwards argues that works are "as much the proper evidence of the act of the soul in receiving Christ, as the act of the soul in receiving Christ is the proper evidence of the principle of faith."[25] Edwards's point is that the new birth attains to the whole of man as a unity of spirit, soul, and body, and it is in this sense that the whole man's accepting of Christ as savior is "properly" the condition of justification. Yet, it is only the "principle or being of faith" (spirit) which is the proper condition for justification absolutely. Because of the unity of spirit, soul, and body, the act of the soul in receiving Christ is necessary evidence and manifestation of that faith. Works (of the body) are necessary evidence and manifestations of the act of the soul. It is this necessary connection that allows Edwards to say that each is a "proper" condition of justification. Edwards presents the hypothetical "if" there were no such necessary connections then the soul's act of faith (and works as evidence) would not be the proper condition of justification. It would still be "the principle or being" of faith that justifies. Christian works are like the outward act of a beggar putting forth his hand and taking the gift offered him. The gift is no less of pure grace for the act of receiving it. As Edwards says, "Practicing holiness is actual accepting that benefit of Christ's purchase, as much as the beggar's taking the gift, and voluntary having it, is the very same as his accepting

---

23. Edwards, "Quaestio," *WJE* 14:61.
24. Edwards, "Misc. 35," *WJE* 13:219.
25. Edwards, "Misc. 859," *WJE* 20:84.

it; or, as the eating food given him is accepting that food."[26] All are the unified acts of the whole man.

In *Misc. 996*, Edwards interacts with the statement in Jas 2:22, "Seest thou how faith wrought with his works, and by works was faith made perfect." Faith being made perfect, says Edwards, is when the act of accepting of and closing with Christ is completed by "doing it practically, as well as in heart." Because of the unity of soul, spirit, and body, the act of closing with Christ is complete, not only by accepting of Christ with the whole soul, "but with the whole man, by giving up all to Christ, and offering our bodies as well as souls a living sacrifice."[27] Christ's call to Matthew to "leave all and come to him" necessitated that Matthew not only consent to do it, but actually do it. Had he fulfilled the condition to "come and follow him," the fulfillment of that condition would have begun as soon as his heart had complied. But the fulfillment of the condition "as being all respected" is not accomplished until he had actually done it. Taking all these *Miscellanies* together, Edwards is saying that works of faith are necessary evidences of the renewed "whole man" in regeneration. There is never a partial re-birth. While it is the "principle or being" of faith alone that justifies, it is "completed" by the compliance of the whole person in both acts of faith and obedience. True faith does not exist in isolation, as if the soul and body were separate parts untouched by the Spirit's work. By "completed" Edwards does not mean there is something lacking in true faith that needs to be supplemented (by works), but only that it comes to "fruition" and completion in the acts of the whole man. "By practice repentance, as the condition of remission of sins, is made perfect. He that is in his heart sensible of his sin and confesses his sin, in him the condition is begun; but 'tis by forsaking of sin that it is made perfect, as the condition of finding mercy. He that confesses and forsakes his sin shall find mercy."[28]

Edwards emphasizes this in several sermons, including a sermon on Heb 12:14: "[f]aith alone Gives the Right to salvation[,] yet . . . Living a Life of Holin[ess] is necessary to the actual Receiving [of] salv[ation]." Faith "is that Qualific[ation] that is Primarily necessary in order to persons Coming to see [Christ,] for tis the very thing by which they are united to [Christ] and Come to have an int[erest] in him. But none have

---

26. Edwards, "Misc. 856," *WJE* 20:83.
27. Edwards, "Misc. 996," *WJE* 20:324.
28. Edwards, "Misc. 996," *WJE* 20:325.

that Faith but H[oly] P[ersons]."²⁹ In a sermon on Gal 5:6a entitled, "Only that sort of faith that works by love avails anything before God," Edwards preaches, "'[T]is only faith without works that Justifies[,] yet [the] Christian Religion secures Obedience to [God] and Good Works." The "proper work of faith in the heart is to Change and Renew the heart." Therefore, "they that say they have faith and don't bring forth . . . Good works are like the dry limbs of a tree that must be Lop[pe]d off." Justifying faith is "faith that is accompanied by works."³⁰

In the twelfth sermon in the series *Charity and Its Fruits* entitled "Christian Graces Concatenated Together," Edwards says, "The graces of Christianity are all linked together or united one to another and within one another, as the links of a chain; one does, as it were, hang on another from one end of the chain to the other, so that if one link be broken, all falls; the whole ceases to be of any effect."³¹ Faith, love, and the other evangelical graces are so tightly bound together that "where there is one, there are all; and when one is wanting, all are wanting. Where there is faith, there is love and hope and humility. Where there is love, there is also trust; and where there is a holy trust in God, there is love to God."³² Faith promotes love, and love is the most essential ingredient in a saving faith. The doctrine of *sola fide* does not require faith to be "alone" in the regenerate believer. At the moment of conversion, the regenerate believer does not only exercise faith. In Edwards, as with Reformed theology, faith is the only act relevant to justification, but it is not the only virtue present. Faith alone justifies, but the faith that justifies is never alone.³³

Receiving Christ and his benefits takes place by faith with the entire soul, not merely the intellect's reception by assent, or only the will's reception by choosing, or only the affections' reception in love, or merely the capacities for action receiving him in obedience. It encompasses all of these at once. This, according to Edwards, is described in various ways

---

29. Edwards, "Heb 12:14," *WJEO* 48, L. 12r., 10r.
30. Edwards, "Gal. 5:6(a)," Beinecke Library, L. 11, 7v.–8r.
31. Edwards, "Charity and Its Fruits," *WJE* 8: 327–28.
32. Edwards, "Charity and Its Fruits," *WJE* 8:328.
33. Both Schafer and Danaher make the mistake of assuming that the doctrine of *sola fide* requires faith to be "alone" in the subject. For instance, Danaher says, "Traditionally, the Puritan doctrine of regeneration holds that the connection between faith and works is an orderly sequential relationship subordinate to the experience of justification." Danaher, *Trinitarian Ethics*, 149.

in Scripture as "coming, believing, trusting, receiving, submitting, etc."[34] Furthermore, saving faith receives the entire Christ in "all his offices." Christ is received both in his priestly as well as kingly office, but "he is justified by his receiving Christ in his priestly office."[35] Edwards explains: "Though the receiving and submitting to Christ in his kingly office directly as such, or as this has a direct respect to the kingly office, is not that which justifies; yet this, as 'tis the proper exercise and expression of trusting in Christ for the benefits of his priesthood, does properly belong to that faith which is the most proper condition or qualification for justification."[36] So close are evangelical works and faith tied together in Edwards, that he can even say that "faith was made perfect by works" (in reference to Jas 2:21–23). But unlike the Roman Catholic doctrine of *fides formata caritate*, evangelical works evidence and manifest an already present justifying faith and do not contribute or add to it.

If there was a shift in Edwards's thinking over time, it was not from a Protestant doctrine of *sola fide* to a Roman Catholic doctrine of works contributing to justification. Rather, it was to a further emphasis on holiness in the Christian life; from affirming that faith alone justifies to the additional affirmation that faith can never be separated from evangelical works in those whom God grants salvation. Stephen Wilson says, "Only charity's habitual nature reveals whether the seeds of redemption have been sown in the heart . . . habits alone elicit what is foundationally desired and willed."[37] If so, then persistent practice of Christian love and evangelical obedience becomes secondarily a means of assurance. If Calvin worried that relying on works as a source of assurance of salvation could easily slide into works righteousness,[38] Edwards found it impos-

---

34. Edwards, "Quaestio," *WJE* 14:61.
35. Edwards, "Faith," *WJE* 21:435.
36. Edwards, "'Controversies' Notebook: Justification," *WJE* 21:360.
37. Wilson, *Virtue Reformed*, 44.
38. According to Randall Zachman, "Calvin is confident that the judgment of conscience is sufficient to disclose the sincerity or hypocrisy of our faith, but the judgment of conscience can never be equated with the judgment of God. The testimony of a good conscience may rightly and necessarily declare the sincerity of our faith based on the genuineness of repentance, but the testimony of conscience is never adequate to declare us justified before God. We can only be certain that we are justified before God when God declares that we are justified in Jesus Christ. The testimony of a good conscience must always accompany, but can never replace, the faith in Jesus Christ that alone justifies us and assures our consciences before the judgment seat of God." Zachman, *Assurance of Faith*, 201.

sible to imagine the truly converted believer not exhibiting, at least to some extent and however incomplete, the virtues of righteousness.

Edwards's covenant theology makes this clear. The Covenant of Grace does, once consented to, place demands on the believer, including a persevering in faith as exhibited by a progressive growth in holiness (sanctification). But those conditions of the Covenant of Grace between Christ and the believer are also the promises of the Covenant of Redemption, already earned by Christ's obedience and applied as the gift of the Holy Spirit. The elect believer's "working" faith, as the ground for union with Christ's justification through his imputed perfect and complete obedience, has already been secured from eternity in the Second Person of the Trinity's covenant obedience. As Edwards says in *Religious Affections*:

> The saints' love to God, is the fruit of God's love to them; as it is the gift of that love. God gave them a spirit of love to him, because he loved them from eternity. And in this respect God's love to his elect is the first foundation of their love to him, as it is the foundation of their regeneration, and the whole of their redemption.[39]

The elect believer's own works, which flow from that union, are neither necessary nor sufficient for adding anything towards justification. In a sermon entitled, "He That Believeth Shall Be Saved," Edwards says:

> But 'tis not because our goodness is sufficient, or can do anything of itself. But 'tis because all whose hearts come to Christ will be good, and if men ben't good, their hearts never will come to Christ . . . They whose hearts come to Christ, they are joined to Christ, and so they belong to him and therefore are saved for his sake . . . And the great reason why God is willing to save good men is not because of the goodness, or for anything they do—for they are sinful unworthy creatures—but because they are joined to Christ.[40]

Good works flow out of the believer's union with Christ, and the believer is justified for Christ's sake. Works are necessary evidence of that union but are never meritorious.

While union with Christ brings about the *duplex gratia* of justification and sanctification, there is a (logical, not temporal or sequential) priority to justification. In the method of justification by the gospel, "a

---

39. Edwards, "Religious Affections," *WJE* 2:249.
40. Edwards, *Sermons of Jonathan Edwards: A Reader*, 115.

person is justified before he has any habitual holiness, or any holiness as an established principle of action."[41] The establishing of holiness as an abiding principle of spiritual life and action is consequent on justification. What this means for Edwards is simply that "God justifies the ungodly." As he preached in a sermon on Titus 3:5, "There are none saved upon the account of their own moral . . . goodness, or any qualification of the person, any good disposition of the heart, or any good actions . . . none [are] saved upon the account of any habitual excellency . . . or any moral or religious habit obtained by frequent acts or any truly gracious habit."[42] Justification and sanctification are received simultaneously in union with Christ, but this does not negate the law-gospel distinction in Edwards, nor does it necessitate abandoning the traditional (logical not temporal) *ordo salutis* of personal redemption.

Edwards can say that "holiness and an active conformity to God's moral nature and will" is "absolutely necessary in order to justification" under the New Covenant, because "it is so ordered in infinite wisdom that holiness shall always follow faith, and God will not give one without the other—the same spirit that works faith in Christ will also at the same time implant principles of holiness." God promises that all that truly believe (exercise true saving faith) will be enabled and inclined to be "universally holy" and he will "uphold them in a way of holiness to the end." Holiness is the natural and necessary consequence and fruit of faith."[43] Faith alone justifies, but the very nature, spirit, and act of a true justifying faith is an active conformity to God's moral nature and will.[44]

Perseverance

The necessity of works in salvation also raises the question of perseverance in faith in justification. In *Justification by Faith*, Edwards argued for the necessity of later acts of faith for the justification that occurs at the moment of conversion. Responding again to charges of antinomianism, that "faith" is a mere "bare assent," he explains both the necessity of good

41. Edwards, "'Controversies' Notebook: Justification," *WJE* 21:371.
42. Edwards, "None Are Saved," *WJE* 14:333.
43. Edwards, "'Controversies' Notebook: Justification," *WJE* 21:356.
44. Edwards, "'Controversies' Notebook: Justification," *WJE* 21:356. Edwards shows how this applies to both the Old and New Covenants, though in different manners. See my previous discussion on the role of faith under the Covenant of Works in chapter 2 and the nature of faith and obedience under the Mosaic covenant in chapter 5.

works as well as the necessity of perseverance in faith for justification (at conversion). In *Misc. 729* Edwards recognizes that perseverance "is acknowledged by Calvinian divines to be necessary to salvation," and yet it seemed to him that this doctrine was insufficiently explained.[45] Is Edwards saying that justification is somehow suspended on faith's perseverance, or that justification is somehow incomplete in the first act of faith? Is "perseverance" in some sense contributory to the first act of faith in the believer's justification? If so, this would leave Edwards's view of justification open to critiques of being outside the bounds of Reformed orthodoxy. While a superficial reading of Edwards's language may lead one to suspect such, a closer reading of Edwards, particularly in the context of his covenant theology, shows that Edwards did not hold to any of these positions. While believers must persevere, it is not that perseverance or continued acts of faith contribute to the sinner's justification (as if the initial forensic pronouncement needed anything else). The question is about the nature of the faith that initially justifies. Is it a persevering faith or not? And, more importantly, the fulfillment of the condition of perseverance comes by way of blessing through the Covenant of Grace.

Edwards discusses a believer's perseverance according to his previous discussions on the definition of faith and the "natural congruity" and "fitness" of the faith-union between the believer and Christ. This union by which the believer has an interest in Christ's righteousness "depends on its being an abiding union." It is "necessary that the soul should abide in Christ, in order to its receiving those lasting benefits of God's final acceptance and favour."[46] Justifying faith is "not a vanishing but a durable faith that justifies."[47] While the sinner is "actually and finally" justified on the first act of faith, a "necessary quality" of that faith is that it has a persevering nature.[48]

> But this fitness lies in perseverance in faith. If it could be so that a man should cease to believe in Christ, and so should not continue to receive him and to be united in his heart to him, it would not be fit that he should continue to be looked upon

---

45. Edwards, "Misc. 729," *WJE* 18:353. In this *Miscellany* Edwards uses the term "salvation" rather than "justification." Since he is talking about that which brings a legal "title to salvation," it is clear he means "justification."
46. Edwards, "Justification by Faith Alone," *WJE* 19:202.
47. Edwards, "Persevering Faith," *WJE* 19:601.
48. Edwards calls this a "property in that faith." Edwards, "Misc. 729," *WJE* 18:304.

> as one with him; and that, although persons are fully justified and accepted as one with Christ on the first act of faith without waiting till a persevering faith has actually had existence. For it may influence before it has actual existence, because it has existence already implicitly and virtually. The first act of faith virtually implies a perseverance in faith, by virtue of its own nature.[49]

Edwards told his congregation: "The love of true saints to Jesus Christ is such that nothing can extinguish or overcome it."[50] He continues: "Though perseverance be not an act performed, till after persons have finished their days: yet perseverance is looked upon as virtually performed in the first act of faith, because that first act is of such a nature as shows the principle to be of a persevering sort."[51] Simply put, a faith that does not persevere is not a Spirit-wrought justifying faith. God justifies completely and eternally on the first act of faith. Persevering in faith witnesses to (is evidence of) the "persevering quality" of that faith, a faith which has already justified the believer and procured a right to everlasting life.

Edwards also argues that persevering faith is at the same time a blessing of the Covenant of Grace, the blessing earned by Christ's obedience in the Covenant of Redemption.[52] Perseverance is also a gift that follows justification. "In its own nature it [faith] implies a full consent to and compliance with a persevering adherence to Christ, and particularly in that act of trust, in that adventuring of all on Christ, mentioned under the last particular; and it not only consents to it, but it *trusts in Christ to grant it*. And such is the divine constitution in the covenant of grace, that they who thus by one act sincerely consent to a persevering faith and holiness, and trust in Christ for it, *have it made sure to 'em*."[53]

In *Misc. 729* Edwards says that perseverance in faith is more than a *sine qua non* of a "title to salvation." In justifying a sinner God has respect to his own promise, and to the fitness of a qualification beheld "as

---

49. Edwards, "'Controversies' Notebook: Justification," *WJE* 21:360–61.

50. Edwards, "Cant. 8:7," *WJEO* 64, L. 1r (my transcription of Edwards's sermon notes).

51. Edwards, "Persevering Faith," *WJE* 19:601.

52. Yazawa, *Covenant of Redemption*," 126–29.

53. Edwards, "'Controversies' Notebook: Justification," *WJE* 21:361 (emphasis mine).

yet only in his promise."⁵⁴ It is possible for God to justify a sinner at the first exercise of faith because God's own covenant promise includes the gift of persevering faith (and the works which are a manifestation of its reality). In his sermon "Grace Never Overthrown," Edwards maintains, "The believer is already actually justified to life, and therefore God will not suffer him to come short of life. Justification is an actual acquittance of a sinner, a final acquittance from guilt, and deliverance from hell, and acceptance to a free title to life. But this is inconsistent with a deliverance from hell, and abiding life being yet suspended on an uncertain perseverance."⁵⁵ Justification is a once-for-all completed act. It is a declaration by God coinciding with the first exercise of faith. But God also justifies on the basis of "continuance in faith . . . because by divine establishment it shall follow."⁵⁶ The certainty of the divine establishment, founded on the covenant promises and the divine decrees, guarantees that the believer's faith will indeed persevere. Thus, whether perseverance is considered in terms of the object of faith (Christ's perseverance and promises) or as the principle and act of faith, justification is not suspended but actually declared on the first exercise of faith.

The Covenant of Grace is the ultimate basis of the "grace to persevere." Eternal life "won't be suspended on our perseverance by our own poor, feeble, broken strength."⁵⁷ "'Tis a Covenant of Works and not a Covenant of Grace that suspends eternal life on what is the fruit of man's own strength."⁵⁸ Furthermore, the gift of perseverance is essential to the New Covenant precisely because the sin of Adam was one of failing to persevere in faithfulness.⁵⁹ It is fundamentally Christ's perseverance in fulfillment of the Covenant of Redemption that is one of the benefits promised and given in the Covenant of Grace. This is why an understanding of Edwards's covenant theology is so important. Edwards explains this in his sermon:

> Adam, according to the tenor of the first covenant, was to persevere in perfect obedience in order to his having a title to life. And so Christ's perseverance in perfect obedience, is the

---

54. Edwards, "Misc. 729," *WJE* 18:355.
55. Edwards, "Charity and Its Fruits," *WJE* 8:347.
56. Edwards, "Justification by Faith Alone," *WJE* 19:203
57. Edwards, "Misc. 695," *WJE* 18:279.
58. Edwards, "Misc. 695," *WJE* 18:278.
59. Edwards, "Freedom of the Will," *WJE* 1:435–36.

condition of our right to life by the second covenant. But 'tis not perseverance in our own personal, imperfect obedience that acquires a right to life. That can't be; for the saints' persevering in holiness is one of the benefits to which a right is acquired by that righteousness. This is one of the things that Christ has purchased for the saints by his righteousness; and therefore 'tis one of the things promised in the covenant of grace.[60]

In the previously cited sermon, "Grace Never Overthrown," Edwards goes on to explain how the covenant arrangements provide the ground for the believer's perseverance:

> The second covenant was introduced to supply what was needed in the first, of which a sure ground of perseverance was the main thing. The first covenant had no defect on God's part who constituted it. It was a holy, just and wise, and perfect constitution; but yet it proved that on our part it was wanting, that we needed something more in order to its being effectual for our happiness; and the thing wanting was some sure ground of perseverance. All the ground which we had under the first covenant was the freedom of our own will, and that was found not to be depended on. God, therefore, has made another covenant. The first was liable to fail, and therefore another was introduced which could not fail, and therefore it is called an everlasting covenant, Isaiah 55:3. The things which can be shaken are removed to make way for that which cannot be shaken. The first covenant had a head and surety which was liable to fail; therefore God has provided one which cannot fail, even his own Son.[61]

Edwards contrasts the "legal" method of justification under the first covenant with the New Covenant "gospel" method. Under the first covenant, justification was dependent and suspended upon an actual perseverance in holiness (through an appointed time of probation) and is not finished and perfect until then. Under the Covenant of Grace (the gospel), a believer is justified at the very "first point or first step of his holy course," i.e., upon the first exercise of saving faith. And while perseverance in holiness is taken into account (in that it must be a persevering faith), God "don't wait till the perseverance of faith has actually existed, the same [justification] being made sure in the very first act of faith as though

---

60. Edwards, "Persevering Faith," *WJE* 19:600.
61. Edwards, "Charity and Its Fruits," *WJE* 8:347.

it had existed."⁶² Under the gospel, justification "is so far from being consequent" on actual perseverance, that it is actually a fruit of the faith by which persons are first justified. It is not only a fruit of faith, but a benefit received, and that God is trusted in for, by that act of faith.⁶³

Final Justification

Edwards does not teach a doctrine of justification through faith *and* works or justification through "faithfulness." But does he introduce a cooperation of works with faith by distinguishing, explicitly or implicitly, between an initial justification and a final or eschatological justification based on works? In this scheme sinners may be said to be justified initially by grace alone (*sola gratia*) and through faith alone (*sola fide*) in this life. But they are also *finally* justified (in the same legal sense) at the final eschaton also partly based on their inherent righteousness and sanctity produced through union with Christ. The logical order between justification and sanctification becomes blurred if not extinguished all together. One recent proponent of such a scheme has argued that Reformed Christians must "move on" from "*ordo salutis* thinking,"⁶⁴ by which he means both the temporal or logical priority of justification over sanctification. Again, it is not the purpose here to insert Edwards into a contemporary theological discussion. However, these issues were also those confronted by Edwards, and his stature in the history of Reformed theology makes his arguments important for more than mere historical purposes.

Lutheran and Reformed scholastics both talk of a "double justification" or *duplex iustitia*. This doctrine of the *duplex iustitia* is not establishing two grounds of standing before God (one of imputed righteousness by faith and another inherent righteousness), nor does it imply that there are two stages to justification, an initial in this life

---

62. Edwards, "'Controversies' Notebook: Justification," *WJE* 21:371.

63. Edwards, "'Controversies' Notebook: Justification," *WJE* 21:371. This reading of Edwards differs from that of J. V. Fesko who, in my opinion, errs in reading Edwards through the lens of Schafer and Hunsinger, or has simply read Edwards out of context. Fesko, *Justification*, 34–39; Fesko, *Covenant of Redemption*, 127–38.

64. Evans, *Imputation and Impartation*, 264–65. N. T. Wright also seems to be a proponent of a final justification by works when he writes, "The whole point about 'justification by faith' is that it is something which happens in the present time (Romans 3.26) as a proper anticipation of the eventual judgment which will be announced on the basis of the whole life led, in the future. (Romans 2.1–16)." Wright, *Paul*, 57.

and a final in the eschaton. Rather, Lutheran and Reformed theologians distinguished between justification as a legal and forensic act whereby God declares the ungodly to be legally just on the basis of Christ's perfect and complete (*condign*) merit imputed to them on the one hand, and the process of sanctification whereby the gracious consequences of that justification are worked out and exhibited in the lives of believers. These two aspects of a believer's righteousness are to be carefully distinguished but never separated. This was what Calvin meant by the *duplex gratia Dei* ("twofold grace of God") and what was taught by Olevianus and others as the *Duplex beneficium* ("double benefit") of the Covenant of Grace.[65] Any "final justification" in the eschaton or at the resurrection is one of vindication. Elect believers are justified in this life through the imputed righteousness of Christ alone and vindicated in the next by their works only as they witness to, declare, or give outward evidence of this initial justification. The view that believers are justified on two grounds, the

---

65. This *duplex gratia Dei* is also found in Luther. The relationship between justification and the ethical life of the believer is brought out most clearly in Luther's 1521 writing *Against Latomus*. While Luther did not use the term "*duplex gratia Dei*," he did discuss justification under the two aspects of grace (*gratia, favor*) and gift (*donum*). The former term signifies a forensically declared righteousness and the latter an effective righteousness. This is not a late thought of Luther but is grasped as early as his *Lecture on Romans* (1515/1516) and is centered on Rom 5:15 (*gratia Dei et donum in gratia*). Luther says in his preface to the German translation of Romans (1522), "Between grace and gift there is this difference. Grace actually means God's favor, or the good will which in himself he bears toward us, by which he is disposed to pour Christ and the Holy Spirit with his gifts into us. This is clear from chapter 5[:15], where St. Paul speaks of 'the grace and gift in Christ' etc." Luther, "Preface to the Epistle of St. Paul to the Romans," *LW* 35:369. The original German reads: "*Gnade und Gabe sind des Unterschieds: daß Gnade eigentlich heißet Gottes Huld oder Gunst, die er zu uns trägt bei sich selbst, aus welcher er geneigt wird, Christum und den Geist mit seinen Gaben in uns zu gießen, wie das aus dem 5. Kapitel (15) klar wird, wo er spricht: 'Gnade und Gabe in Christo' etc.*" Luther, "Drucktext der Lutherbibel 1522–1546: Das Neue Testament. Zweite Hälfte: Episteln und Offenbarung," *WA DB* 7:9, 10–14. The translation in the *American Edition of Luther's Works* (*LW*) appears to separate Christ and the Holy Spirit with his gift from each other: "By which he is disposed to give us Christ *and* to pour into us the Holy Spirit with his gifts." (emphasis mine) While clearly distinguishing these two aspects, Luther does not separate them and understands grace and gift to be so closely related within the donated righteousness of a Christian through Christ that he often speaks of them as one: "But 'the grace of God' and 'the gift' are the same thing, namely, the very righteousness which is freely given to us through Christ." Luther, "Lecture on Romans," *LW* 25:306; cf. Luther, "Römervorlesung (Hs.) 1515/16," *WA* 56: 318, 328–29: "'*Gratia Dei' autem et 'donum' idem sunt sc. Ipsa Iustitia gratis donate per Christum.*" This is an extremely important point. Both grace and gift are not only given through Christ, but in Christ and with Christ.

imputed righteousness of Christ and an inherent righteousness, is one that was defended by the Roman Catholic delegates at the Colloquy at Regensburg (1541).[66]

Turretin discusses a "final justification," but one that is merely declarative. In a section where he discusses "The Time of Justification," Turretin rejects the opinion that a believer's justification is an immanent act in God performed from eternity and the opinion of those who would "throw [justification] forward to the consummation of the world." The latter opinion falsely confuses the declarative with justification itself.[67] On the declarative aspect of "final justification," he says:

> Although our justification will be fully declared on the last day, our good works also being brought forward as the sign and proof of its truth, (Mt. 25: 34-40), still falsely would anyone maintain from this a twofold gospel justification—one from faith in this life (which is the first); the other (and second) from works on the day of judgment (as some hold, agreeing too much with Romanists on this point). The sentence to be pronounced by the supreme Judge will not be so much a new justification, as the solemn and public declaration of a sentence once passed and its execution by the assignment of the life promised with respect to an innocent person from the preceding justification. Thus it is nothing else than an adjudicatory sentence of the possession of the kingdom of heaven from the right given before through justification. And if works are then brought forward, they are not adduced as the foundation of a new justification to be obtained then, but as signs, marks and effects of our true faith and of our justification solely by it.[68]

Works, if they enter at all, merely point in declarative reference to the validity of the believer's initial justification. They are "signs," "marks," or "effects," and do not contribute in any way to justification. It is not so much a "new" justification as it is an "adjudicatory" sentence that the kingdom of heaven, which the believer already has a right to according to their initial justification, is now actually possessed in reality.

Edwards would argue nothing less. In his *"Controversies" Notebook: Justification*, he opens with his opponent John Taylor's insistence

---

66. For a close look at the relevant "Article 5" of the Regensburg Colloquy, see Lane, "Twofold Righteousness," 205-24.
67. Turretin, *Institutes*, 2:682-84.
68. Turretin, *Institutes*, 2:687.

that the believer's full and final justification is of works and not only of grace.[69] Edwards counters that this would be opposing what the Apostle says in Phil 3:8, that at the last judgment believers will be found "in him [Christ]," not having any righteousness of their own (of law) other than the righteousness which is through faith (of gospel grace). Here "faith and works of the law—or our own righteousness, which is of the law—are opposed."[70] Edwards could "allow the distinction between the first and second justification," but the second justification is "no repetition of the first. Men are justified in the sense wherein they are at first, viz. a being accepted as righteous, but once and forever; the second justification is *declarative* only."[71]

Edwards accuses Taylor, and others who hold this view, of mistaking what the word "righteousness" means in the New Testament, i.e., the mercy of God in salvation. Rather, "righteousness" and "works" (perfect obedience to the law) mean the same thing when speaking of justification, particularly by the Apostle Paul. "Righteousness" and its derivatives "is manifestly most properly a forensic term used primarily to express things belonging to judgment or a judicial proceeding." Edwards then puts his argument in the context of his covenant theology. The Covenants of Works and Grace "agree as to the method of justification, and the appointed qualification for it." They both require "holiness and sincere and universal compliance and actual conformity to God's nature and will." They differ, however, in that the Covenant of Works requires the obedience of the self as the condition for justification, whereas the Covenant of Grace is based on the obedience of another, Christ. Edwards opposes these two covenants just as there are only two kinds of righteousness: one inherent and one imputed. Just as the Covenant of Works can never be fulfilled by any one of Adam's posterity, so there can be no confusion or admixture between these two forms of righteousness in the believer's justification (initial or final).

In his earlier treatise on justification, Edwards describes those who would agree with "the Apostle" that persons are admitted into a justified state by the first act of faith only, without any preceding holiness, yet they continue in this justified state by persevering in faith and obedience and it is by this that they are "finally justified." He says this is no different

---

69. Edwards would later refute Taylor in *Original Sin*.

70. Edwards, "'Controversies' Notebook: Justification," *WJE* 21:332.

71. Edwards, "'Controversies' Notebook: Justification," *WJE* 21:338 (emphasis mine).

from saying that a believer's first embracing the gospel by faith is only "conditionally" justified and pardoned. In other words, the believer is not actually pardoned and freed from eternal punishment. This, Edwards says, "is to make just nothing at all of the Apostle's great doctrine of justification by faith alone: such a conditional pardon is no pardon or justification at all, any more than all mankind have, whether they embrace the gospel or no; for they all have Promise of final justification on condition of future sincere obedience as much as he that embraces the gospel."[72]

Edwards did not teach a "two-stage" justification or a final eschatological justification based on works. Elect believers are justified once-and-for-all and completely upon the first exercise of faith and this is not suspended upon any further perseverance, even while such perseverance is a necessary manifestation of saving faith. The justification at the consummation, at the end of the history of redemption, is one of vindication and public declaration of the already justified. Reading Edwards in the context of his covenant theology helps resolve many of the tensions in his discussion of the role of works and perseverance in the redemption of God's elect.

Heavenly Rewards

While the Christian's good works have no interest in the affairs of salvation, they do contribute to degrees of rewards in heaven. Edwards acknowledges that the saints' eternal life in heaven will be manifested by differing degrees of glory proportional to the works accomplished in their earthly life. "'Tis most agreeable to the Scriptures to suppose not only that certain additions to the happiness and glory of the saints are given as a reward of their inherent holiness and good works, but heaven itself with all its glory and happiness. The same heaven and the same happiness that is purchased by Christ's righteousness is in some respect the reward of the saints' own holiness and obedience."[73] This statement must be carefully parsed, and could be easily misinterpreted if lifted out of context. An understanding of Edwards's covenant relationships, particularly the blessings and conditions of the Covenant of Grace, is necessary to understand how he goes on to explain this statement.

72. Edwards, "Justification by Faith Alone," *WJE* 19:167.
73. Edwards, "Misc. 671," *WJE* 18:224.

Although eternal life is the reward of both, Christ's righteousness and the saints' inherent holiness are "far from having a parallel concern in the affair." It is not the reward of both in the same manner for the following reasons:

> 1. The bringing men into a state of salvation and justification, and favor with God and right to eternal life, is the reward of Christ's righteousness alone.
>
> 2. The reward of Christ's righteousness includes both the holiness of the saints, and the reward of it; and it includes their justification, which makes way for their good works being rewardable, and also the reward itself. Salvation in the sum of it is only the reward of Christ's righteousness. The sum of salvation includes the saints' conversion, and justification, and holiness, and good works, and also their consequent happiness. Christ has purchased holiness and happiness both, but only he has purchased one as consequent on the other. But if we speak of salvation as the reward of the holiness of the saints, it must be taken in a more restrained sense, viz. for that happiness that is consequent of their holiness.
>
> 3. That the holiness and good works of the saints are rewardable, is what is merited and purchased by the righteousness of Christ. His righteousness not only purchased the holiness itself, but also purchased that it should be rewardable. 'Tis from Christ's righteousness that their holiness derives the value that it has in the eyes of God; so that eternal life and blessedness is primarily only the reward of Christ's righteousness, and is the reward of the holiness of the saints secondarily and derivatively. Men's holiness is so far from having a parallel concern in this affair with Christ's righteousness, that the rewardableness itself of men's holiness is included in the reward of Christ's righteousness. 'Tis part of the reward of his righteousness that the saints' holiness should be rewarded.[74]

In the Covenant of Redemption, Christ's obedience secures the saints' conversion, justification, holiness, good works, and consequent happiness. The saints' obedience, which itself is a gift, has no concern in justification or the right to eternal life, but is nevertheless "rewardable" of degrees of happiness in heaven. But even this "reward" arises properly

---

74. Edwards, "Misc. 671," *WJE* 18:224–25.

from Christ's righteousness. It is Christ's righteousness that makes the saints' (incomplete and insufficient) works "rewardable."

Edwards's most complete presentation is found in his sermon on 2 Cor 9:6 entitled "Degrees of Glory."[75] In this sermon he presents a number of Scriptural arguments for this doctrine, including 1 Cor 15:41–42 where the glory of the saints at the resurrection is represented by the various degrees of glory in the heavenly bodies. Edwards also finds support in the Lucan parable of the nobleman travelling into a far country to receive for himself a kingdom and entrusting each of his servants with a certain amount of money (Luke 19). Upon returning he rewards each according to how wisely they invested his money. Edwards equates the nobleman's return with Christ's return at the end of history to call his servants to account and to reward them proportionately to their works. Edwards also cites as evidence for this doctrine 1 Cor 3:14–15, Matt 16:27, and John 14:2.

After proving the doctrine from Scripture, Edwards addresses four possible objections to this doctrine. First, if heaven is a place of perfect blessedness, how can there be any more blessedness, or degrees of blessedness? Edwards answers by affirming that perfect happiness is not inconsistent with their being differing degrees of happiness. Whereas only God is perfectly happy in terms of an absolute and infinite perfection, the perfection of the saints in heaven will be finite. But finitude admits of degrees: "Whatsoever is finite has bounds, and that which has bounds, its bounds can be exceeded; those bounds may be either extended or shortened."[76] Perfection in happiness is in two respects, one negative and one positive. Negatively, one can be happy as to be free from all trouble and all evil. Positively, degrees of happiness are proportional to each specific individual's capacity for happiness. "He that is full of happiness, he has perfection of happiness: his capacity being full, he is satisfied, and craves no more. But yet another man's perfection of happiness may exceed his."[77] Some saints are blessed with more capacity for happiness than others, but all are filled to capacity.

A second objection is that one saint deserves no more happiness than another, for all is of free grace. Edwards responds that while all is of free grace, and though the works of the saints deserve no reward, God of

---

75. Edwards, "Degrees of Glory," *WJE* 19:612–27.
76. Edwards, "Degrees of Glory," *WJE* 19:617.
77. Edwards, "Degrees of Glory," *WJE* 19:618.

his own free grace is "pleased to promise a reward to them, to encourage them to diligence in his work and service." A kind father will encourage and reward what is done by a child, even though the child's works remain childish and of no benefit to the father. "Though the best the saints do is exceeding polluted, and deserves nothing . . . yet for Christ's sake he beholds not the pollution, and accepts the sincerity, and testifies his acceptance by a glorious reward."[78]

A third objection is that if eternal life in heaven is given on account of Christ's imputed righteousness alone, why does it not merit as much happiness for one as for another? Edwards counters this objection by affirming that Christ's purchase was eternal life and a perfect happiness respecting everyone's capacity. What Christ did not purchase was each individual's actual capacity for happiness, which was left to the sovereign pleasure of God. Edwards's covenant theology is enlisted in his explanation:

> This is evident, for what Christ did was to fulfill the Covenant of Works for us; but the Covenant of Works did not meddle with this matter. If Adam had fulfilled the law, he and all his posterity would have had perfect happiness. But God would still have been left at liberty to {dispense in this matter according to what rule he pleases}. The angels obtain eternal life by a Covenant of Works, whose condition is perfect abundance. All have performed the condition; but yet some are higher in glory than others, according to their several capacities. That was a thing that their perfect obedience meddled not with, but was determined according to the arbitrary pleasure of God. And if the Covenant of Works don't meddle with that matter, it follows that Christ's righteousness don't; for that only fulfilled the Covenant of Works. If Adam's perfect obedience would not have been concerned in this matter, then Christ's is not.[79]

It is God's sovereign pleasure to decide "how large the vessel" should be in proportion to each saint's holiness and good works.

A final objection is raised that those in lower degrees of glory would be less happy seeing so many above them. But Edwards maintains that in heaven there will be only perfect humility without any remains of pride. Furthermore, since all are filled to their capacity, all their cravings will be satisfied and there will be no need of envy. "[There shall be] perfect

---

78. Edwards, "Degrees of Glory," *WJE* 19:618.
79. Edwards, "Degrees of Glory," *WJE* 19:619.

resignation. Everyone shall now [be] perfectly coincident with the will of God, and perfectly rejoicing in his will; rejoicing in that will of his in so disposing and ordering the various degrees of glory, and assigning them such a degree as he has."[80]

It is the happiness of the saints in heaven that the glory of God's grace is manifest. This is God's supreme end of redemption. Therefore, believers ought to seek out higher degrees of glory so as to render a greater tribute of praise. "Love to God as well as ourselves, ought to stir us up to seek high degrees of glory."[81] This last statement of Edwards's raises the question of the role of self-love and to the objection that this is a manifestation of a selfish spirit. But Edwards says that self-love is a good principle, if well-regulated. "'Tis no irregular thing for us to love our own happiness: 'tis not this that is what is properly called selfishness; but 'tis the inordinancy of self-love: it's being ungoverned that denominates a person selfish."[82] Edwards says in *Religious Affections*, "Self-love...assists as an handmaid, being subservient to higher principles, to lead forth a mind to the view and contemplation, and engage and fix the attention, and heighten the joy and love" of God's own glory and beauty in his work of redemption.[83] Self-love, when directed and regulated by the will and word of God, is a good principle. Furthermore, it is ultimately love to God that should be the highest motive, in that God will be most glorified in them that are highest in glory. The difference between the love of the hypocrite and that of the saint is that "the former rejoices in himself; self is the first foundation of his joy: the latter rejoices in God."[84]

The good works of the saints result in both glorifying God's name and in doing good for others. At the end of his sermon, Edwards implores his congregation to, "Let those things stir us all up earnestly to seek that we may do good; that we may not live in vain; and we may be the instruments of God's glory, and the good of our fellow [creatures]." A Christian should "abound in deeds of charity, and do it with cheerfulness and joyfulness on all occasions, knowing that great is his reward in heaven."[85] Evangelical obedience, while never meritorious in terms of

80. Edwards, "Degrees of Glory," *WJE* 19:620.
81. Edwards, "Degrees of Glory," *WJE* 19:621.
82. Edwards, "2 Cor 9:6," *WJEO* 52, L. 11r (my transcription of Edwards's sermon notes).
83. Edwards, "Religious Affections," *WJE* 2:248.
84. Edwards, "Religious Affections," *WJE* 2:249.
85. Edwards, "Degrees of Glory," *WJE* 19:627.

the believer's justification, is nevertheless rewarded by God's sovereign grace in heaven. God's glorifying himself in the happiness of the saints, the saints' happiness in their glorifying God, and the good works directed to others in this life under the freedom of the gospel, are all tied together in the covenant work of redemption.

Love for God's Holiness

The primary motive for evangelical obedience in Edwards is a love for God's holiness. Implied in all saving faith is a love for God's holiness, which Edwards defines as "conformity of the heart and consent of the inclination to the holiness of God and Christ, and to God's revealed will."[86] Edwards lists a number of ways this is worked out in the life of the redeemed believer, including a "relish" of the supreme "beauty and amiableness" in holiness and a consequent hatred of sin. For a sinner to accept God's offer of a savior, there must also be a conviction of the justice of God's condemnation, which is a necessary consequence of God's holiness and hatred of sin. The necessity of Christ's atoning death attests to the "infinite odiousness" of sin.

An accepting with the heart a salvation offered by Christ implies an acceptance and respect to that means of salvation. Accepting and adhering to Christ as a sufficient mediator in the Covenant of Grace implies "a cordial adhering to and complying with God's moral excellency and holiness." No one can embrace Christ's righteousness as a means of salvation without loving and embracing that very righteousness, not as a means to procure one's own salvation, but as a "cordial approbation and an exceeding esteem" of God's law and authority, his honor and inviolable rights as lawgiver. The way of salvation as revealed in the Covenant of Grace has infinite respect to God's holy nature, in that Christ's atoning sacrifice was "so much done to preserve, honor and magnify" it "as altogether worthy." Acceptance of "that rich and transcendent grace and love of God and Christ exercised and manifested in the salvation of Christ, implies a sight of the transcendent beauty of holiness and cordially embracing it." God's way of redemption, as revealed under the structure of his covenants, is a revelation of his own transcendent beauty and holiness. Faith, as accepting this way of salvation, is not something that is out of mere private interest. "He that accepts God's grace appearing in the

---

86. Edwards, "'Controversies' Notebook: Justification," *WJE* 21:356.

salvation of Christ only as related to his interest, don't sincerely and really accept anything that is divine ... But he that with all his heart embraces that divine grace and love which is manifested in Christ's salvation, must of necessity therein embrace all holiness: for he must entirely delight in such a thing."[87] Edwards concludes that to trust in Christ directly implies a love for Christian practice.

To love God is to love him as he has revealed himself. In *Misc. 777*, "Happiness of Heaven is Progressive," Edwards demonstrates that the knowledge of the "invisible God" can only be a mediate knowledge. This mediate knowledge comes only through images (of which Christ Jesus is the supreme image of the invisible God), words and declarations (God's own Word in Scripture), *a priori* arguments (the necessity of his existence and perfections), or through his effects (providence and his work in redemption). God's glory is principally revealed and manifested through his work of redemption: "The manifestations of God makes of himself in his works are the principle manifestations of his perfections, and the declarations and teaching of Word are to lead to those."[88] Hence, even the beatifical vision of the saints in heaven is beholding what God reveals of himself in the work of redemption. Even the saints in heaven cannot see or behold God's essence or perfections, except by seeing him in Christ the Redeemer and the effects of his perfections in his redemption. Edwards main conclusion in this *Miscellany* is that heaven is a progressive state of ever increasing happiness and enjoyment in "contemplation, praise, and conversation" in contemplating the wonders of God's work of redemption, praising God's glory and love that are displayed therein. To love God, even in this life, is to love his plan of redemption. A love of his plan of redemption is to have a love for his holiness, a love which is expressed in loving works of evangelical obedience.

Conclusion

In this final chapter I have argued that Edwards holds to the non-meritorious necessity of works in the Christian faith. The "non-meritorious" nature of works addresses Arminian errors, while the "necessity" of works speaks to the error of antinomianism. Edwards's language of the necessity of works for justification has raised concerns that he leaned towards

---

87. Edwards, "'Controversies' Notebook: Justification," *WJE* 21:358–59.
88. Edwards, "Misc. 777," *WJE* 18: 427–34.

a more Roman Catholic view of faith and works in his later writings, concerns that are unfounded when reading Edwards closely and in the context of his covenant theology. While Edwards emphasizes the close connection between faith and works, he is saying nothing more than what Reformed theologians have always maintained. Works are "necessary conditions" for justification in that they are necessary evidences of or manifestations of justifying faith. Faith is always accompanied by its fruits by which it is known yet is still that faith alone which justifies the sinner.

I have also shown that Edwards speaks of the necessity of a persevering faith. For Edwards this is about the nature and definition of justifying faith, not that justification is suspended upon faith's perseverance. A believer is once-and-for-all completely justified upon the first act of faith. Perseverance is a manifestation of or witness to the type of faith that once justifies. As such Edwards holds no place for a "final justification" based on works or justification based on "faithfulness." Perseverance is not only of the nature of Spirit-wrought faith but is also a gift and blessing of Christ's own perseverance and righteousness in the Covenants of Redemption and Grace, such that elect believers *will* inviolably persevere in faith.

Finally, evangelical obedience does accrue rewards of future happiness in heaven. Edwards shows that even then, it is still ultimately by Christ's own righteousness that works become "rewardable." The ultimate motivation for evangelical obedience for Edwards is a love of God's holiness, especially as revealed in the Covenant of Redemption.

In each of these areas Edwards has been contested as seeming to fall outside the bounds of Reformed orthodoxy, or at least using language that would suggest such. Understanding the covenant context of Edwards's theology can be a helpful resource in guiding a closer and more authentic reading of Edwards, situating him more firmly within his own New England Puritan Reformed and covenant tradition.

Summary and Concluding Comments

I HAVE ENDEAVORED TO show in this study that one must read Jonathan Edwards as a Reformed covenant theologian, and that explicating his covenant framework and redemptive-historical approach to scriptural exegesis sheds light on and helps interpret the more controversial discussions regarding the "ethics" of Edwards, by which I limit to the role of and motive for "good works," or evangelical obedience, in the salvation and life of the elect believer.

Jonathan Edwards wrote and preached at the transition between two worlds. The "old" world of Puritan traditionalism and Reformed scholasticism was giving way to the "new" world of Enlightenment rationalism. As a theologian and philosopher, he straddled the intellectual realms of both premodern biblical exegesis and the Lockean-Newtonian worldview with its mounting critical assumptions that would lead to modern skepticism. According to Peter Thuesen, "These opposing forces did not overcome him: to his dying day he remained an eclectic thinker who resisted unambiguous identification with either traditional or modern forms of thought."[1] And while Perry Miller in 1949 "chastised the prejudice in academic circles against Edwards and the frequent caricature of him as an antiquarian specimen of Hell-fire preaching from the long-lost times of the Great Awakening,"[2] he nevertheless viewed Edwards as an artist working in the only medium available to him in the eighteenth-century American frontier, namely that of religion and theology. Or, according to philosopher Herbert Schneider, "His philosophical insight was buried under the ruins of his religion. He failed to see the futility of insisting on the Puritan principles."[3] Ola Winslow similarly saw Edwards

1. Thuesen, "Edwards' Intellectual Background," 16–17.
2. Piper, "Personal Encounter," 13–17.
3. Quoted in Murray, *Jonathan Edwards*, xxi.

as a prisoner of an outworn, obsolete theological system: "His bondage seems almost a tragic pity."[4] Edwards would prove far more attractive and serviceable to secular intellectuals when portrayed by Perry Miller as "one of us—close to being an atheist for Niebuhr." This myopic and somewhat narrow vision of Edwards may have gotten Edwardsean scholarship off on the wrong footing.

I maintain that Edwards must be viewed primarily as a Reformed Puritan pastor-theologian, and this by faith and personal intellectual commitment and not by mere historical assimilation. Edwards was foremost a Reformed biblical theologian and pastor. His assurance of Scripture's inerrant authority guided his philosophical speculations on theological subjects and not vice-versa. While his particularistic and fundamentalist commitments may offend more modern sensibilities, the purpose here is not to defend or critique him as such, but to read and understand him as he was and thought of himself, and thereby to read him authentically.

As a biblical theologian in the Reformed tradition, covenant theology was for Edwards the internal scaffolding that gave shape to the biblical story of redemption. It was not a mere ancillary theological construct, but an overarching hermeneutic that guided Edwards's theology of salvation. It was the "big picture" that provided both the comprehensive narrative of his biblical theology as well as the path of individual salvation. Perry Miller was not the first scholar to neglect or misinterpret this aspect of Edwards, but by proposing a division between Edwards's Calvinism and New England federal theology he would raise interpretive difficulties for subsequent Edwardsean scholarship that he inaugurated in the twentieth century. Without a robust view of Edwards's own controlling biblical narrative of the covenants it is difficult to read his more technical theological writings correctly.

As a fountainhead from which his ideas flowed, Edwards's covenant theology provides a clear and comprehensive understanding of his Reformed soteriology and the role of evangelical obedience in justification. At the same time, close attention to the implications of his covenant theology as a controlling paradigm affords a more authentic and accurate interpretation of his more controversial statements and writings, especially those that have been used to make Edwards's seem less orthodox compared to his own Reformed confessional tradition.

---

4. Winslow, *Jonathan Edwards*, 327.

It also prevents him from being read and interpreted through a more Barthian and neoorthodox lens.

Edwards's covenant theology was foundational for his teaching and preaching on the redemptive role of Christ, especially the imputation of the active righteousness of Christ as the only grounds for a believer's justification. The establishment of the eternal rule of righteousness as the basis for mankind's communion with God and the elect believer's eternal happiness is a central theme beginning with the initial Covenant of Works with Adam. It runs through the Covenant of Grace and its republication in the Mosaic covenant dispensation and is grounded in the eternal Covenant of Redemption. It is the basis for the law-gospel distinction in Edwards, as it was for earlier Reformed architects of federal theology. His formulation of the relationships between the covenants, especially in terms of the covenanting parties, built an impenetrable wall between a believer's works and justification under the New Covenant. This must be taken into consideration when interpreting any statement of Edwards regarding faith and works if he is to be read consistently.

Current discussions in Reformed scholarship have begun to question aspects of traditional covenant theology, including the existence of a prelapsarian Covenant of Works, whether the Mosaic covenant is a republication of the Covenant of Works (in some sense), and the presence of a final justification based on works, to name just a few. These issues have important practical implications for how one views the relationship between faith, works, and justification in the Protestant Reformed tradition. Jonathan Edwards, a key transitional figure in the history of Reformed covenant theology, is an important historical resource whose thinking is still relevant to many of these and other current controversies.

Beyond the academic, polemical, and historical, a study of Jonathan Edwards's covenant theology is of immense practical and spiritual importance for the Christian believer. For the "God intoxicated" New England preacher and revivalist, this was no dry academic exercise. Rather, it was a glorious encounter with and participation in the great drama of redemption. It was a joyous and affectionate discovery and embrace of what God had ordained in eternity, what Christ accomplished in history on the cross, and what the Holy Spirit is doing and will complete in the church, Christ's bride. All rightly discerned Christian doctrine, according to Edwards and his Puritan tradition, is immensely practical and spiritually edifying. The goal of all theology or "divinity," whether biblical or systematic, is to promote one's living to God here in this world, in a life of faith and holiness, and to bring one to a life of perfect holiness and happiness in the full enjoyment of God in eternity. To repeat what I said at the outset of this study in the Preface, the study of God's covenanting relationship with his creation as expounded by "America's greatest theologian" shows forth the wonder, joy, and relevance of the Christian faith unfolding in history and continues to be spiritually significant, pastoral, and comforting for today's modern church.

Bibliography

Abernethy, Andrew T. "Jonathan Edwards as Multi-Dimension[al] Bible Interpreter: A Case Study from Isaiah 40–55." *Journal of the Evangelical Theological Society* 56 (2013) 815–30.
Allen, Michael, and Scott R. Swain, eds. *Christian Dogmatics: Reformed Theology for the Church Catholic.* Grand Rapids: Baker, 2016.
Ames, William. *The Marrow of Theology.* Edited and translated by John D. Eusden. Boston: Pilgrim, 1968.
Anderson, Wallace E. "Immaterialism in Jonathan Edwards' Early Philosophical Notes." *Journal of the History of Ideas* 25 (1964) 181–200.
Anonymous. *The Theologia Germanica of Martin Luther.* Translated by Bengt Hoffman. New York: Paulist, 1980.
Aquinas, Thomas. *Summa Theologica.* 5 vols. English Dominican Province Translation. Notre Dame: Christian Classics, 1981.
Arminius, Jacob. "The Priesthood of Christ." In *The Works of James Arminius, Volume 2*, translated by James Nichols and William Nichols, 416–17. Grand Rapids: Baker, 1986.
Asselt, Willem J. van. *The Federal Theology of Johannes Cocceius (1603–1669).* Translated by Raymond A. Blacketer. Leiden: Brill, 2001.
———. "The Fundamental Meaning of Theology: Archetypal and Ectypal Theology in Seventeenth-Century Reformed Thought." *WTJ* 64 (2002) 319–35.
———, and Eef Dekker, eds. *Reformation and Scholasticism: An Ecumenical Enterprise.* Grand Rapids: Eerdmans, 2001.
Atchison, Thomas F. "Towards Developing a Theology of Christian Assurance from 1 John with Reference to Jonathan Edwards." PhD diss., Trinity Evangelical Divinity School, 2004.
Atwood, Christopher S. "Jonathan Edwards's Doctrine of Justification: A New Reading of Edwards's Treatises, Sermons, and 'Miscellanies.'" PhD diss., Wheaton College, 2014.
Augustine. *City of God.* Edited by David Kowles. Translated by Henry Betenson. New York: Penguin, 1972.
———. *The Trinity.* Edited by John E. Rotelle. Translated by Edmund Hill. Brooklyn: New City, 1991.
Baik, Chung-Hun. *The Holy Trinity—God for God and God for Us: Seven Positions on the Immanent-Economic Trinity Relation in Contemporary Trinitarian Theology.* Eugene: Pickwick, 2011.

Baker, J. Wayne. *Heinrich Bullinger and the Covenant: The Other Reformed Tradition.* Athens: Ohio University Press, 1980.

Ball, John. *A Treatise of the Covenant of Grace.* London: Semeon Ash, 1645.

Barrett, John. *Good Will Towards Men, or A Treatise of the Covenants.* London: Samuel Richards, 1675.

Barshinger, David P. *Jonathan Edwards and the Psalms: A Redemptive-Historical Vision of Scripture.* Oxford: Oxford University Press, 2014.

———. "Making the Psalter One's 'Own Language': Jonathan Edwards Engages the Psalms." *JES* 2 (2012) 3–29.

Barth, Karl. *Church Dogmatics.* 31 vols. Translated by G. W. Bromily. Peabody: Hendrickson, 2010.

Bavinck, Herman. *Reformed Dogmatics.* 4 vols. Edited by John Bolt. Translated by John Vriend. Grand Rapids: Baker, 2006.

Beach, Mark J. *Christ and the Covenant: Francis Turretin's Federal Theology as a Defense of the Doctrine of Grace.* Göttenen: Vandenhoeck and Ruprecht, 2015.

Beck, Andreas J., and William de Boer, eds. *The Reception of Calvin and His Theology in Reformed Orthodoxy.* Leiden: Brill, 2010.

Bell, M. Charles. *Calvin and Scottish Theology.* Edinburgh: Handsel, 1985.

Beisner, E. Calvin. *The Auburn Avenue Theology, Pros and Cons: Debating the Federal Vision.* Ft. Lauderdale: Knox Theological Seminary, 2004.

Berkeley, George. *A Treatise Concerning the Principles of Human Knowledge.* Edited by Jonathan Dancy. Oxford: Oxford University Press, 1998.

Berkhof, Louis. *Principles of Biblical Interpretation.* Grand Rapids: Baker, 1950.

———. *Systematic Theology.* Grand Rapids: Eerdmans, 1941.

Berkouwer, G. C. *Sin.* Translated by Philip C. Holtrop. Grand Rapids: Eerdmans, 1971.

———. *The Work of Christ.* Translated by Cornelius Lambregtse. Grand Rapids: Eerdmans, 1965.

Beza, Theodore. *The Christian Faith.* Translated by James Clark. East Essex: Focus Christian Ministries, 1992.

———. *Iesu Christi D. N. Novum Testamentum, Graece & Latine Theodoro Beza Interprete.* Henricus Stephanus, 1567.

Biehl, Craig. *The Infinite Merit of Christ: The Glory of Christ's Obedience in the Theology of Jonathan Edwards.* Jackson: Reformed Academic, 2009.

Bierma, Lyle D. "Federal Theology in the Sixteenth Century: Two Traditions?" *WTJ* 45 (1983) 304–22.

———. *German Calvinism in the Confessional Age: The Covenant Theology of Caspar Olevianus.* Grand Rapids: Baker, 1996.

———. Review of *The Origins of the Federal Theology in Sixteenth-Century Reformation Thought* by David A. Weir. *CTJ* 26 (1991) 483–85.

———. "The Role of Covenant Theology in Early Reformed Orthodoxy." *SCJ* 21 (1990) 453–62.

Bogue, Carl W. *Jonathan Edwards and the Covenant of Grace.* Eugene: Wipf and Stock, 2008.

Bolton, Samuel. *The True Bounds of Christian Freedom.* Edinburgh: Banner of Truth, 1964.

Bombaro, John J. "Beautiful Beings: The Function of the Reprobate in the Philosophical-Theology of Jonathan Edwards." PhD diss., King's College London, 2001.

———. "Dispositional Peculiarity, History, and Edwards's Evangelistic Appeal." *WTJ* 66 (2004) 121–58.

———. *Jonathan Edwards's Vision of Reality: The Relationship of God to the World, Redemption History, and the Reprobate*. Eugene: Pickwick, 2012.

———. "Jonathan Edwards's Vision of Salvation." *WTJ* 65 (2003) 45–67.

Boston, Thomas. *A View of the Covenant of Grace*. Philadelphia, 1827.

———. "The Marrow of Modern Divinity (On the Covenants, the Gospel and the Law)." In *The Complete Works of Thomas Boston, Volume 7*, 143–489. Lafayette: Sovereign Grace, 2001.

Boswell, James. *Life of Johnson*. Edited by R. W. Chapman. Oxford: Oxford University Press, 1998.

Bracken, Joseph A. "Panentheism from a Trinitarian Perspective." *Horizons* 22 (1995) 7–28.

———. "Trinity: Economic and Immanent." *Horizons* 25 (1998) 7–22.

Brakel, Wilhelmus à. *The Christian's Reasonable Service in which Divine Truths Concerning the Covenant of Grace are Expounded, Defended against Opposing Parties, and their Practice Advocated*, 4 vols. Translated by Bartel Elshout. Ligonier: Soli Deo Gloria, 1992.

Brown, John. *A Compendious View of Natural and Revealed Religion*. London: J&C Muirhead, 1817.

Brown, Robert E. *Jonathan Edwards and the Bible*. Bloomington: Indiana University Press, 2002.

Bruce, Willard, "The Distinction between the Law and the Gospel, A Sermon by Martin Luther, Jan. 1, 1532." Translated by Willard Bruce. *Concordia Journal* 18 (1992) 153–62.

Bruggink, Donald J. "Calvin and Federal Theology." *The Reformed Review* 13 (1959) 15–22.

Brunner, Emil. *The Christian Doctrine of God*. Translated by Olive Wyon. Philadelphia: Westminster, 1950.

Bulkeley, Peter. *The Gospel Covenant; or The Covenant of Grace Opened*. 2nd edition. London: Matthew Simons, 1651.

Burgess, Anthony. *Vindiciae Legis: Or, A Vindication of the Morall Law and the Covenants, From the Errours of Papists, Arminians, Socinians, and more especially, Antinomians*. In *XXIX Lectures, Preached at Lawrence-Jury, London by Anthony Burgess, Preacher of God's Word*. London: Thomas Underhill, 1646.

Caldwell, Robert W. *Communion in the Spirit: The Holy Spirit as the Bond of Union in the Theology of Jonathan Edwards*. Eugene: Wipf and Stock, 2006.

Calhoun, D. B. "The Covenant in Bullinger and Calvin." ThM thesis, Princeton Theological Seminary, 1976.

Calvin, John. *Calvin's Commentaries*. 22 vols. Grand Rapids: Baker, 2005.

———. *Institutes of the Christian Religion*. Edited by John T. McNeill and Ford Lewis Battles. 2 vols. Philadelphia: Westminster, 1960.

———. *Selected Works of John Calvin: Tracts and Letters*. 7 vols. Edited by Henry Beveridge and Jules Bonnet. Grand Rapids: Baker, 1983.

Carson, D. A., Peter T. O'Brien, and Mark A. Seifrid, eds. *Justification and Variegated Nomism, Volume 1: The Complexities of Second Temple Judaism*. Grand Rapids: Baker, 2004.

———, eds. *Justification and Variegated Nomism, Volume 2: The Paradoxes of Paul*. Grand Rapids: Baker, 2004.

Casselli, Stephen J. *Divine Rule Maintained: Anthony Burgess, Covenant Theology, and the Place of the Law in Reformed Scholasticism*. Grand Rapids: Reformation Heritage, 2016.

Cherry, Conrad. "The Puritan Notion of the Covenant in Jonathan Edwards' Doctrine of Faith." *CH* 34 (1965) 328–41.

———. "Symbols of Spiritual Truth: Jonathan Edwards as Biblical Interpreter." *Interpretation* 39 (1985) 263–64.

———. *The Theology of Jonathan Edwards: A Reappraisal*. Bloomington: Indiana University Press, 1966.

Cho, Hyun-Jin. *Jonathan Edwards on Justification: Reformed Development of the Doctrine in Eighteenth-Century New England*. Lanham: University Press of America, 2012.

Clarke, Samuel. *Scripture-Doctrine and the Trinity*. London, 1712.

Colacurcio, Michael J. "The Example of Edwards: Idealist Imagination and the Metaphysics of Sovereignty." In *Puritan Influences in American Literature, Illinois Studies in Language and Literature*, edited by Emory Elliott, 55–106. Urbana: University of Illinois Press, 1979.

Cooper, John W. *Panentheism: The Other God of the Philosophers*. Grand Rapids: Baker, 2006.

Crisp, Oliver D. "Jonathan Edwards on the Divine Nature." *Journal of Reformed Theology* 3 (2009) 175–201.

———. *Jonathan Edwards and the Metaphysics of Sin*. Burlington: Ashgate, 2005.

———. "Jonathan Edwards's Ontology: A Critique of Sang Hyun Lee's Dispositional Account of Edwardsian Metaphysics." *Religious Studies* 46 (2010) 1–20.

Dabney, Robert L. *Syllabus and Notes of the Course of Systematic and Polemic Theology*. St. Louis: Presbyterian Publishing Company of St. Louis, 1878. Reprinted as *Systematic Theology*. Carlisle: Banner of Truth, 1996.

Danaher, William J. *The Trinitarian Ethics of Jonathan Edwards*. Louisville: Westminster John Knox, 2004.

Davidson, Bruce W. "Glorious Damnation: Hell as an Essential Element in the Theology of Jonathan Edwards." *Journal of the Evangelical Theological Society* 54 (2011) 809–22.

Dennison, James T., ed. *Reformed Confessions of the 16th and 17th Centuries in English Translation, Volume 4:1600–1693*. Grand Rapids: Reformation Heritage, 2014.

Delattre, Roland A. *Beauty and Sensibility in the Thought of Jonathan Edwards: An Essay in Aesthetics and Theological Ethics*. New Haven: Yale University Press, 1968.

Dickinson, Jonathan. *The True Scripture-Doctrine Concerning Some Important Points of Christian Faith*. Boston, 1741.

Dickson, David, and James Durham. *The Summe of Saving Knowledge, With the Practical Use Thereof*. Edinburgh: Swintoun and Thomas Brown.

Dixhoorn, Chad B. Van. "Reforming the Reformation: Theological Debate at the Westminster Assembly." PhD diss., Cambridge University, 2004.

Duncan, J. Ligon. "The Covenant Idea in Ante-Nicene Theology." PhD diss., University of Edinburgh, 1995.

———. Review of *The Origins of the Federal Theology in Sixteenth-Century Reformation Thought* by David Weir. *Scottish Bulletin of Evangelical Theology* 12 (1994) 55–57.

Dunn, James D. G. "The Justice of God: A Renewed Perspective on Justification by Faith." *JTS* 43 (1992) 1–22.

———. *The Theology of Paul the Apostle*. Grand Rapids: Eerdmans, 1998.

Edwards, Jonathan. *The Blessing of God: Previously Unpublished Sermons of Jonathan Edwards*. Edited by Michael D. McMullen. Nashville: Broadman and Holman, 2003.

———. *The Puritan Pulpit: Jonathan Edwards*. Edited by Don Kistler. Morgan: Soli Deo Gloria, 2004.

———. *Sermons of Jonathan Edwards*. Peabody: Hendrickson, 2005.

———. *The Sermons of Jonathan Edwards: A Reader*. Edited by Wilson H. Kimnach, Kenneth P. Minkema, and Douglas A. Sweeney. New Haven: Yale University Press, 1999.

———. *Treatise on Grace and Other Posthumously Published Writings*. Edited by Paul Helm. Cambridge: James Clarke, 1971.

———. *Works of Jonathan Edwards, Volume 1: Freedom of the Will*. Edited by Paul Ramsey. New Haven: Yale University Press, 1957.

———. *Works of Jonathan Edwards, Volume 2: Religious Affections*. Edited by John E. Smith. New Haven: Yale University Press, 1959.

———. *Works of Jonathan Edwards, Volume 3: Original Sin*. Edited by Clyde A. Holbrook. New Haven: Yale University Press, 1970.

———. *Works of Jonathan Edwards, Volume 4: The Great Awakening*. Edited by C. C. Goen. New Haven: Yale University Press, 1972.

———. *Works of Jonathan Edwards, Volume 5: Apocalyptic Writings*. Edited by Stephen J. Stein. New Haven: Yale University Press, 1977.

———. *Works of Jonathan Edwards, Volume 6: Scientific and Philosophical Writings*. Edited by Wallace E. Anderson. New Haven: Yale University Press, 1980.

———. *Works of Jonathan Edwards, Volume 8: Ethical Writings*. Edited by Paul Ramsey. New Haven: Yale University Press, 1989.

———. *Works of Jonathan Edwards, Volume 9: A History of the Work of Redemption*. Edited by John F. Wilson. New Haven: Yale University Press, 1989.

———. *Works of Jonathan Edwards, Volume 10: Sermons and Discourses 1720–1723*. Edited by Wilson H. Kimnach. New Haven: Yale University Press, 1992.

———. *Works of Jonathan Edwards, Volume 11: Typological Writings*. Edited by Wallace E. Anderson and Mason I. Lowance. New Haven: Yale University Press, 1993.

———. *Works of Jonathan Edwards, Volume 12: Ecclesiastical Writings*. Edited by David D. Hall. New Haven: Yale University Press, 1994.

———. *Works of Jonathan Edwards, Volume 13: The "Miscellanies," (Entry Nos. a–z, aa–zz, 1–500)*. Edited by Thomas A. Schafer. New Haven: Yale University Press, 1994.

———. *Works of Jonathan Edwards, Volume 14: Sermons and Discourses: 1723–1729*. Edited by Kenneth P. Minkema. New Haven: Yale University Press, 1997.

———. *Works of Jonathan Edwards, Volume 15: Notes on Scripture*. Edited by Stephen J. Stein. New Haven: Yale University Press, 1998.

———. *Works of Jonathan Edwards, Volume 16: Letters and Personal Writings*. Edited by George S. Claghorn. New Haven: Yale University Press, 1998.

———. *Works of Jonathan Edwards, Volume 17: Sermons and Discourses, 1730–1733*. Edited by Mark Valeri. New Haven: Yale University Press, 1999.

———. *Works of Jonathan Edwards, Volume 18, The "Miscellanies," (Entry Nos. 501–832)*. Edited by Ava Chamberlain. New Haven: Yale University Press, 2000.

———. *Works of Jonathan Edwards, Volume 19: Sermons and Discourses, 1734–1738*. Edited by M. X. Lesser. New Haven: Yale University Press, 2001.
———. *Works of Jonathan Edwards, Volume 20, The "Miscellanies," 833–1152*. Edited by Amy Plantinga Pauw. New Haven: Yale University Press, 2002.
———. *Works of Jonathan Edwards, Volume 21: Writings on the Trinity, Grace, and Faith*. Edited by Sang Hyun Lee. New Haven: Yale University Press, 2002.
———. *Works of Jonathan Edwards, Volume 22: Sermons and Discourses, 1739–1742*. Edited by Harry S. Stout and Nathan O. Hatch. New Haven: Yale University Press, 2003.
———. *Works of Jonathan Edwards, Volume 23, The Miscellanies," (Entry Nos. 1153–1360)*. Edited by Douglas A. Sweeney. New Haven: Yale University Press, 2004.
———. *Works of Jonathan Edwards, Volume 24: The "Blank Bible."* Edited by Stephen J. Stein. New Haven: Yale University Press, 2006.
———. *Works of Jonathan Edwards, Volume 25: Sermons and Discourses, 1743–1758*. Edited by Wilson H. Kimnach. New Haven: Yale University Press, 2006.
———. *Works of Jonathan Edwards, Volume 26: Catalogues of Books*. Edited by Peter J. Thuesen. New Haven: Yale University Press, 2008.
———. *Works of Jonathan Edwards Online, Volume 27: "Controversies" Notebook*. Jonathan Edwards Center, Yale University, 2008. Last accessed August 1, 2020.
———. *Works of Jonathan Edwards Online, Volume 34: "Original Sin" Notebook*. Jonathan Edwards Center, Yale University, 2008. Last accessed August 1, 2020.
———. *Works of Jonathan Edwards Online, Volume 39: Church and Pastoral Documents*. Jonathan Edwards Center, Yale University, 2008. Last accessed August 1, 2020.
———. *Works of Jonathan Edwards Online, Volume 42: Sermons, Series II, 1723–1727*. Jonathan Edwards Center, Yale University, 2008. Last accessed August 1, 2020.
———. *Works of Jonathan Edwards Online, Volume 43: Sermons, Series II, 1728–1729*. Jonathan Edwards Center, Yale University, 2008. Last accessed August 1, 2020.
———. *Works of Jonathan Edwards Online, Volume 44: Sermons, Series II, 1729*. Jonathan Edwards Center, Yale University, 2008. Last accessed August 1, 2020.
———. *Works of Jonathan Edwards Online, Volume 45: Sermons, Series II, 1729–1731*. Jonathan Edwards Center, Yale University, 2008. Last accessed August 1, 2020.
———. *Works of Jonathan Edwards Online, Volume 47: Sermons, Series II, 1731–1732*. Jonathan Edwards Center, Yale University, 2008. Last accessed August 1, 2020.
———. *Works of Jonathan Edwards Online, Volume 48: Sermons, Series II, 1733*. Jonathan Edwards Center, Yale University, 2008. Last accessed August 1, 2020.
———. *Works of Jonathan Edwards Online, Volume 52: Sermons, Series II, 1737*. Jonathan Edwards Center, Yale University, 2008. Last accessed August 1, 2020.
———. *Works of Jonathan Edwards Online, Volume 54: Sermons, Series II, 1739*. Jonathan Edwards Center, Yale University, 2008. Last accessed August 1, 2020.
———. *Works of Jonathan Edwards Online, Volume 64: Sermons, Series II, 1746*. Jonathan Edwards Center, Yale University, 2008. Last accessed August 1, 2020.
———. *The Works of Jonathan Edwards*. 2 vols. Peabody: Hendrickson, 2007.
Eichrodt, Walter. *Theology of the Old Testament, Volume 1*. Philadelphia: Westminster, 1961.
Elwood, Douglas J. *The Philosophical Theology of Jonathan Edwards*. Columbia: Columbia University Press, 1960.

Eusden, John D. "Natural Law and Covenant Theology in New England." *Natural Law Forum* 47 (1960) 1–30.

Evans, William B. *Imputation and Impartation: Union with Christ in American Reformed Theology. Studies in Christian Thought.* Eugene: Wipf and Stock, 2008.

Ferry, Brian C. "Works in the Mosaic Covenant: A Reformed Taxonomy" in *The Law is Not of Faith: Essays on Works and Grace in the Mosaic Covenant,* edited by Bryan D. Estelle et al., 76–108. Phillipsburg: Presbyterian and Reformed, 2009.

Fesko, J. V. *The Covenant of Redemption: Origins, Development, and Reception.* Göttingen: Vandenhoeck and Ruprecht, 2015.

———. *Justification: Understanding the Classic Doctrine.* Phillipsburg: Presbyterian and Reformed, 2008.

———. *The Theology of the Westminster Standards.* Wheaton: Crossway, 2014.

———. *The Trinity and the Covenant of Redemption.* Fearn: Mentor, 2016.

Fiering, Normal. *Jonathan Edwards's Moral Thought and Its British Context.* Eugene: Wipf and Stock, 1981.

Fisher, Edward. *Marrow of Modern Divinity.* Fearn: Christian Focus, 2009.

Flower, Elizabeth, and Murray G. Murphey. *A History of Philosophy in America.* New York: Putnam, 1976.

Gaffin, Richard B. *By Faith, Not by Sight: Paul and the Order of Salvation.* Phillipsburg: Presbyterian and Reformed, 2006.

Garner, David B. Review of *The Binding of God: Calvin's Role in the Development of Covenant Theology* by Peter Lillback, *TJ* 23 (2002) 291–94.

Gass, Wilhelm. *Geschichte der protestantishen Dogmatic in ihrem Zusammenhange mit der Theologie.* 4 vols. Berlin: Georg Reimer, 1854-1867.

Gerstner, John H. *The Rational Biblical Theology of Jonathan Edwards.* 3 vols. Powhatan: Berea, 1991.

Gill, John. *A Complete Body of Practical and Doctrinal Divinity.* Philadelphia: B. Graves, 1810.

Girardeau, John L. "The Federal Theology." In *Memorial Volume of the Semi-centennial of the Columbia Seminary,* edited by B. M. Palmer, 96–130. Columbia: Presbyterian, 1884.

Goodwin, Thomas. *The Works of Thomas Goodwin.* 12 vols. Edinburgh: James Nichol, 1856.

Greaves, Richard L. "The Origins and Early Development of English Covenant Thought." *The Historian* 31 (1968): 21–35.

Hall, Richard A. S. "Did Berkeley Influence Edwards?" In *Jonathan Edwards's Writings: Text, Context, Interpretation,* edited by Stephen J. Stein, 100–121. Bloomington: Indiana University Press, 1996.

Hart, David Bently. *The Experience of God: Being, Consciousness, Bliss.* New Haven: Yale University Press, 2013.

Hawking, Stephen. *A Brief History of Time.* New York: Bantam, 1990.

Helm, Paul. "Calvin and the Covenant: Unity and Continuity." *EQ* 55 (1983) 65–81.

Henderson, George D. "The Ideal of the Covenant in Scotland." *EQ* 27 (1955) 2–14.

Heppe, Heinrich. *Die Dogmatik des Deutschen Protestantismus in sechzehnten Jahrhundert.* 3 vols. Gotha: Perthes, 1857.

———. *Geschichte des Pietismus und der Mystik in der reformierten Kirche namentlich in der Niederlande.* Leiden: Brill, 1879.

———. *Reformed Dogmatics: Set Out and Illustrated from the Sources*. Revised and Edited by Ernst Bizer. Translated by G. T. Thomson. Grand Rapids: Baker, 1978.

Hodge, Charles. *Systematic Theology*. 3 vols. Grand Rapids: Eerdmans, 1997.

Holifield, E. Brooks. "Edwards as a Theologian." In *The Cambridge Companion to Jonathan Edwards*, edited by Stephen J. Stein, 144–161. Cambridge: Cambridge University Press, 2007.

———. *Theology in America: Christian Thought from the Age of the Puritans to the Civil War*. New Haven: Yale University Press, 2003.

Holmes, Christopher R. J. "The Theological Foundation of the Doctrine of the Divine Attributes and the Divine Glory, with Special Reference to Karl Barth and His Reading of the Protestant Orthodox," *SJT* 61 (2008) 205–23.

Holmes, Stephen R. "Does Jonathan Edwards Use a Dispositional Ontology? A Response to Sang Hyum Lee." In *Jonathan Edwards: Philosophical Theologian*, edited by Paul Helm and Oliver D. Crisp, 99–113. Burlington: Ashgate, 2003.

———. *God of Grace and God of Glory: An Account of the Theology of Jonathan Edwards*. Grand Rapids: Eerdmans, 2001.

Horton, Michael S. "Calvin and the Law-Gospel Hermeneutic." *Pro Ecclesia* 6 (1997) 27–42.

———. *The Christian Faith: A Systematic Theology for Pilgrims on the Way*. Grand Rapids: Zondervan, 2011.

———. *Covenant and Eschatology: The Divine Drama*. Louisville: Westminster John Knox, 2002.

———. *Covenant and Salvation: Union with Christ*. Louisville: Westminster John Knox, 2007.

———. *God of Promise: Introducing Covenant Theology*. Grand Rapids: Baker, 2006.

———. "Law, Gospel, and Covenant: Reassessing Some Emerging Antitheses." *WTJ* 64 (2002) 279–87.

Hunsinger, George. "An American Tragedy: Jonathan Edwards on Justification." *Modern Reformation* 13 (2004) 18–21.

———. "Dispositional Soteriology: Jonathan Edwards on Justification by Faith Alone." *WTJ* 66 (2004) 107–120.

Jenson, Robert W. *America's Theologian: A Recommendation of Jonathan Edwards*. Oxford: Oxford University Press, 1988.

Jeon, Jeong Koo. *Calvin and the Federal Vision: Calvin's Covenant Theology in Light of Contemporary Discussion*. Eugene: Resource, 2009.

———. *Covenant Theology: John Murray's and Meredith G. Kline's Response to the Historical Development of Federal Theology in Reformed Thought*. Lanham: University Press of America, 1999.

———. *Covenant Theology and Justification by Faith: The Shepherd Controversy and Its Impacts*. Eugene: Wipf and Stock, 2006.

Jowers, Dennis W. "An Exposition and Critique of Karl Rahner's Axiom: 'The Economic Trinity *is* the Immanent Trinity and Vice Versa,'" *MJT* 15 (2004) 165–200.

Junius, Francis. "*Vera Theologia.*" In *Opuscula Theologica Selecta, Volume 4*, edited by Abraham Kuyper, 51–52. Amsterdam: Frederic Muller, 1882.

Kaiser, Walter C. "The Old Promise and the New Covenant: Jeremiah 31:31–34." *Journal of the Evangelical Theological Society* 15 (1972) 11–23.

Kang, Kevin. "Justified by Faith in Christ: Jonathan Edwards' Doctrine of Justification in Light of Union with Christ." PhD diss., Westminster Theological Seminary, 2003.

Karlberg, Mark W. "Justification in Redemptive History." *WTJ* 43 (1981) 213–46.

———. "The Mosaic Covenant the Concept of Works in Reformed Hermeneutics: A Historical-Critical Analysis with Particular Attention to Early Covenant Eschatology." PhD diss., Westminster Theological Seminary, 1980.

———. "The Original State of Adam: Tensions within Reformed Theology." *EQ* 59 (1987) 291–309.

———. "Recovering the Mosaic Covenant as Law and Gospel: J. Mark Beach, John H. Sailhamer, and Jason C. Meyer as Representative Expositors." *EQ* 83 (2011) 233–50.

———. "Reformed Interpretation of the Mosaic Covenant." *WTJ* 43 (1980) 1–57.

Kendall, R. T. "The Nature of Saving Faith from William Perkins (D. 1602) to the Westminster Assembly (1643-9)." DPhil diss., University of Oxford, 1976.

Kevan, Ernest F. *The Grace of Law: A Study in Puritan Theology*. Grand Rapids: Soli Deo Gloria, 2015.

Kline, Meredith. "Law Covenant." *WTJ* 27 (1964) 1-20.

———. *Treaty of the Great King: The Covenant Structure of Deuteronomy*. Grand Rapids: Eerdmans, 1963.

Knijff, Cornelis van der. "The Development in Jonathan Edwards' Covenant View." *JES* 3 (2013) 269–81.

———, and Willem van Vlastuin. "Why Edwards Did Not Understand Thomas Boston: A Comparison of Their Views on the Covenants." *JES* 5 (2015) 44–56.

Lane, Anthony N. S. "Twofold Righteousness: A Key to the Doctrine of Justification? Reflections on Article 5 of the Regensburg Colloquy (1541)." In *Justification: What's at Stake in the Current Debates*, edited by Mark Husbands and Daniel J. Treier, 205–224. Downer's Grove: InterVarsity, 2004.

Lee, Sang Hyun. "Grace and Justification by Faith Alone." In *The Princeton Companion to Jonathan Edwards*, edited by Sang Hyun Lee, 130–46. Princeton: Princeton University Press, 2005.

———. *The Philosophical Theology of Jonathan Edwards*. Princeton: Princeton University Press, 1988.

Leigh, Edward. *A System or Body of Divinity: Consisting of Ten Books. Wherein the Fundamentals of the main Grounds of Religion Are Opened*. London: William Lee, 1654.

Leithart, Peter J. "Trinitarian Anthropology: Toward a Trinitarian Re-Casting of Reformed Theology." In *The Auburn Avenue Theology Pros & Cons: Debating the Federal Vision*, edited by Calvin Beisner, 58–71. Fort Lauderdale: Knox Theological Seminary, 2004.

Letham, Robert. "The *Foedus Operum*: Some Factors Accounting for Its Development." *SCJ* 14 (2017) 457–67.

Lillback, Peter A. *The Binding of God: Calvin's Role in the Development of Covenant Theology*. Grand Rapids: Baker, 2001.

———. "The Continuing Conundrum: Calvin and the Conditionality of the Covenant." *CTJ* 29 (1994) 42–74.

———. "Ursinus' Development of the Covenant of Creation: A Debt to Melanchthon or Calvin?" *WTJ* 43 (1981) 247–88.

Lincoln, Charles F. "The Development of the Covenant Theory." *BS* 100 (1943) 134–63.
Lindsay, T. M. "The Covenant Theology." *British and Foreign Evangelical Review* 28 (1879) 521–38.
Locke, John. *Essay Concerning Human Understanding*. Amherst: Prometheus, 1995.
Logan, Samuel T. "Justification and Evangelical Obedience." In *Jonathan Edwards and Justification*, edited by Josh Moody, 95–129. Wheaton: Crossway, 2012.
———. Review of *Tragedy in Eden: Original Sin in the Theology of Jonathan Edwards* by Samuel Storms. *WTJ* 46 (1984) 26–52.
Luther, Martin. *D. Martin Luthers Werke, Kritische Gesamtausgabe [Deutsche Bibel], 7. Band, Drucktext der Lutherbibel 1522–1546: Das Neue Testament. Zweite Hälfte: Episteln und Offenbarung*. Weimar: Herman Böhlau, 1931.
———. *Martin Luthers Werke, Kritische Gesamtausgabe [Schriften], 2. Band, Schriften 1518/19 einschließlich Predigten, Disputationen*. Weimar: Herman Böhlau, 1884.
———. *D. Martin Luthers Werke, Kritische Gesamtausgabe [Schriften], 16. Band, Reihenpredigten über 2. Mose 1524/27*. Weimar: Herman Böhlau, 1889.
———. *D. Martin Luthers Werke, Kritische Gesamtausgabe [Schriften], 36. Band, Predigten 1532*. Weimar: Herman Böhlau, 1909.
———. *D. Martin Luthers Werke, Kritische Gesamtausgabe [Schriften], 56. Band, Römervorlesung (Hs.) 1515/16*. Weimar: Herman Böhlau, 1938.
———. *Luther's Works, Volume 12, Selected Psalms*. Edited by Jaroslav Pelikan. St. Louis: Concordia, 1955.
———. *Luther's Works, Volume 25, Lectures on Romans, Glosses and Scholia*. Edited by Hilton C. Oswald. St. Louis: Concordia, 1972.
———. *Luther's Works, Volume 26, Lectures on Galatians 1535 Chapters 1–4*. Edited by Jaroslav Pelikan and Walter A. Hansen. St. Louis: Concordia, 1963.
———. *Luther's Works, Volume 27, Lectures on Galatians 1535 Chapters 5–6, Lectures on Galatians 1519 Chapters 1–6*. Edited by Jaroslav Pelikan. St. Louis: Concordia, 1964.
———. *Luther's Works, Volume 32, Career of the Reformer*. Edited by George W. Forell. Phildelphia: Fortress, 1958.
———. *Luther's Works, Volume 35, Word and Sacrament I*. Edited by E. Theodore Bachmann. Philadelphia: Fortress, 1960.
Lyall, Francis. "Of Metaphors and Analogies: Legal Language and Covenant Theology." *SJT* 32 (1979) 1–17.
MacLean, Donald John. "Missing, Presumed Misclassified: Hugh Binning (1627–1653), the Lost Federal Theologian." *WTJ* 75 (2013) 261–78.
MacLeod, Donald. "Covenant Theology." In *Dictionary of Scottish Church History and Theology*, edited by Nigel M. de S. Cameron, 214–18. Downers Grove: InterVarsity, 1993.
Marsden, George M. *Jonathan Edwards: A Life*. New Haven: Yale University Press, 2003.
———. "Perry Miller's Rehabilitation of the Puritans: A Critique." *CH* 39 (1970) 91–105.
Mastricht, Petrus van. *The Best Method of Preaching: The Use of Theoretical-Practical Theology*. Translated by Todd M. Rester. Grand Rapids: Reformation Heritage, 2013.
———. *A Treatise on Regeneration*. Edited by Brandon Withrow. Morgan: Soli Deo Gloria, 2002.

McClelland, Joseph C. "Covenant Theology — A Re-Evaluation." *Canadian Journal of Theology* 3 (1957) 182–88.

McClenahan, Michael. *Jonathan Edwards and Justification by Faith*. Burlington: Ashgate, 2012.

McCormack, Bruce L. "A Scholastic of a Higher Order: The Development of Karl Barth's Theology, 1921-1931." PhD diss., Princeton Theological Seminary, 1989.

McCoy, Charles S. "Johannes Cocceius: Federal Theologian." *SJT* 16 (1963) 352–70.

McClymond, Michael J. *Encounters with God: An Approach to the Theology of Jonathan Edwards*. Oxford: Oxford University Press, 1998.

———. "God the Measure: Towards an Understanding of Jonathan Edwards' Theocentric Metaphysics." *SJT* 47 (2000) 43–59.

———, and Gerald R. McDermott. *The Theology of Jonathan Edwards*. Oxford: Oxford University Press, 2012.

McDermott, Gerald R. *Jonathan Edwards Confronts the Gods: Christian Theology, Enlightenment Religion, and Non-Christian Faiths*. Oxford: Oxford University Press, 2000.

———. "Jonathan Edwards on Justification by Faith: More Protestant or Catholic?" *Pro Ecclesia* 17 (2007) 92–111.

McGiffert, Michael. "From Moses to Adam: The Making of the Covenant of Works." *SCJ* 19 (1988) 131–55.

———. "Grace and Works: The Rise and Division of Covenant Divinity in Elizabethan Puritanism." *HTR* 75 (1982) 463–502.

———. "William Tyndale's Conception of the Covenant." *JEH* 32 (1981) 167–184.

Miller, Perry. *Errand into the Wilderness*. New York: Harper and Row, 1956.

———. *Jonathan Edwards*. Amherst: The University of Massachusetts Press, 1949.

———. *The New England Mind: The Seventeenth Century*. Cambridge: Belknap, 1982.

Møller, Jens G. "The Beginnings of Puritan Covenant Theology." *JEH* 14 (1963) 46–67.

Moody, Josh. *Jonathan Edwards and the Enlightenment: Knowing the Presence of God*. Lanham: University Press of America, 2005.

Morimoto, Anri. *Jonathan Edwards and the Catholic Vision of Salvation*. University Park: The Pennsylvania State University Press, 1995.

———. "Salvation as Fulfillment of Being: The Soteriology of Jonathan Edwards and Its Implications for Missions." *Princeton Seminary Bulletin* 20 (1999) 13–23.

Muller, Richard A. *After Calvin: Development of a Theological Tradition*. Oxford: Oxford University Press, 2003.

———. "Calvin and the 'Calvinists': Assessing Continuities and Discontinuities between the Reformation and Orthodoxy, Part One." *CTJ* 30 (1995) 345–75.

———. *Calvin and the Reformed Tradition: On the Work of Christ and the Order of Salvation*. Grand Rapids: Baker, 2012.

———. *Christ and the Decree: Christology and Predestination in Reformed Theology from Calvin to Perkins*. Grand Rapids: Baker, 1986.

———. "The Covenant of Works and the Stability of Divine Law in Seventeenth-Century Reformed Orthodoxy: A Study in the Theology of Herman Witsius and Wilhelmus á Brakel." *CTJ* 29 (1994) 75–100.

———. *Dictionary of Latin and Greek Theological Terms, Drawn Principally From Protestant Scholastic Theology*. Grand Rapids: Baker, 1985.

———. "Diversity in the Reformed Tradition." In *Drawn into Controversie: Reformed Theological Diversity and Debates within Seventeenth-Century British Puritanism*, edited by Michael A. G. Haykin and Mark Jones, 11–30. Göttingen, Germany: Vandenhoeck & Ruprecht, 2011.

———. "Giving Direction to Theology: The Scholastic Dimension," *Journal of the Evangelical Theological Society* 28 (1985) 183–93.

———. "God as Absolute and Relative, Necessary, Free, and Contingent: The *Ad Intra-Ad Extra* Movement of Seventeenth-Century Reformed Language about God." In *Always Reformed, Essays in Honor of W. Robert Godfrey*, edited by R. Scott Clark and Joel E. Kim, 56–73. Escondido: Westminster Seminary California, 2010.

———. *Post-Reformation Reformed Dogmatics: The Rise and Development of Reformed Orthodoxy, Ca. 1520 to Ca. 1725*. 4 vols. 2nd edition. Grand Rapids: Baker, 2003.

———. Review of *The History of the Covenant Concept from the Bible to Johannes Cloppenburg 'De Foedere Dei,'* by David N. J. Poole. *CTJ* 28 (1993) 217–18.

———. Review of *The Origins of the Federal Theology in Sixteenth-Century Reformation Thought*, by David A. Weir. *JR* 72 (1992) 597–98.

———. "Scholasticism Protestant and Catholic: Francis Turretin on the Object and Principles of Theology," *CH* 53 (1986) 193–205.

———. "Toward the *Pactum Salutis*: Locating the Origins of a Concept." *MJT* 18 (2007) 11–65.

———. *The Unaccommodated Calvin: Studies in the Foundation of a Theological Tradition*. Oxford: Oxford University Press, 2000.

Murray, Iain. *Jonathan Edwards: A New Biography*. Carlisle: Banner of Truth, 1987.

Murray, John. "The Adamic Administration." In *Collected Writings of John Murray*, 2:47–59. Carlisle: Banner of Truth, 1977.

———. *The Covenant of Grace: A Biblico-Theological Study*. Phillipsburg: Presbyterian and Reformed, 1988.

———. "Covenant Theology," in *The Encyclopedia of Christianity*, edited by Erwin Fahlbusch et al., III:199–216. Grand Rapids: Eerdmans and Leiden: Brill, 1999.

———. *The Epistle to the Romans*. 2 vols. Grand Rapids: Eerdmans, 1997.

———. *The Imputation of Adam's Sin*. Grand Rapids: Eerdmans, 1959.

Myers, Stephen G. *Scottish Federalism and Covenantalism in Transition: The Theology of Ebeneezer Erskine*. Eugene: Pickwick, 2015.

Neele, Adriaan C. *Before Jonathan Edwards: Sources of New England Theology*. Oxford: Oxford University Press, 2019.

Niesel, Wilhelm. *Reformed Symbolics: A Comparison of Catholicism, Orthodoxy and Protestantism*. Translated by David Lewis. Edinburgh: Oliver and Boyd, 1962.

Oberman, Heiko A. *The Dawn of the Reformation*. Grand Rapids: Eerdmans, 1986.

———. *Forerunners of the Reformation: The Shape of Late Medieval Thought Illustrated by Key Documents*. Philadelphia: Fortress, 1981.

———. *The Harvest of Medieval Theology*. Grand Rapids: Baker, 1963.

———. "The Shape of Late Medieval Thought: The Birthpangs of the Modern Era," in *The Pursuit of Holiness in Late Medieval and Renaissance Religion*, edited by Charles Trinkauswith and Heiko A. Oberman, 3–25. Leiden: Brill, 1974.

Otto, Randall E. "The Solidarity of Mankind in Jonathan Edwards' Doctrine of Original Sin." *EQ* 62 (1990) 205–21.

Owen, John. *Hebrews*. 7 vols. Edited by W. H. Goold. Carlisle: Banner of Truth, 1991.

———. *The Works of John Owen*. 16 vols. Edited by William H. Goold. Carlisle: Banner of Truth, 1998.

Pauw, Amy Plantinga. "'Heaven Is a World of Love': Edwards on Heaven and the Trinity." *CTJ* 30 (1995) 392–400.

———. *The Supreme Harmony of All: The Trinitarian Theology of Jonathan Edwards*. Grand Rapids: Eerdmans, 2002.

Perkins, William. *Art of Prophesying*. Edinburgh: Banner of Truth, 1996.

———. *The Works of That Famous and Worthy Minister of Christ in the Universitie of Cambridge, M. William Perkins*. London: John Legatt, 1631.

Peterkin, Alexander, ed. *Records of the Kirk of Scotland, containing the Acts and Proceedings of the General Assemblies, from the Year 1638 Downwards, Volume 1*. Edinburgh: John Sutherland, 1838.

Peters, Ted. *GOD—The World's Future: Systematic Theology for a Postmodern Era*. Minneapolis: Fortress, 1992.

Peterson, Rodney. "Continuity and Discontinuity: The Debate Throughout Church History." In *Continuity and Discontinuity: Perspectives on the Relationship between the Old and New Testaments*, edited by John S. Feinberg, 17–34. Wheaton: Crossway, 1988.

Petto, Samuel. *The Difference between the Old and New Covenants*. London, 1674.

Pieper, Josef. *Leisure, The Basis of Culture*. South Bend: St. Augustine's, 1998.

Piper, John. "A Personal Encounter with Jonathan Edwards." *The Reformed Journal* 28 (1978) 13–17.

Poole, David N. J. *The History of the Covenant Concept from the Bible to Johannes Cloppenburg "De Foedere Dei."* San Francisco: Mellen Research University Press, 1992.

Rad, Gerhard von. *Old Testament Theology, Volume 1*. New York: Harper and Row, 1962

Rainy, R. "Federal Theology," *Catholic Presbyterian* 5 (1881) 341–49, 427–34.

Ridgley, Thomas. *A Body of Divinity: Wherein the Doctrines of the Christian Religion are Explained and Defended, Being the Substance of Several Lectures on the Assembly's Larger Catechism*. 4 vols. Philadelphia: William W. Woodward, 1814–1815.

Riley, I. Woodbridge. *American Philosophy: The Early Schools*. New York: Dodd, Mead, and Co., 1907.

Roberts, Alexander, and James Donaldson, eds. *The Ante-Nicene Fathers: Translations of the Writings of the Fathers Down to A.D. 325*. 10 vols. Peabody: Hendrickson, 2004.

Robertson, O. Palmer. *The Christ of the Covenants*. Phillipsburg: Presbyterian and Reformed, 1980.

Rohr, John Von. *The Covenant of Grace in Puritan Thought*. Eugene: Wipf and Stock, 1986.

Rollock, Robert. "A Treatise of Our Effectual Calling and of Certain Common-Places of Theology Contained Under It." In *Selected Works of Robert Rollock*, edited by William M. Gunn, 1:29–288. Edinburgh: The Wodrow Society, 1849.

Rolston, Holmes, III. *John Calvin versus the Westminster Confession*. Richmond: John Knox, 1972.

———. "Responsible Man in Reformed Theology: Calvin versus the Westminster Confession." *SJT* 23 (1970) 129–56.

Rupp, Gordon. "The 'Idealism' of Jonathan Edwards." *HTR* 62 (1969) 209–26.

Rutherford, Samuel. *The Covenant of Life Opened, or, a Treatise of the Covenant of Grace Containing Something of the Nature of the Covenant of Works, the Soveraignty of*

God, the Extent of the Death of Christ. Edinburgh: Printed by Andro Anderson for Robert Brown, 1655.

Sailhamer, John H. *The Meaning of the Pentateuch: Revelation, Composition and Interpretation*. Downers Grove: InterVarsity, 2009.

Schafer, T. A. "Jonathan Edwards and Justification by Faith." *CH* 20 (1951) 55–67.

Schaff, Philip, and Henry Wace, eds. *A Select Library of Nicene and Post-Nicene Fathers of the Christian Church*. 28 vols. in 2 series. Peabody: Hendrickson, 2004.

Scheick, William J. "The Grand Design: Jonathan Edwards' History of the Work of Redemption." *Eighteenth-Century Studies* 8 (1975) 300–314.

Schreiner, Susan E. *The Theater of His Glory: Nature and the Natural Order in the Thought of John Calvin*. Durham: Labyrinth, 1991.

Schrenk, Gottlob. *Gottesreich and Bund im alteren Protestanismus vornehmlich bei Johannes Coccejus: Zugleich ein Beitrag zur Geschichte des Pietismus und der Heilgeschichtlichen Theologie*. Gütersloh: Bertelsmann, 1923.

Scott, J. L. "The Covenant in the Theology of Karl Barth." *SJT* 17 (1964) 192–98.

Shedd, William G. T. *Dogmatic Theology*. 3rd ed. Edited by Alan W. Gomes. Phillipsburg: Presbyterian and Reformed, 2003.

Shepherd, Norman. *The Call of Grace: How the Covenant Illuminates Salvation and Evangelism*. Phillipsburg: Presbyterian and Reformed, 2000.

Sibbes, Richard. "A Description of Christ." In *The Complete Works of Richard Sibbes, D. D., Volume 1*, edited by Alexander B. Grosart, 1–31. Edinburgh, 1862–1864. Reprinted, Edinburgh: Banner of Truth, 1973.

Spiegel, James S. "The Theological Orthodoxy of Berkeley's Immaterialism." *Faith and Philosophy* 13 (1996) 215–35.

Spohn, William C. "Sovereign Beauty: Jonathan Edwards and the Nature of True Virtue." *Theological Studies* 42 (2004) 394–421.

Stein, Stephen J. "'Like Apples of Gold in Pictures of Silver': The Portrait of Wisdom in Jonathan Edwards's Commentary on the Book of Proverbs." *CH* 54 (1985) 324–37.

———. "The Quest for the Spiritual Sense: The Biblical Hermeneutics of Jonathan Edwards." *HTR* 70 (1977) 99–113.

Steinmetz, David C. *Luther in Context*. Grand Rapids: Baker, 1995.

Stetina, Karen Spiecker. *Jonathan Edwards' Early Understanding of Religious Experience: His New York Sermons, 1720-1723*. Lewiston: Edwin Mellen, 2011.

Stogdon, Hubert. *Seasonable Advice Relating to the Present Disputes about the Holy Trinity, Address'd to Both Contending Parties*. London, 1719.

Stout, Harry S. "The Puritans and Edwards." In *Jonathan Edwards and the American Experience*, edited by Nathan O. Hatch and Harry S. Stout, 142–59. New York: Oxford University Press, 1988.

Stoute, D. A. "The Origins and Early Development of the Reformed Idea of the Covenant." PhD diss., Cambridge University, 1979.

Strobel, Kyle C. "By Word and Spirit: Jonathan Edwards on Redemption, Justification, and Regeneration." In *Jonathan Edwards and Justification*, edited by Josh Moody, 45–70. Wheaton: Crossway, 2012.

———. *Jonathan Edwards's Theology: A Reinterpretation*. London: T. & T. Clark, 2013.

Studebaker, Steven M. "Jonathan Edwards' Pneumatological Concept of Grace and Dispositional Soteriology: Resources for an Evangelical Inclusivism." *Pro Ecclesia* 14 (2005) 324–39.

———. "Jonathan Edwards's Social Augustinian Trinitarianism: An Alternative to a Recent Trend." *SJT* 56 (2003) 268–85.

———. *The Trinitarian Vision of Jonathan Edwards and David Coffey*. Amherst: Cambria, 2011.

———, and Robert W. Caldwell. *The Trinitarian Theology of Jonathan Edwards: Text, Context, and Application*. Burlington: Ashgate, 2012.

Sweeney, Douglas A. *Edwards the Exegete: Biblical Interpretation and Anglo-Protestant Culture on the Edge of the Enlightenment*. Oxford: Oxford University Press, 2016.

———. "Jonathan Edwards and Justification: The Rest of the Story." In *Jonathan Edwards as Contemporary: Essays in Honor of Sang Hyun Lee*, edited by Don Schweitzer, 151–73. New York: Peter Lang, 2010.

———. "Justification by Faith Alone?" In *Jonathan Edwards and Justification*, edited by Josh Moody, 129–45. Wheaton: Crossway, 2012.

Tanner, Kathryn. *God and Creation in Christian Theology*. Minneapolis: Fortress, 2005.

Thuesen, Peter J. "Edwards' Intellectual Background." In *The Princeton Companion to Jonathan Edwards*, edited by Sang Hyun Lee, 16–33. Princeton: Princeton University Press, 2005.

Tillich, Paul. *The Courage to Be*. New Haven: Yale University Press, 1952.

Tillotson, John. *The Works of the Most Reverend Dr. John Tillotson, Lord Archbishop of Canterbury in Twelve Volumes*. London, 1743.

Tooman, William A. "Edwards's Ezekiel: The Interpretation of Ezekiel in the *Blank Bible* and *Notes on Scripture*," *Journal of Theological Interpretation* 3 (2011) 160–92.

Torrance, James B. "Calvin and Puritanism in England and Scotland—Some Basic Concepts in the Development of 'Federal Theology.'" In *Calvinus Reformator: His Contribution to Theology, Church and Society*, edited by B. J. Van Der Walt, 265–77. Potchefstroom: Potchefstroom University for Christian Higher Education, 1982.

———. "The Contribution of McLeod Campbell in Scottish Theology." *SJT* 26 (1973) 295–311.

———. "The Covenant Concept in Scottish Theology and Politics and Its Legacy." *SJT* 34 (1981) 225–43.

———. "Covenant or Contract? A Study of the Theological Background of Worship in Seventeenth-Century Scotland." *SJT* 23 (1970) 51–56.

———. "Strength and Weaknesses of the Westminster Theology." In *The Westminster Confession in the Church Today: Papers Prepared for the Church of Scotland Panel on Doctrine*, edited by Alasdair I. C. Heron, 40–54. Edinburgh: Saint Andres, 1982.

Trinterud, Leonard J. "The Origins of Puritanism." *CH* 20 (1951) 37–57.

Trueman, Carl and R. Scott Clark, eds. *Protestant Scholasticism: Essays in Reassessment*. Carlisle: Paternoster, 1999.

———. "The Reception of Calvin: Historical Considerations." *Church History and Religious Culture* 91 (2011) 19–27.

Turretin, Francis. *Institutes of Elenctic Theology*. Edited by James T. Dennison. Translated by George Musgrave Giger. Phillipsburg: Presbyterian and Reformed, 1994.

Ursinus, Zacharia. *Commentary on the Heidelberg Catechism*. Phillipsburg: Presbyterian and Reformed, 1985.

Vanhoozer, Kevin. *Remythologizing Theology: Divine Action, Passion, and Authorship*. Cambridge: Cambridge University Press, 2012.

Voetius, Gisbert. "Problematum De Merito Christi, Pars Tetria." In *Selectarum Disputationum Theologicarum, Volume 2*. Ultrajecti: apud Johannem à Waesberge, 1655.

Vos, Arvin. "Scholasticism" In *New Dictionary of Theology*, edited by Sinclair B. Ferguson et al., 621–23. Downers Grove: InterVarsity, 1988.

Vos, Geerhardus. *Biblical Theology: Old and New Testaments*. Carlisle: Banner of Truth, 1996.

———. "The Doctrine of the Covenant in Reformed Theology." In *Redemptive History and Biblical Interpretation: The Shorter Writings of Geerhardus Vos*, edited by Richard B. Gaffin, 234–270. Phillipsburg: Presbyterian and Reformed, 1980.

Waddington, Jeffrey C. "Jonathan Edwards's 'Ambiguous and Somewhat Precarious' Doctrine of Justification?" *WTJ* 66 (2004) 357–72.

———. "Must We Believe? Jonathan Edwards and Conscious Faith in Christ." *The Confessional Presbyterian* 6 (2010) 11–21.

Wainwright, William J. "Jonathan Edwards, William Rowe, and the Necessity of Creation." In *Faith, Freedom, and Rationality*, edited by Jeff Jordan and Daniel Howard-Snyder, 119–133. Lanham: Rowman and Littlefield, 1996.

Ward, Roland S. *God and Adam: Reformed Theology and the Creation Covenant*. Wantim: New Melbourne, 2003.

Warfield, B. B. *The Works of Benjamin B. Warfield, Volume VI: The Westminster Assembly and Its Work*. Grand Rapids: Baker, 2000.

Watson, Thomas. *A Body of Divinity*. Carlisle: Banner of Truth, 2000.

Weber, Otto. *Foundations of Dogmatics*. Translated by Darrell Guder. 2 vols. Grand Rapids: Eerdmans, 1981–1982.

Watts, Isaac. *The Christian Doctrine of the Trinity . . . Asserted and Prov'd [and] . . . Vindicated by Plain Evidence of Scripture, without the Aid or Incumbrance of Human Schemes*. London, 1722.

Weber, Richard M. "The Trinitarian Theology of Jonathan Edwards: An Investigation of Charges Against Its Orthodoxy." *Journal of the Evangelical Theological Society* 44 (2001) 297–318.

Weir, David A. *The Origins of the Federal Theology in Sixteenth-Century Reformation Thought*. Oxford: Clarendon, 1990.

Wenger, Thomas L. "The New Perspective on Calvin: Responding to Recent Calvin Interpretations." *Journal of the Evangelical Theological Society*, 50 (2007) 311–28.

Wilson, Stephen A. *Virtue Reformed: Rereading Jonathan Edwards's Ethics*. Leiden: Brill, 2005.

Winslow, Ola Elizabeth. *Jonathan Edwards 1703–1758: A Biography*. New York: Macmillan, 1940.

Witsius, Herman. *The Economy of the Covenants between God and Man: Comprehending a Complete Body of Divinity*. 2 vols. Escondido: The den Dulk Christian Foundation, 1990.

Woodbridge, Frederick J. E. "Jonathan Edwards." *Philosophical Review* 13 (1904) 401–406.

Woolsey, Andrew A. *Unity and Continuity in Covenantal Thought: A Study in the Reformed Tradition to the Westminster Assembly*. Grand Rapids: Reformation Heritage, 2012.

Wright, N. T. *The Climax of the Covenant: Christ and the Law in Pauline Theology*. Minneapolis: Fortress, 1991.

———. *Paul: In Fresh Perspective*. Minneapolis: Fortress, 2005.
———. *What Saint Paul Really Said*. Grand Rapids: Eerdmans, 1997.
Yazawa, Reita. *Covenant of Redemption in the Trinitarian Theology of Jonathan Edwards: The Nexus between the Immanent Trinity and the Economic Trinity*. Eugene: Pickwick, 2019.
Yoo, Jeongmo. "Jonathan Edwards's Interpretation of the Major Prophets: The Books of Isaiah, Jeremiah, and Ezekiel." *Puritan Reformed Journal* 3 (2011) 160–92.
Zachman, Randall C. *The Assurance of Faith: Conscience in the Theology of Martin Luther and John Calvin*. Minneapolis: Fortress, 1993.
Zandt, Abraham Brooks Van. "The Doctrine of the Covenants Considered as the Central Principle of Theology." *Presbyterian Review* 3 (1882) 28–39.

Name and Author Index

Althaus, Paul, 15n41, 17, 21n67
Ames, William, 55, 80, 237–38
Anderson, Wallace, 96n78, 100, 100n94, 101n98
Aquinas, Thomas, 17, 17n45, 106, 126n189, 226n25, 241n81
Aristotle, 16, 126n189, 234
Arminius, Jacobus, 8n13, 80, 87n40
Augustine, 14, 39, 39n52, 84, 94, 94n64, 106, 114n155, 168, 168n85, 169, 175, 251n116

Baik, Chung-Hun, 107
Ball, John, 31n19, 40, 54–56, 179n15, 184, 187n43
Barrow, Isaac, 71n145
Barshinger, David, 12, 12n34
Barth, Karl, 19, 19n57, 19n59, 20n63, 21, 50n86, 125, 125n87
Bavinck, Herman, 136–38
Bellarmine, Robert, 263
Berkeley, George, 100–102, 100n97, 101n102
Berkhof, Louis, 39, 82n21, 179, 181, 185n37
Beza, Theodore, 26, 30, 37, 81–82
Biehl, Craig, 89, 169n87, 259n147
Bierma Lyle, 29, 32–33, 79
Bizer, Ernst, 20n67
Blake, Thomas, 137
Bogue, Carl, 4, 28n8, 156, 189n50
Bolton, Robert, 179, 185, 187n43, 188

Bombaro, John, 220n3, 227n28, 234n56, 235–36, 247
Boston, Thomas, 12, 40, 142–45, 144n24, 143n21, 186, 186n36, 169n89, 197n66
Boswell, James, 101n102
Bracken, Joseph, 107
Brahe, Jan Jacob, 138
Brakel, Wilhelmus à, 11, 27, 119n167, 144n24
Brown, John (of Haddington), 169n89
Brown, Robert, 11
Bruggink, Donald, 31
Bulkeley, Peter, 84, 136, 139
Bullinger, Heinrich, 21n67, 26, 30n17
Burgess, Anthony, 30n19, 34n34, 57, 57n106, 174

Caldwell, Robert, 253
Calvin, John, xix, 4n4, 14–18, 20, 20n67, 25–26, 30–33, 30n17, 31n21, 33n29, 33n31, 35n40, 36n4, 80–81, 103n114, 168–69, 185n36, 181, 187n43, 222n10, 228, 241n81, 242, 245, 265, 237–38, 251n120, 271, 271n38, 279
Cartwright, Thomas, 29
Channing, William Ellery, 103
Cherry, Conrad, 3–4, 10–11, 71n145, 222–23, 241, 244n97, 256

Clark, R. Scott, 18
Clarke, Samuel, 71n145, 92
Clement of Alexandria, 14
Cloppenburg, Johann, 79, 80n13
Cocceius, Johannes, xx, 33n29, 39, 79, 80n13, 84
Comrie, Alexander, 138
Crisp, Oliver, 96–97, 105, 235n61

Danaher, William, 80–81, 84–87, 87n40, 144n24, 178, 188n47
Dickinson, Jonathan, 68
Dickson, David, 80–81, 84, 86–87, 87n40, 144n24, 178, 188n47
Dixhoorn, Chad Van, 175–76
Duncan, J. Ligon, 13, 20n62, 39n51
Durham, James, 86

Edwards, John, 126
Elwood, Douglas, 97–98

Fenner, Dudley, 29
Ferry, Brenton, xxiin12, 175–82, 184–88, 178n13, 184n34, 185n36, 187n43, 188n47, 216–17
Fesko, J. V., xxiii, 5n7, 77n1, 78n2, 82, 86n38, 278n63

Gass, Wilhelm, 79
Gerstner, John H., 13, 68n135, 91n55, 109, 129n199, 130, 249n111
Gill, John, 169n89
Gomarus, Franciscus, 80
Goodwin, Thomas, 86, 169n89

Hall, Richard, 101
Hart, David Bently, 98n84
Hawking, Stephen, 101n102
Heidegger, Johann Heinrich, 87, 169n89
Helm, Paul, 80, 90n48, 111n140, 112n149
Heppe, Heinrich, 17, 20n67, 31–32, 33n29, 79, 91n52, 169n89

Hobbes, Thomas, 100
Hodge, Charles, 4n6, 33n32, 54n97, 68n135, 136, 139, 179–80, 249n111
Holifield, E. Brooks, 8, 99
Horton, Michael, xvi, 5n7, 35n40, 52, 83n25
Hume, David, 234
Hunsinger, George, 5n7, 219, 227–34, 235, 238, 241, 276n63

Irenaeus, 13, 14, 39, 175

Jenson, Robert, 95–96
Justin Martyr, 13, 175

Karlberg, Mark, 4n6, 19n62, 57n107, 176, 176n7, 177n12, 182, 193n58
Kevan, Ernest, 56
Kimnach, Wilson, 89
Kline, Meredith, xvi–xviii, 185
Knijff, Cornelis van der, 143, 143n21, 151

Lactantius, 13
Lee, Sang Hyun, 97, 226, 234–35, 235n61, 241
Letham, Robert, 30, 119n167
Lillback, Peter, 6n10, 19n62, 20n65, 33, 33n29
Locke, John, 102n107, 234
Luther, Martin, xx, xxiii, 14, 35n40, 36, 79, 227n27, 237, 251n116, 279n65

MacLeod, Donald, 144
Manton, Thomas, 256–57
Mastricht, Petrus van, 11–12, 12n31, 26, 38, 105, 237–38, 242, 264–65, 265n14
McClenahan, Michael, 229, 231–33, 233n53, 233n54, 244n97, 253n128, 256, 263

McClymond, Michael, 4n5, 5n7, 102n105, 137, 140–43, 151, 189–90
McDermott, Gerald, 4n5, 5n7, 137, 140–43, 151, 190, 238n74
McGiffert, Michael, xxiin12, 19n56, 20n65, 30
Melanchthon, Philip, 35n40, 31–32
Miller, Perry, 4, 8, 10, 13–14, 18–20, 19n56, 32, 103, 104n115, 135, 237, 237n69, 290–91
Moody, Josh, 101, 104n115, 259n147
Morimoto, Anri, 5n7, 71n145, 219, 234–39, 234n56, 241, 241n81, 245
Muller, Richard, xx, 11, 15, 17–18, 18n52, 19n62, 20–21, 20n67, 26, 29, 30n19, 32–35, 78–79, 124–26, 176, 176n8, 251
Murray, John, xix, 31, 177n12, 180–81, 181n29, 249n111

Neele, Adriaane, xixn9, 4n4, 9, 12n31, 82

Oberman, Heiko, 17, 57n107
Oecolampadius, Johannes, 80, 80n13
Olevianus, Kaspar, 29, 33, 79, 80n13, 279
Osiander, Andreas, 237–38
Owen, John, 55–56, 56n102, 80n13, 123, 178–79, 187n43, 188n47

Pauw, Amy Plantinga, 89, 90n48, 96, 114n155, 151n45, 153, 262
Perkins, William, 38, 85
Peters, Ted, 107
Petto, Samuel, 198n68
Polanus, Amandus, 125–26
Poole, David, 30, 32
Preston, John, 40, 137

Rahner, Karl, 234n56, 106
Ramsey, Chevalier, 94n64

Ramsey, Paul, 99–100, 242, 265
Rawlin, Richard, 226
Ridgley, Thomas, 169n89
Robertson, O. Palmer, xvi
Rollock, Robert, 26, 29, 29n12, 38, 50, 54, 137
Rolston, Holmes III, 30, 32
Rupp, Gordon, 100
Rutherford, Samuel, 56n104, 86, 144n24

Schafer, Thomas, 5n7, 71n145, 219–22, 224–27, 231, 235, 237–39, 270n33, 278n63
Scheick, William, 200
Schrenk, Gottlob, 79
Schweizer, Alexander, 20n67
Sedgwick, Obadiah, 86, 184n34
Shedd, William G. T., 136, 139
Sibbes, Richard, 135n214
Stein, Stephen, 10, 12
Steinmetz, David, 17
Stetina, Karen, 11
Sweeney, Douglas, 4n5, 12n32, 218, 259n147, 262n3

Tanner, Kathryn, 98n84
Taylor, John, 249n111, 280–81, 281n69
Tertullian, 13
Tillich, Paul, 239
Tillotson, John, 71n45, 229, 229n35, 232, 233n54
Torrance, James B., 17, 20n63, 30, 30n19, 32, 50
Trinterud, Leonard, 19n56, 20n65, 25–26, 30, 30n17, 31n21
Trueman, Carl, 18
Turretin, Francis, xxiin14, 12, 12n31, 54, 56–58, 56n103, 57n108, 87, 91, 105, 136, 138–39, 155, 169n89, 181, 187n44, 228, 231–33, 238, 241n81, 242–43, 264, 280

Ursinus, Zacharias, 26, 29, 37

Vanhoozer, Kevin, 107–8, 108n130
Voetius, Gisbertus, 38n48, 80n13, 83–84
Vos, Geerhardus, 18n53, 27, 179–80, 185

Waddington, Jeffrey, 220n3, 225, 234n56, 244n97
Watson, Thomas, 85
Weber, Hans Emil, 17, 20n67
Weber, Otto, 125n187
Weber, Richard, 89–90, 92, 122
Weir, David, 21n62, 28–29, 29n12
Whitby, Daniel, 71n145
Whitefield, George, 262, 262n4
Whittelsey, Chauncy, 103
Wilson, John, 200

Wilson, Stephen, 271
Winslow, Ola, 290–91
Witsius, Herman, 12, 27, 32, 33n29, 39–40, 80, 80n13, 84, 136, 138, 144n24, 155, 179, 181, 187
Wollebius, Johannes, 126
Woolsey, Andres, 20n63, 80
Wright, N. T., 6, 278n64

Yazawa, Reita, xviin7, 77n1, 97

Zachman, Randall, 271n38
Zwingli, Ulrich, 14, 26

Subject Index

Abraham, xxii, xvii, 21, 153
ad extra-ad intra. See Trinity
Adam, xvii, 15, 21, 24, 26, 30–31,
    65, 67–68, 70
    covenant headship of, xix, 28,
        34, 39–40, 42–46, 50, 54,
        56–57, 59–60, 62–63, 68,
        71–75, 84, 128, 131–32,
        248–49
    status integritatis of, 24
    unity in, 72, 76, 248–50,
        249n111
    See also original sin
Adamic administration, xix, 26
adoption, 166n77, 190, 206
aesthetics, xxiv, 88, 95–96, 104–5,
    134. *See also* beauty
Amyraldianism, 175
Anabaptist/pietist traditions, 2, 14
ANE vassal-suzerain treaties, xvii
antinomianism, xxiii, 1, 8, 76, 139,
    142, 153, 175, 218, 220, 239,
    263, 273, 288
archetypal/ectypal theology, 83, 106,
    124–25
Aristotelian philosophy, 11, 17, 234
Arminianism, xxiii, 3, 8, 26, 71, 80,
    87, 171, 175, 218, 220, 223,
    231–32, 239, 242, 263, 288
assurance, 87, 167, 246
Auburn Avenue theology, 7
Augsburg Confession, 16
Augustine, 168–69, 175, 239
baptism, xvii, 191, 215n116. *See also*
    sacraments

Jesus', 80, 113
beauty, xxiv, 96, 99, 104–5, 206n90,
    215, 224–25, 247, 254, 286,
    287; *see also* aesthetics
Belgic Confession, 16
berith, xvi, 30, 44. *See also*
    covenant(s)
bicovenantalism, 30, 50, 146, 151
Bride of Christ. *See* Mystical Bride
    (Body) of Christ
Calvin against the Calvinists, 20, 32
Calvinism, 4
    Barth, Karl on, 20
    Miller, Perry on, 18–19
Catholicism. *See* Roman
    Catholicism
central dogma theory, 15, 29–30,
circumcision, xvii, 168, 176, 191. *See*
    also sacraments
circumincession/perichoresis, 114
Colloquy at Regensburg, 278–79
concursus, 29, 127, 236
Council of Peace, 27. *See also*
    Covenant of Redemption
covenant(s) (*berith, diatheke/*
    diatithemai, foedus, pactum,
    testamentum)
    Abrahamic, xvi, 31, 143, 198,
        205
    biblical (scriptural), xvi–xviii
    church, xviin7
    creation, of, 26, 48
    definition of, xvi, 149
    favor, of, 26
    friendship, of, 26

covenant(s) (*continued*)
  innocence, of, 26–27
  law, of, 26
  life, of, 26–27, 48
  love, of, 26
  national (other than with Israel), xviin7
  nature, of, xix, 26, 33, 56
  Noahic, xvi
  Northampton half-way, xxii, 159, 162, 188
  signs and seals of, xvi–xvii, 80
  theological, xvii–xviii
  See also Covenant of Works
  Covenant of Grace (*foedus gratiae/gratuitum, foedus gratiae evangelicum*), xvi–xviii, 4, 7, 24, 27, 31, 37, 39, 50, 61, 63, 75–77, 83, 85, 136–73
    application of salvation to individual believers, as, 135, 137, 151, 247
    Christ's last will and testament, as, 162
    conditions (conditionality) of, xxiii–xxiv, 4, 20, 31, 126, 136, 140, 143–45, 157–62, 171, 206 207, 209, 253, 272, 281
    Covenant of Redemption, in relation to, 137–39, 145, 151–56, 164, 168, 227, 272
    covenanting parties of, 86, 132, 145–46, 152–55, 159–62, 167, 171
    Edwards, Jonathan on, xxi, 41–43, 134, 136, 139–72, 152–57, 168
    hidden and revealed in the Mosaic covenant, 188, 191–95, 197–98, 204, 212–17
    marriage covenant, as a, 44, 48, 64, 136, 142, 151–52, 154, 158–68, 171, 202, 230, 248, 246, 252–53, 251, 259
    Mosaic covenant, in relation to, xxii, 172, 174, 176–77, 183, 186–88, 191–206, 217

    origins of, 137–39
    progressive revelation of the Covenant of Redemption in history, as, 51, 78, 135, 145, 151, 153, 156, 158, 160, 167–68, 171
    promises (blessings) of Christ in, 164–71, 274–76, 283–84, 253, 289
    Reformed theology on, 137–39
covenant nomism, 6
Covenant of Redemption (Council of Peace, *foedus redemptionis, foedus sempiternum, pactum salutis*), xvi–xviii, xxi, 4, 7, 24, 26, 46, 77–135, 229, 247–49
  biblical foundations of, 81–82
  Calvin, John on, 80
  Coccesius, Johannes on, xx, 79
  conditions of, 148, 157, 164, 168, 171
  Covenant of Grace, in relation to, 137–39, 145, 151–56, 164–67, 227, 272
  Covenant of Works, in relation to, 131–33, 135, 148–50, 168, 277
  definition of, xx
  development and confessionalization of, 84–87
  Edwards, Jonathan on, xx, 41, 43–44, 51, 59, 62–63, 75–76, 88–135
  evangelical obedience, implications for, 133–34
  Father and Son, as a new arrangement between, 117–22
  Holy Spirit's role in, 88, 90, 99, 120–23, 135, 166, 253, 272
  Luther, Martin on, xx, 79
  medieval scholasticism, in, xx
  origin of, xx, 79–81
  parties to, 86–87, 118, 131–33, 153–55, 159–62, 167, 171

SUBJECT INDEX 319

promises of (blessings obtained by) Christ in, 156, 162, 166–68, 223, 226–27, 230, 247, 253, 272, 275–76, 283–84, 289
Reformed theology, on, 78–87,
Son, as a new authority for, 120–22
speculative doctrine, as, 78–81
submission of the Son to the Father in, 84
systematic theology, in, 83–84
Trinity, as a work of the whole, 122–25
covenant theology, xix, 13–19
ante-Nicene theologians on, 13–14
Barth, Karl on, 19
Calvin, John on, 14–15
historiography of, xix, 23, 28–33,
Luther, Martin on, 14
Lutheranism, in, 14
Miller, Perry on Puritan, 18
post-Reformation theology, in, 15
See also federal theology
Covenant of Works, xvi–xviii, 4, 7, 24–77, 83–85, 142, 161, 276–77
abrogated by Adam's disobedience, xx, 41, 44, 60, 70–72, 77, 256, 281
Adam's consent to, 45–46
Calvin, John on, 31–33
Covenant of Redemption, in relation to, 131–33, 135, 148–50, 168, 277
definition of, xix, 26, 40
Edwards, Jonathan on, 40–76
established and proposed under the Old Covenant, 195–96, 207
eternal rule of righteousness, as, xxi, 48, 62–63, 71, 74, 76, 89, 168–69, 198, 248
eternal and never abrogated in terms of judgment, 70–77, 141, 149–50, 152

exhibited and proposed under the Mosaic covenant, 195, 197–98, 207, 208, 216–17
exhibited under the New Covenant, 196
fulfilled by Jesus Christ, xx–xxi, 119, 131–32, 137, 140–41, 148–50, 164–67, 185, 196, 204, 213, 249, 272
gracious nature of, 49–51, 56–57, 60–61, 75, 133
origin of, 28–31
pedagogical use of, 150
reasonable and just, as, 65–67
Reformed scholastic theology, in, 24–25, 28, 30 - 40
requirement of complete and perfect obedience in, 67–70, 76–77, 131, 140, 148, 150, 208, 281
unchangeable and eternal, as, 60, 64–65
creator-creation distinction, 55–56, 97–98, 107, 117
Decalogue, 202–3
deism, 100
diatheke (diatithemai), xvi, 81, 162. *See also* covenant(s)
dispositional ontology, 5, 233–39, 245
dispositional soteriology, 728–29, 237–39
duplex gratia, 221, 251, 264–65, 272, 279, 279n65
duplex iustitia, 278
Edwards, Jonathan
biblical interpretation/exegesis of, 10–13, 93
biblical theologian, as, xix, xxiv, 9–11, 93, 134, 219
Covenant of Grace, on (*see under* Covenant of Grace)
Covenant of Redemption, on (*see under* Covenant of Redemption)
Covenant of Works, on (*see under* Covenant of Works)
eschatological vision of, xxiii

Edwards, Jonathan (*continued*)
  law and gospel, on (*see under* law and gospel)
  Mosaic covenant (*see under* Mosaic Covenant)
  philosopher/speculative theologian, as, 8, 92–105, 134
  Puritan Reformed pastor, as, xix, xxiv, 134, 219, 258–59
  redemptive history of, 1, 3, 61, 133, 158, 199–202, 257
  redemptive-historical theology of, xxiv, 3–4, 51, 165, 199
  Trinitarian theology of, 89–151, 134
Edwards, Jonathan, *Miscellanies*
  Misc. ff, 96
  Misc. gg, 66
  Misc. pp, 100
  Misc. 2, 71n145, 144, 147–48, 153, 156–57
  Misc. 11, 112
  Misc. 22, 66
  Misc. 27a, 99
  Misc. 27b, 228, 236
  Misc. 30, 42, 71–72, 140–41, 149, 152–53
  Misc. 33, 255
  Misc. 35, 42, 62n120, 75, 268
  Misc. 37, 44n60, 254
  Misc. 66, 253n126
  Misc. 69, 62
  Misc. 77, 222
  Misc. 87, 94, 104
  Misc. 92, 94
  Misc. 94, 91–92, 92n58, 94, 99, 109n33, 110, 111n140, 135n214
  Misc. 103, 95
  Misc. 104, 97
  Misc. 117, 104, 110
  Misc. 135(151), 97
  Misc. 165, 157
  Misc. 171, 132
  Misc. 188, 96
  Misc. 238, 110n138
  Misc. 250, 149, 189, 195
  Misc. 292, 12n31
  Misc. 299, 45, 46n71, 255
  Misc. 306, 66
  Misc. 308, 110n140
  Misc. 334, 113
  Misc. 348, 66n131
  Misc. 332, 94, 97
  Misc. 336, 113
  Misc. 337, 201
  Misc. 362, 115
  Misc. 367, 65
  Misc. 370, 115
  Misc. 384, 250
  Misc. 385, 247
  Misc. 405, 115
  Misc. 412, 261, 267
  Misc. 415, 128
  Misc. 436, 195–96
  Misc. 439, 189, 192, 195, 197, 206
  Misc. 441, 190
  Misc. 483, 248
  Misc. 507, 255
  Misc. 517, 114n155
  Misc. 568, 254
  Misc. 589, 74
  Misc. 612, 151n45
  Misc. 617, 141, 143, 144, 151, 151n45, 159, 160, 162, 165, 166, 167
  Misc. 625, 151n45
  Misc. 629, 243
  Misc. 671, 282–83
  Misc. 695, 62, 276
  Misc. 697, 99
  Misc. 700, 66n131
  Misc. 702, 95
  Misc. 704, 41n56, 51n87, 127, 128
  Misc. 717, 22, 75, 149
  Misc. 729, 274, 274n48, 275–76
  Misc. 741, 95
  Misc. 769, 129–30
  Misc. 777, 288
  Misc. 782, 224n101
  Misc. 807, 151n45
  Misc. 809, 171
  Misc. 825, 151, 156, 259

SUBJECT INDEX   321

Misc. 832, 151n45
Misc. 847, 262
Misc. 849, 236
Misc. 856, 268–69
Misc. 859, 268
Misc. 861, 268
Misc. 876, 268
Misc. 880, 48, 97
Misc. 884, 44, 69
Misc. 901, 151n45
Misc. 919, 151, 151n45, 152
Misc. 996, 268, 269
Misc. 1021, 151n45
Misc. 1030, 63, 64, 268
Misc. 1062, 115, 118, 120–24, 131, 168
Misc. 1069, 151n45
Misc. 1074, 44, 48
Misc. 1091, 147, 151, 151n45, 153, 154–55, 160–61
Misc. 1130[a], 257
Misc. 1159, 247
Misc. 1215, 45, 46
Misc. 1253, 94n64
Misc. 1280, 132n210
Misc. 1352, 203
Misc. 1353, 166n77, 189, 190–92, 194, 198, 202–6
Misc. 1354, 47 205, 206n90, 207–10, 212–14
Edwards, Jonathan, sermons
  A Divine and Supernatural Light (Matt 16:17), 233n54, 243–44
  All God's Methods Are Most Reasonable (Isa 1:18–20), 45–46, 65–67, 66n132
  Application on Love to Christ (Jas 1:2), 112
  Blessings of God (Hos 13:9), 118–19
  Christ the Light of the World (John 8:12), 111
  Degrees of Glory (Cor 9:6), 285–86
  God Doesn't Thank Men for Doing Those Things He Commands Them (Luke 17:9), 54, 58–59, 59n111
  God Glorified in Man's Dependence (1 Cor 1:29–31), 111, 223, 233n54, 258
  God Never Changes His Mind (Num 23:19), 7, 71
  God Never Fails in Any Instance of Faithfulness (Ps 111:5), 46, 62–63
  Glorious Grace (Zech 4:7), 50, 54, 59, 61
  He That Believeth Shall Be Saved (Mark 16:15–16), 272
  Jesus Christ the Same Yesterday, Today, and Forever (Heb 13:8), 155, 167–68
  Justification by Faith Alone (Rom 4:5), 63, 74, 119, 131n207, 198, 221, 224–26, 229–32, 252–54, 256–57, 266–67, 274, 276, 282
  Persevering Faith (Heb 10:38–39), 274–77
  Profitable Hearers of His Word (Matt 15:23), 26
  Sermon on 1 Cor 11:13, 89
  Sermon on 2 Sam 23:5, 156
  Sermon on Cant 8:7, 275
  Sermon on Deut 10:13, 210–11
  Sermon on Eph 3:10, 106n122
  Sermon on Gen 3:11, 70, 73–74
  Sermon on Gal 2:17, 263
  Sermon on Gal 2:20, 130
  Sermon on Gal 3:16, 129n199
  Sermon on Gal 5:6(a), 270
  Sermon on Hab 2:4, 266
  Sermon on Heb 12:14, 269–70
  Sermon on John 1:16, 156
  Sermon on John 14:23, 109
  Sermon on Rom 4:16, 49, 133, 266
  Sermon on Rom 6:14, 60–61
  Sermon on Rom 8:29–30, 130
  Sinners in the Hands of an Angry God (Deut 32:35), 67

Edwards, Jonathan, sermons (*cont.*)
  The Importance and Advantage of a Thorough Knowledge of Divine Truth (Heb 5:12), xxv, 9, 134n213
  The Spiritual Blessings of the Gospel Represented by a Feast (Luke 14:6), 261n1
  The Torments of Hell Are Exceeding Great (Luke 16:24), 67n134, 68
  The Warnings of Scripture Are in the Best Manner Adopted to the Awakening of Sinners (Luke 16:31), 67n134
  There Are None Saved by Their Own Righteousness (Tit 3:5), 273
  There is Much of the Goodness and Mercy of God Appearing in the Commands He has Given Us (Deut 10:13), 52–53
  Threefold Work of the Holy Ghost (John 16:8), 109, 115, 123, 164n74, 242, 245–46, 248
  True Grace, Distinguished from the Experience of Devils (Jas 2:19), 263n9
Edwards, Jonathan, works
  An Humble Inquiry, xxii, 188–89
  Apocalypse Series, 218n1
  Charity and Its Fruits, 265, 270, 276–77
  Concerning the End for Which God Created the World, 9, 10, 94, 95, 97, 99, 142, 241–42, 243–44, 272, 286
  "*Controversies*" *Notebook*, 44, 190
  "*Controversies*" *Notebook: Justification*, 54, 169, 205, 214–16, 226, 229, 232, 233n54, 255–56, 271, 273, 275, 278, 280–81, 287–88
  Discourse on the Trinity, 88, 105, 109–14, 123
  Faith, 47
  Freedom of the Will, 276
  History of the Work of Redemption, xxiv, 5n8, 51, 74, 124, 147–50, 153, 190, 199–200, 202–3
  On the Nature of True Virtue, 99, 110, 265
  Master's Quaestio: A Sinner is Not Justified in the Sight of God Except Through the Righteousness of Christ Obtained by Faith, 220, 271, 229n35, 263, 267–68
  Miscellaneous Observations on Important Theological Subjects, 109
  Miscellaneous Remarks, 47
  Misrepresentations Corrected and Truth Vindicated, 46n71
  Notes on Scripture, 12, 44–46, 52n90, 64, 74, 189, 190
  Of Atoms, 102
  Religious Affections, 4n4, 12n31, 12n32, 98
  Resolutions, 10
  The Great Christian Doctrine of Original Sin Defended, 44, 68, 105, 249–50, 249n111, 281n69
  The Mind, 103–5, 109n133, 112, 114n69
  Treatise on Grace, 88, 90, 90n48, 112, 113, 116
  Types of the Messiah, 211
election, 17, 18, 126–30, 131, 171. See also predestination
emanation/remanation, 95
empiricism, 234
eternal (divine) decrees, 17, 66, 77–78, 83, 88, 124–31, 134, 276
eternal life, xx, 13–14, 27, 42–43, 45, 48–49, 53–54, 56–57, 59, 61–63, 67, 71–73, 76, 130–32, 140, 161, 165, 168, 172, 192, 196
  Adam, as promised to under the Covenant of Works, 169–71, 169n89

evangelical obedience, xv–xvi, xviii,
    xxiii, xxiv, 3, 7–8, 10, 23,
    40, 76, 78, 88, 133–34, 145,
    155. *See also* good works;
    sanctification
  consequence of justification, as,
    212, 222, 224–25, 230, 273,
    275, 278
  distinguishing characteristic of
    faith, as, 207, 232, 261, 276
  evidence of faith, as, 207,
    209–11, 216, 261, 267–80,
    231, 289
  fruit of faith, as, 205, 207, 216,
    231
  love for God's holiness, as, 261,
    287–88
  necessary for (as a condition of)
    salvation, 261, 264, 267–70,
    273, 289, 231–33
  non-meritorious necessity of,
    260–89, 220, 259
faith, xvi–xxii, xxv, 2–5, 8, 10–11,
    21–24, 34–36, 38, 40, 46–48,
    71, 74, 88, 126, 145, 155–56,
    162, 194
  condition, as, 48, 140–43, 146,
    148, 266–67, 224, 253
  consent, as, 46–48, 269, 253
  hearing and yielding to the voice
    of God, as, 47, 207, 209
  natural and moral fitness of,
    240, 252–57
  nature of saving, 266–89,
    224–25
  non-meritorious nature of, 164,
    168, 210, 212, 223–25, 245,
    255–56
  obedience and, 8, 162, 172, 174,
    105–16
  promise of the Covenant of
    Redemption, as, 166
  reason and, 92
  uniting to Christ, as, 172, 191,
    224, 252–53
federal theology, 24, 15, 17–18, 20,
    25, 34, 75. *See also* covenant
    theology

federal vision, 7
fides formata caritate, 221, 224–25,
    271. *See also* under Roman
    Catholicism: relationship
    between grace (justification)
    and works in
foreknowledge, 129
Formula Consensus Helvitica, 87
Gallican Confession, 16
God the Father (as first person of
    the Trinity), 109–12, 115
God's glorification of himself in
    creation, xxiii, 53, 89, 94–95
God's glorification of himself in
    redemption, 89, 95, 288
God's self-communication, 53, 88–
    89, 93–100, 107–8, 111–12,
    129, 134
good works, xv, 2–3, 40, 54, 58, 78,
    133, 155. *See also* evangelical
    obedience; sanctification
gospel, free offer of, 148, 157–58
grace, 56, 60–61, 63, 90, 113
  law and, 40, 50–51
heaven, 89, 99, 284–88
  promise of the New Covenant,
    as, 171
heavenly rewards, 261, 282–87, 289
Heidelberg Catechism, 16, 37
hell, 99
historia salutis, 199–202, 239. *See
    also* redemptive history
historical-redemptive theology;
    see redemptive-historical
    theology
Holy Spirit, xxi, 112–17, 21–23,
    241–45
  blessing of Christ's obedience,
    as, 166, 168, 191, 223, 230
  Covenant of Redemption, role
    in (*see under* Covenant of
    Redemption)
  filoque (dual procession of), 116
  hiddeness of, 116
  Old Covenant, presence in, 179,
    192, 206
idealism, 67, 88, 93, 100–104, 134
immanence, 98–99, 98n84, 107

imputation (of Christ's
    righteousness), xxiii, 43, 49,
    76, 135, 150, 169, 217, 220,
    225–27, 245, 259
infusion of righteousness (virtues),
    264–65, 264–65, 271, 278–
    80, 285, 219, 237, 240–45
Jesus Christ
    active and passive obedience of,
        27, 76, 164, 164n74, 213, 220
    ascension of, 206
    covenant head, as, xx, 34, 42–44,
        46, 62–63, 74–75, 146, 246
    covenant mediator, as, 82–84,
        86, 119, 132, 136, 142, 146,
        155–56, 158, 160, 190, 193,
        205, 214, 246, 249, 287
    covenant surety, as, xxiii, 76, 83,
        86, 119, 136, 155, 167–68,
        171
    Covenant of Works fulfilled
        by (*see under* Covenant of
        Works)
    fulfillment of Old Testament
        prophecy, as, 82
    Old Testament antitype, as, 82,
        196, 203, 213, 215
    Second Adam, as, 85, 119, 132,
        145, 147, 150, 161
    Second Person of the Trinity, as,
        78, 83, 86, 93, 104, 110–12,
        115, 205, 213–14
justification, xvii, xxi–xxii, xxiii,
    1–6, 10, 12–13, 40, 49, 88,
    128, 130, 155, 162, 165, 172,
    190–1, 237, 245–52
    faith alone, by, 40, 133, 192,
        206, 206n90, 209, 212, 216,
        221, 231–32, 234, 260, 263,
        267–70, 278, 289 (*see also*
        sola fide)
    final (second), xxiv, 278–82, 289
    forensic, 23, 221, 226, 230, 237,
        239, 245, 250–52, 164, 274,
        279, 279n65
law
    ceremonial, 178–79, 195–96,
        203–4, 213, 216

civil or judicial, 178, 195–96,
    203–4, 216
communion, as, 53, 65, 75
God's nature, as reflecting, 49,
    51
letter and spirit of, 193–95, 197,
    204, 209–10, 216–17
love, not opposed to, 49, 51–53,
    60, 75
merciful, as, 49, 52–53, 211
moral, 178, 183–84, 195–96,
    199, 203–4, 216
law and gospel, xix, xxii–xxiii, 1,
    7–8, 23–25, 35–40, 71,
    176–77, 180, 192
    Edwards, Jonathan on, 40, 43,
        47–50, 59, 61, 76, 78, 88,
        136, 150, 152, 162, 168, 172,
        190–91, 196, 198, 201, 203,
        216, 259
    Luther, Martin on, 36–37
law of nature; *see* natural law
legalism, 1, 25, 30, 40, 49, 51
Lord's Supper, xvii, 35n40, 191. See
    also sacraments
Lutheranism, 2, 35
merit, 40, 49, 54–59
    condign (*meritum de condigno*),
        57–58, 57n107
    congruity (*meritum de congruo*),
        57–58, 57n107, 224
    covenantal (*meritum ex pacto*),
        57, 57n107, 59
monocovenantalism, 6, 21
Mosaic covenant, xvi, xxii, 4, 7, 31,
    174–217
    antithesis (discontinuity) with
        the New Covenant, 177–81,
        216
    complex mixed covenant, as a,
        186, 189–90, 202–3, 217
    Covenant of Grace, in relation
        to, xxii, 172, 174, 176–77,
        183, 186–88, 191–206, 217
    Covenant of Grace hidden and
        revealed in, 188, 191–95,
        197–98, 204, 212–17
    early church on, 175
    Edwards, Jonathan on, 188–217

hypothetical covenant, as a, 184–85, 186, 195–98
misinterpretation theory of, 181, 216
national covenant with Israel, as, 179, 188, 193, 203–4, 211, 216
Old Testament saints saved in the same manner as the New Testament under, 165, 190, 205–16, 231
pedagogical (schoolmaster or tutor) use of, xxii, 7, 149, 184, 186, 188, 198–99, 204, 209, 217
principle of abstraction in, 180, 216
promise–fulfillment of the New Covenant, as, 180–81, 216
Reformed theology on, 174–86,
republication of Covenant of Works, as, xxii, 7, 176–77, 181–83, 186–87, 192–93, 195, 198, 202–4, 216–17
substance and accidents of, 178, 187, 192, 216
typological, as, 185–86, 191, 203–4, 211–12, 217
Moses, xvii, xxii, 31, 36, 69, 153
Mystical Bride (Body) of Christ, 156, 162, 167, 171, 207, 259–60, 247
Nadere Reformatie, 10
natural law (law of nature), 30, 56, 58, 64, 68–70
neonomianism, xxiii, 7, 71, 76, 136, 146, 153, 172, 220, 239
neoorthodoxy, 20 - 21
neoplatonism, 97
Newtonian worldview, 96
nominalism, late medieval, 14, 234
ordo salutis, xxiii, 8, 24, 61, 78, 133, 165, 199–202, 222–23, 239, 247, 251, 273–78
original sin, 67–68, 132, 148–50, 262, 248–50, 249n111. *See also under* Adam: unity in
pactum, xvi, 79, 80–81, 83. *See also* covenant(s)

pactum salutis, xx, 7, 27, 44, 78, 81, 83, 85, 134, 137. *See also* Covenant of Redemption
pantheism/panentheism, 96–100, 103, 107
Passover, 191
Pelagianism, 242
perseverance in faith, xxiii, 2, 145, 165, 166, 261–62, 272–73, 281, 289
postmodernism, 102
predestination, 15, 26, 28–30, 32, 83, 88, 131. *See also* election
principium cognoscendi, 15
principium essendi, 15
protoevangelium, xxi
redemptive history, 179, 204. *See also historia salutis*
 Edwards, Jonathan, of (*see under* Edwards, Jonathan)
redemptive-historical theology, xxiii, 10, 12, 20, 76, 146, 257, 242
 Edwards, Jonathan, of (*see under* Edwards, Jonathan)
Reformed tradition, 2, 11, 15–16
regeneration, 166–68, 222–23, 237, 242–44, 262, 289
reprobation, 128–29
Roman Catholicism, 218, 239
 relationship between grace (justification) and works in, 2, 221, 224–25, 230–31, 240–52, 260, 271 (*see also fides formata caritate*)
 Edwards, Jonathan's theology as consistent with, 3–4, 260, 262–63, 218–20, 224, 227–28, 234–45, 257, 271, 280, 288
sacrament(s), xix, 14, 16, 33, 33n29, 46n71, 139, 191–92, 251n116
sanctification, xxi, xxiii, 1–7, 21, 190, 203, 262–63, 272, 278–79, 222–24. *See also* evangelical obedience; good works
scholastic(ism), 16–18

Scots Confession, 16
Socinianism, 242
sola fide, xviii, 35n40, 36, 221, 232, 234, 260, 270, 270n33, 271, 278. *See also under* justification: faith alone, by
sovereignty of God, xvi, xxi, xxiv, 4, 27–28
subordination(ism), xx–xxi, 83, 115, 118, 120–22, 124
substance, 102–3, 234
testament, 162. *See also* covenant(s)
Tetrapolitan Confession, 16
Thirty-Nine Articles of the Church of England, 16
transcendence, 98–99, 98n84, 107, 287
Tree of Life, as covenantal sign, xix, 14, 33, 45
Tree of the Knowledge of Good and Evil, as covenantal sign, xix, 64, 68–69
tricovenantalism, xvii, 24, 31, 41, 44, 50, 75, 151
Trinity
  ad extra-ad intra, xx–xxi, 27, 77, 83, 88, 94, 106, 108, 112, 124–26
  economic, 89, 106–8, 118, 121–24
  immanent (ontological), 88, 106–17, 120, 134
  Edwards, Jonathan on (*see under* Edwards, Jonathan: Trinitarian theology of)
  love between Persons of, 94–96, 105, 110–16, 245–46
typology, xxiv, 7, 10, 12, 153, 215
union with Christ, xxi, 85, 156, 159, 165, 167–70, 221, 228–31, 237–42, 245–52, 259, 264, 272–74
Westminster Confession, 17, 19, 84, 87, 90, 177, 179, 187, 263–64
Westminster Larger Catechism, 84–85, 90, 183–84
Westminster Seminary in Philadelphia, 6
Westminster Shorter Catechism, 85, 90

Scripture Index

OLD TESTAMENT

Genesis
1:26	108, 123
1:26–27	34
1:27–30	43
2:17	34n34, 68, 72, 248
3:11	70, 70n141, 70n142, 72, 73n151
3:15	xii, xviii
20:13	108

Exodus
2:4	108
19:8	197n66
20:6	202
20:20	197, 208
24:5–8	203
32	189
33:14	111
34:5–7	192

Leviticus
18:4–5	34
18:5	180, 182
26:12	42–46, 192

Numbers
23:19	71

Deuteronomy
4:33	199
5:29	207n92, 208
6:4	108
8:18	55
9	190
9:5	213
10:13	52, 210, 211n101
10:16	168
10:20	163
26:16–19	55
30:6	168
39:1–6	192
39:3–15	192
30:19	192

Joshua
24:19–27	208

1 Samuel
4:8	109

2 Samuel
23:5	13n85, 156

Nehemiah
9:18	108

Job
31:33	34, 45

Psalm

51:6	227n30
111:5	46, 46n47, 62
119	256

Proverbs

8	111
8:30	112

Canticles (Song of Solomon)

8:7	275n50

Isaiah

1:18–20	45, 65
1:19	209n97
6	109
16:6	108
33:15–16	210
41:16	109
53:10	80n14
55:3	277
56:6	163

Jeremiah

4:4	168
31:18–19	168
31:31–34	31

Ezekiel

11:19	168
18:30–32	168
18:31	168
33	208
36:26	168

Daniel

4:8	109

Hosea

6:7	34, 24n36, 44
13:9	118

14:2	168

Habakkuk

2:4	266, 266n18

Zechariah

4:7	43, 54, 59, 61
6:13	82n222

NEW TESTAMENT

Matthew

3:13	80n15
7:21	210
7:26	210
15:23	261
16:17	37
16:27	284
19:16–30	185, 197
19:16–17	34
22:37–39	34

Mark

10:17–31	185n36, 197

Luke

2:21	80n15
14:16	261
16:24	68
17	58
17:9	54, 58, 59n111
17:10	56, 58
18:18–30	185n36, 197
19	284
22	81
22:29	81, 81n19, 162
24:44–47	175

John

1	111

1:1	111
1:13	37
1:16	156, 156n59
1:17	177
1:18	148
6:37	130, 130n202, 130n203
8:12	111
10:16	130n202
10:17–18	164
14:2	284
14:5	111
14:23	109
14:28	84
16	245
16:8	109, 123
17:2	130n202
17:9	130n202

Acts

2:32–33	113
3:25	163
8:30	175

Romans

1:17	34
1:18–32	69
2:1–16	278n64
2:14–15	34
3:9	175
3:20–22	37
3:26	278n64
3:27	37, 45n66
3:28	228
4	175
4:16	49, 49n82, 133, 266, 266n17
5	7n15, 21
5:5	113
5:12–21	34
5:13–14	69
5:15	279n65
6:14	60, 61n115, 73, 116, 117
7:10	34, 45, 45n66
8:3–4	34, 38
8:7	265
8:29–30	128n196, 130n203, 130n204
8:29	128, 130, 130n202
9:6	175
10	180
10:5	34, 45, 45n66, 182
11:6	60, 61

1 Corinthians

1:24	111
1:30	37
2:10	114
2:14	265
3:14–15	284
10	175
11:13	89
14:24–28	124n182
15:22	170
15:28	121n170
15:41–42	284
15:44–52	170
15:50	170

2 Corinthians

3:5	265
3:6	194
3:14	113
4:4	111
9:6	284, 286n82

Galatians

2:17	263, 263n7
2:20	130n202
3:11–12	34
3:12	182
3:13	38
3:16	85, 129n99, 138
3:17	198
3:19	160
3:23–24	36, 211
3:23, 25	179
3:24	184
4:4–5	34
5:6a	270, 270n30

Ephesians

1:4	129
1:6	247
1:23	85
2:2, 5	264
3:10	106

Philippians

2:5	111
2:8–9	84
3:8	281

Colossians

1:14	111

2 Timothy

1:9	130n202
2:15	36
2:19	130n202

Titus

3:5–6	113
3:5	273

Hebrews

1:3	111
1:5	120
8:10	162
9	81
9:18–23	203
11:19	215
12:14	269, 270n29
13:8	155, 167

James

2:18	263
2:19	263n9
2:21–23	271
2:22	269
3:14–26	228
3:14	228

1 John

1:5	111
4:8, 16	112
4:12–13	113
4:18	113

Revelation

4	109
21:27	130n202
22:5	121
22:14–20	200n72
22:14	45, 45n66
22:17	149

www.ingramcontent.com/pod-product-compliance
Lightning Source LLC
Chambersburg PA
CBHW071150300426
44113CB00009B/1157